Minimal Maximal

Alexander Calder

Alexander Calder

Minimal Maximal

Nationalgalerie
Staatliche Museen zu Berlin

PRESTEL
Munich · London · New York

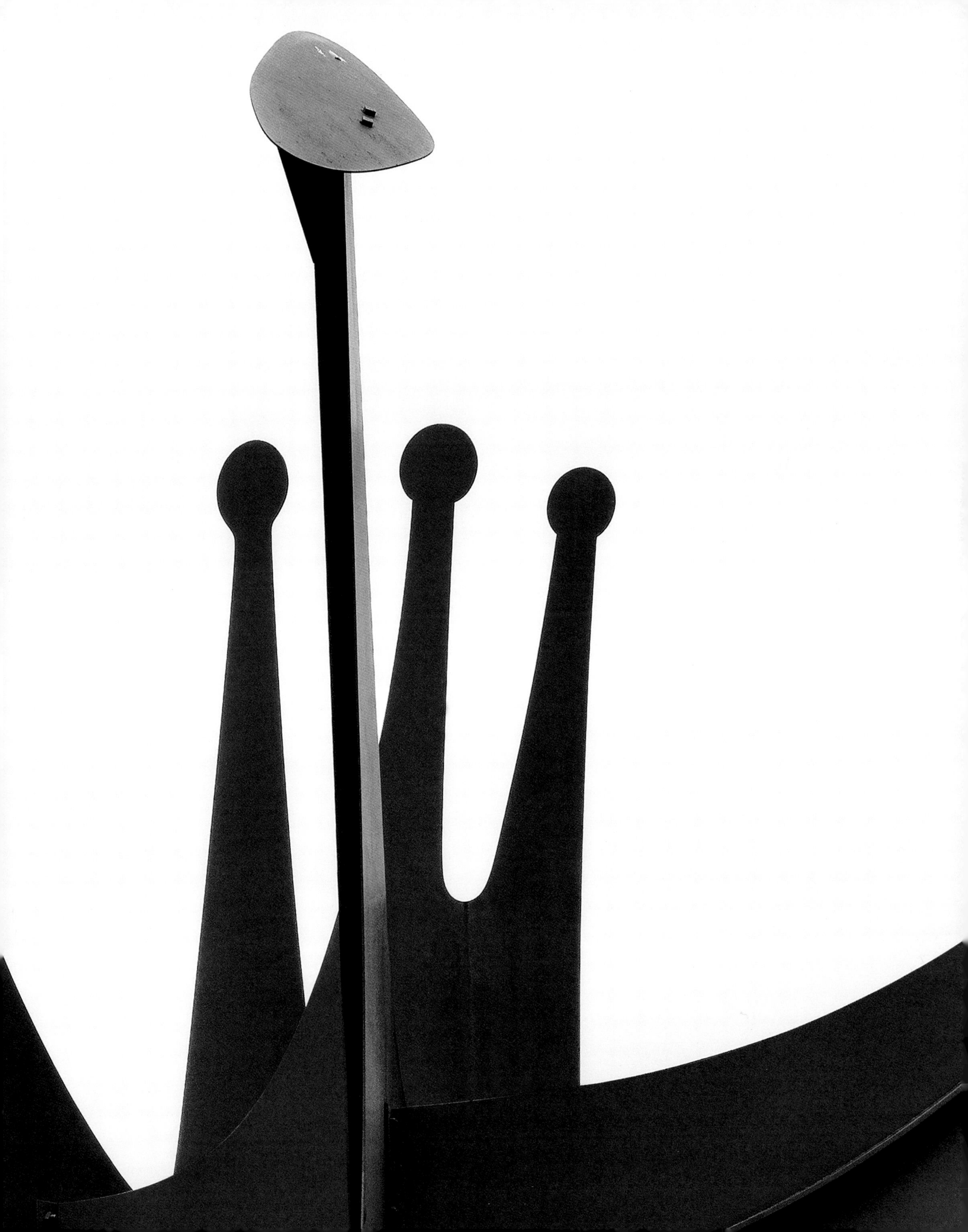

1 *Têtes et queue*, 1965, Stahl, Bolzen, Farbe, 550 × 470 × 330 cm / sheet metal, bolts, paint, 216 1/2 × 185 × 130 in., Staatliche Museen zu Berlin, Nationalgalerie

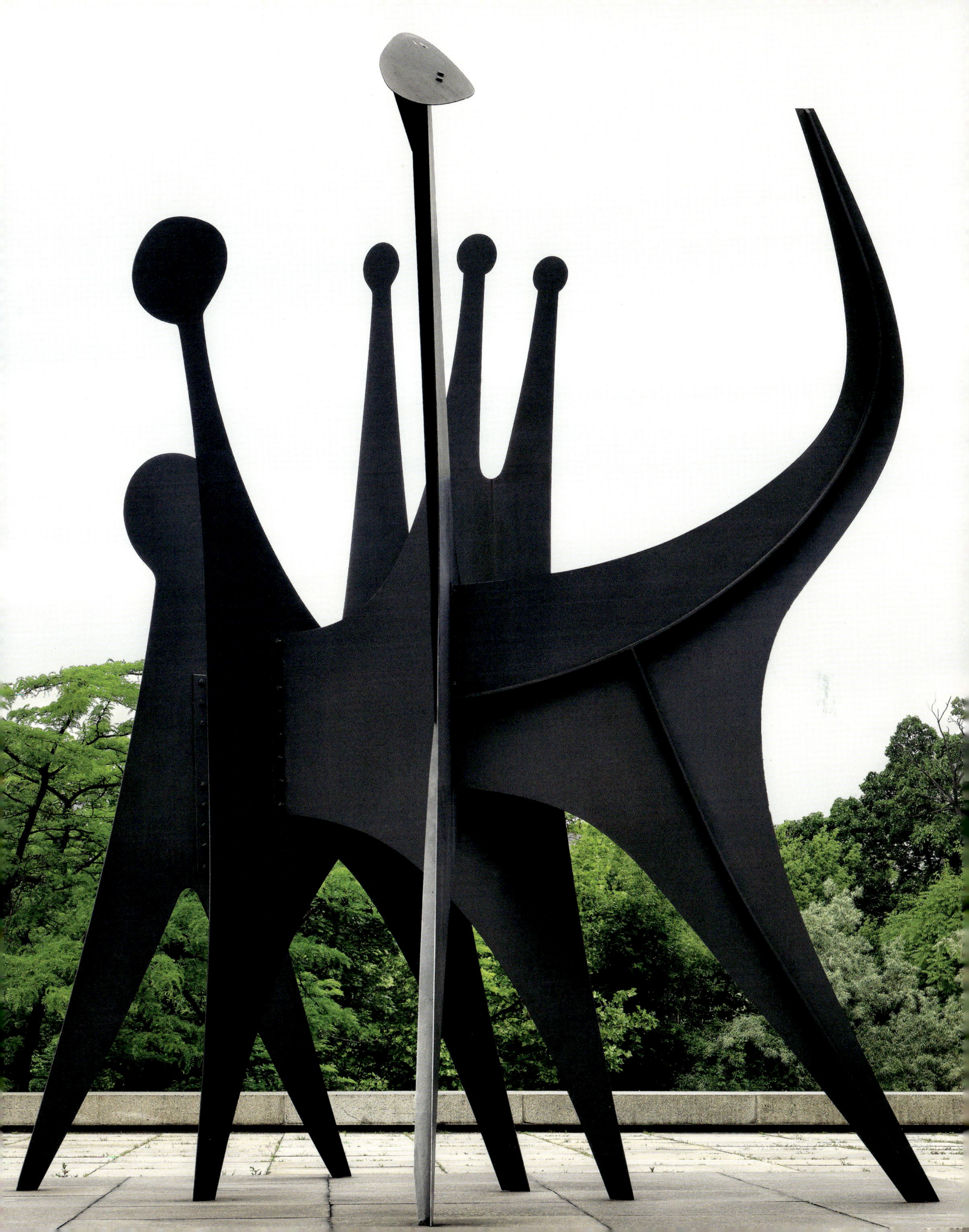

Grußwort

Lange bevor feststand, mit welcher Ausstellung wir nach der mehrjährigen Sanierungszeit die Neue Nationalgalerie wiedereröffnen würden, stand für die FREUNDE DER NATIONALGALERIE schon fest, dass sie dieses Vorhaben unbedingt unterstützen würden: Mies van der Rohes „Tempel der Moderne" muss im neuen Kleid gebührend gefeiert werden! Die Neue Nationalgalerie ist als Museum einzigartig, weil sich hier Kunst- und Raumerlebnis auf eine einmalige Weise verbinden, sodass Kunstbetrachtung nicht nur zu einer geistigen, sondern auch zu einer physischen Erfahrung wird. Die Neue Nationalgalerie ist und bleibt unsere ganz große Liebe, nicht nur, weil sie der Anlass für die Wiederbegründung der FREUNDE im Jahr 1977 war, sondern vor allem wegen der vielen unvergesslichen Momente, die wir in diesem Haus in den vergangenen Jahrzehnten erleben durften.

Dass von den Verantwortlichen Alexander Calder ausgewählt wurde, um die Neue Nationalgalerie mit einer großen Ausstellung in der oberen Halle wiederzueröffnen, ist für die FREUNDE ein Doppel-Glück! Denn die erste Skulptur, die der Verein für die Sammlung der Neuen Nationalgalerie gleich im Jahr 1978 ankaufte, war die Arbeit *Untitled* (um 1948, Abb. 62) von Alexander Calder. Dank der freundlichen Vermittlung unseres langjährigen Mitglieds Folker Skulima und des heldenhaften Verzichts von Heiner und Ulla Pietzsch, die schon vor der Nationalgalerie mit dieser Arbeit von hoher künstlerischer Qualität liebäugelten, konnte diese Arbeit erworben werden und gehört noch heute zu den absoluten Highlights der Sammlung.

Die gelungene Präsentation der Ausstellung verdanken wir Joachim Jäger, Udo Kittelmann und Maike Steinkamp sowie dem ganzen Team der Neuen Nationalgalerie. Die organisatorische Umsetzung und Kommunikation der Ausstellung lag wie üblich in den Händen des Vereins-Teams – hier gebührt unser Dank einmal mehr André Odier, Katharina von Chlebowski und Lutz Driever für ihren unermüdlichen und kreativen Einsatz.

Seine Skulpturen seien Dinge, die man mit Vergnügen betrachte, sagte Calder einmal über seine Arbeiten – geben wir uns also mit Freude diesem Vergnügen hin!

Gabriele Quandt
Vorsitzende
Freunde der Nationalgalerie

Greeting

Long before it was decided which exhibition we would present for the reopening of the Neue Nationalgalerie following several years of renovation work, it was clear that the FREUNDE DER NATIONALGALERIE patrons' association would support the project: after all, the new look of Ludwig Mies van der Rohe's "temple of modernism" had to be properly celebrated! As a museum, the Neue Nationalgalerie is unparalleled because it combines the experience of art and space in a unique way, such that viewing art becomes both an intellectual and a physical experience. And the Neue Nationalgalerie is and remains our greatest love, not only because it was the reason for the reinstatement of the FREUNDE in 1977 but also and above all because of the many unforgettable moments we have enjoyed here over the past decades.

That the work of Alexander Calder has been chosen to reopen the Neue Nationalgalerie with a major exhibition in the upper hall is a double stroke of luck for the FREUNDE! Indeed, the first sculpture acquired by the association for the Neue Nationalgalerie's collection, which took place almost immediately, in 1978, was Alexander Calder's *Untitled* (ca. 1948; fig. 62). Thanks to the gracious intervention of our longtime member Folker Skulima and the valiant sacrifice of Heiner and Ulla Pietzsch, who had already been eyeing this work of outstanding artistic quality, it became possible to purchase the sculpture for the Neue Nationalgalerie. Today, it remains one of the collection's absolute highlights.

We owe the successful presentation of the exhibition to Joachim Jäger, Udo Kittelmann, and Maike Steinkamp, as well as the entire staff at the Neue Nationalgalerie. The organizational implementation and communication of the exhibition lay, as usual, in the hands of the association's team—here we extend our thanks once again to André Odier, Katharina von Chlebowski, and Lutz Driever for their tireless and creative efforts.

Calder once said that his sculptures were things to be looked at with pleasure—let us surrender ourselves to this delight!

Gabriele Quandt
Chairwoman
Freunde der Nationalgalerie

[Calder] läßt aus seiner Plastik weg, was seit Thutmes in Aegypten als das A und O aller Plastik galt: die Masse, die Körperlichkeit. An die Stelle des Tones, Holzes, Steines, Erzes setzt er die – Luft, einfach die Luft, gleichviel, ob Höhenluft oder Kellerluft, dünne Luft oder dicke Luft. Und er macht die Luft räumlich durch sauber hingestellte Konturen aus Draht. Mit einem Minimum an Mitteln hext er frappante Wirkungen.

Adolf Behne[1]

Grußwort

Während das Werk meines Großvaters zu seinen Lebzeiten und auch danach überall auf der Welt zu sehen war, gab es in Berlin erstaunlicherweise nur eine einzige monografische Werkschau in einem Museum, und das vor über fünfzig Jahren.[2] Es war mir deshalb eine riesige Freude, als Udo Kittelmann beim Anblick einer Reihe kleiner stehender Mobiles in meinem Büro in New York City eine Ausstellung seiner Arbeiten in der Neuen Nationalgalerie vorschlug. Kurator Joachim Jäger und Kuratorin Maike Steinkamp führten das Projekt mit erfahrener Hand zum Erfolg: *Alexander Calder. Minimal / Maximal* spürt Themen wie Räumlichkeit und Maßstab, Leere und Körperhaftigkeit nach, die sich unvorhersagbar und doch harmonisch wie ein roter Faden durch das Œuvre meines Großvaters ziehen. Durch den Verzicht auf Masse bei seinen Mobiles, Stabiles und den sogenannten Standing Mobiles eröffnete Calder grenzenlose Möglichkeiten der Kommunikation mit seinen Werken: Mit einem Minimum an Mitteln „hexte" er Unermesslichkeit. In Ludwig Mies van der Rohes einzigartiger gläserner Halle schafft diese Ausstellung einen Resonanzraum, in dem Betrachterinnen und Betrachter das Werk meines Großvaters erleben und an seiner transformativen Energie partizipieren können.

Im Kern geht es bei *Alexander Calder. Minimal / Maximal* um Aktivierung – doch nicht nur um die Aktivierung, die man erlebt, wenn man sich auf die ästhetische Erfahrung etwa eines Mobiles in Bewegung einlässt, sondern auch um Aktivierung im Zuge alltäglicher und doch elementarer Geschehnisse. Die Ausstellung ist begleitet von Veranstaltungen rund um Calders Schachspiel von 1944, Klangperformances von *Chef d'orchestre* aus dem Jahr 1966 sowie der feierlichen Enthüllung des spektakulären Calder BMW Art Car (Künstlerexemplar) von 1975.

Alexander S. C. Rower
Stiftungspräsident
Calder Foundation, New York

1 Adolf Behne, „Plastik als Luftakt: Alexander Calder in der Galerie Neumann-Nierendorf", in: *Welt am Abend*, 11.4.1929.

2 Akademie der Künste, Berlin (West), *Alexander Calder*, 21. Mai – 16. Juli 1967.

[Calder] leaves out of his sculpture what has been regarded as the alpha and omega of all sculpture since Thutmose in Egypt: mass, corporeality. For clay, wood, stone, ore he substitutes—air, simply air, no matter whether mountain air or cellar air, thin air or thick air. And he makes the air spatial through cleanly arranged contours made of wire. With a minimum of means he conjures striking effects.

Adolf Behne[1]

Greeting

My grandfather's work has been shown the world over, both during and after his lifetime, yet, surprisingly, only one monographic museum exhibition has taken place in Berlin, and that over fifty years ago.[2] It was therefore an immense thrill when Udo Kittelmann, spotting a suite of small-scale standing mobiles in my New York City office, proposed a show of Calder's work at the Neue Nationalgalerie. Expertly shepherded into fruition by the curators Joachim Jäger and Maike Steinkamp, *Alexander Calder: Minimal / Maximal* explores themes of space and scale—of voids and volumes—that penetrate my grandfather's oeuvre in unpredictable yet harmonic ways. By omitting mass in his mobiles, stabiles, and standing mobiles, Calder opened up unlimited possibilities for engagement; through a "minimum of means," he conjured immensities. Set within Ludwig Mies van der Rohe's exquisite glass hall, this presentation creates a resonant space for viewers to experience my grandfather's work and take part in its transformative energy.

At its essence, *Alexander Calder: Minimal / Maximal* is about activation—not only that which occurs when engaged in an aesthetic experience, such as a mobile in motion, but also in the ordinary yet vital events of the everyday. Included in this expansive exhibition are events organized around my grandfather's 1944 chess set, sound performances of *Chef d'orchestre* from 1966, and a special unveiling of the spectacular 1975 Calder BMW Art Car, Artist's Proof.

Alexander S. C. Rower
President
Calder Foundation, New York

1 Adolf Behne, "Plastik als Luftakt: Alexander Calder in der Galerie Neumann-Nierendorf," *Welt Am Abend*, April 11, 1929. Translated into English as "Sculpture as Aerial Act: Alexander Calder at the Galerie Neumann-Nierendorf," https://calder.org/bibliography/welt-am-abend-1929 (accessed February 11, 2021).

2 Akademie der Künste Berlin (West), *Alcxander Calder*, May 21 to July 16, 1967.

Vorwort

Der Bildhauer Alexander Calder ist durch sein Hauptwerk *Têtes et queue* (1965) seit Jahrzehnten eng mit der Neuen Nationalgalerie verbunden. Die Außenskulptur wurde zur Eröffnung von Ludwig Mies van der Rohes Architekturikone aufgestellt und kehrt nun mit der Wiedereröffnung des Museums auf dessen Terrasse zurück. 1929 besuchte der Künstler Berlin zum ersten Mal und faszinierte damals mit seinen filigranen Raumobjekten nicht nur den Kunstkritiker Adolf Behne nachhaltig. Dieser sprach über Calders Plastiken als von einem „Luftakt", einer Verräumlichung der Luft, welche der Bildhauer mit einem Minimum an Mitteln zu erreichen wusste. Nach seinem Debüt in Berlin 1929 waren Calders Werke hier nur noch einmal im musealen Kontext zu sehen, 1967 in einer Ausstellung in der Akademie der Künste in Berlin (West). Über fünfzig Jahre später kehren seine Arbeiten nun nach Berlin zurück. Dabei haben Calders Objekte nichts von ihrer Faszination verloren, was sie vor allem ihrem partizipativen, den Raum einnehmenden Charakter verdanken. Insbesondere die grazilen Miniaturen und das von Calder Mitte der 1940er-Jahre entwickelte Schachspiel waren der Auslöser zu dieser Ausstellung, sind es doch gerade diese ungewöhnlichen Objekte, die den dynamischen, sozialen Aspekt von Calders Arbeiten besonders deutlich aufscheinen lassen. Mit unserer Begeisterung für diese Arbeiten traten wir in einen Dialog mit Alexander S.C. Rower, dem Enkel Calders und Präsidenten der Calder Foundation, der die Idee einer Ausstellung Calders in der Neuen Nationalgalerie enthusiastisch aufnahm. Die Ausstellung entstand in enger Kooperation mit der Calder Foundation, für deren großes Engagement und zahlreiche Leihgaben wir uns herzlich bei Alexander S.C. Rower und seinem Team, insbesondere Lily Lyons, Melissa Claus und Susan Braeuer Dam, bedanken möchten. Auch den anderen Leihgebern sind wir zu großem Dank verpflichtet, die uns ihre teils monumentalen Arbeiten für die Präsentation überlassen. Staffan Ahrenberg von *Cahier d'Arts* stellt Faksimiles des 1944 von Calder entwickelten Schachspiels zur Verfügung, wodurch die Besucherinnen und Besucher die einzigartige Möglichkeit erhalten, vor Ort eine Partie Schach zu bestreiten. Das gelungene Ausstellungsdesign verdanken wir erneut dem Büro mvprojekte. Die Projektkoordination und Logistik stemmte Katharina Wippermann, der wir, wie dem gesamten Team der Neuen Nationalgalerie, herzlich für ihre zuverlässige, engagierte Arbeit danken. Barbara Delius war für die Koordination des Katalogs verantwortlich, der wir für ihren unermüdlichen Einsatz ebenso zu Dank verpflichtet sind wie den Autoren, die in ihren Kurzbeiträgen pointierte Analysen zu ausgewählten Aspekten von Calder Werk lieferten.

Ohne den finanziellen und organisatorischen Beitrag der FREUNDE DER NATIONALGALERIE hätte die Ausstellung nicht umgesetzt werden können. Ihre kontinuierliche Unterstützung machen solche anspruchsvollen internationalen Projekte der Nationalgalerie überhaupt noch realisierbar. Vielen Dank!

Joachim Jäger
Udo Kittelmann
Maike Steinkamp

Foreword

For decades, the sculptor Alexander Calder has been closely associated with the Neue Nationalgalerie through his masterpiece *Têtes et queue* (1965). The outdoor sculpture was installed for the opening of Ludwig Mies van der Rohe's architectural icon and now, with the museum's reopening, returns to its terrace. In 1929 the artist visited Berlin for the first time and deeply fascinated the art critic Adolf Behne, among others, with his filigree spatial objects. Behne spoke of Calder's sculptures as being an "aerial act," a spatialization of air that the sculptor achieved with a minimum of means. After his debut in Berlin in 1929, Calder's works were on view here only once in a museum setting, in 1967, at an exhibition at the Akademie der Künste in what was then West Berlin. More than fifty years later, his works are now returning to Berlin. Calder's objects have lost none of their allure in the meantime, which primarily stems from their participatory, expansive character. In particular, the delicate miniatures and the chess set Calder developed in the mid 1940s were the catalysts for this exhibition, as it is precisely in these unusual pieces that the dynamic, social aspect of Calder's oeuvre shines through most brightly. With our enthusiasm for these works, we entered into a dialogue with Alexander S.C. Rower, Calder's grandson and the president of the Calder Foundation, who wholeheartedly embraced the idea of a Calder exhibition at the Neue Nationalgalerie.

The show was developed in close collaboration with the Calder Foundation, and we sincerely thank Alexander S.C. Rower and his team, especially Lily Lyons, Melissa Claus, and Susan Braeuer Dam, for their great commitment and numerous loans. We are also deeply indebted to the other lenders, who have made their works—some of them monumental—available to us for this presentation. Staffan Ahrenberg from *Cahiers d'Art* has provided facsimiles of the chess set Calder designed in 1944, giving visitors the unique opportunity to play a game of chess on site. We once again owe the successful exhibition design to the firm myprojekte. The coordination and logistics were in the capable hands of Katharina Wipperman, and we are grateful to her and the entire staff at the Neue Nationalgalerie for their reliable and dedicated work. Barbara Delius was responsible for coordinating the catalogue, and we are as indebted to her for her tireless efforts as we are to the authors, who in their short essays delivered pointed analyses on selected aspects of Calder's work.

Without the financial and organizational contributions of the FREUNDE DER NATIONALGALERIE, the exhibition could not have been realized. Their continuous support is what makes such ambitious international projects at the Nationalgalerie possible in the first place. Thank you very much!

Joachim Jäger
Udo Kittelmann
Maike Steinkamp

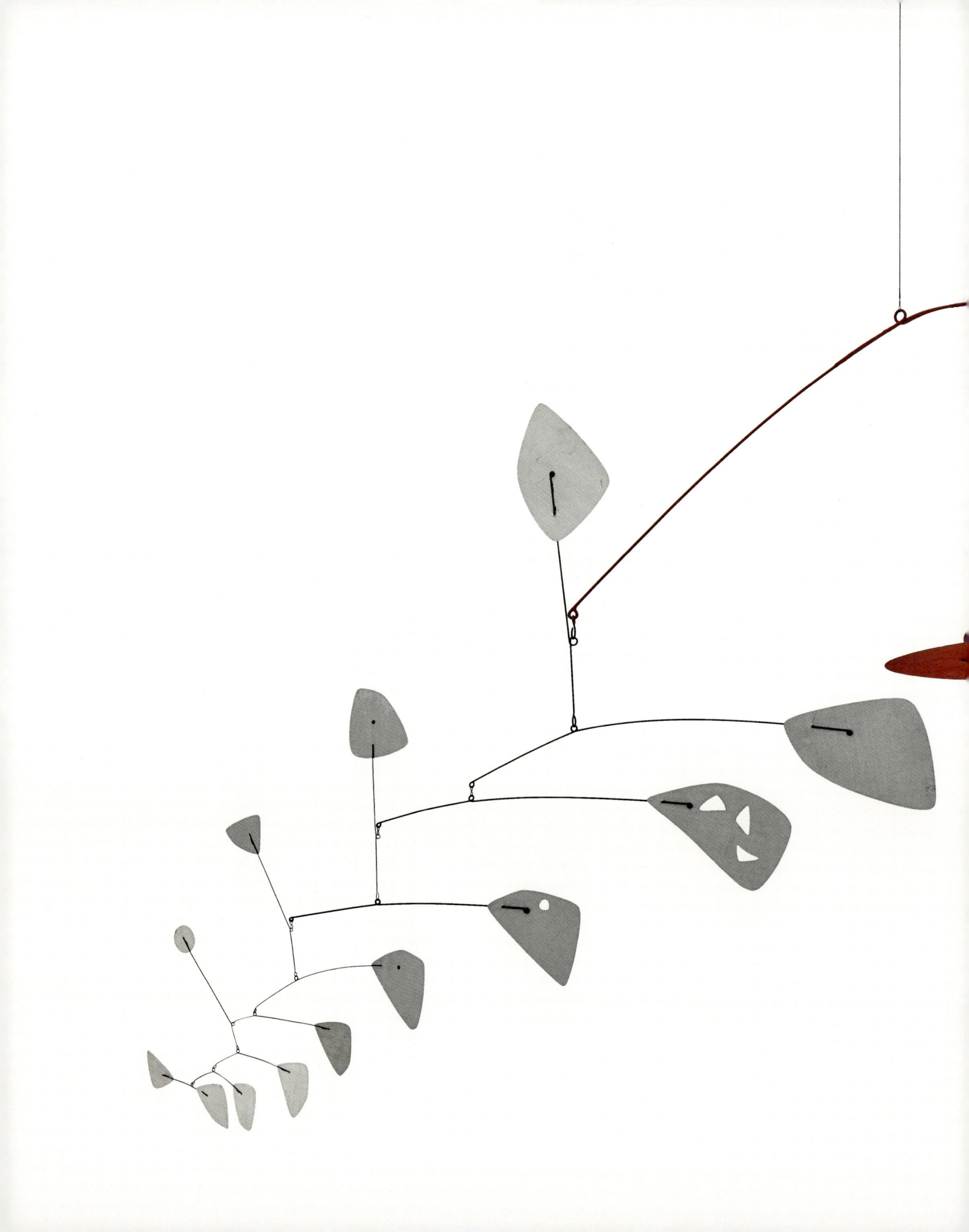

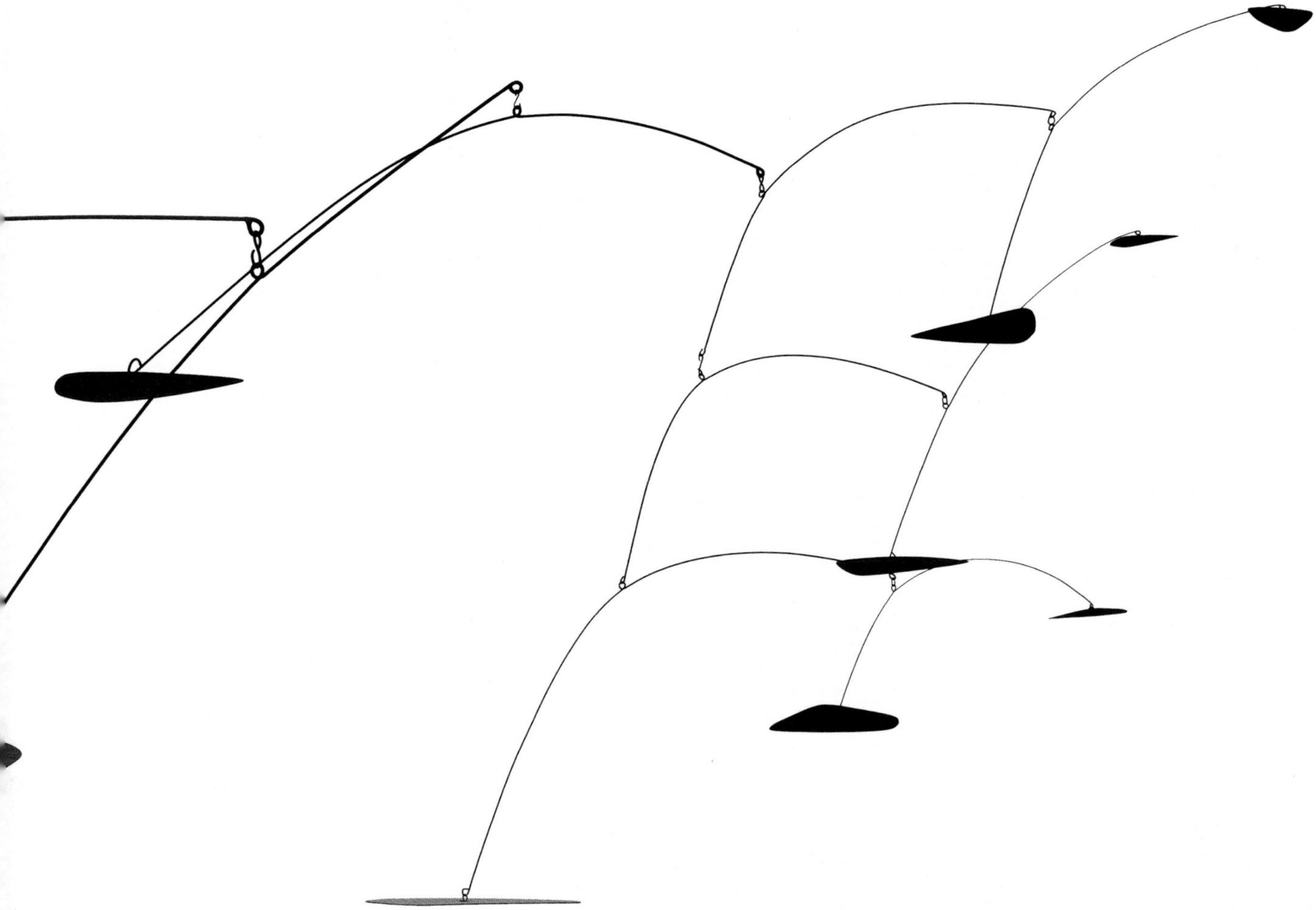

2 *Otto's Mobile*, 1952, Metall, Aluminium, bemalt, 533,4 × 243,8 cm / sheet metal, aluminum, painted, 210 × 96 in., Fondation Beyeler, Riehen/Basel

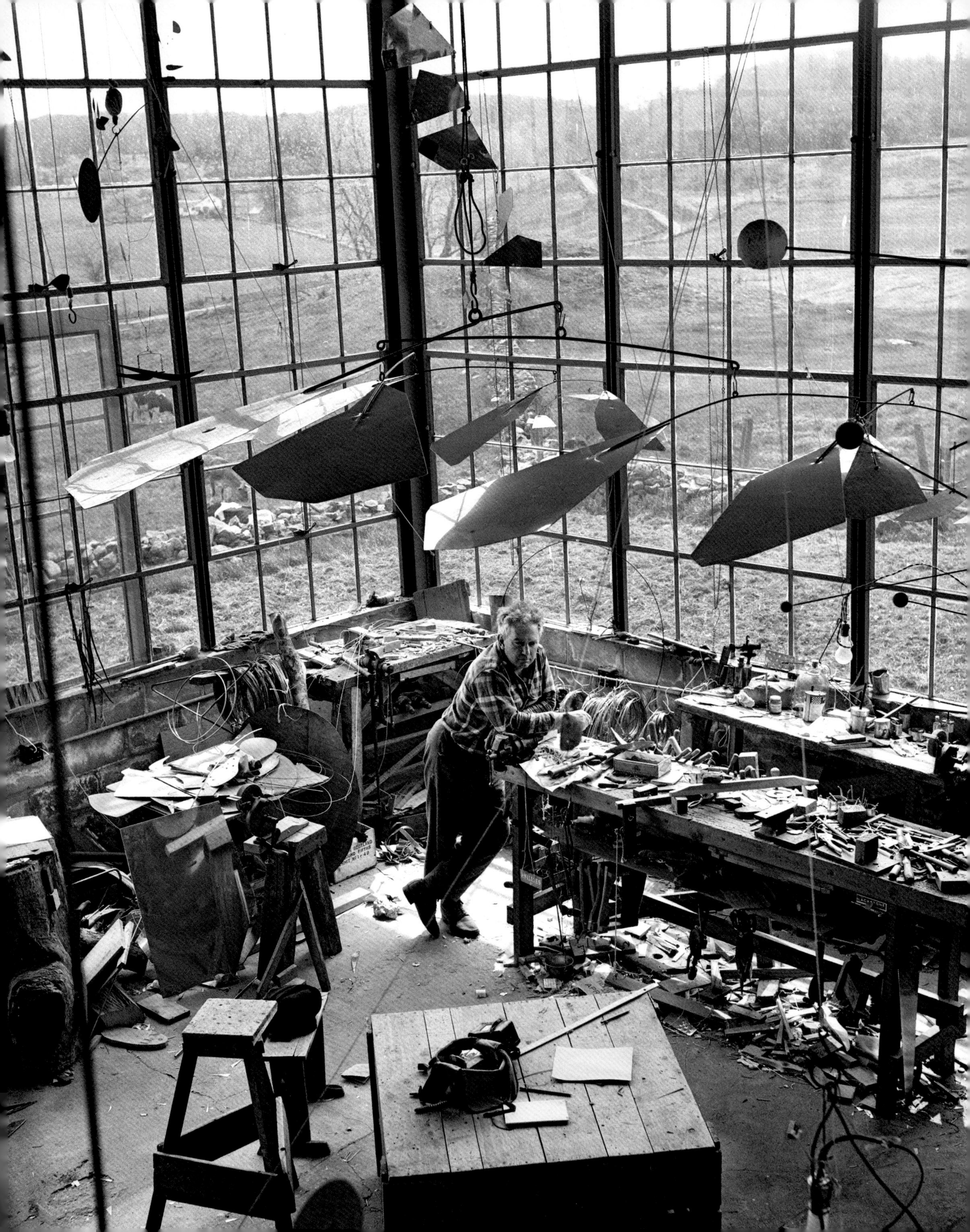

Der Raum als Bühne

Joachim Jäger und Maike Steinkamp

Die Kunst von Alexander Calder ist von spektakulären Wechseln der Maßstäbe geprägt. So gibt es seine beweglichen, von der Decke hängenden Mobiles in vielerlei Spielarten und Größen. Mal legte Calder diese Mobiles fragil und zierlich als kleine Drahtgebilde an, mal waren es weiter in den Raum ausgreifende, leicht wippende Schwebeskulpturen, dann wieder schuf er große und schwere, zumeist mehrfarbige Schwenkobjekte. Ähnliches gilt für die Standskulpturen, die oft in dynamisch gebogenen Formen vom Boden aufragenden sogenannten Stabiles. Calder entwickelte zunächst Formate für Innenräume, freistehende, klare Elemente, orientiert am menschlichen Maßstab. In den 1950er-Jahren traten teils monumentale Skulpturen hinzu, die er oft gezielt für weitläufige Parks oder als „urbane Signale“[1] vor modernen Gebäuden entwarf und die diese Orte bis heute markant prägen. Weniger bekannt sind Calders Miniaturen, die vermehrt seit Mitte der 1940er-Jahre entstanden. In ihrer fragilen Zartheit und durch die Möglichkeit, sie in die Hand zu nehmen, entwickeln diese Miniaturen eine ganz besondere Aura. Nahezu zeitgleich entwarf er sein legendäres Schachspiel aus dem Jahr 1944 (Abb. 82). Es besteht aus roten und blauen Holzfiguren sowie einem einfachen Spielbrett und visualisiert auf eindrucksvolle Weise, wie Calder die Barriere zwischen Kunst und sozialer Interaktion überwindet.

Die Ausstellung *Alexander Calder. Minimal/Maximal* spürt diesem besonderen Verhältnis von Größe, Maßstab und Raum nach, das mit Calders Skulpturen verbunden ist. Es geht dabei nicht um eine simple Gegenüberstellung von klein und groß oder bewegt und unbewegt, sondern vielmehr um die jeweiligen Raumerfahrungen, die damit einhergehen. Bewusst möchte die Präsentation den Blick auf einen Aspekt von Calders Kunst lenken, der bislang wenig beachtet wurde: Die Möglichkeit, dass die Betrachterinnen und Betrachter aktiv mit den Skulpturen und ihrem Umfeld in Verbindung treten, indem sie sich um sie herum bewegen, sie möglicherweise in Bewegung setzen oder sie gar „benutzen“, wie etwa das Schachspiel.

3 Calder in seinem Atelier in Roxbury / Calder in his Roxbury studio, 1941, Foto / photo Herbert Matter

Die Neue Nationalgalerie, erbaut von Ludwig Mies van der Rohe, ist der ideale Raum für eine solche Ausstellung (Abb. 4). Nicht nur waren Mies und Calder Zeitgenossen, deren Biografie und Werk geradezu exemplarisch für die westliche Avantgarde stehen. Beide haben mit ihrem Lebenswerk den Aufbruch und die Befreiung der Künste im 20. Jahrhundert maßgeblich beeinflusst, gelten geradezu als „Heroen" einer solchen Moderne. Beide, Mies und Calder, verbindet zusätzlich, dass sie betont für eine möglichst offene Anlage ihrer Werke eintraten. Alexander Calder erreichte dies, indem er bei seinen Mobiles und Stabiles jeden Bezug auf Wirklichkeiten vermied und stattdessen abstrakt und poetisch bestimmten Themenfeldern nachging, was eine freie Lesart der Werke erlaubte. Immer wieder bezog er sein Publikum bewusst mit ein. Mies van der Rohe wiederum schuf Gebäude, die nicht mehr fest von Außenwänden umschlossen waren, sondern die sich – spätestens seit seinem epochalen Deutschen Pavillon für die Weltausstellung in Barcelona (1929) – öffneten, von fließenden Formen und Strukturen gekennzeichnet waren. Die Neue Nationalgalerie lässt sich in seinem Schaffen als Endpunkt einer langen Entwicklung solcher Architekturen sehen. Der Berliner Bau, den Mies in den 1960er-Jahren als letztes von ihm selbst noch vollständig geplantes Gebäude schuf, gilt als sein großes Vermächtnis. Gerade die lichtdurchflutete Halle, dieser sich scheinbar endlos in die Weite der Stadt erstreckende Raum, steht für ein Prinzip der Offenheit, dem sich auch Calder verschrieben hatte. Es ist vielleicht kein Zufall, dass Calders Atelier in Roxbury (im US-Bundesstaat Connecticut) ebenfalls ein Haus mit großen Fensterflächen war, in dem sich die Licht- und Schattenwirkung seiner raumgreifenden Arbeiten besonders eindrucksvoll entfalteten (Abb. 3). Und noch ein weiteres Thema verbindet Mies und Calder: die Nähe zum Theater. Beide waren von den performativen, interaktiven Räumen des Theaters, auch des Zirkus, stark beeinflusst. Mies van der Rohe sprach sogar explizit von einer „Bühne", als er nach dem Sinn und Nutzen der Ausstellungshalle der Neuen Nationalgalerie gefragt wurde, die aufgrund ihrer Größe in den 1960er-Jahren nahezu unbespielbar erschien. Heute dagegen, im Rückblick auf eine Ära der Moderne, präsentiert sich die Halle als idealer Ort für die Inszenierung von Skulpturen, als eine perfekte Bühne, auf der sich die Werke von Calder, im Kleinen wie im Großen, in außergewöhnlicher Weise erleben lassen.

Die Eroberung des Raumes

Der 1898 geborene und aus einer Künstlerfamilie stammende Alexander Calder wurde von Kindheit an zur künstlerischen Arbeit ermuntert. Nach dem Abschluss als Maschinenbauingenieur wandte er sich 1923 der bildenden Kunst zu. Parallel zu seinem Studium an der Art Students League of New York arbeitete er als Zeichner und Illustrator. Ab 1926 zog es ihn wiederholt für längere Zeit nach Paris, wo er bald zu der künstlerischen Avantgarde um Marcel Duchamp, Joan Miró, Piet Mondrian, Hans Arp, Fernand Léger und den Surrealisten gehörte. In dieser Zeit entwickelte er seinen berühmten

Cirque Calder (1926–1931), ein Ensemble von kleinen Objekten, Tieren und Artisten aus Draht, Stoff, Holz, Kork und anderen gefundenen Materialien. Seine Vorstellungen an den verschiedensten Orten waren für das Publikum immersive Erfahrungen aus Musik, Adrenalin und Aktion (Abb. 12). Aus Draht waren auch seine Porträts von Freunden und bekannten Persönlichkeiten sowie Darstellungen von Zirkusfiguren, die in diesem Zeitraum entstanden (Abb. 5, 6) und die Kritiker in den späten 1920er-Jahren als „Zeichnungen in der Luft" beschrieben.[2] Sowohl der Zirkus als auch seine frühen Drahtkonstruktionen führen vor Augen, wie Calder mit seinen Objekten nicht nur den sie umgebenden Raum mit einbezieht, sondern die Betrachterinnen und Betrachter zugleich aktiv in den performativen Prozess integriert. Noch klarer tritt dieses Verständnis in Calders ersten Mobiles zutage, die seit 1931 entstanden und deren nunmehr abstrakte Formen durch den kleinsten Luftzug in Bewegung versetzt werden konnten. „Von dem Begriff ‚Abstraktion'" – so berichtet Calder in seiner Autobiografie – „hatte ich keine bewusste Vorstellung, kein Gefühl dafür", bis er Piet Mondrian im Oktober 1930 in dessen Atelier besuchte.[3] Dabei waren es weniger die einzelnen Kunstwerke, die ihn beeindruckten, als Mondrians Gestaltung und Vereinnahmung des Raumes, durch die sich ihm das Gefühl vermittelte, in einem neoplastischen Kunstwerk zu stehen (Abb. 60).[4] Im Anschluss an dieses Ereignis – nach einem kurzen Intermezzo mit abstrakten Formen in der Malerei – schuf Calder stehende Konstruktionen aus Draht, Holz und Metall, in denen er sich gänzlich von seinen figurativen Anfängen löste, ebenso wie die ersten, teils motorisierten Mobiles. Die stehenden Konstruktionen, wenig später von dem Künstler Hans Arp als „Stabile" benannten Objekte, bewegten sich nicht von allein, sondern ermöglichten durch ihre Mechanik oder aber durch die Bewegung der Betrachtenden im Raum und die Inszenierung mithilfe von Licht und Schatten immer wieder neue, spektakuläre Ansichten (Abb. 7).

Minimal / Maximal

In die 1930er-Jahre fällt auch die Entstehung von Calders ersten großen Objekten wie *Devil Fish* (1937), die erste Arbeit aus vernieteten Stahlplatten und maßstäblich nach einem Modell gefertigt (Abb. 41). Mit einer Gesamthöhe von 119 cm blieb *Devil Fish* jedoch noch wesentlich kleiner und graziler als es die Stabiles waren, die Calder ab den 1950er-Jahren schuf. Insbesondere der technische Fortschritt der Stahlproduktion eröffnete dem Bildhauer sowohl in den Dimensionen als auch künstlerisch ganz neue Perspektiven. Dies führte unter anderem dazu, dass er verstärkt an der Schnittstelle zwischen Skulptur und Architektur arbeitete.[5] So erhielt Calder ab den späten 1950er-Jahren eine Vielzahl von Aufträgen für monumentale Plastiken im öffentlichen Raum. Durch die Modernität des Materials und ihre bewegten Elemente präsentieren sich die in dieser Phase entstandenen Objekte majestätisch und klar, aber zugleich dynamisch in der städtischen Kulisse – eine Konfrontation, die der Künstler gezielt herbeiführte. Herausragende Beispiele für diese neuen künstlerischen Ansätze im Spätwerk sind etwa Skulpturen wie *Les Trois Ailes* (Abb. 25) und *Les Triangles* (Abb. 31, beide 1963). Wie weit sich die Dynamik der sich nach allen Seiten hin öffnenden Skulptur durch hoch aufragende, geschwungene Stahlplatten treiben ließ, zeigt

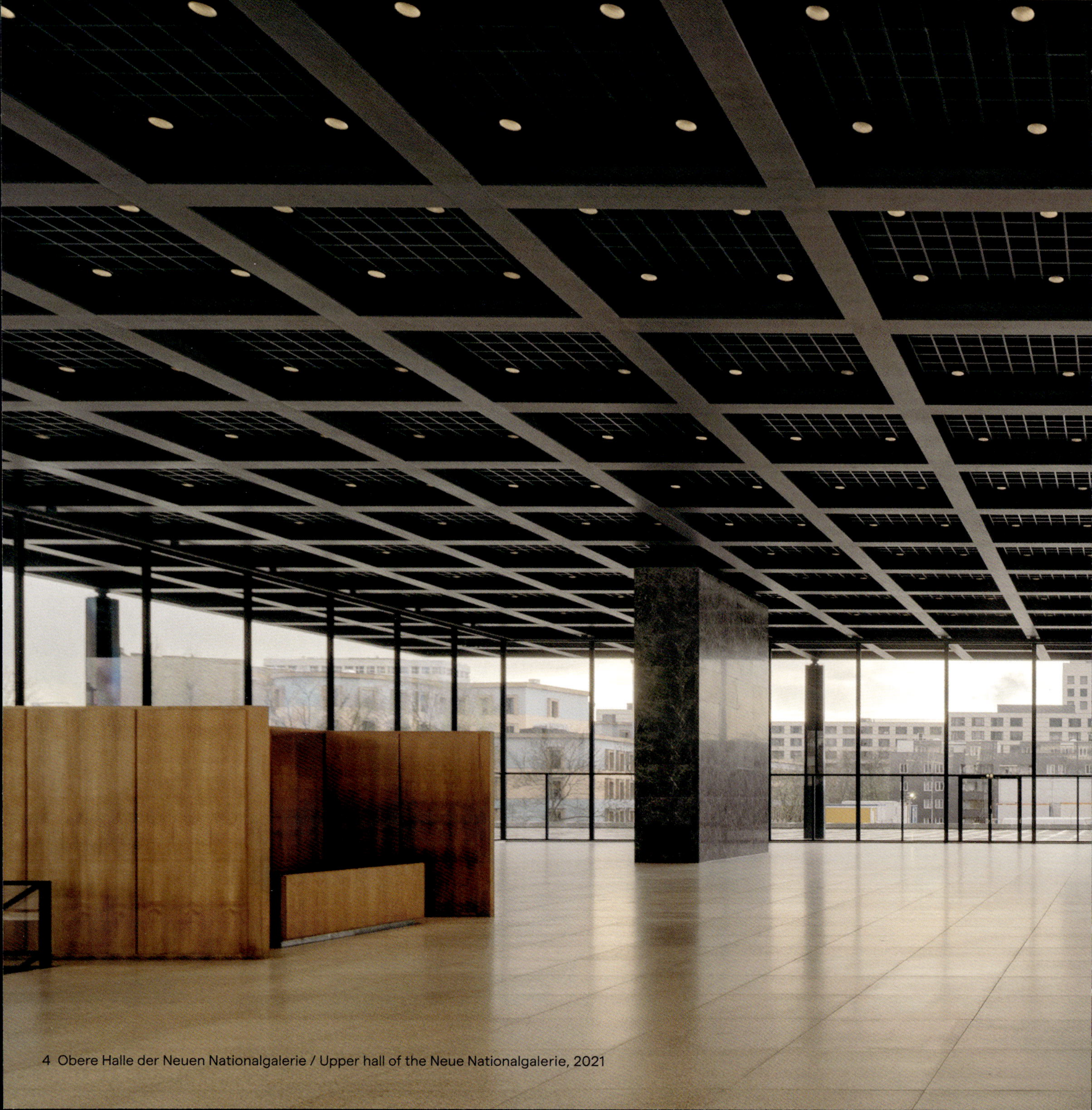

4 Obere Halle der Neuen Nationalgalerie / Upper hall of the Neue Nationalgalerie, 2021

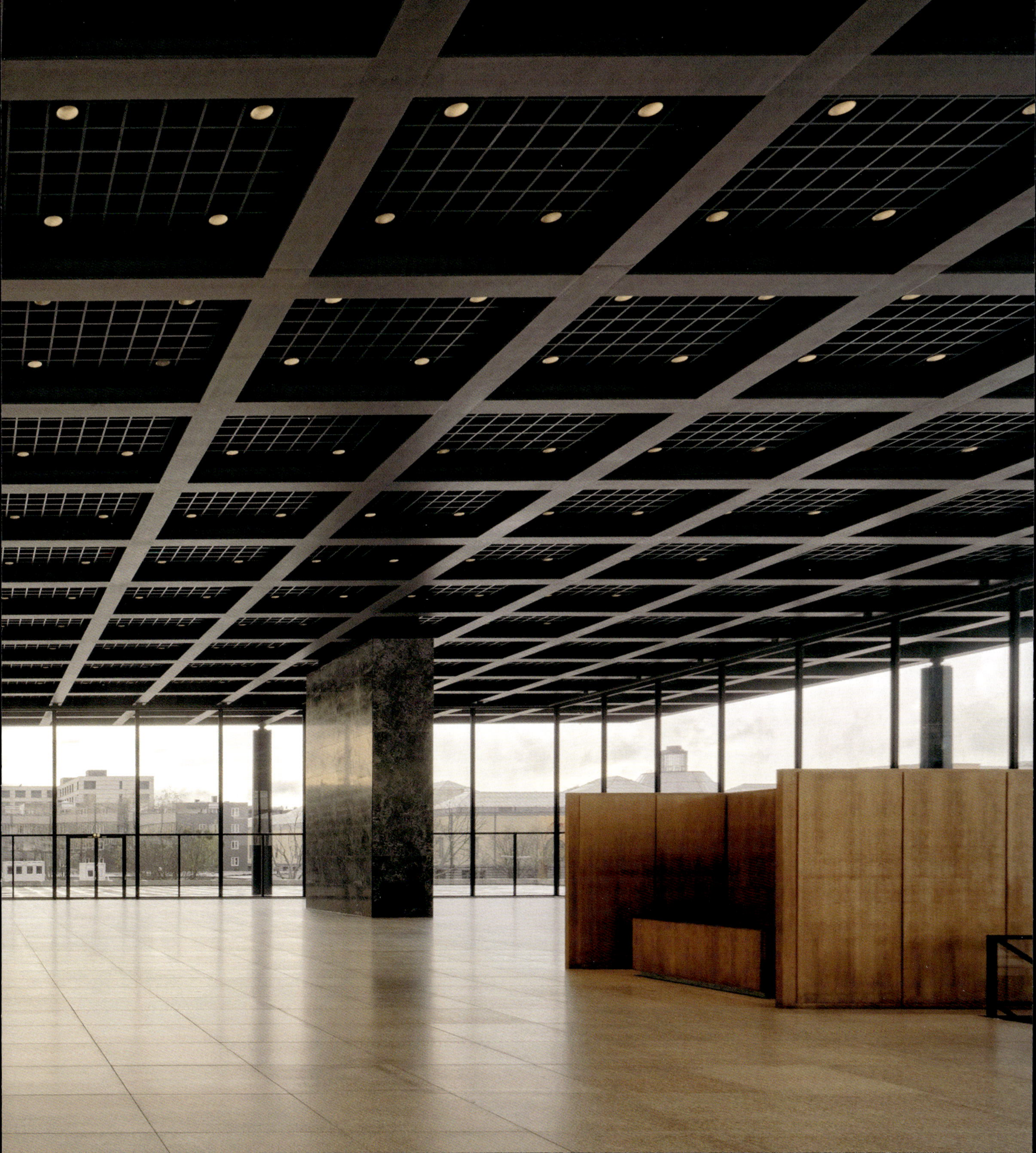

schließlich sein monumentales Spätwerk *Five Swords* (1976, Abb. 8). Das leuchtend rote, fast expressiv ausgreifende Objekt zeigt sich von jeder Seite anders und ist in seiner Vielschichtigkeit überhaupt nur zu erfassen, indem man die Skulptur umschreitet, sie aus der Nähe ebenso wie mit größerem Abstand betrachtet. Allein die Größe verleiht den säbelförmigen Armen eine erhebliche, fast einschüchternde Wucht. Die Versetzung der Skulptur von der weitläufigen Landschaft des Hudson Valley im Bundesstaat New York, wo sie seit den 1980er-Jahren steht, in den Innenraum, in die Halle von Mies van der Rohe, soll genau diese vielschichtige Wahrnehmungsmöglichkeit ins Zentrum rücken. Was geschieht, wenn ich mich dieser Skulptur nähere? Welche konkreten Räume eröffnen sich mit der Skulptur in diesem Umfeld und durch den Dialog mit den Besucherinnen und Besuchern?

Auch bei den Mobiles in Calders Werk ist nach 1950 eine erhebliche Veränderung des Maßstabs erkennbar. Insbesondere Auftragsarbeiten für bestimmte Gebäude nahm er häufig zum Anlass, die Dimensionen der Objekte zu vergrößern. So entstand beispielsweise für die Eingangshalle des heutigen John F. Kennedy International Airport[6] das großformatige Mobile *.125* (1957), das den Raum im Atrium des Flughafens klar definiert und so neue Perspektiven im Zusammenspiel mit der Architektur eröffnet (Abb. 11). Auch andere bedeutende Mobiles der 1950er-Jahre wie *Blizzard* (1950, Abb. 72) oder *Otto's Mobile* (1952, Abb. 2) mit ihrer teils horizontalen, teils vertikalen Ausrichtung transformieren die sie umgebenden Räumlichkeiten fortwährend und erlauben durch ihre Bewegungen, diesen kontinuierlich neu zu erfahren. Die nach Fertigstellung vergebenen Titel der Arbeiten rufen zuweilen eigene Welten auf. Auch wenn sie nicht als Deutungsgrundlagen gedacht sind, lenkt Calder den Blick durch bestimmte Titel auf spezifische Geometrien, so bei *Les Triangles*, auf die Macht der Natur, etwa bei *Blizzard*, oder er verweist auf die

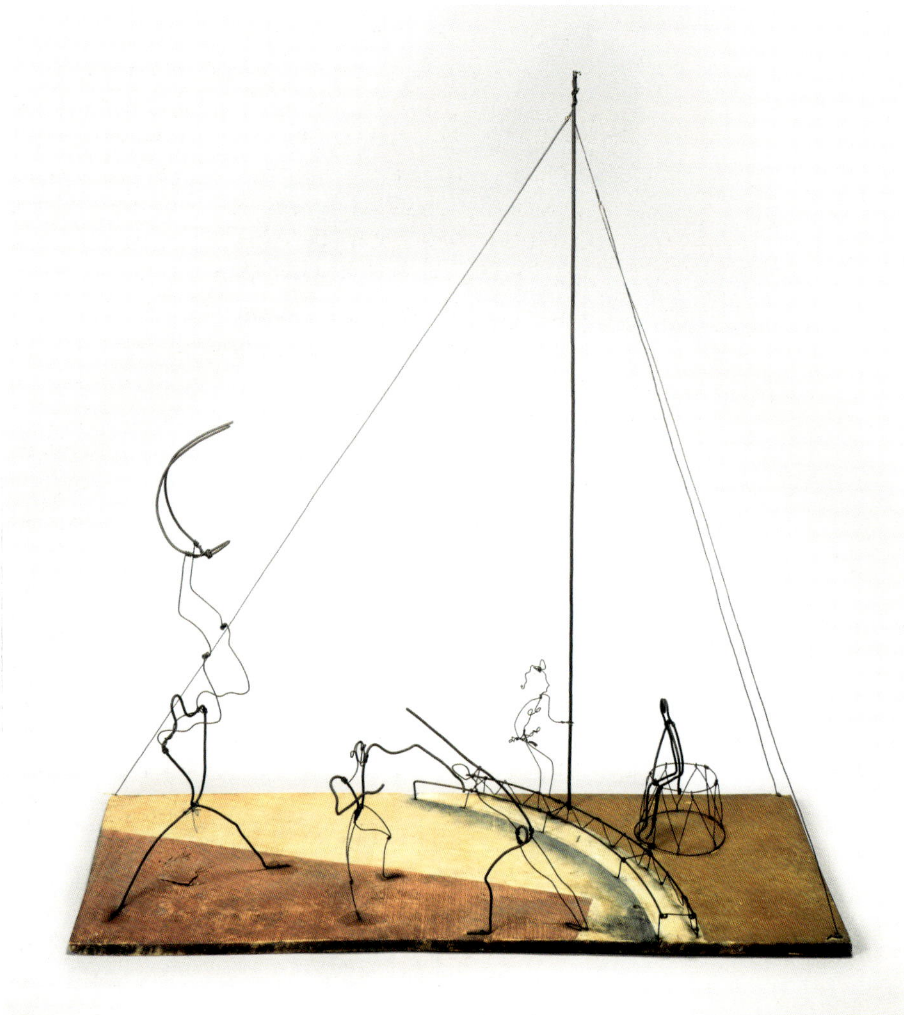

5 *Circus Scene*, 1929, Draht, Holz, Farbe, 127 × 118,7 × 46 cm / wire, wood, paint, 50 × 46¾ × 18⅛ in., Calder Foundation, New York

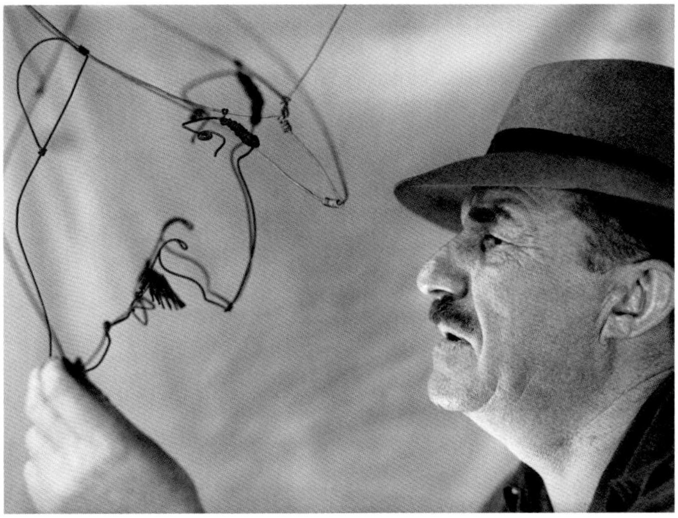

6 Fernand Léger mit seinem Drahtporträt *Fernand Léger* (1930) von Calder, 1934 / Fernand Léger with his wire portrait *Fernand Léger* (1930) by Calder, 1934, Foto / photo Walter Limot

metallene Substanz seiner Kunst, wie bei *Otto's Mobile*, das nicht nur nach dem Vorstandsvorsitzenden der Meta-Mold Aluminum Company, Otto Spaeth, benannt ist, sondern in der amerikanischen Aussprache auch eine phonetische Assoziation mit „automobile" (sich selbst bewegend) herstellt.[7]

Zeitlebens arbeitete Calder mit verschiedenen Primär- und Sekundärfarben, setzte aber vor allem auf Schwarz und nutzte Farbtöne, um „Disparität" innerhalb der Objekte zu erzeugen. So ließ er starke Kontraste entstehen, welche die Skulpturen deutlich aus dem städtischen oder landschaftlichen Umfeld hervortreten lässt. Diese Farbauswahl findet sich auch bei seinen Kleinstobjekten wieder, die ihrerseits Formen und Konstellationen aufgreifen, die er in seinen Großskulpturen nutzte. So gibt es auch unter seinen Miniaturen Stabiles oder die sogenannten Standing Mobiles, die auf einer Metallbasis bewegliche Drahtkonstruktionen balancieren (Abb. 17). Entstanden sind diese kleinen Werke aus übriggebliebenen Metallteilen der Großskulpturen oder aber aus gefundenen Objekten wie zum Beispiel einem Löffel, der zum geschwungenen, beweglichen Fundament für ein an seinem Stiel befestigtes, winziges Mobile wird (Abb. 80). Calders Minimals sind dabei oft mehreres zugleich: Modelle für größere Skulpturen, künstlerische Experimente und auch eigenständige Arbeiten, die demonstrieren, dass ein Objekt, das ebensogut gewaltig und groß hätte sein können, durch sein kleines Format nichts an Ausdruckskraft einbüßt.[8] Dennoch, die Miniaturen fordern eine völlig andere Auseinandersetzung mit dem Raum von ihren Betrachtern. Sie verlangen Aufmerksamkeit und Konzentration. Statt einem öffentlichen Auftritt, einem Spektakel der raumfüllenden Großobjekte, lassen sich die Miniaturen nur in einer intimen, fast privaten Vorstellung erleben.[9]

Gerade diese Erfahrung des Intimen, des Persönlichen, auch im Rahmen einer großen öffentlichen Ausstellung zu ermöglichen, war ein zentraler Ausgangspunkt des Projekts *Alexander Calder. Minimal/ Maximal*. Zu festen Zeiten werden einige der kleinen Objekte in der Ausstellung auch außerhalb der schützenden Vitrinen, im direkten Dialog mit den Besucherinnen und Besuchern vorgestellt. Fast alle Miniaturen sind leicht zu bewegen, sie sind nicht ortsgebunden, im Gegenteil waren sie zum Mitnehmen, im Wortsinne als „mobile" Skulpturen und Begleiter gedacht. Dies zeigt sich insbesondere in dem sehr persönlich angelegten *Louisa's 43rd Birthday Present* für die Frau des Künstlers (Abb. 15). Es besteht aus einer Zigarrenbox mit fünf winzigen Standing Mobiles, die – der Schachtel entnommen und auf dem Tisch arrangiert – selbst zu einer eigenen kleinen Ausstellung werden. Dieses Herausnehmen, dieser aktive Umgang mit den Skulpturen war etwas, das Calder bereits in seinem Frühwerk anstrebte. Schon seine Zirkusfiguren beschrieb er als „Miniatur-Instrumente".[10] Immer wieder fertigte er Objekte an, die zur Beteiligung einluden, sei es, um sie durch Anpusten in Bewegung zu versetzen oder um mit ihnen zu spielen, wie die drei Schachspiele, die er Anfang der 1940er-Jahre herstellte (Abb. 82). In der Ausstellung haben die Besucherinnen und Besucher die Möglichkeit, mit Faksimiles der von Calder entwickelten Schachfiguren zu spielen – ganz so, wie es zu ihrer Entstehungszeit vorgesehen war. Die Schachbegeisterung teilte Calder mit vielen Künstlern seiner Zeit. Auch wenn er ein weniger passionierter Spieler war als Marcel Duchamp oder Max Ernst, hat ihn die interaktive und soziale Komponente des Spiels in jeder Hinsicht fasziniert.

Eine besondere Aktivierung im Raum kennzeichnet *Small Sphere and Heavy Sphere* (1932/33, Abb. 23), das erste hängende Mobile und eine frühe betont performative Arbeit. Sie besteht aus Flaschen und anderen von Calder so genannten Impedimenta (Hindernissen) – Glasflaschen, einer Holzkiste, einer Blechdose und einem vom Künstler gefertigten Gong – sowie zwei an langen Schnüren kreisenden Kugeln. Die Gegenstände können von den Besucherinnen und Besuchern individuell auf dem Boden arrangiert und immer wieder neu angeordnet werden. Die rote, gusseiserne Kugel wird, zusammen mit ihrem etwas kleineren, weißen Gegenpart aus Holz, bei jeder Installation der Arbeit neu ins Spiel gebracht. Wird die rote Kugel in Bewegung gesetzt, schwingt auch die weiße und löst durch die stets unterschiedlichen Bewegungsverläufe und zahlreichen Kollisionen oder Beinahe-Berührungen mit den Objekten eine visuell wie klanglich unvorhersehbare, überraschende Reaktion aus.[11] „Calder wollte, dass *Small Sphere and Heavy Sphere* als *Idee* existierte – eine Idee, die wieder und wieder frisch umgesetzt wird –, wobei die *Idee* der einzige gleichbleibende Aspekt der Arbeit sein sollte."[12]

Mit dieser (heute leider kaum mehr durchführbaren) Idee, dass die Betrachterinnen und Betrachter das Kunstwerk selbst in Gang setzen, nahm Calder bereits Ansätze der interaktiven Kunst der 1960er-Jahre wie Zero, Happening oder Konzeptkunst vorweg. Dabei ist die enge Kopplung von Klang und Bewegung, die den besonderen Reiz von *Small Sphere and Heavy Sphere* ausmacht, ein oft wiederkehrendes Moment in Calders Arbeit. Es zeigt sich zum Beispiel an dem großen, aus roten ovalen Metallplatten bestehenden Standmobile *Chef d'orchestre* (1966), das der Bildhauer eigens für ein Musikstück des Komponisten Earle Brown entwickelte. Die Skulptur fungiert in der für vier Schlagwerker konzipierten Performance sowohl als

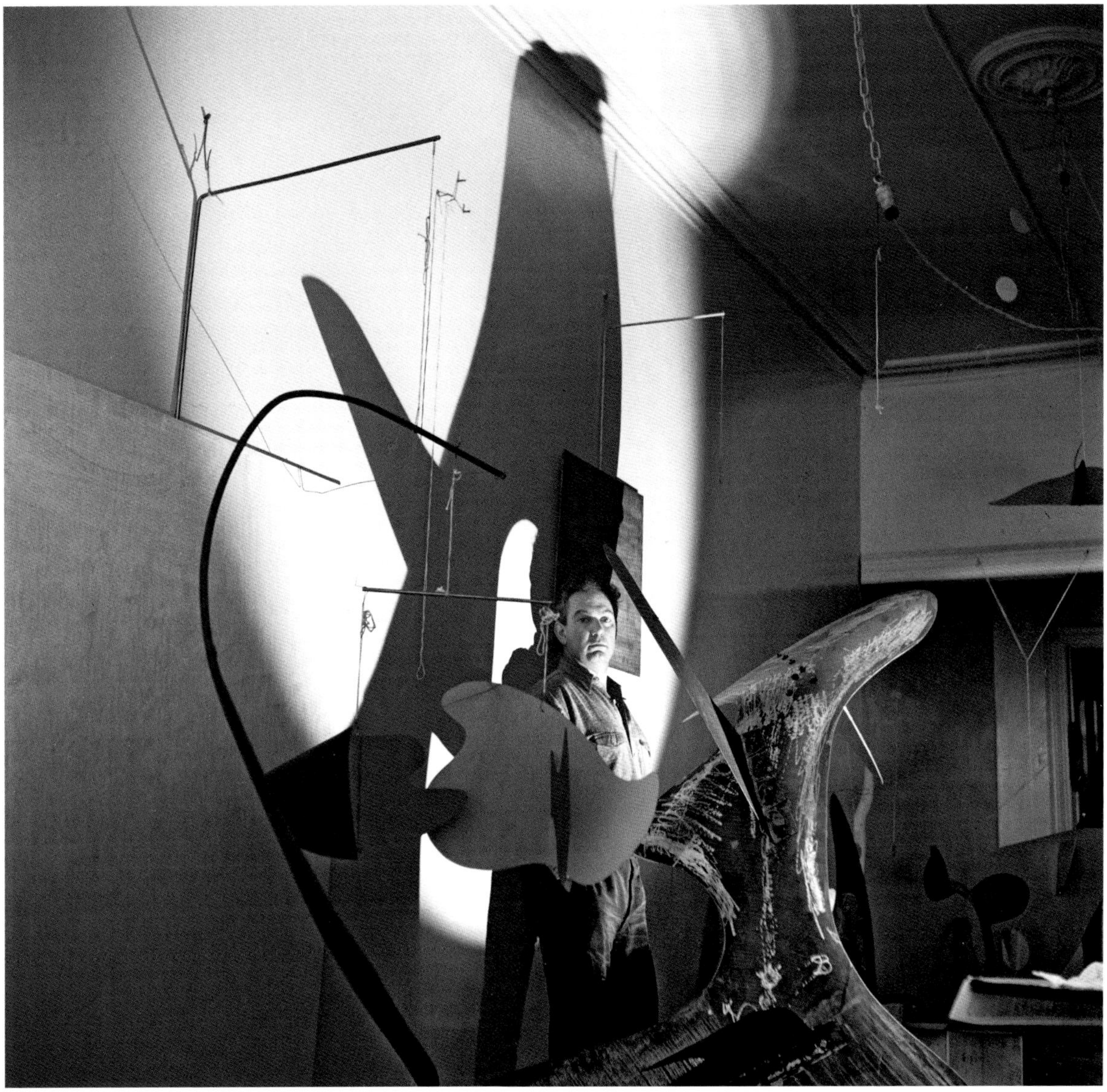

7 Calder mit *White Panel* (1936) und *Devil Fish* (1937, vor Fertigstellung) in seinem New Yorker Laden-Atelier, 1936 / Calder with *White Panel* (1936) and *Devil Fish* (1937, before completion) in his New York City storefront studio, 1936, Foto / photo Herbert Matter

„Dirigent", der das Tempo vorgibt, wie auch ihrerseits als Schlaginstrument (Abb. 10). Auch hier verbinden sich Objekt, Klang, Raum und die Anwesenden zu einem künstlerischen Gesamterlebnis.

Der Raum als Bühne

Für Calder war ein Kunstwerk keine abgeschlossene Erzählung. Vielmehr begriff er es als „Ereignis" beziehungsweise als „Erlebnis".[13] Dieses Erleben wird durch die unterschiedlichen Assoziationsebenen ermöglicht, die den Betrachtenden in verschiedenen Umgebungen – Architektur, Natur, Museum – angeboten werden, mit starken Rückkopplungen auf die Skulpturen selbst. Durch ihre farblichen Kontraste, durch Bewegung, unerwartete Perspektiven oder Einblicke verzahnen sie sich mit der Umgebung und rufen ein ganzheitliches Raumempfinden hervor, wie es viel später erst zeitgenössische „Installationen" ermöglichen sollten. Tatsächlich hat Calder die Bewegung von Personen und das Umherschweifen des Blicks immer mitgedacht. Der umgebende Raum fungierte aus Calders Sicht als Bühne, auf der seine Arbeiten eine visuelle wie auch physische Verbindung mit dem Publikum eingehen.

Den Raum als Bühne zu begreifen, diese Auffassung spiegelt sich auch in Calders Interesse am Theater, dem Varieté und natürlich dem Zirkus wider. Während er mit seinem *Cirque Calder* selbst ein entscheidender Akteur war, entwickelte er später für diverse Inszenierungen Mobiles und Stabiles, die den Bühnenraum aktivierten, etwa 1936 für Eric Saties sinfonisches Drama *Socrate*, Henri Pichettes Schauspiel *Nucléa* (1952) oder für seine eigene und gleichzeitig persönlichste Produktion *Work in Progress* (1968) am Teatro dell'Opera in Rom (Abb. 13).[14] Schon in seinen frühen Ausstellungen war Calder darauf bedacht, seine Skulpturen zu inszenieren, sei es beispielsweise in Form von gezielt gesetztem Schlaglicht und dem so erzeugten Schattenwurf, oder aber durch die Bewegung der einzelnen Elemente seiner Arbeiten, die von leichten Berührungen der Besucherinnen und Besucher ausgelöst wurde. Diese Aktivierung durch das Publikum forderte Calder bereits bei seiner Retrospektive im Museum of Modern Art in New York 1943 explizit ein.[15] Auch in späteren Jahren war es auf Ausstellungen gestattet, die Werke zu berühren, bis steigende Besucherzahlen die Objekte zu stark in Mitleidenschaft zogen (Abb. 14).[16]

Bereits 1935 hatte James John Sweeney, ein guter Freund Calders und der Kurator seiner Retrospektive im Museum of Modern Art, die interaktive Wirkung dieser Kunst erkannt:

„[...] in einem Saal voller [Werke] Calders stellen wir eine deutlich ausgeprägtere Lebendigkeit fest, die auf irgendeine Weise mit den Raumverhältnissen, der Architektur, der Anordnung von Linien und Farben wie auch dem Rhythmus der Objekte zu tun hat. Calders Sprache ist eine der Schlichtheit; sein Schaffen ist zutiefst verbunden mit unserem heutigen Umfeld."[17]

Dieser starke Bezug zum Umraum, den Sweeney hier anspricht, gerade auch jener zum jeweiligen sozialen und gesellschaftlichen Umfeld der Arbeiten, prägt das gesamte Schaffen Calders – ganz gleich, ob es sich um monumentale Großskulpturen oder Miniaturen handelt. Während seiner künstlerischen Laufbahn wechselte Calder immer wieder vom Kleinen zum Großen und wieder zurück. Maßstab, Größe und Größenverhältnisse sind neben Farben, Kontrasten, der Verschiedenheit von Form und Bewegung zentrale Werkzeuge seines Schaffens und der Schlüssel zu Calders eigener Definition von Skulptur als einem „sozialen" Objekt. Es war sein größtes Anliegen, dass wir uns seinem Werk intuitiv nähern, damit interagieren, es in seiner Komplexität wahrnehmen und seine Arbeiten und ihre Umgebung als Erfahrungsraum begreifen. Seinen Skulpturen ist keine feste Bedeutung eingeschrieben, vielmehr werden wir als Publikum zum unmittelbaren Erleben der Objekte aufgefordert. Es ist eine große Freiheit und Offenheit, die sich daher mit Calders Kunst verbindet und die zu seinen Lebzeiten viel radikaler und visionärer war, als man das heute vielleicht wahrnimmt. Der visuelle wie partizipative Erfahrungsraum, den Calder mit seinen Skulpturen eröffnet, ist ein wesentlicher Grund dafür, dass der Künstler weltweit so populär geblieben ist: Seine Werke wirken nicht einengend oder festgelegt, sondern bleiben variabel und offen.

1 Maurice Bruzeau: *Calder à Saché*, New York 1975, Neuauflage 1979, S. 15.

2 Siehe z. B. Gros: „Sculpture sur fil de fer", in: *Paris-Midi*, 2.2.1929; Paul Fierens, *Journal des Débats*, 3.2.1929.

3 Alexander Calder: *Calder: An Autobiography with Pictures*, hg. von Jean Davidson, New York 1966, S. 113.

4 Vgl. Jed Perl: *Calder. The Conquest of Time. The Early Years, 1898–1940*, New York 2017, S. 340f.

5 Emily Caplan Reed: „Sculpture and Architecture: Building Calder's Global Network", in: *Alexander Calder: Radical Inventor/Inventeur radical*, hg. von Elizabeth Hutton Turner und Anne Grace, Ausst.-Kat. Montreal Museum of Fine Arts; National Gallery of Victoria, Melbourne, Mailand 2018, S. 169–180, hier S. 169.

6 Damals Idlewild Airport.

7 Calder nannte das Werk in einem Brief vom 9.3.1953 (Archiv der Calder Foundation) „Otto's Mobile", in Publikationen wurde es seinerzeit jedoch auch als „Ottomobile" bezeichnet, so etwa im *Milwaukee Journal*, 25.2. und 27.3.1953, in der *New York Times*, 7.6.1953 und in *Time*, 63, Nr. 21, 24.5.1954.

8 Vgl. Jed Perl: „Alexander Calder: Multum in Parvo", in: *Multum in Parvo*, Ausst.-Kat. Dominique Levy Gallery, New York 2015, S. 11–19, hier S. 13.

9 Vgl. ebd.

10 „Futurist Toys for Advanced Kiddies Created by Calder, Artist-Engineer", in: *New York Herald* (Paris), 4.8.1927, S. 7, zit. in Elizabeth Hutton Turner: „Alexander Calder and the Case for Radical Invention", in: Ausst.-Kat. Montreal/Melbourne (wie Anm. 5), S. 23–43, hier S. 32.

11 Vgl. Gryphon Rue Rower-Upjohn: „Calder und der Klang", in: *Alexander Calder. Avantgarde in Bewegung*, Ausst.-Kat. Kunstsammlung Nordrhein-Westfalen, Düsseldorf, München 2013, S. 99–111, hier S. 104. Eine erste Version wurde 1933 in der Galerie Pierre Colle gezeigt. Diese existiert heut nicht mehr. Kurze Zeit später schuf Calder eine zweite Version, die in der Ausstellung der Neuen Nationalgalerie zu sehen ist.

12 Alexander S. C. Rower: „Calder's Grand Proposition", in: *Calder: Small Sphere and Heavy Sphere*, Ausst.-Kat. Pace Gallery, New York 2019, S. 20.

13 Alexander S. C. Rower: „Approximations of Perfection", in: *Calder: Monumental*, Ausst.-Kat. Denver Botanic Gardens, Denver 2017, S. 13.

14 Ausführlich zu den Theaterproduktionen vgl. *Alexander Calder. Performing Sculpture*, hg. von Achim Borchardt-Hume, Ausst.-Kat. Tate Modern, London 2015.

15 Vgl. Jed Perl: *Calder. The Conquest of Space. The Later Years, 1940–1976*, New York 2020, S. 95.

16 Vgl. ebd., S. 96.

17 James Johnson Sweeney: „Alexander Calder's Mobiles", in: *Mobiles by Alexander Calder*, Ausst.-Kat. The Renaissance Society of The University of Chicago, Chicago 1935, https://calder.org/bibliography/mobiles-by-alexander-calder-1935/james-johnson-sweeney-alexander-calders-mobiles (abgerufen am 21.2.2021).

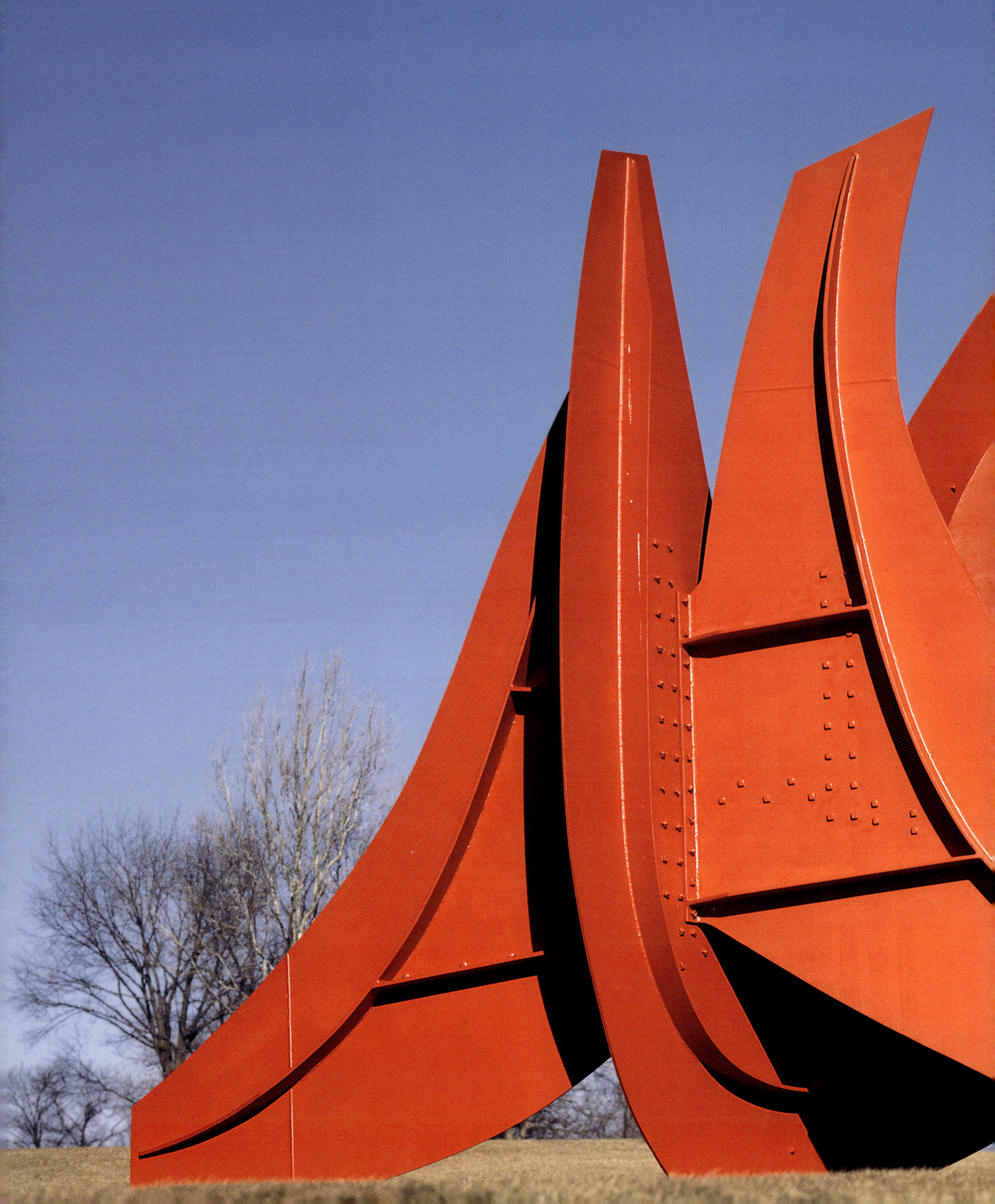

8 *Five Swords*, 1976, Stahl, Bolzen, Farbe, 541 × 671 × 884 cm / sheet metal, bolts, paint, 213 × 264 × 348 in., Calder Foundation, New York

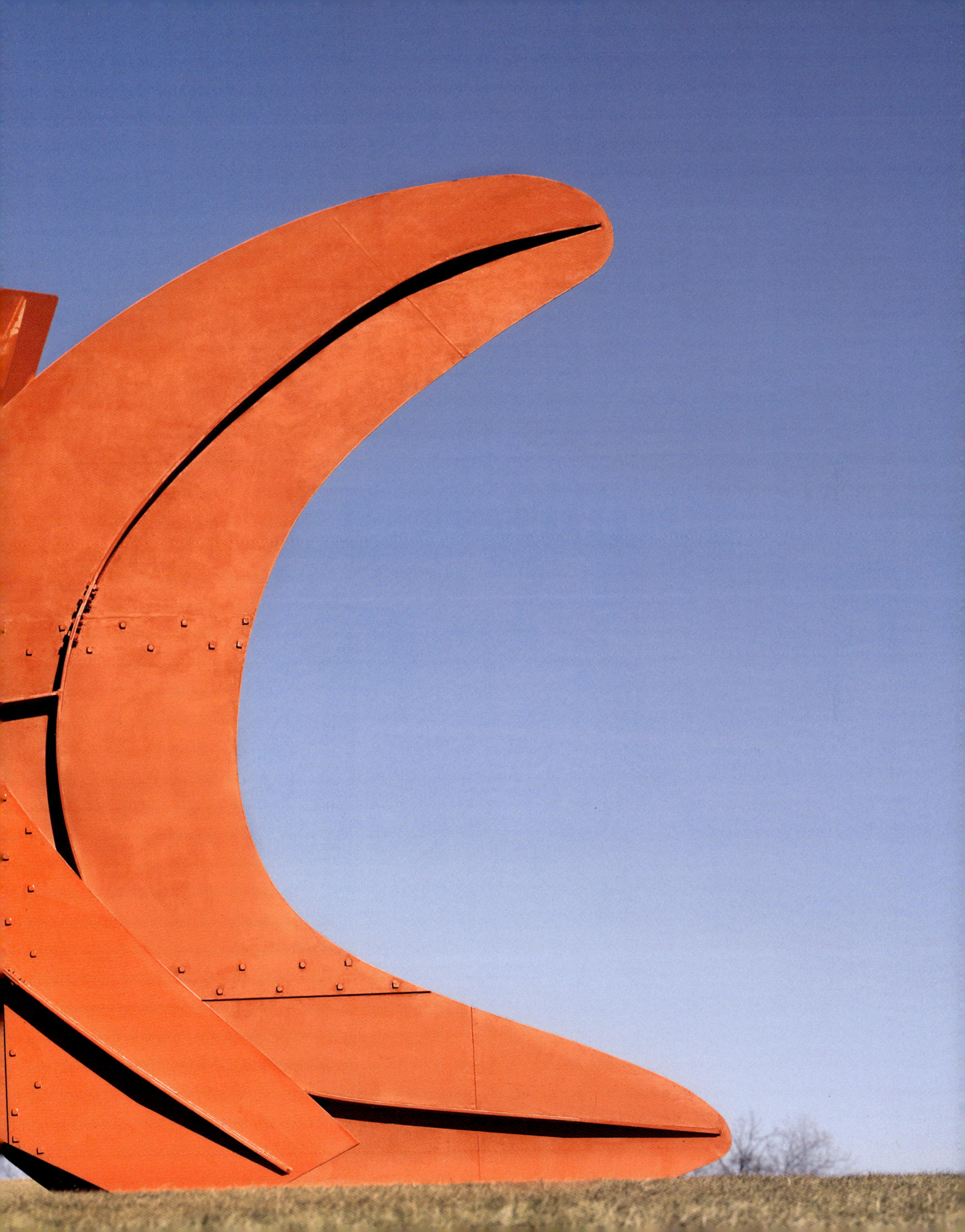

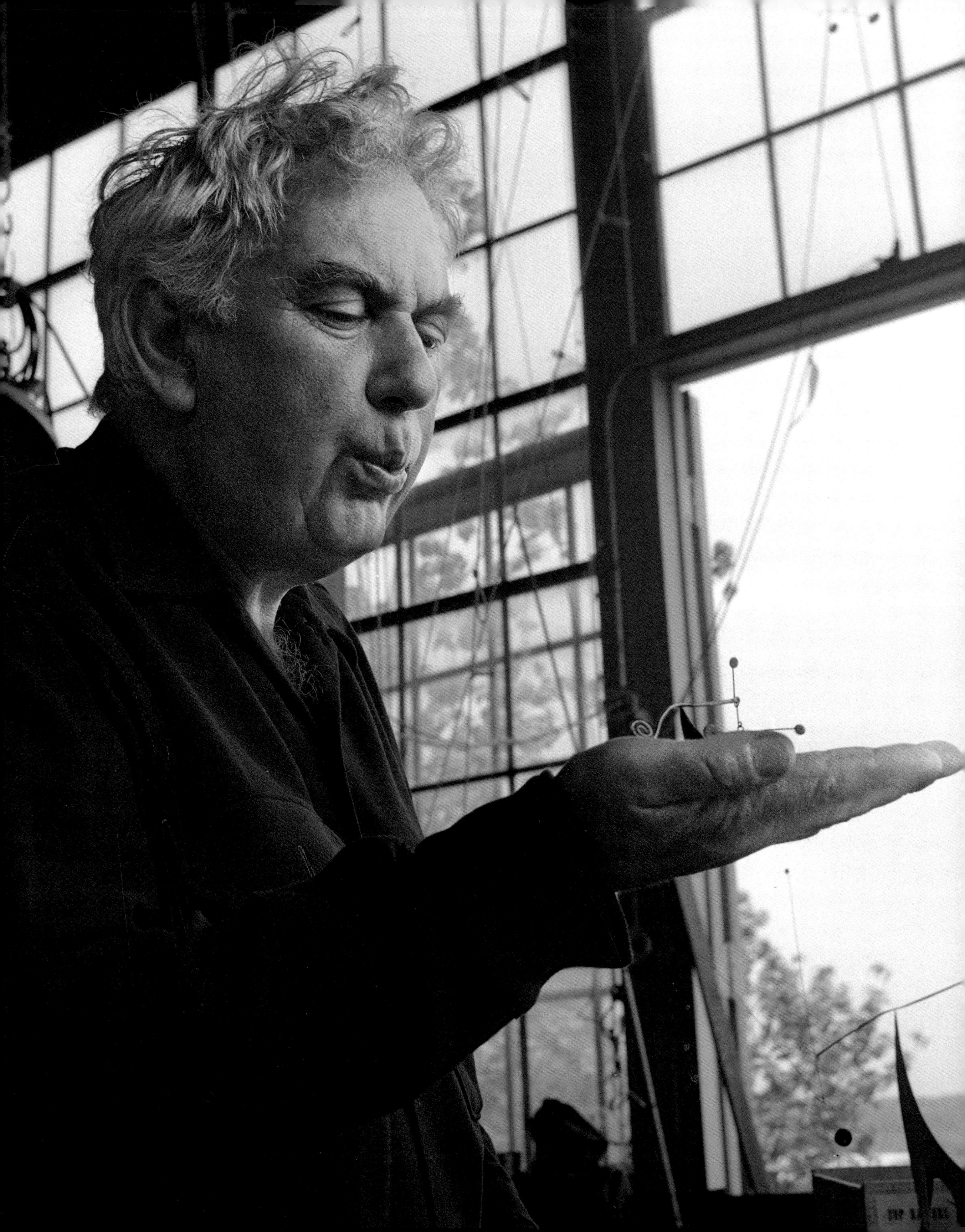

Space as Stage

Joachim Jäger and
Maike Steinkamp

The art of Alexander Calder is distinguished by its striking diversity of scale. His ceiling-mounted mobiles alone come in many variations and sizes. Some are small, fragile structures made of wire, others are spatially expansive, gently teetering floating sculptures, and still others are large and heavy, mostly multicolored pivoting objects. His standing sculptures, the so-called stabiles, which frequently lift upward in dynamic curved shapes, present a similar variation. Calder first developed pieces for interiors; free-standing, distinct components, oriented on a human scale. Beginning in the 1950s these were joined by sculptures, some of them monumental, meant to stand in spacious parks or as "urban signal[s]"[1] in front of modern buildings, works that impressively define their sites to this day. Less well known are Calder's miniatures, which he began to produce in greater numbers in the mid 1940s. Their delicacy and the fact that you can hold them in your hand lend them a particular aura. At the same time, he developed his legendary chess set from 1944 (fig. 82), an object consisting of red and blue wooden pieces and a simple board, which impressively visualizes how Calder was crossing boundaries of social interaction as art.

The exhibition *Alexander Calder: Minimal/Maximal* explores the special relationship between scale and space associated with Calder's sculptures. It doesn't simply present a juxtaposition of large and small or mobile and fixed; rather, it focuses on the particular spatial experiences that accompany the pieces. The presentation deliberately calls attention to an aspect of Calder's art that has as yet received little notice: the opportunity for viewers to socially engage with the

9 Calder in seinem Atelier in Roxbury, um 1960 / Calder in his Roxbury studio, ca. 1960, Foto / photo Hélène Hoppenot

sculptures and their surroundings by moving around them, perhaps setting them in motion, or even "using" them, as in the case of the chess set.

The Neue Nationalgalerie, built by Ludwig Mies van der Rohe, is the ideal venue for such an exhibition (fig. 4). Mies and Calder were not only contemporaries whose biographies and works virtually exemplify the Western avant-garde. With their life's work, both importantly influenced the liberation of the arts in the twentieth century and are considered "heroes" of modernism. What both Mies and Calder also had in common was that they emphatically championed the most open layout possible for their works. Calder achieved this in that he avoided any reference to realities in his mobiles and stabiles, and instead pursued abstract and poetically determined notions, inviting a free reading of them. He deliberately involved his audience time and again. Mies van der Rohe, in turn, created buildings that were no longer firmly enclosed by outer walls, but that—beginning at the latest with his epochal German Pavilion at the International Exposition in Barcelona (1929)—opened out and were defined by flowing forms and structures. The Neue Nationalgalerie can be seen as the end point of a long evolution of such constructions in his work. Realized in the 1960s, the Berlin building, which was the last structure still completely designed by Mies himself, is considered his ultimate legacy. The light-filled hall, a space that appears to extend endlessly outward into the expanse of the city, stands for the principle of openness, to which Calder was also committed. It might not be a coincidence that Calder's studio in Roxbury, Connecticut, was likewise a building with huge windows in which the light and shadow effects of his expansive works unfolded in a particularly impressive manner (fig. 3). There is something else that links the two: their sense of theater. Both were greatly influenced by the performative, interactive spaces of the theater as well as that of the circus. When asked about the meaning and uses of the exhibition hall in the Neue Nationalgalerie, the size of which seemed almost unusable in the 1960s, Mies quite explicitly spoke of it as a "stage." Today, however, looking back on an era of modernism, the hall offers itself as an ideal venue for presenting sculptures, a perfect stage on which Calder's works, both large and small, can be experienced in an extraordinary way.

The Conquest of Space

Born into an artist family in 1898, Alexander Calder was encouraged to create from a young age. After studying mechanical engineering, he turned to fine art in 1923, and while studying at the Art Students League of New York he also worked as a draftsman and illustrator. Beginning in 1926 he repeatedly enjoyed extended stays in Paris, where he soon fell in with the avant-garde artists Marcel Duchamp, Joan Miró, Piet Mondrian, Hans Arp, Fernand Léger, and the Surrealists. It was in this period that he developed his famous *Cirque Calder* (1926–31), an ensemble of small objects, animals, and figures made of wire, fabric, wood, and cork, among other found materials; he regularly gave performances that immersed audiences in live experiences of music, adrenaline, and action (fig. 12). In these same years he

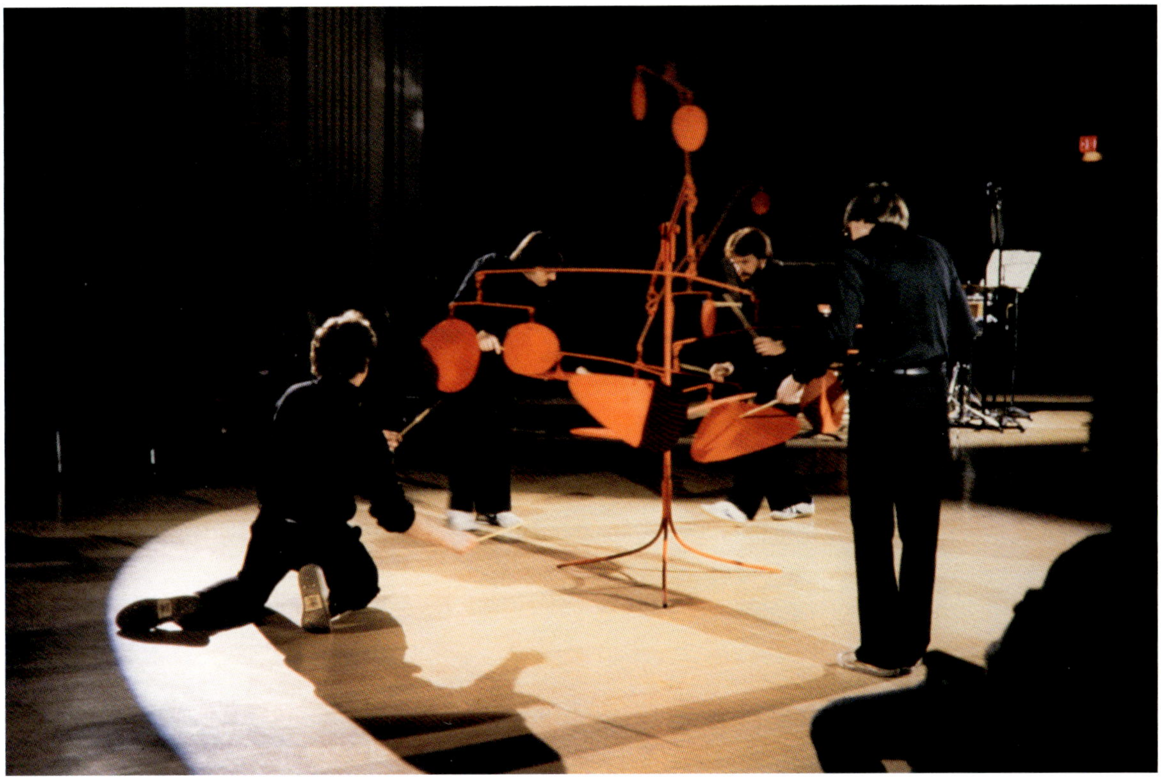

10 Aufführung der Komposition *Calder Piece* (1963–1966) von Earle Brown / Performance of Earle Brown's composition *Calder Piece* (1963–66), New Gallery of Contemporary Art, Cleveland, 1982

made wire portraits of friends and well-known personalities as well as representations of circus figures (figs. 5, 6), described by critics in the late 1920s as "drawings in space."[2] Both the circus and his early wire constructions demonstrate how Calder not only incorporated the surrounding space with his objects but also actively integrated viewers into the performative process. This becomes even more apparent in the first mobiles he made beginning in 1931, whose abstract shapes could be set in motion by the slightest flow of air.

As he recounted in his autobiography, Calder "did not consciously know or feel the term 'abstract'" until October 1930, when he visited Mondrian's studio.[3] It was not the individual works of art that impressed him but rather the way Mondrian had designed and used the space, which gave him the feeling of standing within a Neo-Plastic work of art (fig. 60).[4] After that visit—following a brief experiment with abstract forms in painting—Calder produced standing constructions in wire, wood, and sheet metal, in which he completely disassociated himself from his figurative beginnings, as well as his first mobiles, some of them motorized. The former objects, which the artist Hans Arp dubbed "stabiles," didn't move by themselves but disclosed new, spectacular views owing to their mechanics or to the movement of viewers in the space and the deliberate deployment of light and shadow (fig. 7).

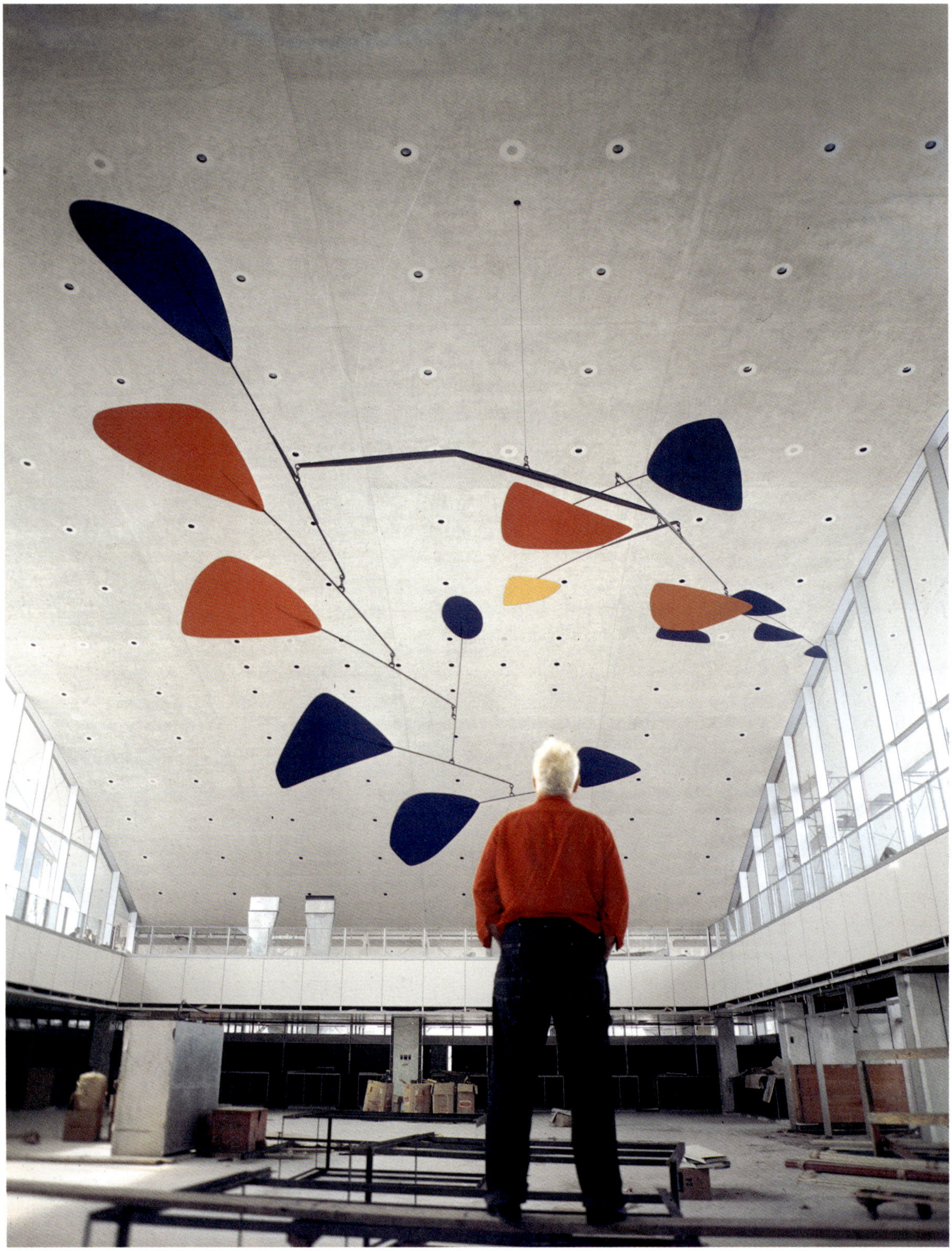

11 Calder und *.125* (1957), Idlewild Airport (heute John F. Kennedy International Airport) / Calder and *.125* (1957), Idlewild Airport (now John F. Kennedy International Airport), New York, 1957

Minimal/Maximal

In the 1930s Calder began to create large-scale objects such as *Devil Fish* (1937), the first work he made from bolted sheet metal and enlarged from a maquette (fig. 41). But at only sixty-eight inches tall, *Devil Fish* was still considerably smaller and more graceful than the stabiles Calder began creating in the 1950s. Technical advances in steel construction in particular offered the sculptor entirely new possibilities, both in terms of scale and artistically. One of the consequences of this was that he increasingly worked at the interface between sculpture and architecture.[5] Calder thus received a number of commissions for monumental sculptures in public spaces beginning in the late 1950s. With the modernity of the material and their moving elements, the objects produced in this period stand majestically and clearly but at the same time dynamically in the urban setting—a confrontation that the artist effected deliberately.

Outstanding examples of these new, artistic approaches in his late work are such sculptures as *Les Trois Ailes* (fig. 25) and *Les Triangles* (fig. 31, both 1963). Finally, his monumental piece *Five Swords* (1976; fig. 8) shows how dynamic a sculpture open on all sides could become with the use of towering, curved steel plates. The bright red, almost expressively thrusting work appears differently from every side, and its complexity can only be appreciated by walking around it, viewing it both close up and from farther away. Their size alone lends the saber-shaped arms a considerable, almost intimidating presence. The sculpture's recent removal from the expansive landscape of New York's Hudson Valley, where it has stood since the 1980s, and installation in Mies van der Rohe's hall in Berlin is bound to highlight this complex perception. What happens if I approach this sculpture? What sort of space does the sculpture generate in this setting and in its dialogue with viewers?

A considerable change of scale is also apparent in Calder's mobiles made after 1950. He often used commissions for specific buildings as a chance to work with larger dimensions. For the International Arrivals Building at what is now John F. Kennedy International Airport[6] in New York, for instance, he created the huge mobile *.125* (1957), which clearly defined the space in the terminal's atrium and thus opened up new perspectives in its interplay with the architecture (fig. 11). Other important mobiles from the 1950s, such as *Blizzard* (1950; fig. 72) and *Otto's Mobile* (1952; fig. 2), with their partly horizonal, partly vertical orientation, continually transform the spaces around them and, with their movements, allow viewers to experience them in continuously new ways. At times the works' titles, given after the fact of creation, evoke worlds of their own. Although not meant to be assets for interpretation, these titles call attention to specific geometries, as in *Les Triangles*; to the power of nature, as in *Blizzard*; or to a work's metal substance, as in *Otto's Mobile*, named after the director of the Meta-Mold Aluminum Company, Otto Spaeth; the title is also a pun involving the phonetic association between "Otto Mobile" and "automobile" ("moving by itself").[7]

Throughout his life, Calder utilized a range of primary and secondary colors in his work, with a preference for black and a tendency to use colors to heighten "disparity" within a composition—an approach that produces strong contrasts and makes the sculptures stand out clearly in their urban or landscape settings. This same range of colors is also found in his smallest pieces, which employ the shapes and combinations used in his large sculptures. It is seen, for example, among his miniature stabiles or so-called standing mobiles, which balance moving wire constructions on a metal base (fig. 17). These small works were created out of leftover scraps of metal from large sculptures or out of found objects, such as a spoon, which forms the

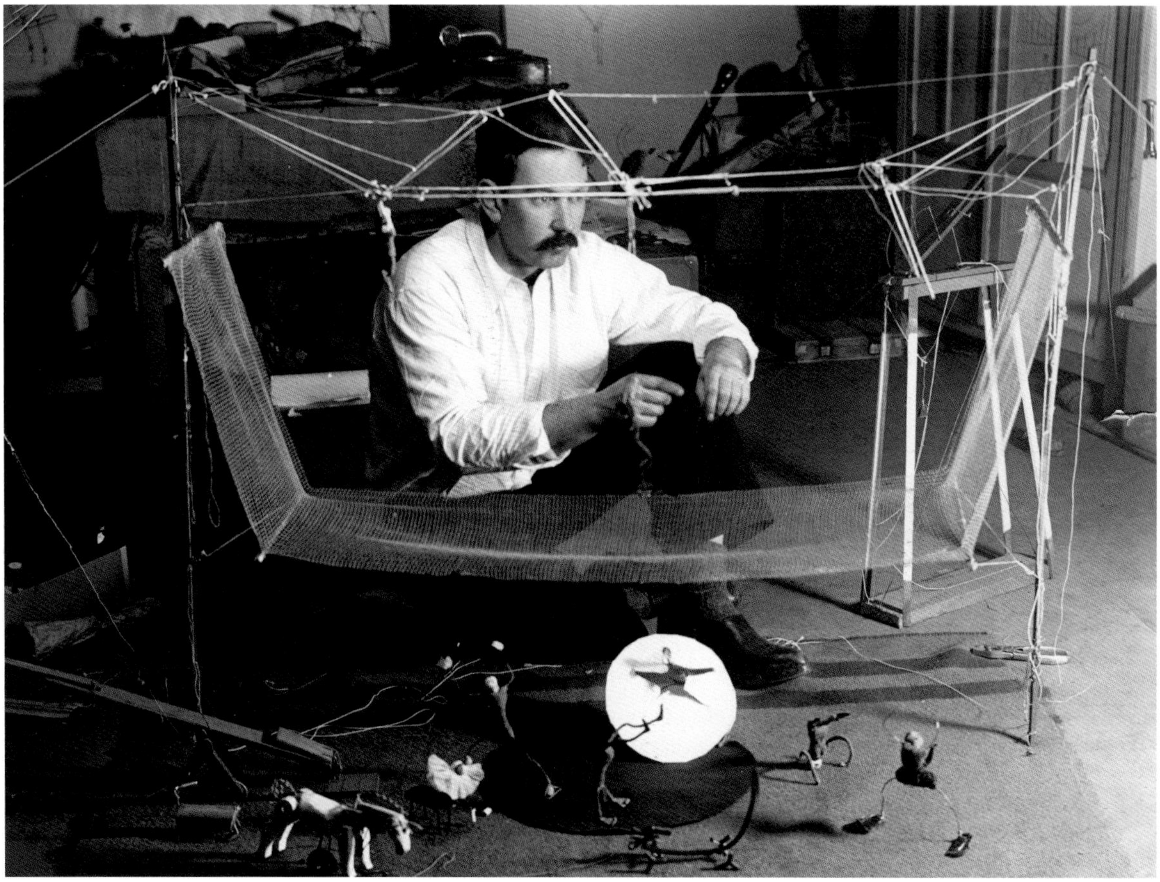

12 Calder mit / with *Cirque Calder*, 1929, Foto / photo Sacha Stone

curvaceous, movable foundation for a tiny mobile attached to its handle (fig. 80). Calder's "minimals" are often several things at once: models for larger sculptures, artistic experiments, and even independent works that demonstrate that an object that could also have been large and formidable suffers no loss of expressiveness in its small format.[8] Nevertheless, the miniatures force the viewer to engage with space in an entirely different way. They require attention and concentration. Instead of providing a public performance, a spectacle of large, space-filling objects, the miniatures can be appreciated only in an intimate, almost private setting.[9]

It was precisely this experience of the intimate, the personal, and also transposing it to the context of a large, public exhibition, that was a central starting point of the *Minimal/Maximal* project. At specific times, some of the small objects in the show are being presented outside the protective display cases in direct dialogue with viewers. Almost all the miniatures are easy to move, they are not tied to a specific site; on the contrary, they were meant to be "mobile" sculptures in a literal sense, pieces that could be carried about. This is particularly true of the very personal *Louisa's 43rd Birthday Present*, created for the artist's wife (fig. 15). It consists of a cigar box containing five tiny standing mobiles, which when removed from the box and arranged on a table make up a small exhibition on their own. The idea of taking sculptures out of their case and enjoying them was important to Calder from the start. He even described his circus figures as "miniature instruments."[10] He routinely made objects that invited interaction, whether setting them into motion with a breath, or playing with them, as in the case of the three chess sets that he produced in the 1940s (fig. 82). In the present exhibition, visitors have a chance to play with facsimiles of the chess pieces Calder designed—just as they were intended to be. Calder shared an interest in chess with many of his artist contemporaries. Though he may not have been as passionate about it as Marcel Duchamp or Max Ernst, he was altogether intrigued by the interactive and social aspects of the game.

A special kind of activation in space characterizes *Small Sphere and Heavy Sphere* (1932/33; fig. 23), the first suspended mobile and an early, distinctly performative work. It consists of what Calder called "impedimenta"—glass bottles, a wooden crate, a tin can, and a gong made by the artist—as well as balls suspended on two long strings. The items are meant to be set up on the floor by the viewer and can be repeatedly rearranged. The red cast-iron ball, together with its somewhat smaller white counterpart made of wood, is brought into play in a new way with each installation. When the viewer pushes the red ball, the white one moves, and its numerous collisions and near misses with the impedimenta trigger unexpected, surprising visual and aural reactions.[11] "Calder intended *Small Sphere and Heavy Sphere* to exist as an *idea*—one that can be freshly realized over and over again—with the *idea* being the only fixed aspect of the composition."[12]

With the (today unfortunately no longer feasible) intention that the viewer him- or herself set the work of art in motion, Calder anticipated some of the ideas of the interactive art of the 1960s such as Zero, Happenings, or Conceptual Art. The close coupling of sound and movement, which accounts for the special charm of *Small Sphere and Heavy Sphere*, is a recurring feature in Calder's work. It is found, for instance, in the large standing mobile *Chef d'orchestre* (1966), composed of red oval metal plates, which the artist developed especially for a piece of music by the composer Earle Brown. In the performance, conceived for four percussionists, the sculpture functions both as the "conductor," who sets the tempo, and as a percussion instrument itself (fig. 10). Here again, object, sound, space, and viewer combine to produce a total artistic experience.

Space as Stage

For Calder, a work of art was not a self-contained narrative. Rather, he thought of it as an "event," or an "experience."[13] This experience is made possible by the different levels of association offered to the viewer in different settings—architecture, nature, museum—with their significant feedback to the sculptures themselves. With their color contrasts, movement, and unexpected perspectives or insights, they mesh with their surroundings and generate an integrated, or holistic, sense of space, just like contemporary "installations" would make possible much later. Calder always factored in the viewer's movements and his or her shifting gaze. To his mind, the surrounding space functioned as a stage, one on which his works enter into visual as well as physical contact with the audience.

Calder's concept of space as stage is also reflected in his interest in theater, music halls, and of course the circus. Whereas he himself was still an integral player with his *Cirque Calder*, he later developed mobiles and stabiles that activated stages for various productions, such as for Eric Satie's symphonic drama *Socrate* in 1936, Henri Pichette's play *Nucléa* (1952), and his own, most personal production *Work in Progress* (1968) at Rome's Teatro dell'Opera (fig. 13).[14] Even in his early exhibitions Calder was concerned about how his sculptures were

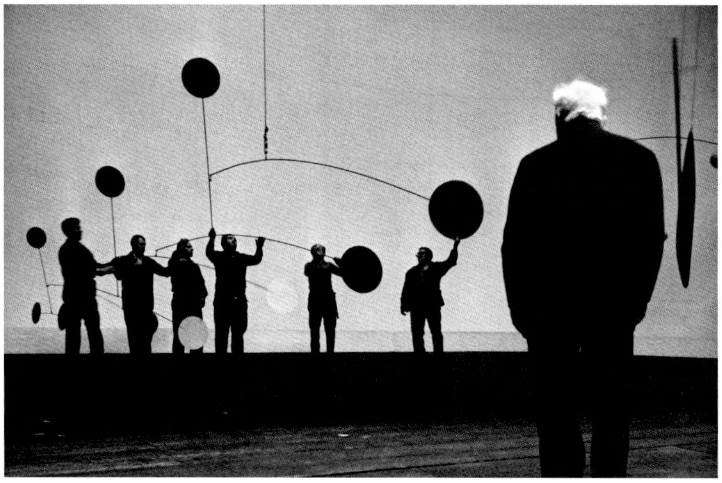

13 Calder bei einer Probe zu *Work in Progress*, Teatro dell'Opera, Rom / Calder during a rehearsal for *Work in Progress*, Teatro dell'Opera, Rome, 1968, Foto / photo John G. Ross

staged, whether in the form of special lighting that cast the desired shadows, or the way individual elements of his works might move in response to the gentle touches of viewers. At his retrospective at New York's Museum of Modern Art in 1943 he already explicitly insisted on such activation by the public.[15] Even in later years, visitors were permitted to touch the works in exhibitions, until increasing attendance figures meant that the works suffered too much damage (fig. 14).[16]

As early as 1935 James Johnson Sweeney, a good friend of Calder's and the curator of his retrospective at the Museum of Modern Art in 1943, recognized the interactive influence of Calder's art:

In a roomful of Calder's [works] we are conscious of a definite heightening of vitality that does associate itself somehow or other with the space-relationships, the architectonics, the line- and color-organizations, as well as the rhythms of the objects. Calder's idiom has the fibre of simplicity; his work bears an integral relationship with our contemporary environment.[17]

The strong reference to the surrounding space that Sweeney addresses here, especially to the given social and societal environment of the works, characterizes Calder's entire oeuvre—no matter whether monumental sculptures or miniatures. Throughout his artistic career, Calder often shifted from small to large and back again. Scale, size, and proportion, along with colors, contrasts, and the diversity of shapes and movement, are central tools of his creative work and the key to Calder's own definition of sculpture as a "social" object. His greatest concern was that we approach his art intuitively, interact with it, perceive it in its complexity, and understand his works and their surroundings as experiential spaces. There is no fixed meaning inscribed in his sculptures; rather we as the audience are invited to experience the objects directly. A great freedom and openness is thus associated with Calder's art, which was far more radical and visionary during his lifetime than we perhaps recognize today. The visual as well as participatory space that Calder reveals with his sculptures is a major reason why the artist continues to be so popular worldwide: his works don't appear confining or fixed but remain variable and open.

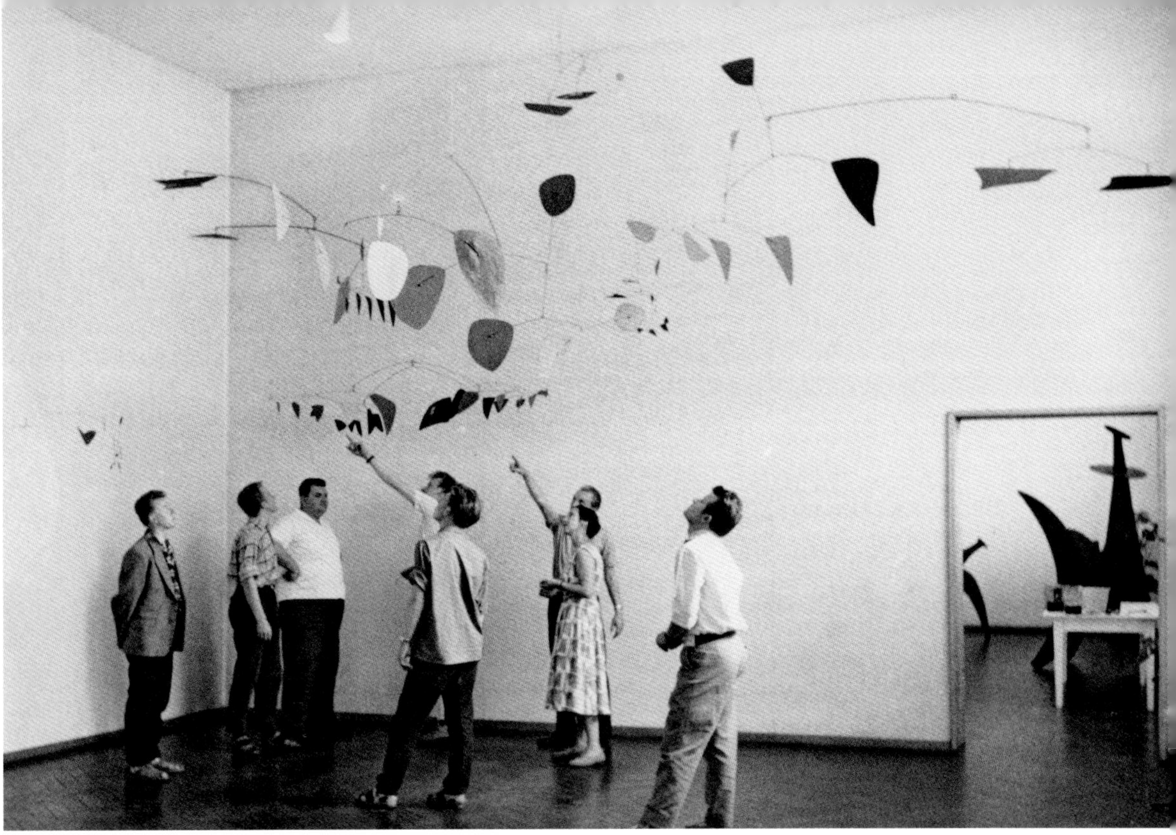

14 Ausstellungsansicht / Installation view, *Alexander Calder: Stabilen, Mobilen*, Stedelijk Museum, Amsterdam, 1959

1 Maurice Bruzeau, *Calder à Saché* (1975; repr., New York, 1979), p. 15.

2 See, among others, Gros, "Sculpture sur fil de fer," *Paris-Midi*, February 2, 1929; and Paul Fierens, *Journal des Débats*, February 3, 1929.

3 Alexander Calder, *Calder: An Autobiography with Pictures*, ed. Jean Davidson (New York, 1966), p. 113.

4 See Jed Perl, *Calder: The Conquest of Time: The Early Years: 1898–1940* (New York, 2017), pp. 340–41.

5 Emily Caplan Reed, "Sculpture and Architecture: Building Calder's Global Network," in *Calder: Radical Inventor / Inventeur radical*, ed. Elizabeth Hutton Turner and Anne Grace, exh. cat. Montreal Museum of Fine Arts; National Gallery of Victoria, Melbourne (Milan, 2018), pp. 169–80, here p. 169.

6 Then the Idlewild Airport.

7 Calder titled the work "Otto's Mobile" in a letter dated March 9, 1953 (Calder Foundation archives), but it was also published at the time as "Ottomobile," including in articles in the *Milwaukee Journal*, February 25 and March 27, 1953; *New York Times*, June 7, 1953; and *Time* 63, no. 21 (May 24, 1954).

8 Cf. Jed Perl, "Alexander Calder: 'Multum in Parvo,'" in *Multum in Parvo*, exh. cat. Dominique Levy Gallery (New York, 2015), pp. 11–19, here p. 13.

9 Cf. ibid.

10 "Futurist Toys for Advanced Kiddies Created by Calder, Artist-Engineer," *The New York Herald* (Paris), August 4, 1927, p. 7, cited in Elizabeth Hutton Turner, "Alexander Calder and the Case for Radical Invention," in exh. cat. Montreal and Melbourne 2019 (see note 5), pp. 23–43, here p. 32.

11 Cf. Gryphon Rue Rower-Upjohn,"Calder and Sound," in *Alexander Calder: Avant-Garde in Motion*, exh. cat. Kunstsammlung Nordrhein-Westfalen, Düsseldorf (Munich, 2013), pp. 99–111, here p. 104. A first version was shown at the Galerie Pierre Colle in 1933. That one no longer exists; a short time later Calder made a second version, which is displayed in the exhibition at the Neue Nationalgalerie.

12 Alexander S. C. Rower, "Calder's Grand Proposition," in *Calder: Small Sphere and Heavy Sphere*, exh. cat. Pace Gallery (New York, 2019), pp. 9–21, here p. 20.

13 Alexander S. C. Rower, "Approximations of Perfection," in *Calder: Monumental*, exh. cat. Denver Botanic Gardens (Denver, 2017), p. 15.

14 For a detailed overview of the theater productions, see *Alexander Calder: Performing Sculpture*, ed. Achim Borchardt-Hume, exh. cat. Tate Modern (London, 2015).

15 See Jed Perl, *Calder: The Conquest of Space: The Later Years: 1940–1976* (New York, 2020), p. 95.

16 Ibid., p. 96.

17 James Johnson Sweeney, "Alexander Calder's Mobiles," in *Mobiles by Alexander Calder*, exh. cat. The Renaissance Society of the University of Chicago (Chicago, 1935), https://calder.org/bibliography/mobiles-by-alexander-calder-1935/james-johnson-sweeney-alexander-calders-mobiles/ (accessed February 21, 2021).

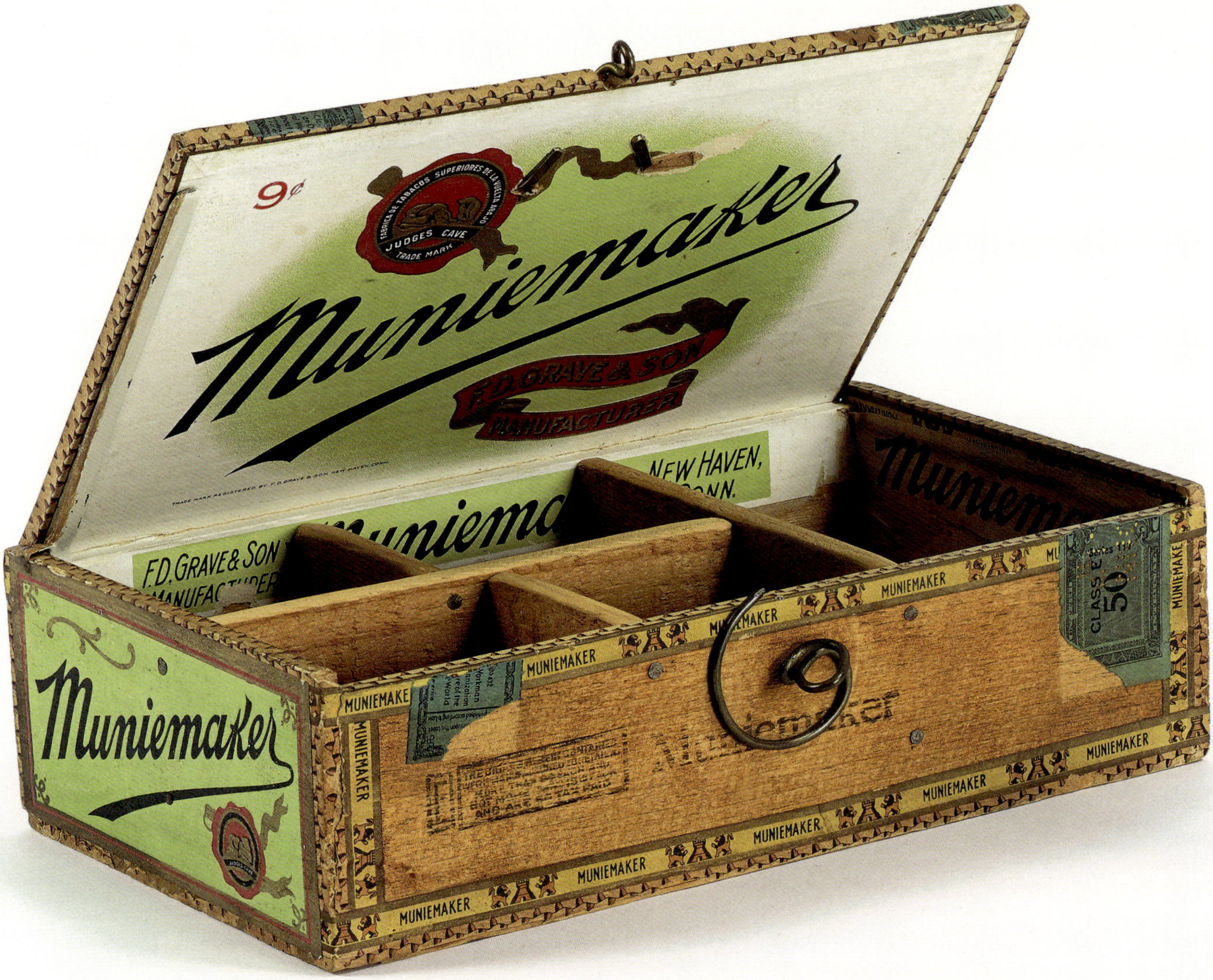

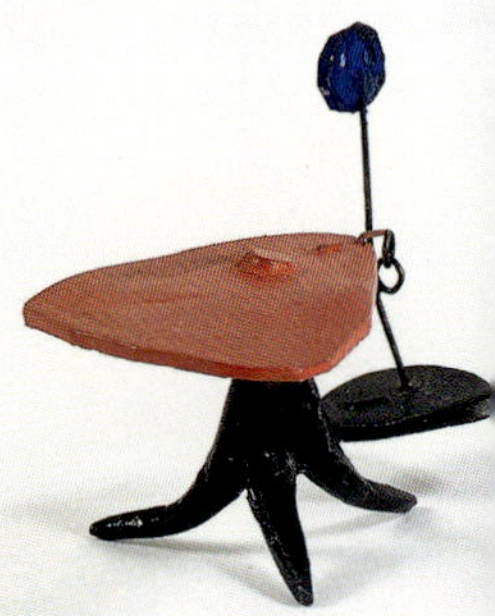

15 *Louisa's 43rd Birthday Present*, 1948, Blech, Holz, Draht, Filz, Zigarrenkiste, Farbe; Kiste: 6,4 × 22,1 × 12,9 cm / sheet metal, wood, wire, felt, cigar box, paint; box: 2 ½ × 8 ¹¹⁄₁₆ × 5 ¹⁄₁₆ in., Calder Foundation, New York

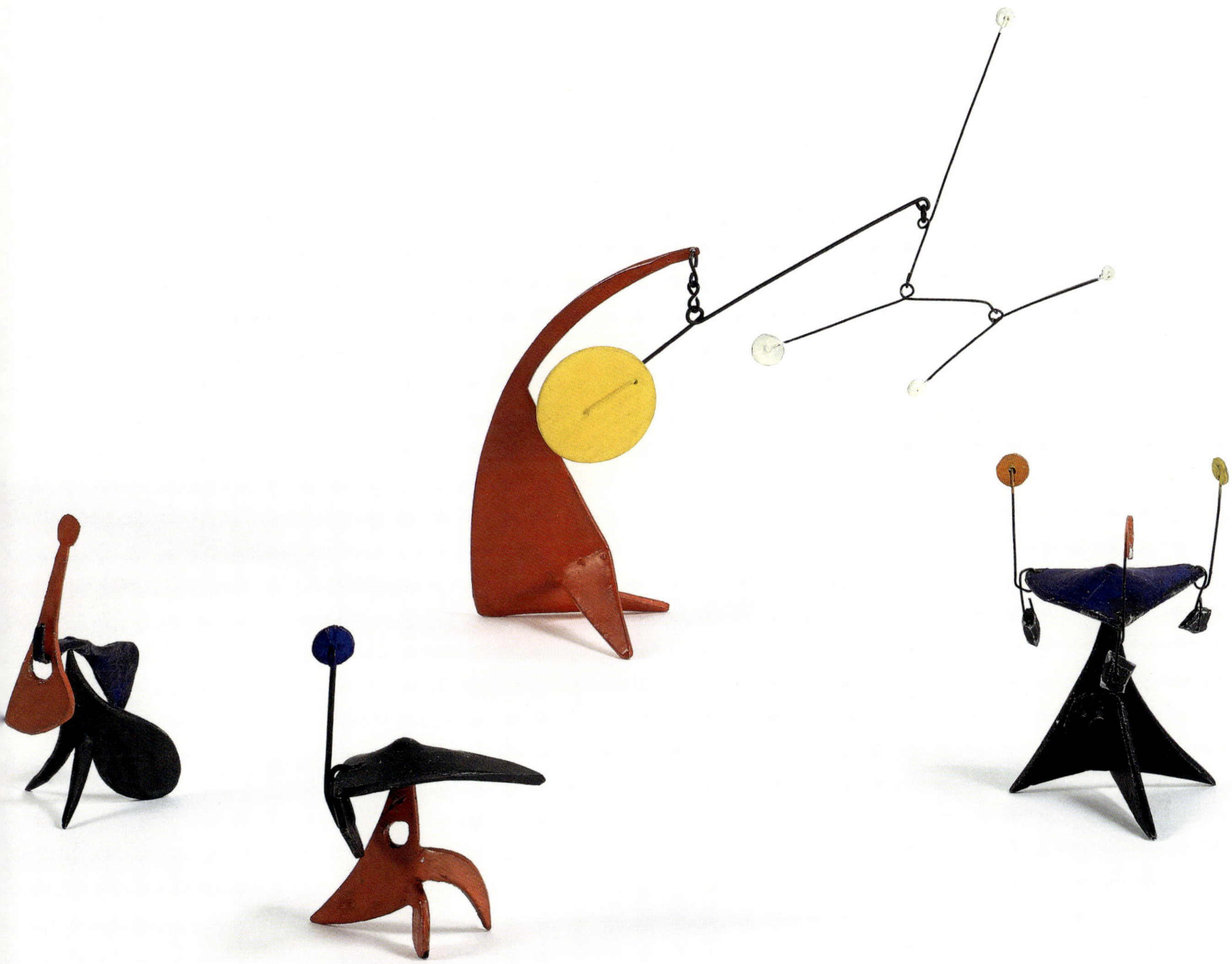

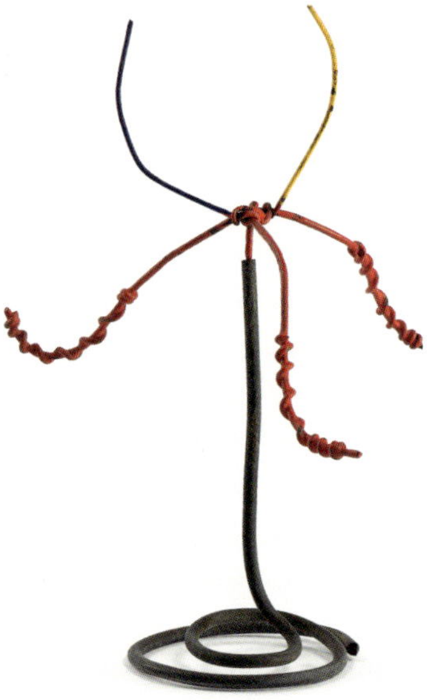

16 *Untitled*, um 1945, Draht, Farbe, 14 × 10,2 × 10,2 cm / ca. 1945, wire, paint, 5 ½ × 4 × 4 in., Calder Foundation, New York

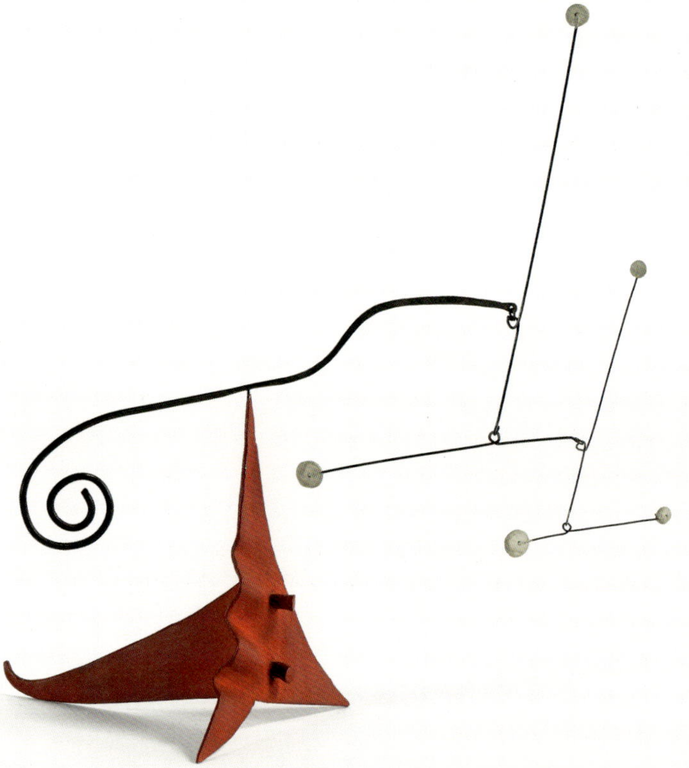

17 *Untitled*, um 1946, Blech, Messing, Draht, Farbe, 21,6 × 21,6 × 10,2 cm / ca. 1946, sheet metal, brass, wire, paint, 8 ½ × 8 ½ × 4 in., Calder Foundation, New York

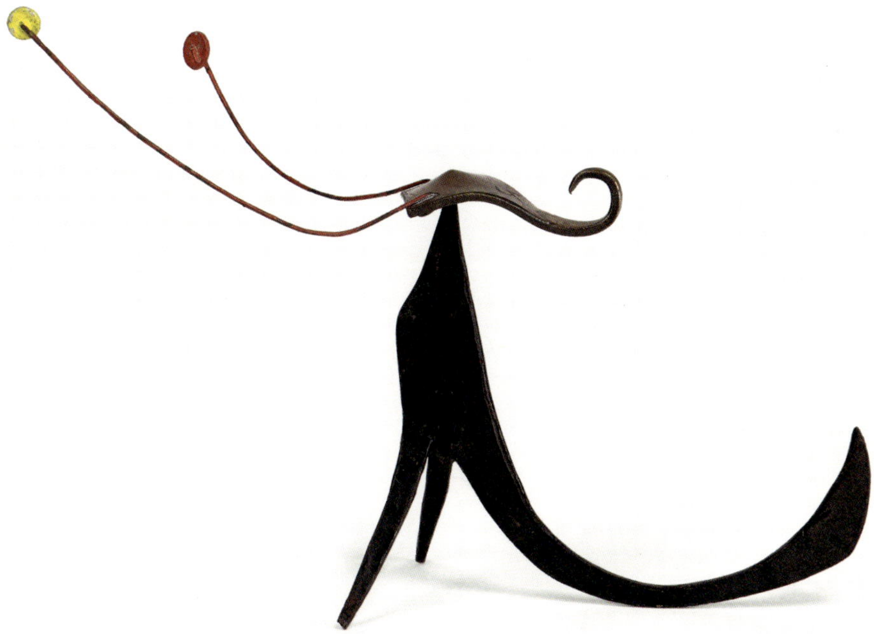

18 *Untitled*, um 1955, Blech, Messing, Draht, Farbe, 16,5 × 17,8 × 10,2 cm / ca. 1955, sheet metal, brass, wire, paint, 6½ × 7 × 4 in., Calder Foundation, New York

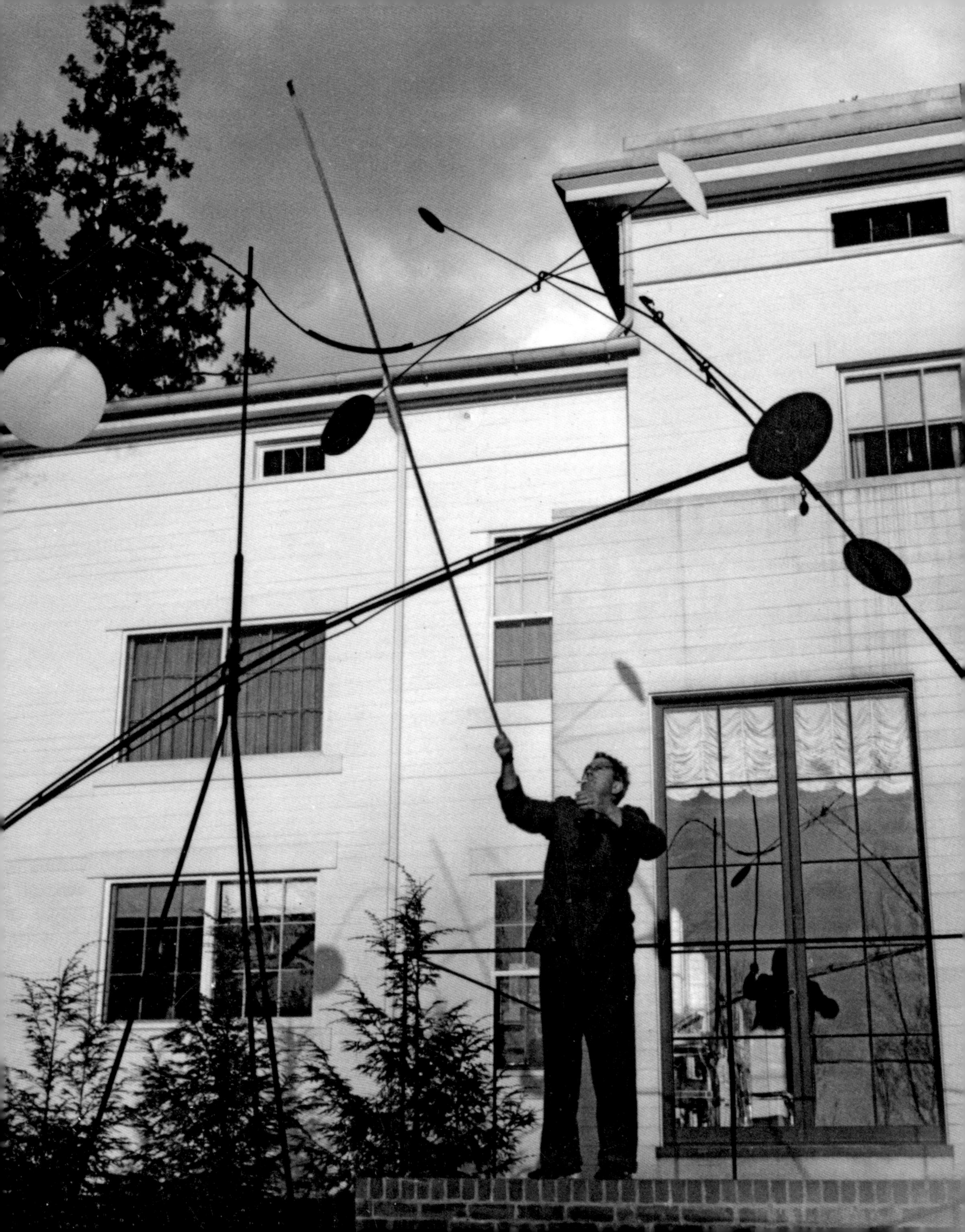

Innerer und äußerer Raum

Robert Slifkin

Irgendwann im Frühjahr 1926 stellte Alexander Calder für sein neues Atelier in Downtown New York eine Sonnenuhr her. Er bog Draht zu einer Art Wetterhahn und richtete dessen gespreizte Zehen so aus, dass der wandernde Schatten des langen Hahnenbeins daran die Uhrzeit anzeigte. Die Sonnenuhr selbst ist nicht erhalten, was vielleicht dafür spricht, dass Calder ihr anfangs keinen besonderen Wert beimaß oder sie nicht einmal als Kunstwerk einstufte. Später jedoch nahm er eine Skizze davon in seine Autobiografie auf (Abb. 20) und bezeichnete die Figur als wichtigen Meilenstein seines Schaffens, als seinen „ersten Versuch, ein Tier mit Draht wiederzugeben“[1]. Noch bevor Pablo Picasso und Julio Gonzales ab 1928 erste Metallplastiken schufen (Abb. 22), verankerten Calders lineare, offene Formen die Bildhauerei eindeutiger als je zuvor in der Welt des realen Raums. Calders Sonnenuhr ließ jedenfalls durch die geniale Verknüpfung eines schlichten Drahtgebildes mit einer weit entfernten Lichtquelle und dem von ihr erzeugten Schlagschatten bereits die nahezu grenzenlose räumliche Ausdehnung dieser neuartigen Form plastischen Arbeitens erahnen.

Das Entfaltungspotenzial von Skulpturen im Raum erforschte Calder wie kaum ein anderer Künstler. Durch die Verweigerung der materiellen Solidität, die mit herkömmlichen Werken der Bildhauerei aus Stein, Holz oder Ton verbunden ist, und durch den Verzicht auf repräsentative Sockel oder Podeste verlieh die moderne Plastik dem Raum rings um das ausgestellte Werk einen ästhetischen Eigenwert – das mag wie ein kunsthistorischer Gemeinplatz klingen, doch schmälert dies nicht die zentrale Rolle des Raums in Calders Werken. Mit ihren schwungvollen biomorphen Formen, die oft über ihre materiellen Grenzen hinauszuwachsen scheinen, und den verschlungenen Pfaden, auf denen sich seine Mobiles bewegen, aktivieren Calders Werke kraftvoll und oft sehr deutlich den sie umgebenden Raum. Vor allem aber korreliert die von Objekten wie dem *Rooster Sundial* suggerierte räumliche Expansion die endlose Weite des Universums mit dem intimen Maßstab des Körpers und seines baulichen Umfeldes und bezieht die Betrachterinnen und Betrachter sowohl durch ihre Wahrnehmung als auch durch ihre physische Interaktion in erheblichem Maße ein.

Dieser partizipatorische Aspekt seiner Kunst, den Calder früh anhand von Spielzeug und Schmuck ausgelotet hatte (später auch bei seinem Schachspiel; Abb. 82), zeichnet viele seiner Skulpturen aus. Sechs Jahre nach der Erfindung des *Rooster Sundial* stellte Calder sein vermutlich erstes hängendes Mobile aus: *Small Sphere and Heavy Sphere* (1932/33, Abb. 23). Die Installation besteht aus zwei ungleich großen, unterschiedlich schweren Kugeln, die von den Enden einer Metallstange über einer Ansammlung gefundener Gegenstände hängen, darunter mehrere Glasflaschen, eine Blechdose, eine

19 Calder mit *Well Sweep* (1936) in Farmington, Connecticut / Calder with *Well Sweep* (1936) in Farmington, Connecticut, 1938, Foto / photo Herbert Matter

Holzkiste und ein kleiner Gong. Die verblüffend simple Konstellation wirkt wie eine Kreuzung zwischen einem schiefen Pendel und einer Dampforgel. Die Besucherinnen und Besucher durften das Werk aktivieren, indem sie die Eisenkugel so anstießen, dass die kleinere Holzkugel im Kreis schwang und dabei – hier und da mit klangvollem Effekt – gegen einen der auf dem Boden verteilten Gegenstände stieß, die Calder selbst *impedimenta* (Hindernisse) nannte.[2] Durch die beiden umeinander kreisenden Kugeln und den Einsatz von „Mechanismen wie Gravitation und Fliehkraft", auf den der Kunstkritiker Paul Recht in einer Rezension der ersten Ausstellung des Werks 1933 hinwies, definierte *Small Sphere and Heavy Sphere* die Grundlagen für Calders Mobiles. Die physikalischen Gesetze des Universums wurden zu elementaren Faktoren, die Struktur und Erscheinungsbild der Werke bestimmen, sie mit ihrer Umgebung verknüpfen und vor allem die mit dem Werk interagierenden menschlichen Körper einbinden.[3]

Wie diese beiden ausgesprochen minimalistischen Beispiele für Calders Schaffen zeigen, braucht es nicht unbedingt kolossale Größe, um Maßstab und räumliche Ausdehnung zu thematisieren. Selbst das materiell bescheidenste aller Werke ist in der Lage, eine wesentliche Interaktion zwischen Betrachtenden und Objekt herbeizuführen. In dieser Hinsicht ist Calders Kunst gekennzeichnet durch eine dreifache Wechselbeziehung zwischen dem Werk, der materiellen Welt ringsum und den menschlichen Körpern, die sich im selben physikalischen Raum befinden. Calder wurde klar, dass alle aus Materie bestehenden Gebilde, seien es raffinierte moderne Skulpturen oder „stellare Beziehungen" gigantischer Ausmaße, innerhalb ein und desselben Kontinuums im Universums existieren, zu dessen Urkräften sie in einem wechselseitigen Wirkungsverhältnis stehen;[4] inbegriffen sind hier auch alle Lebensformen – von den so oft von Calder skizzierten Tieren bis zu den Menschen, die sich mit seinen Kunstwerken auseinandersetzen und gelegentlich physisch mit ihnen interagieren. Wiederholt plädierte er für ein expansives, räumlich vernetztes Verständnis der Bildhauerei, so etwa 1951:

„[...] das meinen Werken zugrunde liegende Formempfinden beruht auf dem System des Universums oder einem Teil davon. [...] Was ich damit meine: Die Vorstellung von frei im Raum schwebenden Körpern unterschiedlicher Größe und Dichte, vielleicht auch ungleicher Farbe und Temperatur, die umgeben und durchdrungen sind von gasförmigen Schwaden und von denen manche sich in Ruhe befinden, während andere auf eigentümliche Weise in Bewegung sind, ist in meinen Augen die ideale Quelle der Form."[5]

In einer seiner frühesten publizierten Äußerungen über die eigene Kunst erklärte Calder zudem, ein Kunstwerk könne „aus Volumen, Richtung und begrenzten Räumen innerhalb des großen Raums, des Universums" bestehen.[6]

Die Wechselwirkungen, die Calder zwischen seinen Werken und diesen universellen Kräften erkannte, veränderten in seinen Augen auch die Beziehung zwischen Betrachtenden und Werk. Die unsichtbaren Flugbahnen

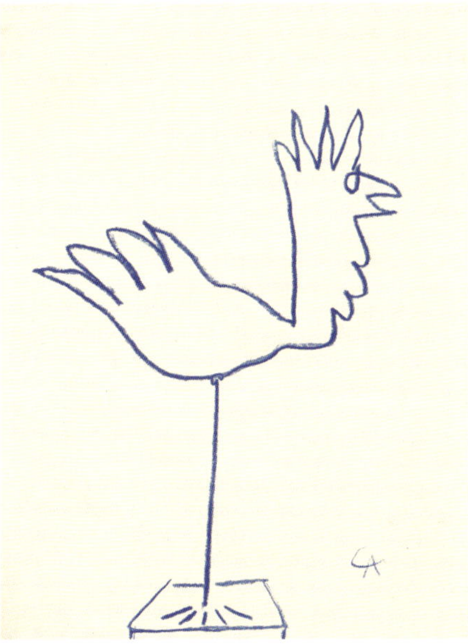

20 *Rooster Sundial* (1926), 1965, Tinte auf Papier, 22,9 × 20,3 cm / ink on paper, 9 × 8 in.

und wandernden Schatten der einzelnen Komponenten seiner Mobiles versinnbildlichen die ausladende Reichweite seiner Kunst, die sich über die materiellen Grenzen des Objekts hinweg in dessen architektonisches Umfeld und die natürliche Landschaft erstreckt und die Menschen einbezieht, die sich mit diesen Sehbedingungen auseinandersetzen. All das prädestiniert seine Werke geradezu für die Neue Nationalgalerie, deren gläserne Hülle die Grenzen zwischen der Ausstellungsfläche im Inneren und der Umgebung verschwimmen lässt. Ihr Architekt Ludwig Mies van der Rohe, der Calder um 1939 kennengelernt hatte, erklärte in einem frühen Statement über seine Vision für diese Art von Museum: In solchen Räumen, in denen der Unterschied zwischen Innen und Außen aufgehoben ist, sei ein Kunstwerk potenziell „ein Raumelement vor einem sich wandelnden Hintergrund".[7]

Calder formulierte seine Auffassung von Kunst als Widerhall der physikalischen Gesetze des Universums bereits in den 1930er-Jahren und setzte diese Form der Interaktion mit Werken wie *Small Sphere and Heavy Sphere* kinetisch, visuell und konzeptuell um. In den ersten Jahrzehnten nach dem Zweiten Weltkrieg setzte sich die Idee, dass sich Plastiken in den Raum hinein ausdehnen und die Betrachtenden direkt einbeziehen, auch bei anderen Kunstschaffenden als ästhetische Strategie durch. David Smith etwa verschweißte Metallteile zu bedrohlich wirkenden abstrakten Figuren, die aggressiv in den umgebenden Raum ausgreifen und eine Art dynamische Energie, ja etwas Beängstigendes ausstrahlen (Abb. 21). Viele Vertreterinnen und Vertreter der folgenden Bildhauergeneration, die dem Minimalismus zugerechnet werden, schufen karge geometrische Formen, deren monumentale Größe etwa nach Meinung von Robert Morris „Beziehungen vom Werk selbst loslöst und zu einer Funktion von Raum, Licht und dem Sehfeld des Betrachters macht"[8] (Abb. 24).

Calder dürfte mit seinen frühen Mobiles der 1930er-Jahre als Erster die expressive, ausgeprägt partizipatorische Aktivierung des Raums vollzogen haben, die in der Nachkriegszeit zum Merkmal eines Großteils der Bildhauerei wurde. Eine explizite Theorie dazu entwickelte jedoch erst der US-amerikanische Künstler Herbert Ferber 1954 in seinem Essay „On Sculpture". Einige Kunstschaffende seiner Generation, so Ferber, sahen in der Bildhauerei nun eine „Kunst der Ausdehnung". Während die herkömmliche Skulptur aufgrund ihrer Masse „an ihre eigene Mitte gefesselt" war, sei die zeitgenössische Plastik „zentrifugal", sie „scheut die Mitte". Obwohl Ferber Calder in

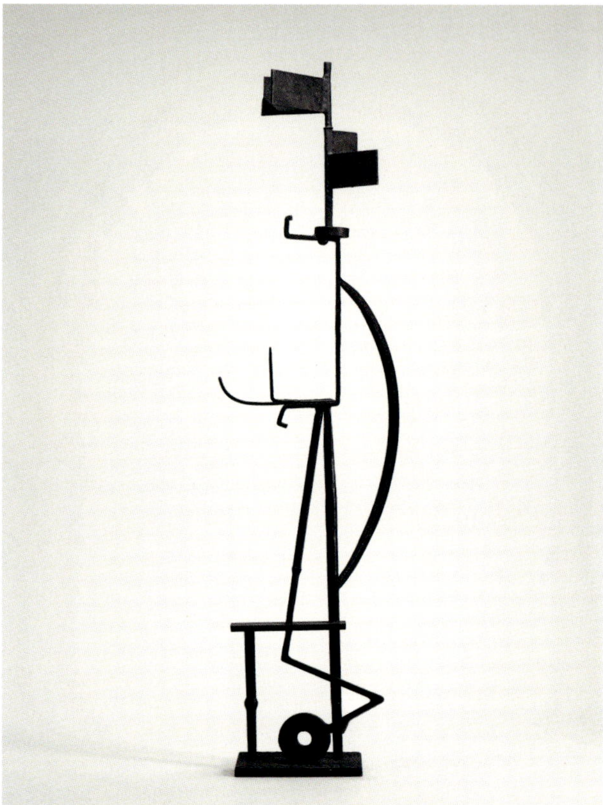

21 David Smith, *Sentinel 1*, 1956, Stahl, 227,7 × 42,9 × 57,5 cm / steel, 89 5⁄8 × 16 7⁄8 × 22 5⁄8 in., National Gallery of Art, Washington, DC. Gift of the Collectors Committee

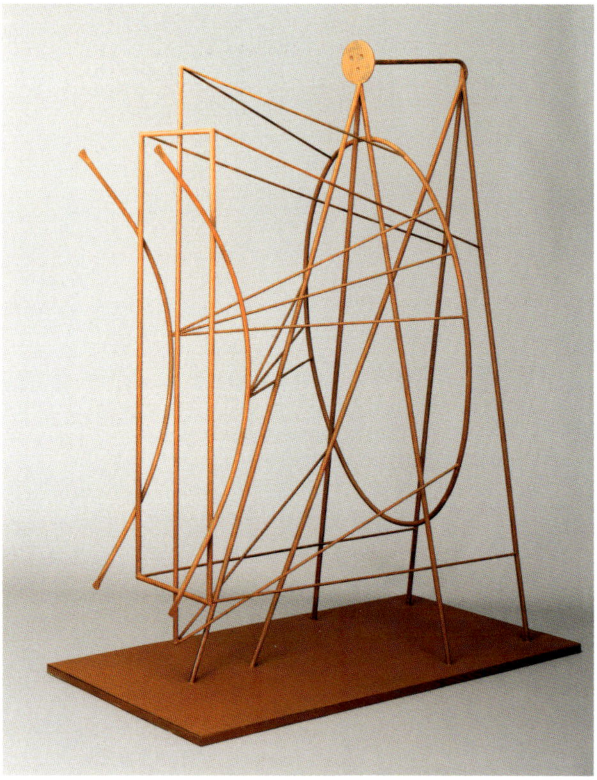

22 Pablo Picasso, Projekt für ein Denkmal für Guillaume Apollinaire, 1962 (vergrößerte Version nach Modell von 1928), Stahl, Farbe, 198 × 75 × 159,7 cm / Pablo Picasso, Project for a Monument to Guillaume Apollinaire, 1962 (enlarged version after 1928 maquette), painted steel, 78 × 29 7⁄8 × 62 7⁄8 in., The Museum of Modern Art, New York. Gift of the artist

seinem Essay nicht erwähnt, passt seine Charakterisierung der neuartigen Skulpturen als „offene, luftige, diskontinuierliche, frei im Raum schwebende Formen" eindeutig zu dessen Arbeiten. In einem anderen Essay zählt Ferber Werke seines älteren Kollegen zu denjenigen, die „den Raum nicht verdrängen", sondern „die Leere unter Spannung halten".[9] Bereits *Small Sphere and Heavy Sphere* hatte nach Ansicht von Paul Recht ahnen lassen, dass Calders Mobiles durch „Gravitation und Fliehkraft" eine existenzielle, wenn nicht gar kosmische Bedeutung annehmen, indem die immer kleiner werdenden Umlaufbahnen der Kugeln „atemberaubende visuelle Variationen über das Thema der Fatalität entstehen ließen". Für viele Künstlerinnen und Künstler, die noch unter dem Eindruck der Traumata des Zweiten Weltkrieges arbeiteten, erhielten solche Verkörperungen entropischer Energieabflüsse und zentrifugaler Ausdehnung im Raum eine wirkmächtige allegorische Bedeutung und Ausdruckskraft; sie verweisen auf das schwierige Verhältnis der Menschheit zur zunehmend rationalisierten, technologisch vermittelten Welt.[10]

Angesichts der leuchtenden Farben und heiteren Ausstrahlung von Calders Werken (und der relativ wenigen Kriegsbezüge in seinem Schaffen ebenso wie in seiner Biografie) erscheint es intuitiv widersinnig, seine Arbeiten in Beziehung zu den düsteren expressionistischen Skulpturen der Nachkriegsgeneration oder zum gedämpften, distanzierten Minimalismus der 1960er-Jahre zu setzen. Doch auch Calder war für solche zentralen Fragen empfänglich, etwa die nach dem prekären Verhältnis der Menschen zu ihrer veränderten Umwelt im 20. Jahrhundert. Man könnte sogar sagen, dass Calders ureigenes Gespür für die enge Verbindung zwischen Kosmos und Kultur vermehrt in den Vordergrund rückte, als die Menschheit sich mit der Atombombe „die Urkraft des Universums" zunutze machte: „die Kraft, aus der die Sonne ihre Energie schöpft", wie es US-Präsident Harry Truman in seiner Radioansprache wenige Stunden nach dem Angriff auf Hiroshima formulierte.[11] Doch während die Plastiken von Bildhauern wie Smith und Ferber durch den Eindruck räumlicher Expansion ähnlich der Mechanik einer Zentrifuge die gefährlichen Interdependenzen zwischen Mensch und Technologie zum Ausdruck bringen, bieten Calders Arbeiten eine ebenso verräumlichte, jedoch weniger drastische Vision des Unvorhersehbaren, das im Ineinandergreifen von menschlicher Erfindungsgabe und der Natur liegt.

Das meinte nach meiner Ansicht Jean-Paul Sartre, als er – bezeichnenderweise ein Jahr nach dem Abwurf der US-Atombomben auf Japan – schrieb, Calders Mobiles seien „weder etwas Lebendiges noch etwas Mechanisches [...]", sondern „lyrische Schöpfungen und zugleich technische, beinahe mathematische Gebilde und überdies auch das eindrucksvolle Symbol der Natur [...]".[12] Viele der kleinen Mobiles, die Calder in den 1940er- und 1950er-Jahren schuf, bewegen sich auf der Schwelle zwischen dem Organischen und dem Mechanischen. Das kleine stehende Mobile ohne Titel aus der Zeit um 1946 (Abb. 17) etwa besteht aus einer locker gewickelten Spirale und einem Gegengewicht aus zwei verschieden großen, umgedrehten T-Elementen, deren Spitzen mit kleinen Scheiben betont sind. Der von der Spirale zu den T-Elementen verlaufende Stab könnte eine evolutionäre Entwicklungslinie von der Urzeit zur technologischen Gegenwart (oder Zukunft) darstellen. Zwischen den beiden Enden des Stabes besteht zudem eine Spannung aus Animation und Mechanisierung, denn die eigentlich starren, schematisch-geometrischen T-Elemente haben dank ihrer Aufhängung einen ausladenden Bewegungsradius und weisen so eine stärkere kinetische Wandelbarkeit auf als die Spirale, deren Form auf dem Weg durch den Raum unverändert bleibt. Sartre sah diese Paradoxa. Er schilderte die Bewegungen eines Mobiles, die „mit ihren unberechenbaren Pfaden immer aufs neue überraschen und dann doch wieder in ihre ursprüngliche Stellung zurückkehren".[13] Auf diese Weise schaffen Calders Arbeiten ein fragiles Gleichgewicht nicht nur zwischen Organischem und Anorganischem, Ordnung und Unordnung, sondern auch zwischen Orientierung und Desorientierung. In Verbindung mit unkonventionellen Werkstoffen wie Blech und Draht, die seinen Werken den Anschein ausgefeilter Mechanik verleihen, drückt sich in diesen Dualismen die Vorstellung aus, das Leben sei unweigerlich von Kräften bestimmt, die trotz aller Anstrengungen, sie zu beherrschen, nicht steuerbar sind.

Die Kontrolle der Menschen über ihre Umgebung war und ist jedoch niemals absolut, und wie es scheint, hat bislang jeder Versuch, etwas durch Technologie beherrschbar zu machen, ebenso viel Unordnung wie Fortschritt gebracht. Mit den beweglichen Elementen der Mobiles ebenso wie den Schatten und Lichtreflexen der Skulpturen im Außenraum und nicht zuletzt durch den Anreiz von Calders Arbeiten zur Interaktion entstehen, wie der Künstler bemerkte, kompositorische Permutationen in „endlosen Kombinationen". Dadurch verweisen sie auf die immer deutlicher werdende Dominanz des menschlichen Willens innerhalb des Universums und zugleich auf die komplexen, oft unvorhersagbaren Prozesse, die jeden Versuch vereiteln, solche universellen Kräfte zu kontrollieren und zu messen.[14] Manche der für den Außenraum vorgesehenen Großskulpturen wie *Les Trois Ailes* (1963, Abb. 25) mit ihren kraftvollen Vertikalen, deren Schatten womöglich uralte monumentale Konstruktionen wie Obelisken und Sonnenuhren heraufbeschwören, und winzige Arbeiten wie das oben angesprochene stehende Mobile aus der Zeit um 1946 mit seinen frei schwebend vom Wind bewegten Anhängseln mögen volkstümliche plastische Gebilde wie Wetterfahnen evozieren, doch keines dieser Objekte dient in

23 *Small Sphere and Heavy Sphere*, 1932/33, Gusseisen, Stab, Draht, Holz, Schnur, Faden, Farbe, Hindernisse, Höhe 317 cm / cast iron, rod, wire, wood, cord, thread, paint, impedimenta, height 125 in., Calder Foundation, New York. Mary Calder Rower Bequest, 2011

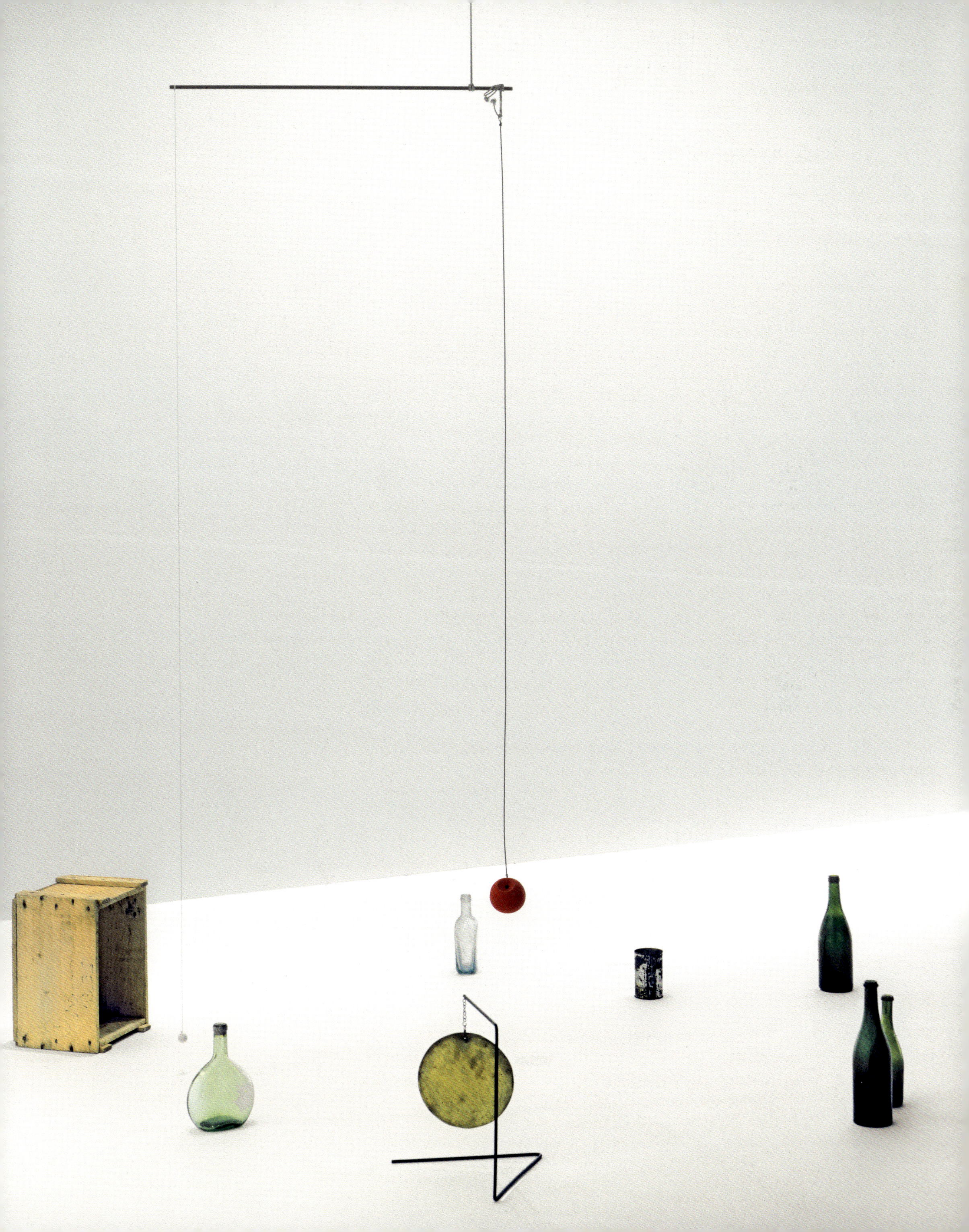

irgendeiner Form konkret der Orientierung. Ohne Kalibrierung oder auch nur eine klare Position in Relation zu den Himmelsrichtungen sind sie im Vergleich zu traditionellen Vorrichtungen dieser Art als Orientierungshilfe nutzlos. Doch auf komplexe, subtile Weise erfassen sie die Effekte auf ihr unmittelbares Umfeld.[15]

Anders als traditionelle Skulpturen, von Sonnenuhren oder Wetterfahnen ganz zu schweigen, reagieren Calders Objekte auf die Kräfte von Naturphänomenen gleichermaßen wie auf die Energie menschlicher Akteure (und die von ihnen geschaffenen technischen Innovationen). Diese technische Interdependenz spiegelte sich zunächst in Calders Idee, seine Mobiles mithilfe von Motoren in Bewegung zu versetzen (und heutzutage bewegen sich die nicht motorisierten Exemplare eher im Luftzug von Klimaanlagen als im Wind). Vor allem aber zeigt sie sich in ihren Materialien, im genialen Einsatz eindeutig von Menschenhand hergestellter Werkstoffe wie Blech und vor allem Draht. Im Gegensatz zu Stein oder Holz, das nach Calders Worten „eine Maserung aufweist, die man berücksichtigen muss", besitzen Komponenten wie „Draht, Stäbe, Blech Festigkeit [...] und reagieren schnell auf jegliche Art der Bearbeitung, der man sie unterzieht". Diese skulpturale Offenheit nach allen Richtungen, die solche unkonventionellen Werkstoffe erlaubten, war für Calder der Inbegriff räumlicher Ausdehnung und Interaktivität, sie demonstrierte in seinen Augen die „enge Allianz zwischen Physik und Ästhetik".[16]

Die Arbeit mit Draht und Metall gestattete es Calder, eine neue Beziehung zwischen seiner Kunst und der Welt herzustellen. Das Kunstwerk wurde unabhängig von seiner Größe zu einem konstituierenden Element seiner Umgebung. Dies war zum einen dank der linearen Offenheit und strukturellen Beweglichkeit möglich, die das Metall gewährleistet, zum anderen aufgrund der Assoziation dieses Werkstoffs mit funktionalen Alltagsgegenständen. Diese gedankliche Verbindung zum Beispiel mit Handwerkzeugen stiftet zum partizipativen Engagement an, ein Schlüsselelement der Kunst Calders. So gesehen könnte man sagen, dass Werke wie *Small Sphere and Heavy Sphere* und *Les Trois Ailes* uns weniger auf die Natur mit ihrem Rhythmus der Jahreszeiten und Wetterphänomene verweisen als vielmehr auf Möglichkeiten einer weitgehend harmonischen Koexistenz in einer zunehmend technologisch vermittelten Welt, in der die Grenzen zwischen künstlichem und natürlichem Leben äußerst unscharf geworden sind. Ein Objekt wie *Les Trois Ailes* mit seinen Industriebolzen und riesigen lackierten Stahlflächen, die ebenso anmutig wie dynamisch zu organisch wirkenden Formen angeordnet sind, das Sonnenlicht einfangen und ringsum Schatten werfen, lässt sich als Monument des unabhängig vom Menschen fortbestehenden Reichs der Natur auch in der Epoche des Anthropozäns lesen. Auf einer anderen Ebene hinterfragen Arbeiten wie *Small Sphere and Heavy Sphere* und *Les Trois Ailes* vielleicht untergründig die Zielstrebigkeit, mit der die moderne Zivilisation die Natur durch Technologie zu beherrschen versucht. Zugleich mögen sie veranschaulichen, dass kosmische, meteorologische oder mikroskopische Kräfte, die nicht dem menschlichen Willen unterliegen, unsere Umwelt nach wie vor bestimmen. Während wir Menschen entschlossen scheinen, uns diesen Kräften mehr und mehr zu entfremden, selbst wenn dies unser Untergang sein könnte, erinnern uns Calders Werke an die wechselseitige Abhängigkeit und die in unserer Sterblichkeit angelegte Verbindung mit der Natur.

1 Alexander Calder: *Calder: An Autobiography with Pictures*, hg. von Jean Davidson, New York 1966, S. 72.

2 Alexander Calder zu James Johnson Sweeney, 28.8.1943, Archiv der Calder Foundation.

3 Paul Recht: „Dans le mouvement, les sculptures mouvantes", in: *Mouvement*, 1, Juni 1933, S. 49, zitiert in: Jed Perl: *Calder. The Conquest of Time. The Early Years, 1898–1940*, New York 2017, S. 414f.

4 Alexander Calder: „À Propos of Measuring a Mobile", Manuskript, Archives of American Art, Smithsonian Institution, 1943.

5 Alexander Calder: „What Abstract Art Means to Me", in: *Museum of Modern Art Bulletin*, 18, 3, Frühjahr 1951, S. 8f., hier S. 8.

6 Alexander Calder: „Comment réaliser l'art?", in: *abstraction-création. art non figuratif*, 1, 1932, S. 6.

7 Ludwig Mies van der Rohe: „Museum for a Small City", in: *Architectural Forum*, 78, 5, Mai 1943, S. 84f., hier S. 84: „Das erste Problem besteht darin, das Museum als zentralen Ort zu etablieren, an dem man sich an Kunst erfreuen kann, ohne dass sie dort gefangen gehalten wird. Durch die Platzierung der Plastiken im Skulpturengarten verwischt sich bei diesem Gebäude die Grenze zwischen dem Kunstwerk und der Gemeinschaft des Lebendigen. Ebenso viel räumliche Freiheit genießen Skulpturen im Inneren, denn dank des offenen Grundrisses sieht man sie vor dem Hintergrund der umliegenden Hügel. Der entstehende architektonische Raum wirkt eher definierend als begrenzend. Für ein Werk wie Picassos *Guernica* findet sich in einem konventionellen Museum nicht leicht der richtige Platz. Hier kommt es viel besser zur Geltung und wird zu einem Element im Raum vor einem sich wandelnden Hintergrund."

8 Robert Morris: „Notes on Sculpture 2", in: *Artforum*, 4, Februar 1966; Wiederabdruck in Robert Morris: *Continuous Project Altered Daily: The Writings of Robert Morris*, Cambridge, MA, 1993, S. 11f., hier S. 15.

9 Herbert Ferber: „On Sculpture", in: *Art in America*, 42, Dezember 1954, S. 262–265, 307f., hier S. 263, 262; ders.: „Twenty Five Years of Sculpture", in: *Bennington College Bulletin*, 7, Herbst 1955, S. 12f., hier S. 13. Für eine zeitgenössische Analyse von Ferbers Konzept des zentrifugalen und zentripetalen Raumes siehe Otis Gage: „ART: Sculpturama", in: *Arts and Architecture*, 72, 2, Februar 1955, S. 4, 8–10, 30, hier S. 10. Ausgehend von Ferbers Essay kommt Gage zu dem Schluss, Calders Mobiles seien „eindeutig zentrifugal", ohne jedoch „physisches oder ästhetisches Unbehagen auszulösen" (S. 10).

10 Recht 1933 (wie Anm. 3), S. 49, zitiert in: Perl 2017 (wie Anm. 3), S. 415. Robert Morris schrieb in seinem Essay „Aligned with Nazca", in: *Artforum*, 14, 2, Oktober 1975, Wiederabdruck in: Morris 1993 (wie Anm. 8), S. 143–173, hier S. 173: „Der Raum selbst hat eine andere Bedeutung erlangt. Früher war er zentrifugal und zäh, er konnte monumentale Impulse absorbieren. Heute ist er zentripetal und intim; er verlangt nach Abgrenzung und Einfriedung."

11 „Statement by the President Announcing the Use of the A-Bomb at Hiroshima", 6.8.1945, Miller Center, University of Virginia, https://millercenter.org/the-presidency/presidential-speeches/august-6-1945-statement-president-announcing-use-bomb (abgerufen am 11.2.2021).

12 Jean-Paul Sartre: „Les Mobiles de Calder", in: *Calder*, Ausst.-Kat. Galerie Louis Carré, Paris 1946, o. S.; dt. Übersetzung: „Die Mobiles von Calder", in: *Alexander Calder*, Ausst.-Kat. Akademie der Künste Berlin (West), Berlin 1967, S. 21–23, hier S. 23.

13 Ebd.

14 Alexander Calder: „Mobiles", in: Myfanwy Evans (Hg.): *The Painter's Object*, London 1937, S. 62–67, hier S. 67.

15 Jed Perl zufolge könnte Calder in der Anderson Gallery in New York, wo er gelegentlich ausstellte, einen Wetterhahn-Typus aus dem frühen 19. Jahrhundert gesehen haben, siehe Perl 2017 (wie Anm. 3), S. 186. Auch nach Meinung von Eleanor Munro besitzt ein Mobile von Calder „alle Qualitäten einer Wetterfahne – bis auf deren Funktion". Eleanor Munro: „Exploration in Forms", in: *Perspectives USA*, 16, Sommer 1956, S. 160–172, hier S. 165.

16 Calder 1943 (wie Anm. 4).

Inner and Outer Space

Robert Slifkin

Sometime in the spring of 1926, finding himself in a new studio in downtown New York and without a clock, Alexander Calder fashioned a sundial out of wire in the shape of a rooster, calibrating the radiating talons of the figure to register the moving shadow produced by its elongated vertical leg. While the sculpture was subsequently lost (suggesting, perhaps, the artist's initial ambivalence about its worth, or even its very status as sculpture), Calder later included a sketch of it in his autobiography (fig. 20) and identified it as an important milestone in his practice, describing it as his "first effort to represent an animal in wire."[1] In advance of Pablo Picasso and Julio Gonzales, who began to use metal in their sculptural output in 1928 (fig. 22), Calder's linear, open forms brought sculpture into the world of real space like never before. Indeed, by aligning his modest, ingenious wire configuration with shadows and lights produced by a distant source, Calder's sundial suggested the almost limitless spatial expansiveness proposed by this new mode of sculpture.

Calder explored the spatially expansive implications of modern sculpture like few other artists. And while it is something of an art-historical truism to note how modern sculpture, by rejecting the material solidity associated with traditional statuary made out of stone, wood, or clay along with any sort of framing devices like a plinth or podium, made the surrounding space in which it was exhibited aesthetically significant, there is no getting around the centrality of space in Calder's work. With their buoyant biomorphic shapes that often seem to extend beyond their material limits, not to mention the circuitous paths traced by his mobiles, Calder's artworks powerfully and oftentimes visibly activate the space around them. Moreover, and just as importantly, the spatial expansiveness suggested by works such as the *Rooster Sundial*, which connected the vastness of the universe with the intimate scale of the body and its architectural settings, invited a crucial degree of engagement, both perceptual and physical, on the part of the beholder.

If this participatory aspect of Calder's art was first explored in his various toys and jewelry (and continued to be explored later in his career in such works as the chess set; fig. 82), it would equally distinguish many of his sculptures. Six years after creating his *Rooster Sundial* the artist would exhibit what is understood to be his first hanging mobile, *Small Sphere and Heavy Sphere* (1932/33; fig. 23). Consisting of two balls of unequal size and weight hanging on either end of a metal rod and suspended above a collection of found objects, including various glass bottles, a tin can, a wooden crate, and a small gong, this disarmingly simple sculpture seemed to operate somewhere between a skewed pendulum and a percussive calliope. Viewers were invited to activate the work by swinging the larger iron ball, setting the smaller wood ball off on a circuitous trajectory around—and occasionally striking to clangorous effect—what the artist called the "impedimenta" on the floor.[2] With its spherical forms orbiting around one another and, as the critic Paul Recht noted in a review when the work was first exhibited in 1933, "using means like gravity and centrifugal force," *Small Sphere and Heavy Sphere* established the basic lexicon for Calder's mobiles. Here, the physical laws of the universe became constituent factors in the very structure and semblance of the work of art, connecting the artwork with the world around it and crucially involving the human bodies that interact with it.[3]

As these two notably minimal examples of Calder's art suggest, questions of scale and spatial extension need not depend on massive size, so that even the most materially modest of works is able to summon a fundamental interaction between viewer and object. Calder's art is in this regard distinguished by its tripartite interrelation between the work of art, the material world around it, and the human bodies that share the physical space of the work and the world. The artist astutely comprehended how all material entities, from delicately wrought modern sculptures to massive "stellar relationships" (as well as all forms of life, from the animals he often sketched to the human bodies that engaged with and sometimes physically interacted with his artworks), existed within the same continuous universe of forces that acted upon them and upon which they acted.[4] Calder repeatedly advocated for just such an expansive and spatially interconnected understanding of sculpture, asserting in 1951 that:

The underlying sense of form in my work has been the system of the Universe, or part thereof. . . . What I mean is that the idea of detached bodies floating in space, of different sizes and densities, perhaps of different colors and temperatures, and surrounded and interlarded with wisps of gaseous condition, and some at rest, while others move in peculiar manners, seems to me the ideal source of form.[5]

Likewise, in one of his earliest published statements, the artist proposed that a work of art could be made "out of volumes, motion, spaces bounded by the great space, the universe."[6]

For Calder, recognizing the ways in which his creations interacted with these universal forces likewise entailed a new relationship between viewer and object. The invisible trajectories of the constituent parts of a mobile as well as the shifting shadows cast by them epitomize this capacious scope of his art, which extends beyond the material limits of the object to include its architectural setting, the natural landscape, and the human subjects who encounter these viewing conditions. In this way, his work seems especially well suited to be exhibited at the Neue Nationalgalerie, a structure whose glass exterior walls make permeable the boundaries between interior gallery space and its surroundings. As the building's architect, Ludwig Mies van der Rohe, who first met Calder around 1939, noted in an early declaration of his vision for this sort of a museum, such spaces that blurred the distinction between interior and exterior would allow works of art to become "an element in space against a changing background."[7]

While Calder would first formulate his conception of an art that would be commensurate to the physical laws of the universe in the 1930s and produce works such as *Small Sphere and Heavy Sphere* that performed this sort of interaction in visual and kinetic and conceptual ways, the interest in sculpture's capacity to extend into space and involve the viewer would become a defining aesthetic strategy for many artists in the decades following World War II. Artists such as David Smith used the welding technique to create looming abstract figures that seemed to aggressively jut out into their environment and invest the surrounding space with a sense of dynamic energy if not anxiety (fig. 21). The following

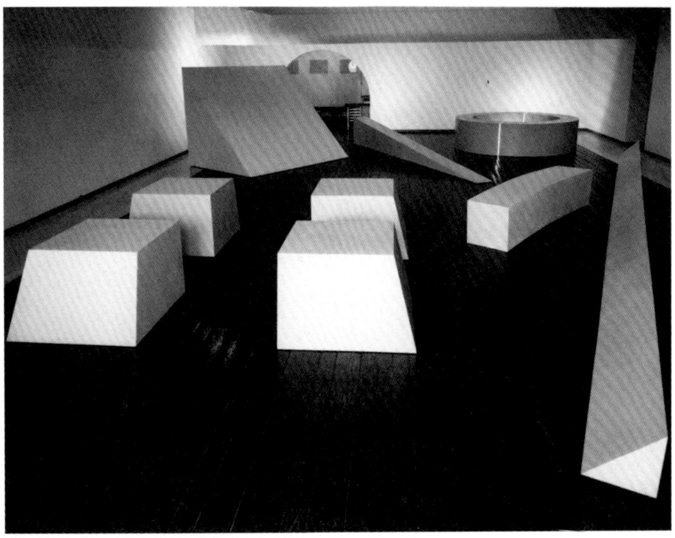

24 Robert Morris, Ausstellungsansicht / installation view, *Robert Morris – One Man Exhibition*, Dwan Gallery, Los Angeles, 1966

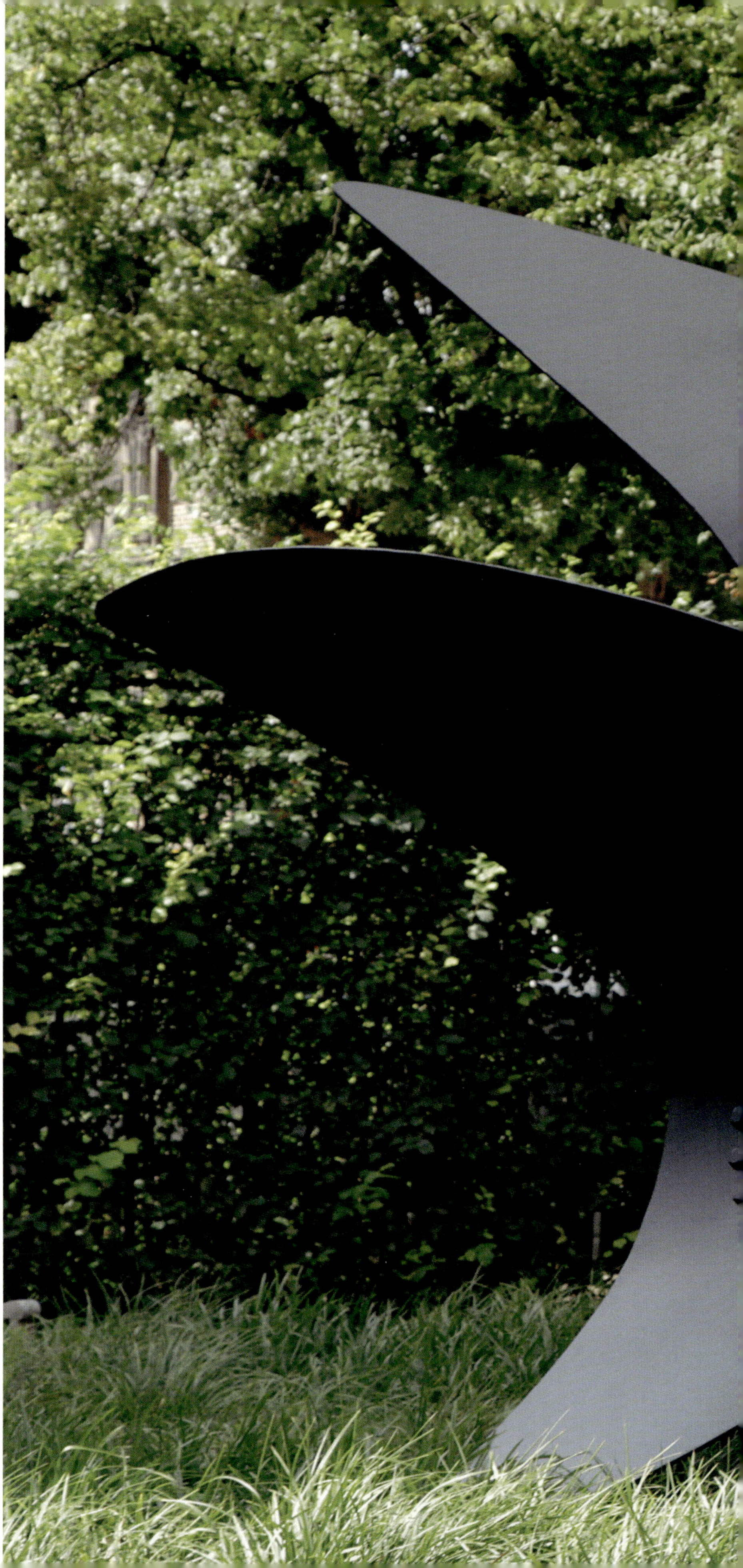

25 *Les Trois Ailes*, 1963, Stahl, Bolzen, Farbe, 380 × 450 × 266 cm / sheet metal, bolts, paint, 149 5⁄8 × 177 1⁄8 × 104 3⁄4 in., Musée National d'Art Moderne, Centre Georges Pompidou, Paris

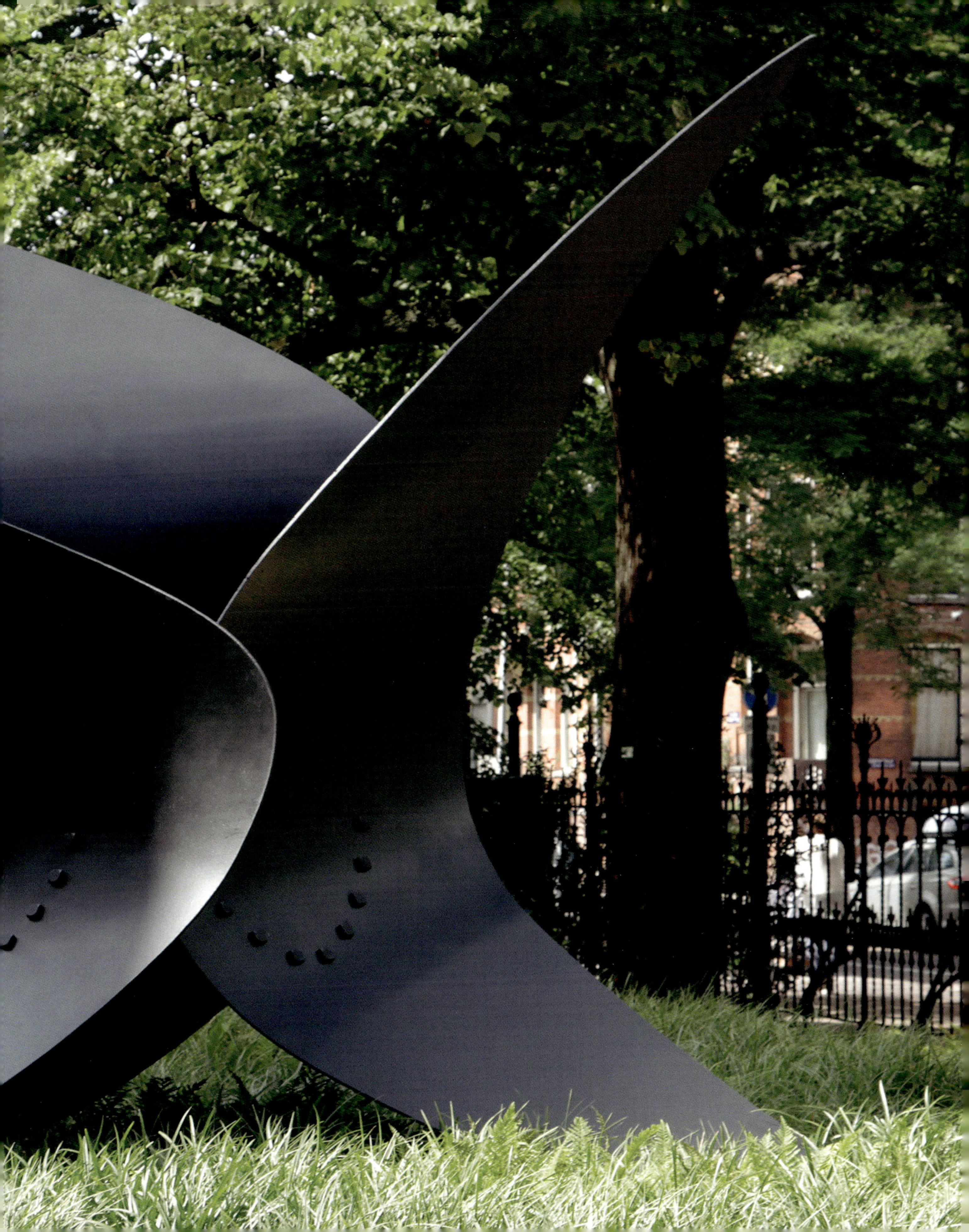

generation of sculptors associated with Minimalism such as Robert Morris would create austere, geometric forms whose monumental scale, according to the artist, takes "relationships out of the work and makes them a function of space, light, and the viewer's field of vision"[8] (fig. 24).

While this expressive and notably participatory activation of space characteristic of a great deal of postwar sculpture was arguably first materialized in Calder's early mobiles in the 1930s, it was most explicitly theorized by the American artist Herbert Ferber in an essay from 1954. In the text, simply titled "On Sculpture," Ferber described how the sculpture of a number of artists of his generation "has now become an art of extension." Unlike traditional sculpture, which, because of mass, "was tied to its own center," contemporary sculpture, he argued, "has become 'centrifugal'" and "shuns the center." While Ferber's essay doesn't mention Calder, his description of the new sculpture's "open, airy, discontinuous forms, suspended in space" certainly seems to summon the older artist's work, and in another essay he would number Calder among those whose works "do not displace space; they hold the void in tension."[9] If *Small Sphere and Heavy Sphere* had already implied, as Recht noted in his review, how Calder's use of "gravity and centrifugal force" invested his mobiles with an existential if not cosmic significance, so that the decreasing orbits of the balls "produced the most extraordinary visual variations on the theme of fatality," for numerous artists working in the wake of the trauma of the war, such figurations of entropic energy drain and centrifugal spatial expansion took on powerful allegorical significance and expressive effect, suggesting humanity's precarious relationship to the increasingly rationalized and technologically mediated world.[10]

Because of the characteristically bright and sanguine appearance of Calder's art (and the paucity of references to war in the artist's oeuvre and biography) it might seem counterintuitive to align his works with the darkly expressionistic sculptures of the postwar generation or the mute, impassive Minimalism of the 1960s. But Calder's art was equally attuned to these central questions regarding humanity's precarious relationship to its altered environment in the twentieth century. In fact, it could be argued that Calder's particular sensitivity to the interconnection between the realms of the cosmos and culture took on newfound significance in the nuclear era, a moment in history in which humanity, according to the US president Harry Truman in a radio address given hours after the attack on Hiroshima, had harnessed "the basic power of the universe. The force from which the sun draws its power."[11] If sculptors like Smith and Ferber created works that expressed the perilous interdependence of humanity and technological power through a sense of spatial expansion that could be compared to the mechanics of the centrifuge, Calder's work offers an equally spatialized, if distinctly less strident, vision of the unpredictability that occurs when human ingenuity intersects with nature.

This, I think, is what Jean-Paul Sartre was getting at when he wrote (notably one year after the US's deployment of the atomic bomb) that Calder's mobiles "are neither entirely alive nor wholly mechanical," and "at once lyrical inventions, technical, almost mathematical combinations and the tangible symbol of Nature."[12] Many of the small mobiles Calder produced in the 1940s and 1950s seem to vacillate between the organic and mechanical. For instance, in the small untitled standing mobile from around 1946 (fig. 17), a loosely configured spiral is counterbalanced by an expanding pair of inverted "T's," whose ends are punctuated by small circles so that the wire line traced from one end to the other suggests a sort of evolutionary progression from a primordial past to the technological present (or future). Another degree of tension between animation and mechanization is performed in the opposing ends, where the more rigidly geometrical and diagrammatic

"T's," which are secured to the mobile with interconnecting hoops that allow a wide range of movement, exhibit more kinetic variability than the more sinuous spiral form, which retains its shape as it travels through space. Sartre noted these paradoxes, describing how the movement of a mobile is "constantly disconcerting" in its unpredictable trajectories, by "always returning to their original position."[13] In this way, Calder's work posits a delicate equilibrium between not only the organic and inorganic but also order and disorder as well as orientation and disorientation. These dualistic themes, coupled with the artist's use of unconventional materials like metal and wire that invest his objects with a sense of mechanical ingenuity, present a vision of life ineluctably tethered to forces beyond its control, even as it constantly tries to master them.

Yet human control of the environment has never been absolute, and it seems that each attempt at technological mastery has produced as much disorder as development. Calder's works, with their invitation for human activation and, as the artist noted, the "infinite combinations" of compositional permutations engendered by the moving parts of his mobiles as well as the changing shadows and highlights that affect the appearance of the outdoor pieces, indicate respectively the increasingly overriding influence of human will within the universe as well as the complex and oftentimes unpredictable processes that frustrate attempts to control and measure such universal forces.[14] While certain large-scale outdoor works such as *Les Trois Ailes* (1963; fig. 25), with its strong vertical forms whose shadows might summon early monumental structures like obelisks and sundials, and smaller works like the aforementioned untitled standing mobile from around 1946, with its moving appendages cantilevered to catch the wind, might likewise suggest vernacular sculptural forms like weathervanes, neither object offers any sort of specific orientational purpose. Without calibration or, for that matter, a specific siting in relation to the cardinal directions, their capacities for orientation, at least as such traditional structures have registered this information, seem inconsequential, even as they register the effects of their immediate surroundings in complex and subtle ways.[15]

Unlike traditional monuments—not to mention sundials or weathervanes—Calder's works seem to register not so much the forces of natural phenomena but just as often respond to the energy of human actors (and the technical innovations they have created). If such technical interdependency was initially manifested in the artist's idea of using motors to propel the motion of his mobiles (and nowadays the nonmotorized versions are more likely to move in response to the currents of air conditioning than the wind), it was perhaps most materially expressed in the ingenious use of conspicuously manufactured materials like metal and in particular metal wire. Unlike stone or wood, which, as he wrote, "has a grain which must be reckoned with," materials like "wire, rods, sheet metal have strength . . . and respond quickly to whatever sort of work one may subject them to." For Calder the newfound multi-oriented flexibility enabled by these unconventional materials epitomized the spatial extension and invitation for interaction and thus, according to the artist, demonstrated "a close alliance between physics and aesthetics."[16]

Working in wire and metal allowed Calder to establish a new relationship between his art and the world, one in which the art object, no matter its size, became a constituent element within its surrounding environment, not only because of the linear openness and structural nimbleness permitted by metal but also because of the material's associations with useful, everyday objects. These associations with functional and handheld objects like tools encouraged the participatory engagement that was crucial to Calder's art. In this way, works like *Small Sphere and Heavy Sphere* and *Les Trois Ailes*, one might argue, orient their beholders not so much to the natural world of seasonal rhythms and meteorological phenomena as they suggest ways of living in relative harmony within an increasingly technologically mediated world, where the boundaries between artificial and natural life have become fundamentally indistinct. With its industrial bolts and massive planes of painted steel that are gracefully and dynamically arrayed into organically allusive forms that catch the light of the sun and project shadows upon its surroundings, a work like *Les Trois Ailes* can be seen as a monument to the persistence of the natural, nonhuman realm in what we would now call the age of the Anthropocene. If on one level works like *Small Sphere and Heavy Sphere* and *Les Trois Ailes* can be seen as sly interrogations of modern civilization's single-minded determination to control nature through technology, these works nonetheless point to the ways that nonhuman forces, whether cosmic, meteorological, or microscopic, continue to inflect the world around us. As humans appear to be bent on increasingly alienating themselves from these forces—even at the peril of their own self-destruction—Calder's art reminds us of our continued interdependence and mortal bond with the natural world.

1 Alexander Calder, *Calder: An Autobiography with Pictures*, ed. Jean Davidson (New York, 1966), p. 72.

2 Alexander Calder to James Johnson Sweeney, August 28, 1943, Calder Foundation archives.

3 Paul Recht, "Dans le mouvement, les sculptures mouvantes," *Mouvement* 1 (June 1933), p. 49, cited in Jed Perl, *Calder: The Conquest of Time: The Early Years: 1898–1940* (New York, 2017), pp. 414–15.

4 Alexander Calder, "À Propos of Measuring a Mobile," manuscript, Archives of American Art, Smithsonian Institution, 1943.

5 Alexander Calder, "What Abstract Art Means to Me," *Museum of Modern Art Bulletin* 18, no. 3 (Spring 1951), pp. 8–9, here p. 8.

6 Alexander Calder, "Comment réaliser l'art?," *abstraction-création: art non figuratif*, no. 1 (1932), p. 6. English translation courtesy Calder Foundation.

7 Ludwig Mies van der Rohe, "Museum for a Small City," *Architectural Forum* 78, no. 5 (May 1943), pp. 84–85, here p. 84. "The first problem is to establish the museum as a center for the enjoyment, not the internment of art. In this project the barrier between the artwork and the living community is erased by a garden approach for the display of sculpture. Interior sculpture enjoys an equal spatial freedom, because the open plan permits them to be seen against the surrounding hills. The architectural space thus achieved becomes a defining rather than confining space. A work such as Picasso's *Guernica* has been difficult to place in the usual museum gallery. Here it can be shown to greatest advantage, and becomes an element in space against a changing background."

8 Robert Morris, "Notes on Sculpture 2," *Artforum* 4 (February 1966); reprinted in Robert Morris, *Continuous Project Altered Daily: The Writings of Robert Morris* (Cambridge, MA, 1993), pp. 11–21, here p. 15.

9 Herbert Ferber, "On Sculpture," *Art in America* 42 (December 1954), pp. 262–65, 307–08, here pp. 263, 262; Ferber, "Twenty Five Years of Sculpture," *Bennington College Bulletin* 7 (Fall 1955), pp. 12–13, here p. 13. For a contemporaneous analysis of Ferber's conception of centrifugal and centripetal space, see Otis Gage, "ART: Sculpturama," *Arts and Architecture* 72, no. 2 (February 1955), pp. 4, 8–10, 30, here p. 10. Gage, drawing upon Ferber's essay, notes that Calder's mobiles are "*really* centrifugal" yet "do not give rise to either a physical or esthetic malaise" (p. 10).

10 Recht 1933 (see note 3), p. 49; cited in Perl 2017 (see note 3), p. 415. Robert Morris, in his essay "Aligned with Nazca," *Artforum* (October 1975), reprinted in Morris 1993 (see note 8), pp. 143–73, here p. 173, writes that "Space itself has come to have another meaning. Before it was centrifugal and tough, capable of absorbing monumental impulses. Today it is centripetal and intimate, demanding demarcation and enclosure."

11 "Statement by the President Announcing the Use of the A-Bomb at Hiroshima," August 6, 1945, Miller Center, University of Virginia, https://millercenter.org/the-presidency/presidential-speeches/august-6-1945-statement-president-announcing-use-bomb (accessed February 11, 2021).

12 Jean-Paul Sartre, "Les Mobiles de Calder," in *Alexander Calder: Mobiles, Stabiles, Constellations*, exh. cat. Galerie Louis Carré (Paris, 1946), pp. 9–19, here pp. 18–19. Published in English as "Calder's Mobiles," in *The Aftermath of War: Jean-Paul Sartre*, trans. Chris Turner (Calcutta, 2008), https://calder.org/bibliography/alexander-calder-mobiles-stabiles-constellations-1946/jean-paul-sartre-les-mobiles-de-calder/ (accessed February 8, 2021).

13 Ibid., p. 18.

14 Alexander Calder, "Mobiles," in *The Painter's Object*, ed. Myfanwy Evans (London, 1937), pp. 62–67, here p. 67.

15 Perl 2017 (see note 3), p. 186, suggests that Calder may have seen an early nineteenth-century variant of a rooster at the Anderson Gallery in New York, where he occasionally exhibited. Likewise, Eleanor Munro writes that a mobile by Calder "shares every quality of the weathervane except its function." Eleanor Munro, "Exploration in Forms," *Perspectives USA* 16 (Summer 1956), pp. 160–72, here p. 165.

16 Calder 1943 (see note 4).

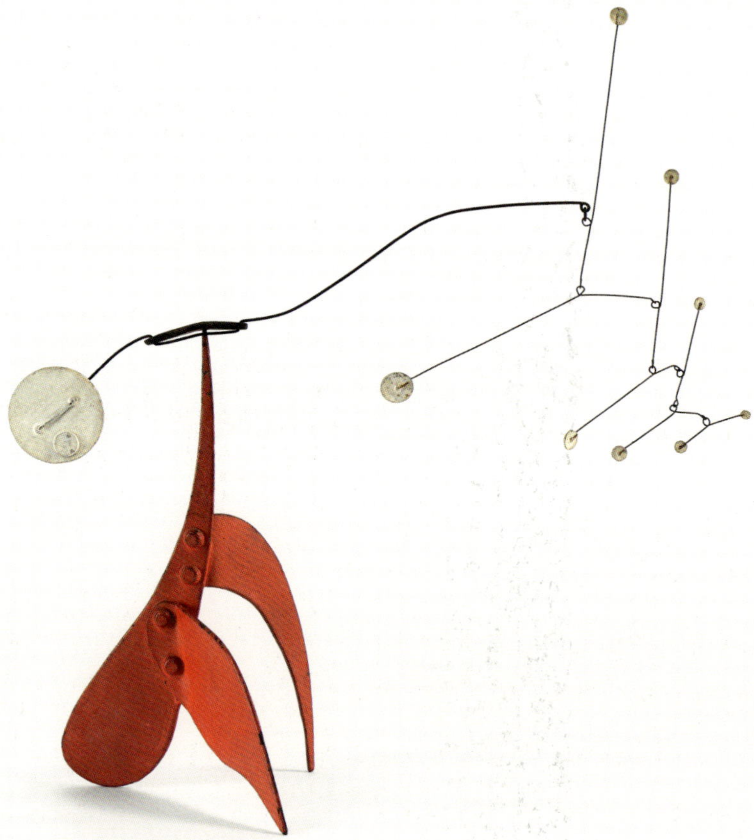

26 *White Counterbalance*, 1948, Blech, Draht, Farbe, 26,7 × 25,4 × 7,6 cm / sheet metal, wire, paint, 10 ½ × 10 × 3 in., Calder Foundation, New York

27 Calder pustet auf ein stehendes Mobile / Calder blowing on a standing mobile, 1969, Foto / photo Claude Gaspari

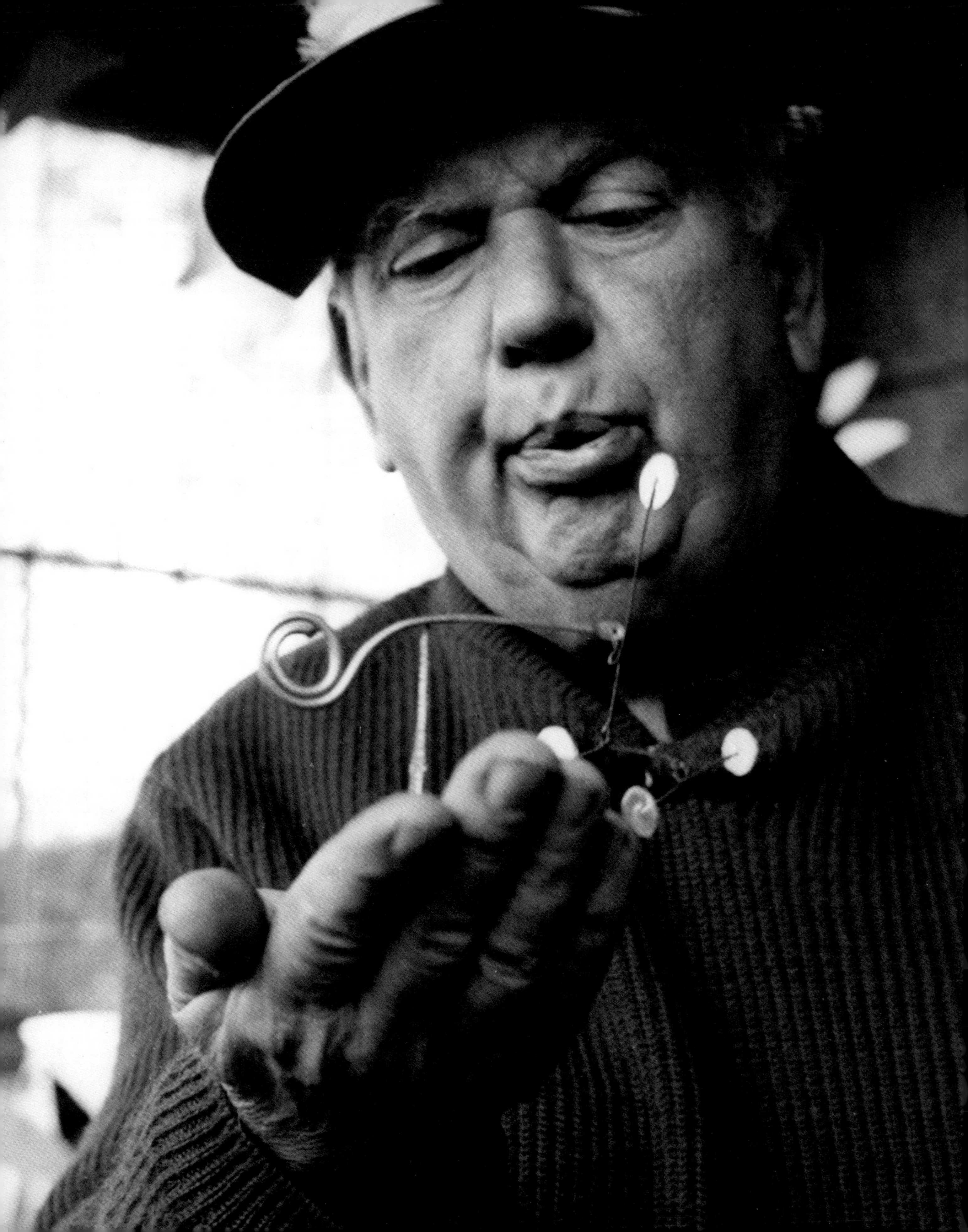

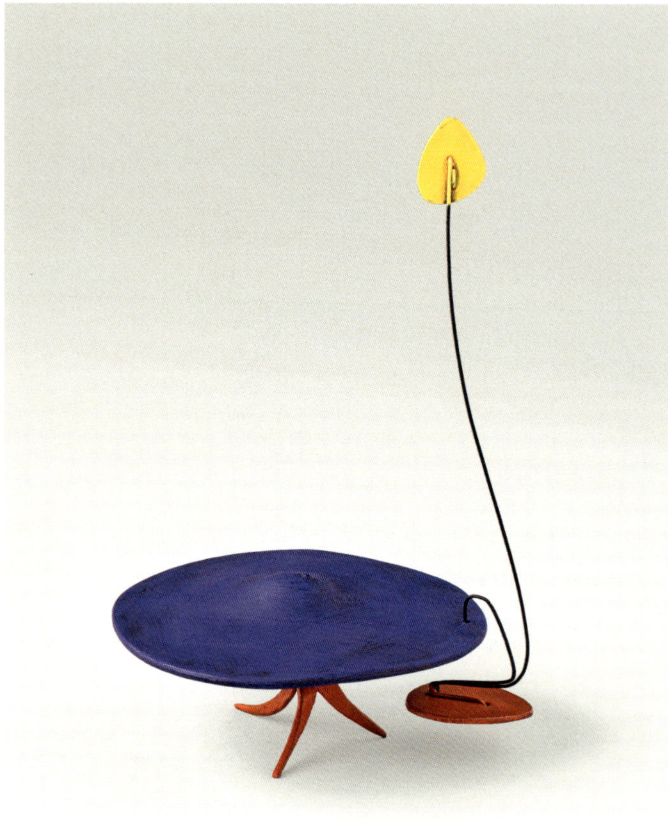

28 *Toadstool with Feather*, 1948, Blech, Draht, Farbe, 18,4 × 12,1 × 10,8 cm / sheet metal, wire, paint, $7\frac{1}{4} \times 4\frac{3}{4} \times 4\frac{1}{4}$ in., Calder Foundation, New York

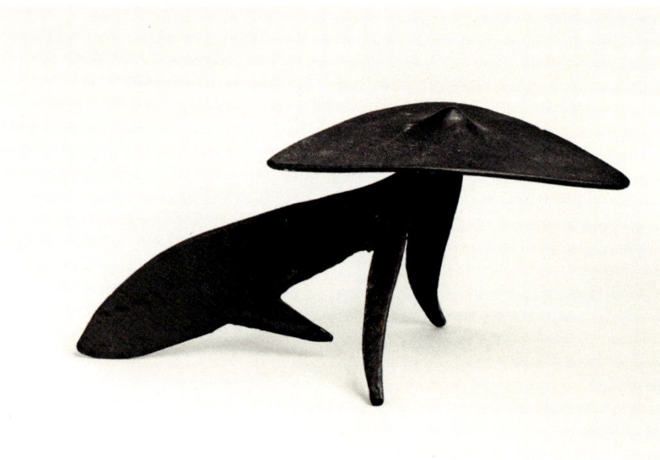

29 *Untitled*, um 1950, Blech, Farbe, 5,1 × 10,2 × 4,8 cm / ca. 1950, sheet metal, paint, $2 \times 4 \times 1\frac{7}{8}$ in., Calder Foundation, New York

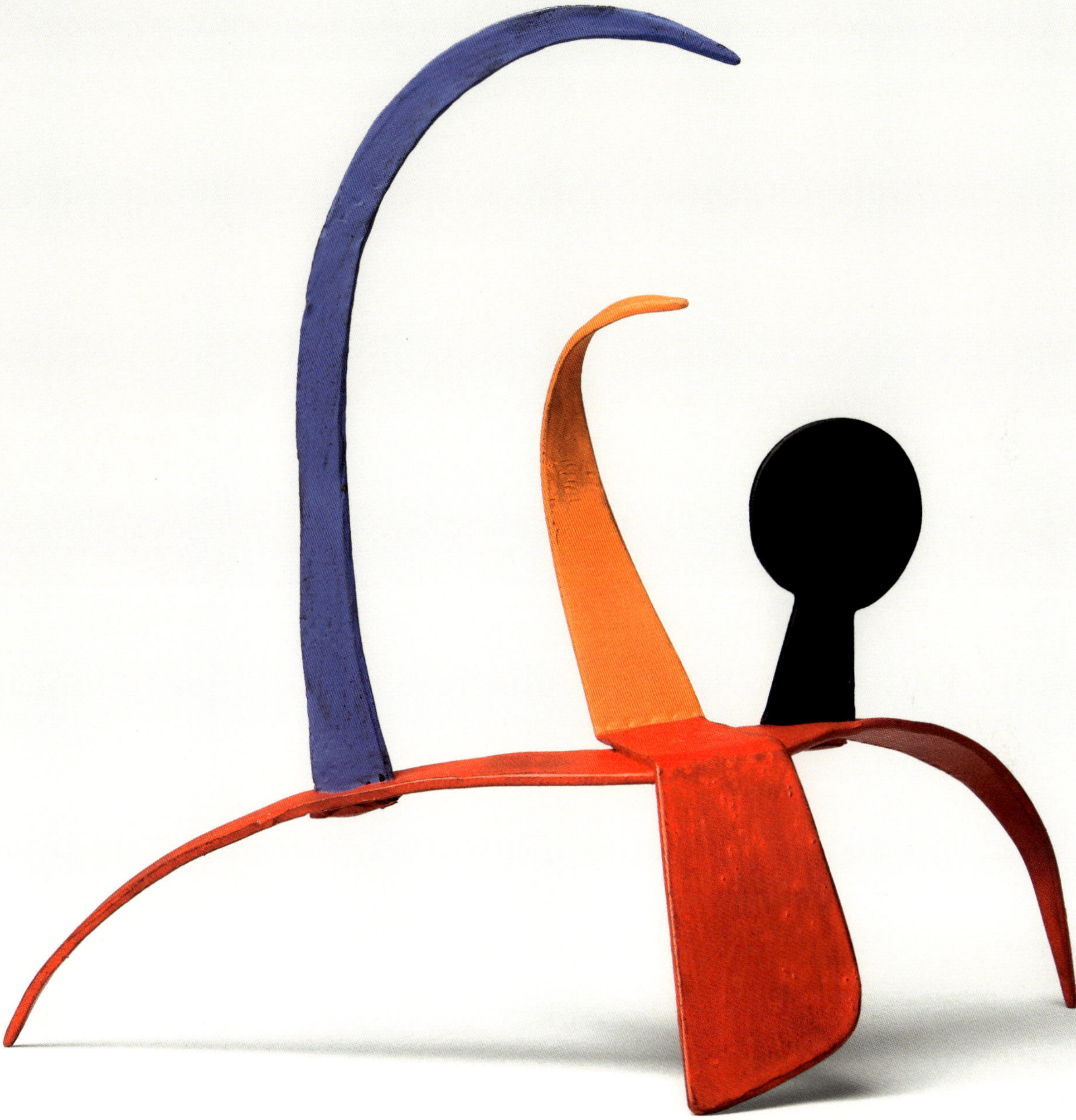

30 *Untitled*, um 1946, Blech, Farbe, 12,7 × 17,8 × 8,9 cm / ca. 1946, sheet metal, paint, 5 × 7 × 3½ in., Collection David and Ezra Nahmad

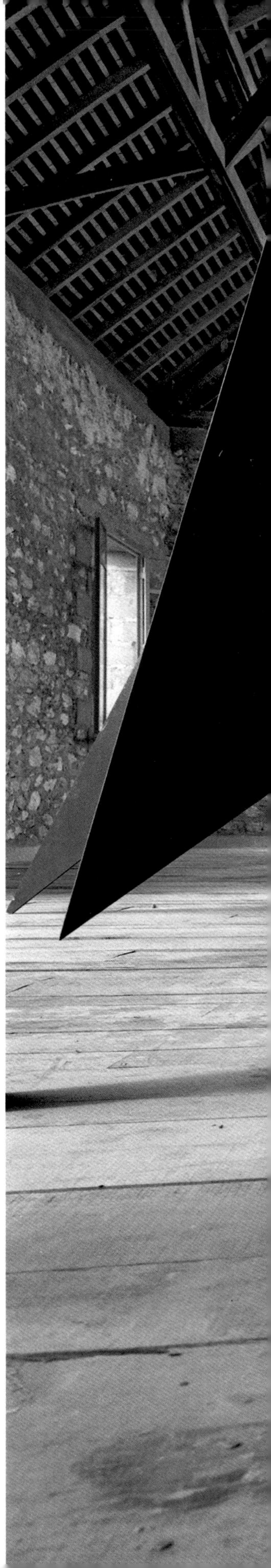

31 *Les Triangles* und Modell (1962) im Atelier Le Carroi / *Les Triangles* and maquette (1962) in the Le Carroi studio, 1963, Foto / photo Ugo Mulas

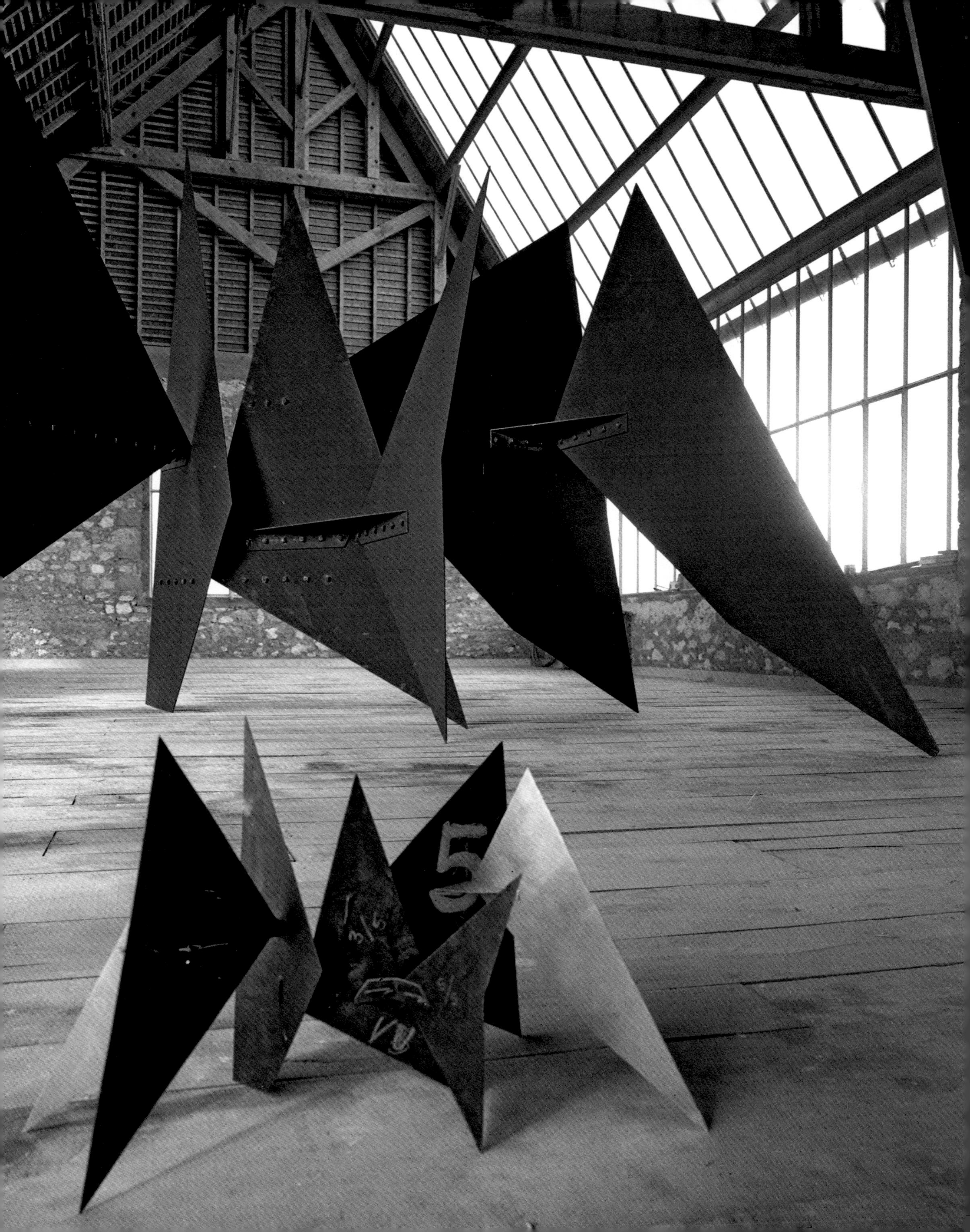

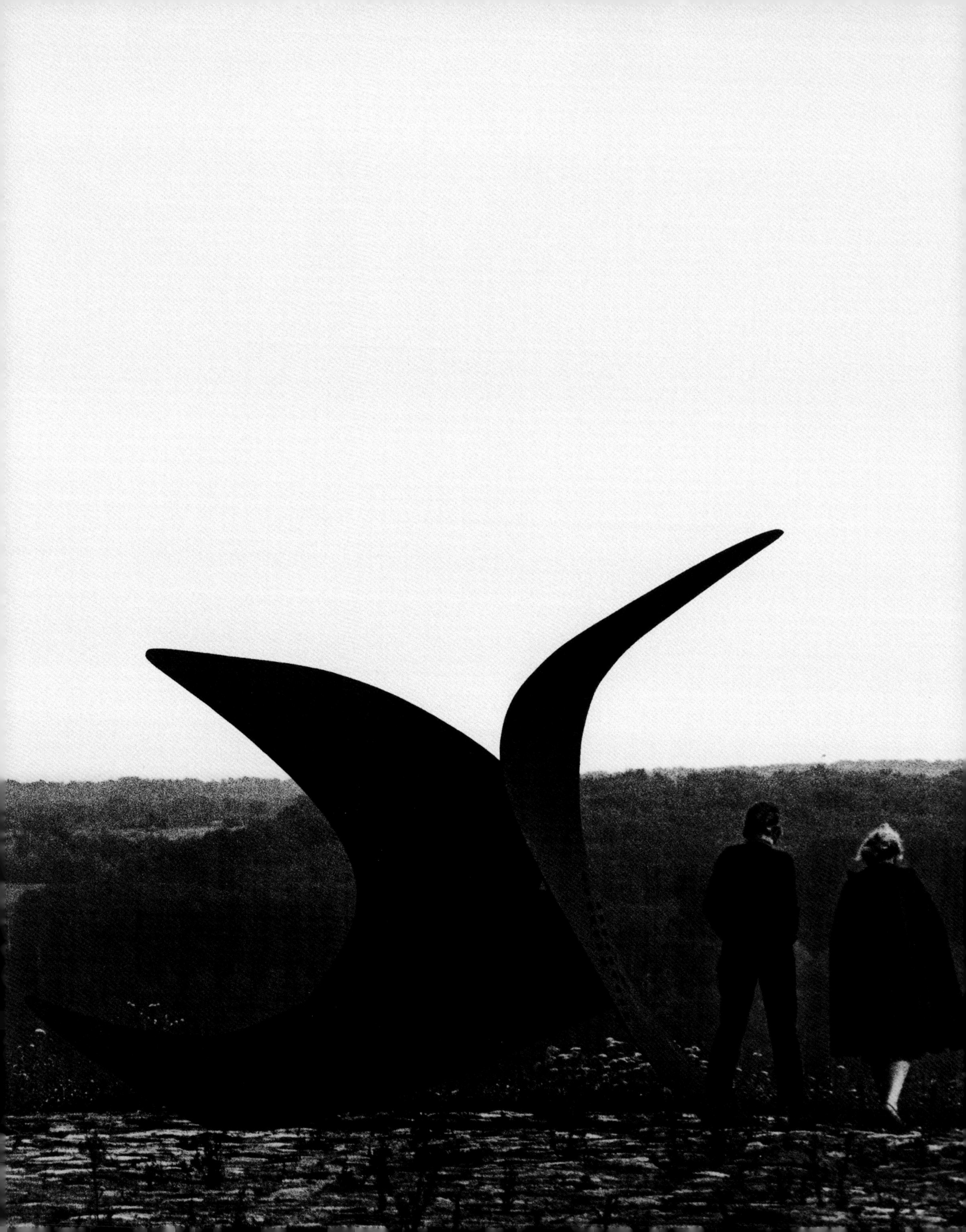

„Maßstab“ ist eine poetische, soziale und kulturelle Größe. Sie steuert Überlegungen zu Ästhetik und Funktionalität und sogar die materielle Qualität der Kunst in einem bestimmten zeitlichen und räumlichen Rahmen.[1] Um Kunstwerke verstehen und wertschätzen zu können, müssen wir sie in ihren realen Maßen in unserem Umfeld, in Museen, Galerien und öffentlichen Räumen erleben, auf sie zugehen oder um sie herum, so wie es Alexander Calder für seine Werke empfahl: „Ein Stabile sollte man umrunden oder durchqueren. Ein Mobile tanzt vor einem.“[2] Ohne gewisse Anhaltspunkte fällt es in der Tat schwer, den Maßstab eines Objekts zu erfassen, zumal es auf der Netzhaut stets neu skaliert wird und die sensorische und kognitive Wahrnehmung jedes Körpers durch seine eigenen Maße begrenzt ist.[3] Auf welche erlernten Berechnungen oder Raummaße stützen wir uns außerdem, um Größe und Maßstab zu ermitteln? Für Calder hatte diese Fragestellung eine ästhetische Tragweite, da er immer in großen Dimensionen dachte und sich der physikalischen Zusammenhänge des Universums bewusst war, selbst wenn seine Hände an etwas Kleinem arbeiteten.[4]

Für Calder war Kunst phänomenologisch, ein poetischer Gestus, heraufbeschworen durch Unermessliches, bestehend „aus Masse, Richtung und begrenzten Räumen innerhalb des großen Raums, des Universums“.[5] Eine seiner zentralen Theorien basiert auf dem von ihm beobachteten „Ungleichgewicht […] zwischen Form, Masse und Bewegung“[6] und lässt sich auf die relationalen Maße und Größenverhältnisse beziehen, mit denen kosmische Ereignisse sichtbar gemacht werden. Mit den jeweils verfügbaren Materialien strebte Calder sein Leben lang danach, „alle Elemente in Bewegung [zu versetzen]“[7], sie aufzuzeichnen, nachzuverfolgen, zu harmonisieren und/oder die Wahrnehmung von Bewegung auf andere Art zu dokumentieren.

Dafür stimmte Calder sein Bewusstsein realer Bewegungen zunächst auf grafische Rhythmen ein. So erstmals 1925, als er mit umgehängtem Zeichenbrett, Papier, Tusche und einem japanischen Pinsel in den Zoos im Central Park und in der Bronx Tiere skizzierte (Abb. 33). Bei diesen Streifzügen entstanden Hunderte Strichzeichnungen, die er im Jahr darauf unter dem Titel *Animal Sketching* publizierte.[8] In Paris wurde Calder 1927 bekannt mit seinen Versuchen, Bewegungsabläufe zu erfassen. Mittels simpler Geräte wie Hebel und Flaschenzügen bewegte er die Figuren seines Miniatur-Zirkus' aus Kork, Stoffresten, Papier, Holz, Draht und Schnur (Abb. 5, 12).[9] Im Jahr darauf faszinierte er das Publikum in einer Dokumentation des ACME Filmstudios mit einem Porträt der amerikanischen Modedesignerin Elizabeth „Babe“ Hawes, das er aus Draht in die Luft zeichnete (Abb. 35).

Elizabeth Hutton Turner

Calder und das Problem des Maßstabs

32 Louisa Calder und Antonia Mulas mit *Le Faucon* (1963) / Louisa Calder and Antonia Mulas with *Le Faucon* (1963), Saché, 1963, Foto / photo Ugo Mulas

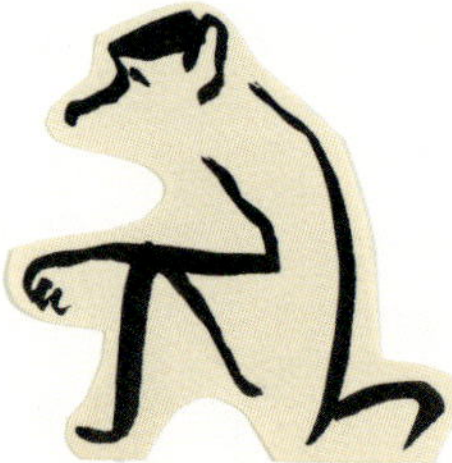

33 *Untitled* (Monkey), 1925, Tinte auf Papier, 7,3 × 7,3 cm / ink on paper, 2 7/8 × 2 7/8 in., Calder Foundation, New York. Mary Calder Rower Bequest, 2011

Nach der Ablösung vom Blatt Papier hin zu Drahtvektoren eröffneten ihm diese Zeichnungen eine neue Möglichkeit der Wahrnehmung, die den räumlichen Umrisslinien plastische Werte durch Volumen und Form verlieh.[10] Zwei im rechten Winkel überkreuzte Drahtringe ergaben für ihn eine Kugel (Abb. 34). Zwei oder mehr Blechstücke, in Form geschnitten und im Winkel miteinander vernietet, standen für einen Festkörper, der konkav oder konvex sein konnte. Dem, was Calder „Befreiung von der Erde" nannte, kam er seiner Meinung nach dann am nächsten, wenn er Konstruktionen aus Draht, flächigen und plastischen Elementen variierender Größe und Dichte mit unterschiedlichem Bewegungsspielraum an „einem sehr langen Faden" und/oder einem freitragenden Gestell aufhängte.[11]

Bis 1936 hatte Calder zwei unterschiedliche Formate für seine visuellen Erkundungen und psychologischen Abenteuer entwickelt: das zu tatsächlichen Bewegungen fähige Mobile aus Abfolgen frei hängender, aneinandergefügter Metallstäbe, die Formen aus Blech und Holz in der Schwebe halten, und das Stabile aus festen, miteinander verschraubten Metallplatten, die sich wechselseitig durchdringen und dafür gemacht sind, fest inmitten einer bewegten Welt zu stehen oder dort aufzusetzen. Beide aktivierten und balancierten größere Kräfte und Gegenkräfte und modellierten linienhafte Szenarien im Raum. Bezeichnenderweise machte Calder keine präzisen Vorgaben für die „richtige Größe" dieser von Zufällen bestimmten Konstruktionen, sondern nutzte die Möglichkeit, bei Auftragsarbeiten die Entwürfe nach Bedarf „für einen bestimmten Standort"[12] zu expandieren und zu kontrahieren. Eine „ganze Gattung faltbarer Objekte" sei entstanden, so Calders Schilderung, als er eine Lösung finden musste, um seine Arbeiten in Luftpostpaketen mit den vorgeschriebenen Maßen 46 × 25,4 × 5 cm nach Paris zu seiner ersten Ausstellung nach dem Zweiten Weltkrieg befördern zu können. Eines der kleinsten Objekte war *Grand Piano, Red*, mit rund 24 × 25 cm, eines der größten mit rund 250 × 200 cm *The S-Shaped Vine*, das aufgestellt fast raumhoch war und sehr viel Platz beanspruchte (Abb. 40, 36).[13]

Calder war der Auffassung, dass sich die Maße eines Objekts beliebig verändern ließen, je nachdem, inwieweit der Künstler durch die Proportionierung Balance und Harmonie schaffen konnte. Bei seinem Bühnenbild für eine Aufführung von Erik Saties sinfonischem Drama *Socrate* beim Hartford Festival in Connecticut 1936 füllte Calder den gesamten Bühnenraum (9 × 3,7 m) mit einer gut zwei Meter hohen Kugel aus zwei sich überkreuzenden Drahtringen, die um ihre eigene Achse rotierte, sich vertikal auf und ab sowie horizontal von hinten nach vorn über die Bühne bewegte. Eine gut 75 cm breite, rote Metallscheibe schwang an einem Seil über die gesamte Bühne, und ein aufrecht stehendes weißes Rechteck (305 × 91 cm) wurde auf dem Boden abgelegt und mit der schwarzen Rückseite nach vorn immer wieder aufgerichtet (Abb. 37). Zeitlich auf die drei Sokratischen Dialoge des Dramas abgestimmt (die ersten beiden neun Minuten, der dritte 18 Minuten lang), bewegte sich das Bühnenbild im Einklang mit der Schilderung der letzten Momente vor Sokrates' Tod. Einem Zuschauer zufolge war alles so perfekt mit Saties Komposition abgestimmt, dass „es schien, als bewege die Musik das Bühnenbild".[14]

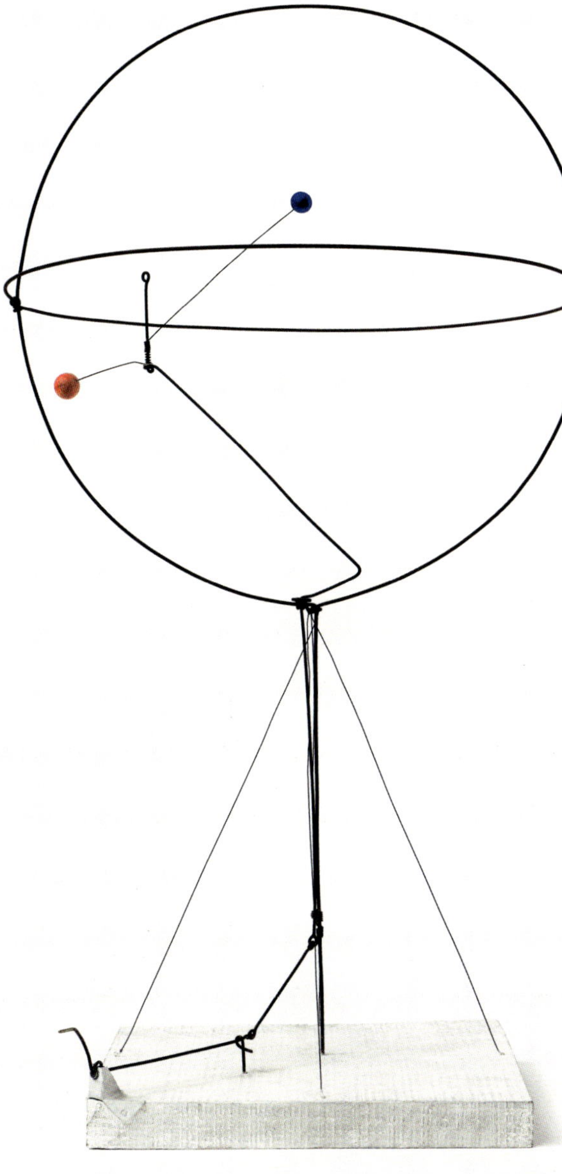

34 *Two Spheres Within a Sphere*, 1931, Draht, Holz, Farbe, 80 × 43,2 × 43,2 cm / wire, wood, paint, 31½ × 17 × 17 in., Calder Foundation, New York. Mary Calder Rower Bequest, 2011

Calder träumte letztlich von einem „Werk von einer ganz großen Spannweite".[15] Er berichtete, dass ihn zu Beginn seiner Laufbahn die Szene aus einem Film über einen Marmorsteinbruch faszinierte, in der ein riesiger, tonnenschwerer Block mit eleganter Leichtigkeit angehoben und bewegt wurde.[16] Er war überzeugt, ein Werk von solchen Dimensionen realisieren zu können, und das aus gutem Grund: Er hatte nicht nur das Publikum für seine neuen Metallobjekte begeistert, sondern wusste als Sohn und Enkel zweier bedeutender US-amerikanischer Bildhauer auch, wie man mithilfe von Modellen, Rastern und Punktiergeräten eine skalierbare Welt erschafft, die ein scheinbar grenzenloses Potenzial der Vergrößerung von Kunstwerken für den öffentlichen Raum birgt. Für seine freistehenden Stabiles aus Metallplatten fertigte Calder nach der klassischen Methode zunächst Arbeitsmodelle an und schnitt dann aus Papier Vorlagen in der angestrebten Größe zu, die in der Gießerei auf Metall übertragen wurden. Für *Devil Fish* (Abb. 41) etwa erstellte er zunächst aus Metall eine knapp 90 cm hohe Maquette. Die schließlich 172 cm hohe Plastik wurde 1937 in der Pierre Matisse Gallery ausgestellt, zusammen mit einem weiteren, über 213 cm hohen Stabile mit dem Titel *Big Bird*. Zwischen dessen gespreizten Beinen stand auf dem Fußboden rund ein Dutzend kleiner Metallmodelle für andere potenziell vergrößerbare Objekte (Abb. 42).[17]

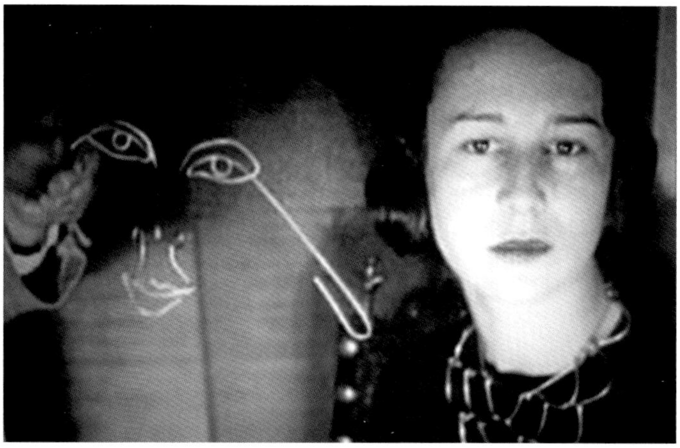

35 Elizabeth „Babe" Hawes mit ihrem von Calder gefertigten Drahtporträt, Filmstill / Elizabeth "Babe" Hawes and Calder's wire portrait of her, film still from *Sculptor Discards Clay to Ply His Art in Wire*, ACME Film Company, 1928

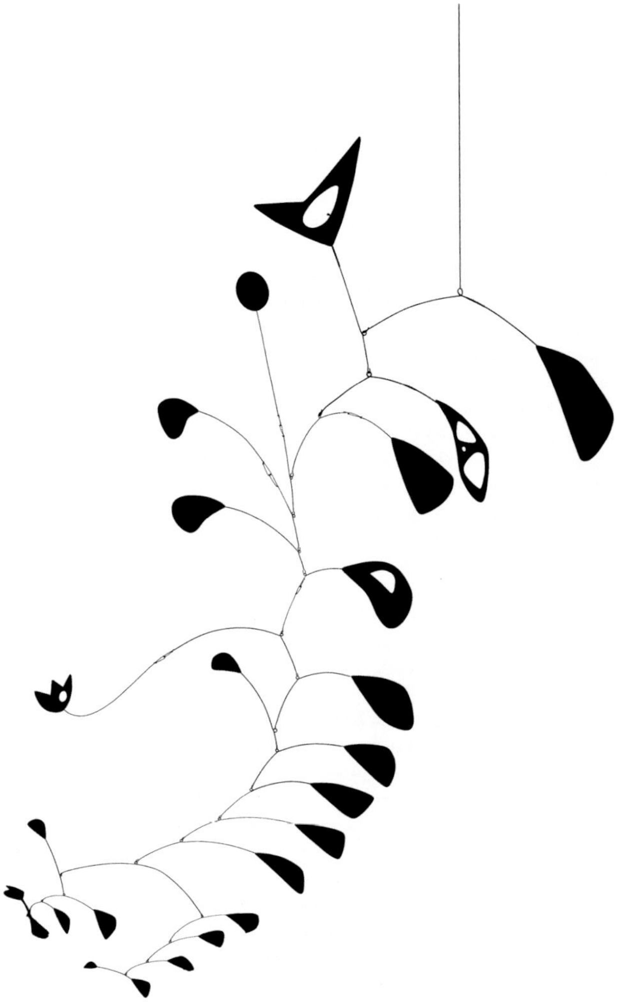

36 *The S-Shaped Vine*, 1946, Blech, Farbe, Draht, 250,2 × 200,7 cm / sheet metal, paint, wire, 98 ½ × 79 in., The Eli and Edythe L. Broad Collection, Los Angeles

Mit der Abkehr von Gewicht und Masse herkömmlicher Skulpturen, an deren Stelle er Volumen und Transparenz setzte, vertraute Calder vor allem auf die materiellen Eigenschaften und Funktionen der modernen Industrie und deren Maschinen, um seine Werke in dem Maße wachsen zu lassen, wie es die Großprojekte im öffentlichen Raum verlangten. Vor allem aber bediente er sich trotz der kontrapunktischen Bewegungen, Geschwindigkeiten und Richtungen, die seine Arbeiten für sich reklamieren, grundsätzlich derselben Sprache und Materialien wie die Architekten des International Style, die fließende Strukturen aus Stahlgittern und Glaswänden konzipierten und in der Nachkriegszeit eine „neue Monumentalität" forderten. Wie die Kunsthistorikerin Emily Reed feststellte, wirkt mindestens einer der in der 1943 erschienenen Abhandlung über Architektur „Neun

Punkte über Monumentalität" so, als hätten die Autoren dabei an Calder gedacht: „Bewegliche Elemente können das Aussehen der Bauten ständig verändern. Diese beweglichen Elemente werfen immer wieder andere Schatten, sobald sie dem Wind oder mechanischem Antrieb ausgesetzt sind, und können zu einer Quelle neuartiger architektonischer Wirkungen werden."[18] Im Jahr 1958 arbeitete Calder an gleich drei öffentlichen Aufträgen mit drei verschiedenen Gießereien.[19] In dieser Zeit drohte der mutige Ansatz zu kolossaler Größe zum Prüfstein für Calders maßgeschneiderte, zu Modellen zurechtgeschnittene und gefaltete Metallplatten zu werden.

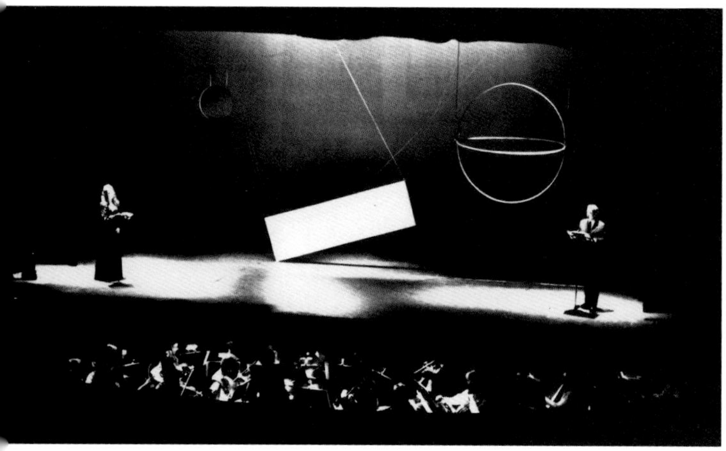

37 Rekonstruktion von Calders Bühnenbild für / Reconstruction from Calder's decor for Erik Satie, *Socrate*, 1936 (Foto einer Aufführung / photograph of a performance, Beacon Theatre, New York, 1977)

Wie der Künstler im Rückblick schilderte,[20] waren seinen Projekten durch Größe keine Grenzen gesetzt, sondern höchstens durch das Austarieren der Kapazitäten: gerade verfügbare Ressourcen, sein Zeitplan und seine Anwesenheit bei Treffen mit den zuständigen Projektteams, die Auslastung der Gießerei, seine Anweisungen an die Ingenieure und Techniker, die das Modell vergrößerten und die Dicke und mechanische Belastbarkeit der Platten berechneten, letzte Korrekturen durch Calder selbst und seine Schlussabnahme während der Aufstellung sowie die Größe und Stärke des Montagekrans und die Erfahrung der Schweißer. All das musste zusammenwirken für ein Werk, das er mit seiner Signatur versah. 1962 erhielt der Künstler die Chance, ein Objekt in einem bis dahin unerreichten Maßstab zu erschaffen. Der italienische Kunstkritiker, Historiker und Kurator Giovanni Carandente beauftragte ihn für das Festival dei Due Mondi (Fest der zwei Welten) in Spoleto mit einer Plastik, die wie ein Stadttor eine Kreuzung vor dem Bahnhof überspannen sollte. Calder lieferte ein kleines Modell für ein Objekt, das er später *Teodelapio* nannte (Abb. 43). Die fünfbeinige Konstruktion besitzt einen zum Himmel strebenden Pfeil als Kopf und eine ausladend geschwungene Kruppe. Der Mittelteil wölbt sich nach oben, damit der Verkehr darunter hindurchfließen konnte. Als bei der Installation des großen Objekts statische Probleme auftraten, erhielt Calder ein aufgeregtes Telegramm und fuhr mit dem nächsten Zug nach Spoleto. Schon vom Abteilfenster aus erspähte er sein Werk und war begeistert von der Größe und Ausdehnung der Plastik, die der Stahl- und Schiffsbaukonzern Italsider anhand seines Modells gefertigt hatte. Calder war beeindruckt: „Maße können täuschen, und ich war überrascht, als ich sah, dass dieses Objekt höher als breit war, denn ich hatte es genau anders herum in Erinnerung."[21] Calder schenkte die Skulptur der Stadt. Bis heute ragt ihr hoher Pfeil weithin sichtbar über die umgebenden Gebäude in den Himmel, in gerader Linie auf einen Punkt in den Weiten des Universums zielend.

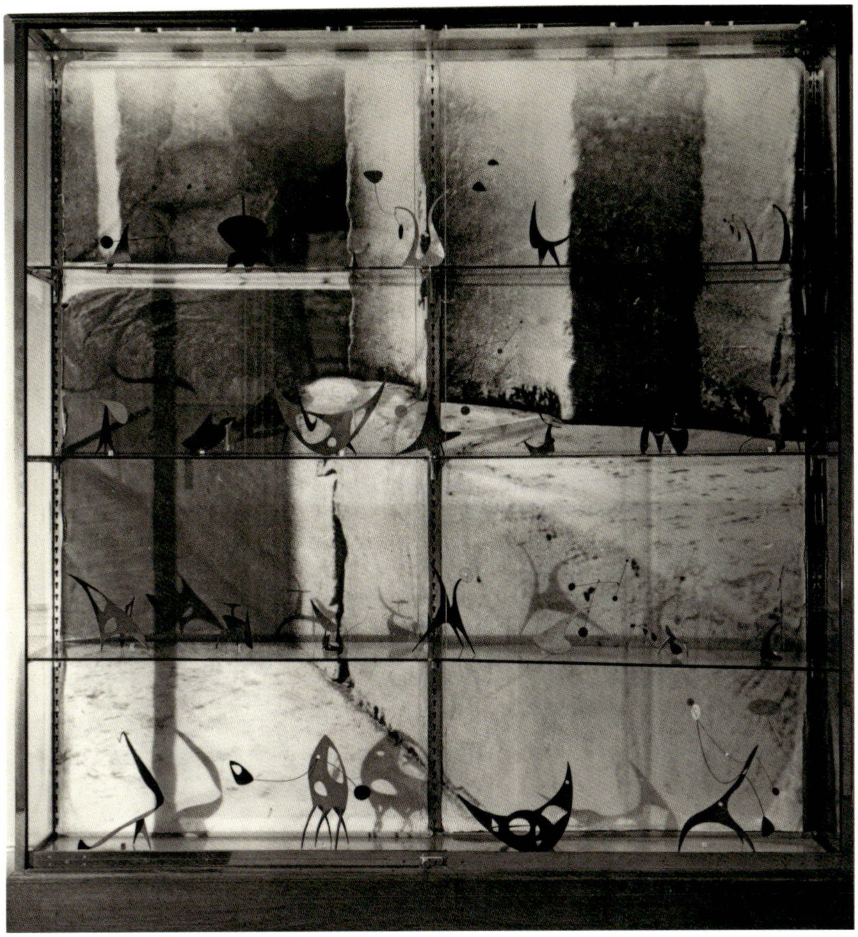

38 Vitrine mit Werken Calders in der Ausstellung / with Calder works in the exhibition *Alexander Calder: Mobiles, Stabiles, Constellations*, Galerie Louis Carré, Paris, 1946

Zwar lässt Calders Arbeitsprozess das Glücksgefühl anklingen, das die Entdeckung „einer neuen Möglichkeit von Schönheit“[22] mit sich bringt, doch schreibt er dem – tatsächlichen oder implizierten – Hauch von Unendlichkeit in den Bewegungen der Objekte keinerlei Zielbestimmung oder gar Rückweg vor. Nach Jean-Paul Sartres Meinung arbeitete Calder mit unsichtbaren Kräften: „Sie haben zu viele und zu komplizierte Federn und Rädchen, als daß irgendein Mensch – auch nicht ihr Schöpfer – alle ihre möglichen Wandlungen voraussehen könnte.“[23] Die Betrachterinnen und Betrachter sollen selbst ihren Eindrücken nachspüren. Für Hans Richter beispielsweise führte der Weg „vom Zirkus zum Mond“, so der Titel seines Films über Calders Arbeit von 1963. Calder selbst erklärte: „Dass andere begreifen, was mir durch den Kopf geht, erscheint mir unerheblich, solange ihnen etwas durch den ihren geht.“[24]

1 Auf die Frage, warum er sich als Realist betrachte, antwortete Calder: „Weil ich das erschaffe, was ich sehe. Das Problem ist nur, es zu sehen. Wenn man sich etwas vorstellen kann, es im Raum heraufbeschwören kann, dann kann man es auch erschaffen, und im Handumdrehen ist man Realist. Das Universum ist real, aber man kann es nicht sehen. Man muss es sich vorstellen. Tut man das, kann man bei seiner Wiedergabe realistisch sein." Alexander Calder: „Alexander Calder", Interview von Katharine Kuh, in: *The Artist's Voice: Talks with Seventeen Modern Artists*, New York und Evanston, IL, 1962, S. 38–51, hier S. 42.

2 Ebd.

3 Jennifer Roberts: „Introduction: Seeing Scale", in: *Scale*, Chicago/Paris 2016, S. 10–24, hier S. 12.

4 Jed Perl: „Alexander Calder: Multum in Parvo", in: *Alexander Calder: Multum in Parvo*, Ausst.-Kat. Dominique Lévy Gallery, New York 2015, S. 10–19, hier S. 19.

5 Alexander Calder: „Comment réaliser l'art?" in: *abstraction-création. art non figuratif*, Nr. 1, 1932, S. 6.

6 Calder 1962 (wie Anm. 1), S. 39.

7 Alexander Calder: „Que ça bouge – à propos des sculptures mobiles", Manuskript, 8.3.1932, Calder Foundation Archives.

8 Alexander Calder: *Animal Sketching*, New York 1926, S. 53.

9 André Legrand-Chabrier: „Un petit cirque à domicile", in: *Candide*, Nr. 171, 23.6.1927, S. 7. Siehe auch: „Futurist Toys for Advanced Kiddies Created by Calder, Artist-Engineer", in: *New York Herald* (Paris), 4.8.1927, S. 7.

10 James Johnson Sweeney: „Alexander Calder", in: *Calder*, Ausst.-Kat. Fondation Maeght, Saint-Paul-de-Vence 1969, S. 7–11, hier S. 8; James Johnson Sweeney: „Alexander Calder", in: *Calder*, Boston 1971, S. 5–8, hier S. 6.

11 Alexander Calder: „What Abstract Art Means to Me", in: *Museum of Modern Art Bulletin*, 18, Nr. 3, Frühjahr 1951, S. 8–9, hier S. 8.

12 Calder 1962 (wie Anm. 1), S. 42.

13 Alexander Calder: *Calder: An Autobiography with Pictures*, hg. von Jean Davidson, New York 1977, S. 188f.

14 Arnauld Pierre: „Staging Movement", in: *Alexander Calder: 1898–1976*, hg. von Marla Prather, Ausst.-Kat. National Gallery of Art, Washington, D.C.; San Francisco Museum of Modern Art, Washington, D.C., 1998, S. 329–347, hier S. 344. Siehe auch Calders Beschreibung seines Bühnenbilds für *Socrate* in: Alexander Calder: „Mobiles", in: Myfanwy Evans (Hg.): *The Painter's Object*, London 1937, S. 62–67, https://calder.org/bibliography/the-painters-object-1937/ (abgerufen am 26.2.2021).

15 Paul Klee: „Manchmal träume ich ein Werk von einer ganz großen Spannweite durch das ganze elementare, gegenständliche, inhaltliche und stilistische Gebiet [...]", in: Paul Klee: Das bildnerische Denken. Schriften zur Form- und Gestaltungslehre, hg. und bearb. von Jürg Spiller, Basel/Stuttgart 1956, S. 95.

16 Calder 1937 (wie Anm. 14).

17 Alexander S. C. Rower: „Calder in Nature", in: *Calder*, Ausst.-Kat. Storm King Art Center, Mountainville, NY, 2003, S. 13–17, hier S. 13f.

18 Sigfried Giedion, Fernand Léger und Josep Lluís Sert: „Neun Punkte: Über Monumentalität – ein menschliches Bedürfnis", in: Sigfried Giedion (Hg.): *Architektur und Gemeinschaft. Tagebuch einer Entwicklung*, Hamburg 1956, S. 40–42, hier S. 41f., zitiert in: Emily Reed: „Sculpture and Architecture: Building Calder's Global Network", in: *Alexander Calder: Radical Inventor/Inventeur radical*, hg. von Elizabeth Hutton Turner und Anne Grace, Ausst.-Kat. Montreal Museum of Fine Arts; National Gallery of Victoria, Melbourne Montreal 2018, S. 169–178, hier S. 176.

19 Calder 1977 (wie Anm. 13), S. 258.

20 Siehe Calders Erläuterungen zu seinen großen Stabiles in: Robert Osborn: „Calder's International Monuments", in: *Art in America* 51, Nr. 2, März/April 1969, S. 90–100.

21 Alexander Calder: „Memorandum on *Teodelapio*", 6.8.1962, in: *Calder*, hg. von Giovanni Carandente, Ausst.-Kat. Palazzo Vela, Turin, Mailand 1983, S. 226: „Ich sah *Teodelapio* zum ersten Mal vom Zug aus und war begeistert von seiner Größe und Ausdehnung. Maße können täuschen, und ich staunte darüber, dass dieses Objekt höher als breit war, denn ich hatte es genau anders herum in Erinnerung."

22 Calder 1932 (wie Anm. 7).

23 Jean-Paul Sartre: „Les Mobiles de Calder", in: *Calder*, Ausst.-Kat. Galerie Louis Carré, Paris 1946, o. S.; dt. Übersetzung: „Die Mobiles von Calder", in: *Alexander Calder*, Ausst.-Kat. Akademie der Künste Berlin (West), Berlin 1967, S. 21–23, hier S. 21.

24 Calder 1951 (wie Anm. 11), S. 8. Für diese Information danke ich Susan Braeuer Dam: Susan Braeuer Dam: „The Mobile Object", in: *Calder: Small Sphere and Heavy Sphere*, Ausst.-Kat. Pace Gallery, New York 2019, S. 22–37, hier S. 34.

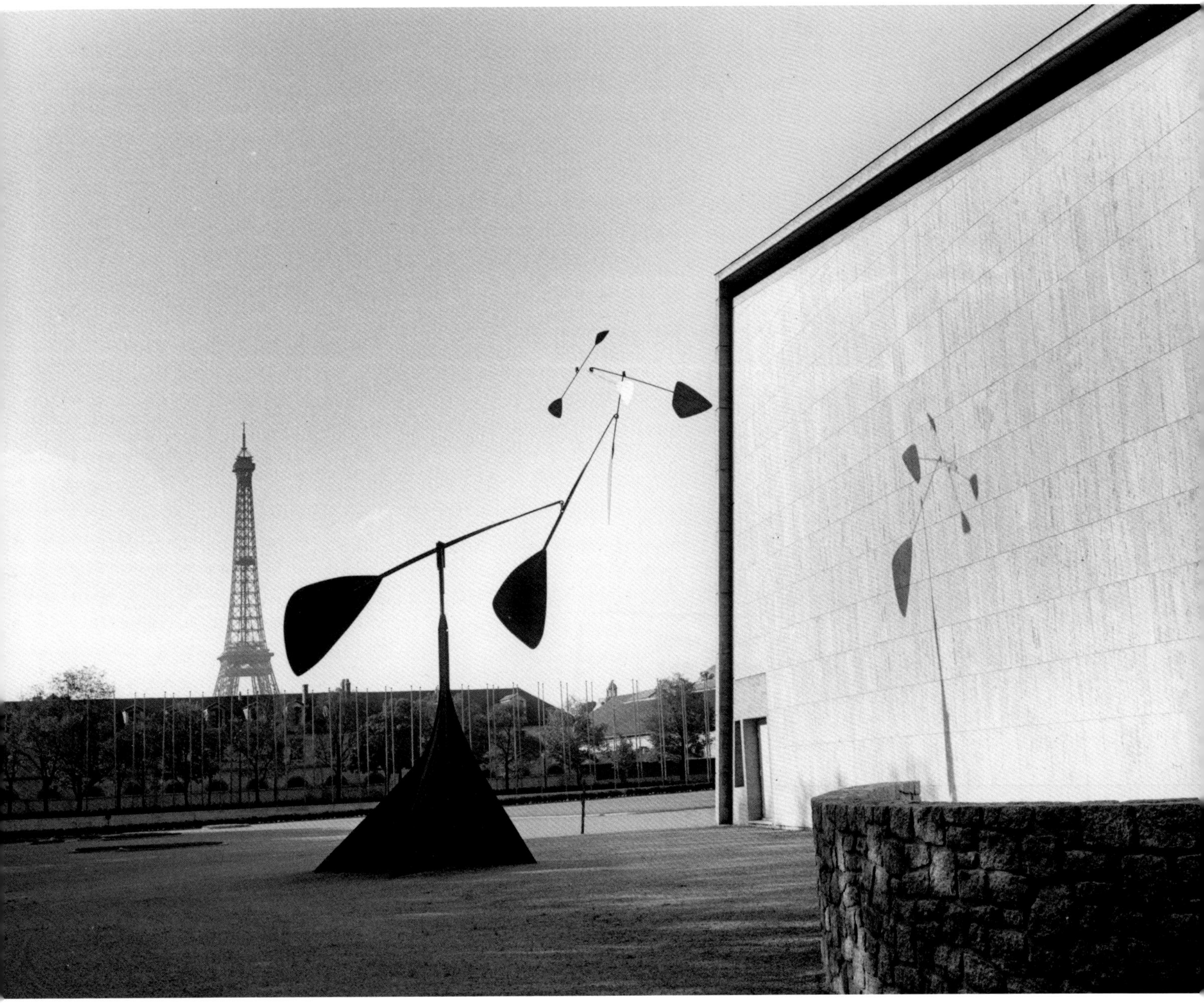

39 *Spirale*, 1958, Stahl, Stab, Bolzen, Farbe, Höhe 914 cm / sheet metal, rod, bolts, paint, height 360 in., Palais de l'Unesco, Paris

Calder and the Problem of Scale

Elizabeth Hutton Turner

Scale is a poetic, social, and cultural metric. It governs considerations of aesthetics and functionality, and even the material quality of art in a given time and space.[1] Experiencing the actual sizes of works of art in our midst, in museums, galleries, and public spaces where one can walk up to or around them, is central to our understanding and appreciation—much as Alexander Calder recommended for his own inventions both stabile and mobile. As he said: "You have to walk around a stabile or through it—a mobile dances in front of you."[2] In fact, without certain cues, it is hard to see scale when vision itself rescales all objects upon the retina and each body's sensory cognitive apparatus is limited by its own scale.[3] What other learned calculations or spatial measures help us to know size and scale? This problem held aesthetic meaning for Calder, who was always thinking big—always cognizant of the physics of big space, even when his hands were working small.[4]

As Calder defined it, art was phenomenological—a poetic gesture summoned from immensities, as he said, "out of volumes, motion, spaces bounded by the great space, the universe."[5] One of his observational theories—what he called, "the disparity... between form, masses and movement"[6]—can be understood as the relational measures and extents of scale used to bring those cosmic occurrences into view. With the materials he had at hand, Calder made it his lifelong task to trace, track, harmonize, and/or otherwise account for an awareness of, as he said, how to "put all the elements in motion."[7]

Calder began this enterprise by attuning his awareness of actual movement to graphic rhythms. He first performed the connection in 1925 while walking through the zoos in both Central Park and the Bronx, strapped with a tray equipped with paper, India ink, and a Japanese brush. Out of these walks emerged hundreds of single line drawings (fig. 33) that he published the following year in a drawing manual entitled *Animal Sketching*.[8] In 1927 Calder became newsworthy in Paris, for pursuing motion-capture through his performances of miniature circus figures—created out of cork, bits of cloth, paper, wood, wire, and string animated by simple machines such as levers and pulleys (see figs. 5, 12).[9] Within a year, he had once more captured the public imagination in an Acme newsreel that featured him launching a line of wire into the air as he configured the likeness of the American fashion designer Elizabeth "Babe" Hawes (fig. 35).

When Calder's drawing left the page as a wire vector, it opened a new channel of awareness conferring sculptural values of volume and shape upon contours traced through space.[10] As he saw it, two circles of wire intersecting at right angles denote a sphere (fig. 34). Two or more sheets of metal cut into shapes and mounted at angles imply a solid, perhaps concave or convex. Calder believed he had best approximated what he called "this freedom from the earth" by suspending wire, planar, and solid constructions of varying sizes and densities, with varying capabilities for movement, from "a very long thread" and/or along a cantilevered armature.[11]

By 1936 Calder had devised two distinct formats for visual exploration and psychological adventure—one, the mobile, that is to say, susceptible to real movement consisting of suspended arrays of linked wire extensions balancing metal and wood shapes; the other, the stabile, consisting of propped intersections of fixed planar shapes, bolted together and made to stand or touch down amid a world in movement. Both leveraged and balanced larger forces and counter forces, and sculpted linear scenarios in space. Revealingly, Calder made no exact specifications regarding a "right size" for these contingent structures. Instead, he delighted at the capacity of commissioned works to expand and contract their designs, as he said, "for a particular spot."[12] Calder once told the story of how a "whole race of objects that were collapsible" was born by solving the problem of fitting his work into the long dimensions of a regulation airmail package—eighteen inches long, ten inches wide, and two inches thick—for his first show in postwar Paris. Among the smallest was *Grand Piano, Red* (fig. 40), measuring nine and five-eighths by ten inches. One of the largest was *The S-Shaped Vine* (98 ½ × 79 in.), which, when recapitulated, reached nearly floor to ceiling and occupied a substantial area (fig. 36).[13]

To Calder, dimension itself was an arbitrary expansion or contraction, depending upon the proportioning power of the artist toward equilibrium and harmony. For a performance of composer Erik Satie's symphonic drama *Socrate* at the Hartford Festival in 1936, Calder took the full measure of the thirty-by-twelve-foot stage with two seven-foot intersecting steel hoops, rotating and moving from the back to the front of the stage and also vertically; a thirty-inch-wide suspended red metal disk, crossing the stage from end to end; and a ten-by-three-foot-tall standing white rectangular panel, made to turn and fall and rise again to reveal the back side as a black pylon (fig. 37). This composition, also measured by time in the opera's three dialogues—the first two in nine minutes and last in eighteen minutes—was made to move in accord with the libretto's narration of the final moments of Socrates's life. According to one viewer, it was all so perfectly coordinated with the measure of Satie's score that "it seemed as if the music moved the set."[14]

Calder clearly dreamed of "a work of really great breadth."[15] As he once explained, early in his career, he was captivated by an image from a movie of a marble quarry, where something of great size and mass was hoisted and made to move with great ease and delicacy.[16] Moreover, he believed that realizing such an all-encompassing work could be within his grasp—and with good reason. Not only had he won a public following for his new metal objects, but, as the son and grandson of two notable American sculptors, he also possessed a familiarity with the methods of creating a scalable world with models, grids, and pointing machines that bore a seemingly limitless potential for proliferating works of public art. With the advent of his own free-standing sheet metal stabiles, such as *Devil Fish* (fig. 41), which was first created as a thirty-five-inch-tall metal "sketch," or maquette,

Calder adopted the classical method of sketching models for fabrication and then cutting full-scale paper patterns for foundry enlargement. When fully realized, the five and a half-feet-tall *Devil Fish* was shown at the Pierre Matisse Gallery in 1937, the display that also included another large stabile, measuring over seven-feet-tall, called *Big Bird*, standing astride a dozen small metal sketches for other, potentially enlargeable works arrayed beneath it on the gallery floor (fig. 42).[17]

By discarding the weight and mass of conventional sculpture in favor of volume and transparency in his own practice, Calder essentially placed confidence in certain material features and functions of modern industry and machinery that enabled his works to grow along with great civic projects. Most importantly, though his work laid claim to contrapuntal movements, speeds, and directions, Calder essentially spoke in the same language and with the same materials as architects who were designing floating structures of gridded steel and glazed walls in the International Style and calling for "a new monumentality" in the postwar era. As the art historian Emily Reed has noted, at least one of the points in the treatise entitled "Nine Points on Monumentality," published in 1943, seemed to have been written invitation with Calder in mind: "Mobile elements can constantly vary the aspect of the buildings. These mobile elements, changing positions and casting different shadows when acted upon by wind or machinery, can be the source of new architectural effects."[18] At one point in 1958 Calder was fully occupied with three public commissions employing three foundries.[19] At the time, the emboldening question of colossal scale loomed as a test for his configured metal sheets, cut and folded into maquettes.

As Calder later recounted,[20] his projects seemed to have acknowledged no limits of scale, only balanced contingencies: the resources of the situation; Calder's personal schedule and ability to be present with the project team of a given community; the capacity of the foundry; his direction of the skilled engineers and technicians enlarging the design, calculating the thickness of the metal, the tolerance for the load; and, during installation, the artist's final supervision and adjustments; the size and strength of the derrick; and the experience of the welders. All were meant to arrive at a single solution for his signature. In 1962, the occasion for unprecedented scale arrived by way of a commission from the Italian art critic, historian, and curator Giovanni Carandente to create a sculpture for the Festival dei Due Mondi (Festival of two worlds), in Spoleto, near Rome. The work was to span an intersection in front of the Spoleto train station as a gateway to the city. Calder supplied a small maquette of a work he later called *Teodelapio* (fig. 43)—a five-legged object with a launching arrow at its head, with undulating curved haunches and an arched middle section to permit the flow of traffic. When problems of stability arose during the process of installing the enlargement, Calder was frantically summoned by telegram and soon arrived in Spoleto by railway. At first sight from the train, Calder was delighted at the size and expanse of the work that the Italsider ship building firm had made from his maquette. As he said, "Dimensions can be deceiving—and I was surprised to learn that the object was taller than it was wide—as I had thought I had remembered the contrary."[21] A gift to the city, Calder's sculpture's tall arrow can still be seen

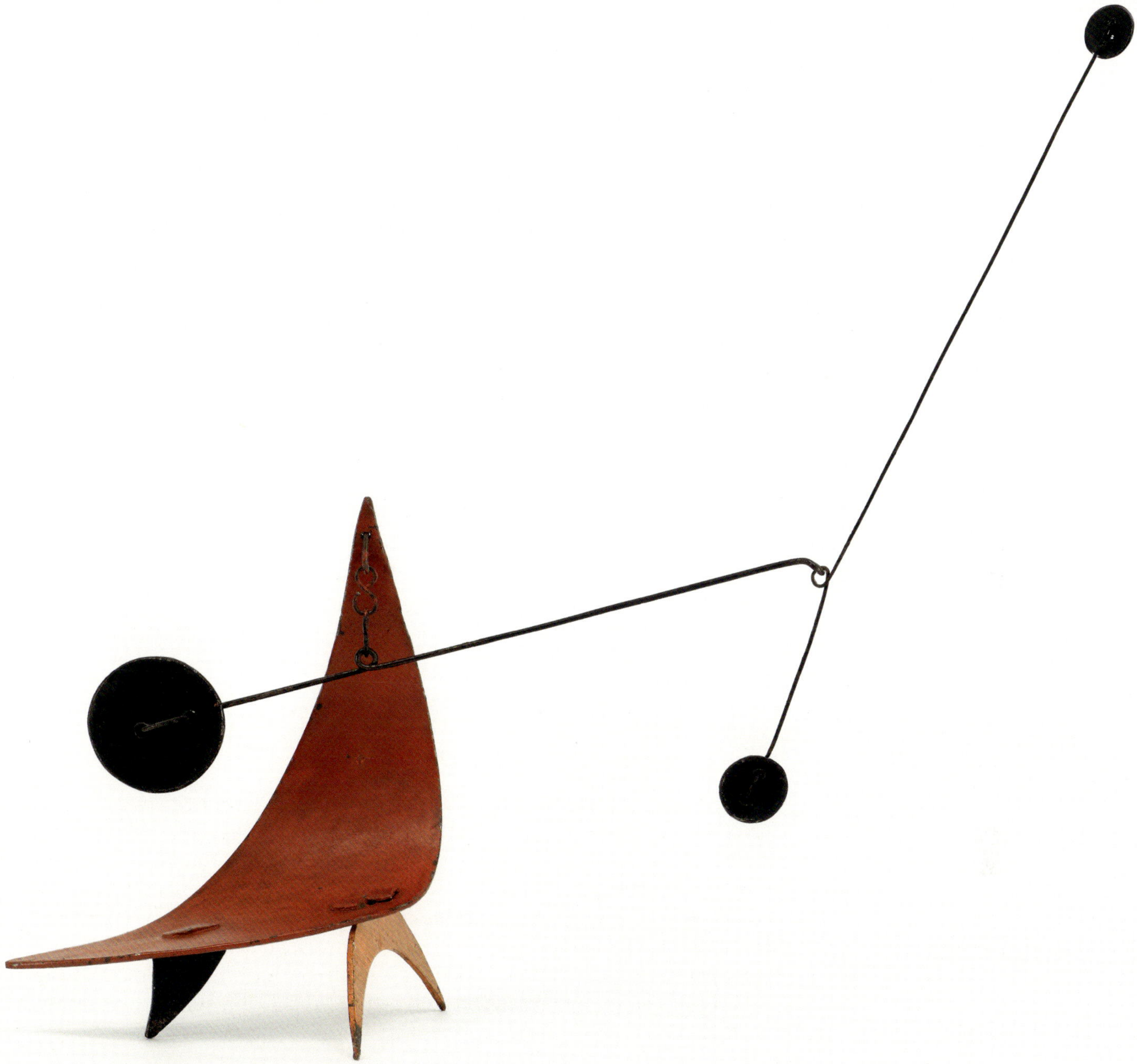

40 *Grand Piano, Red*, 1946, Blech, Draht, Farbe, 24,5 × 25,4 × 7,6 cm / sheet metal, wire, paint, 9 ⅝ × 10 × 3 in., Calder Foundation, New York

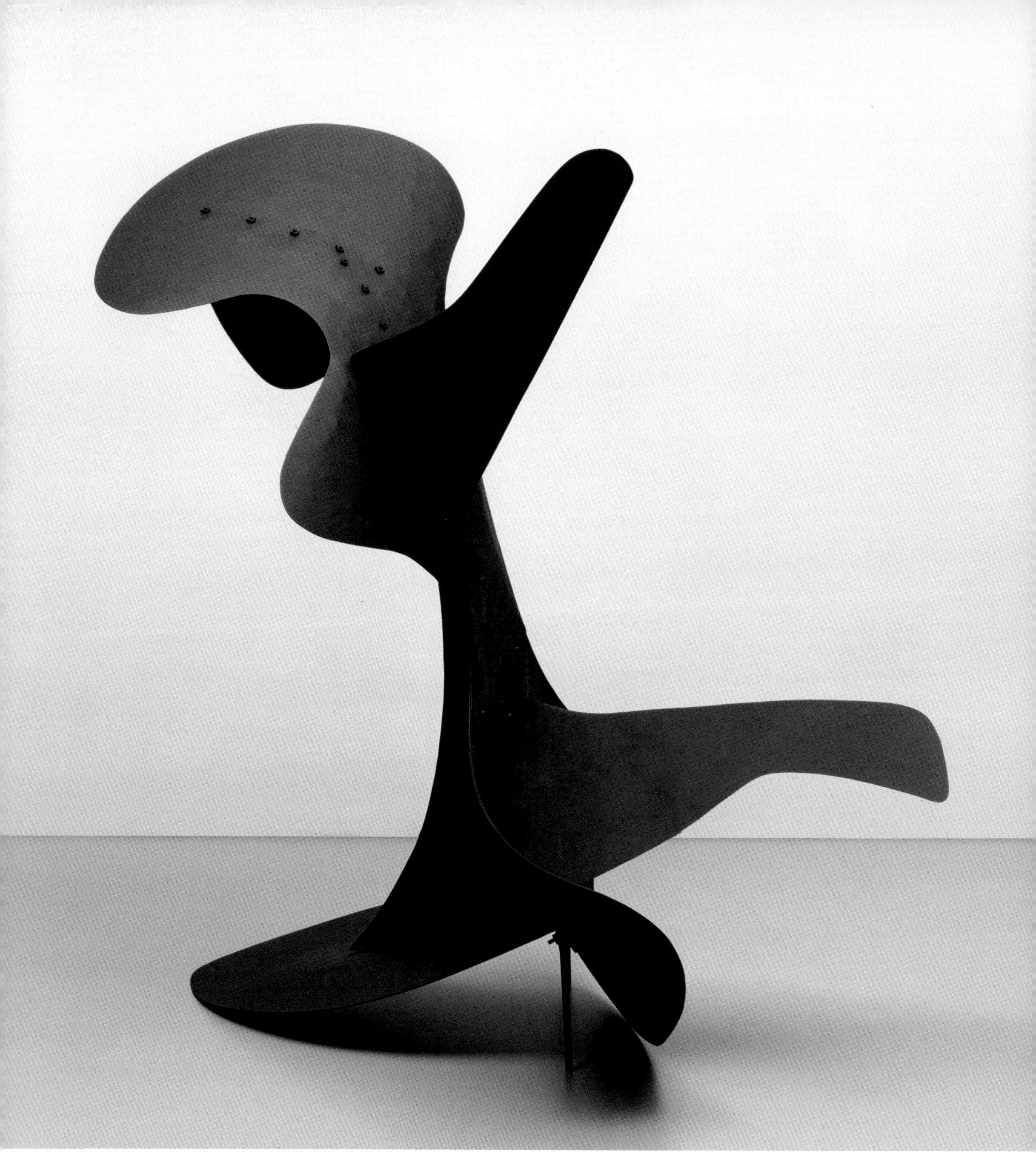

41 *Devil Fish*, 1937, Blech, Bolzen, Farbe, 172,7 × 162,6 × 119,4 cm / sheet metal, bolts, paint, 68 × 64 × 47 in., Calder Foundation, New York

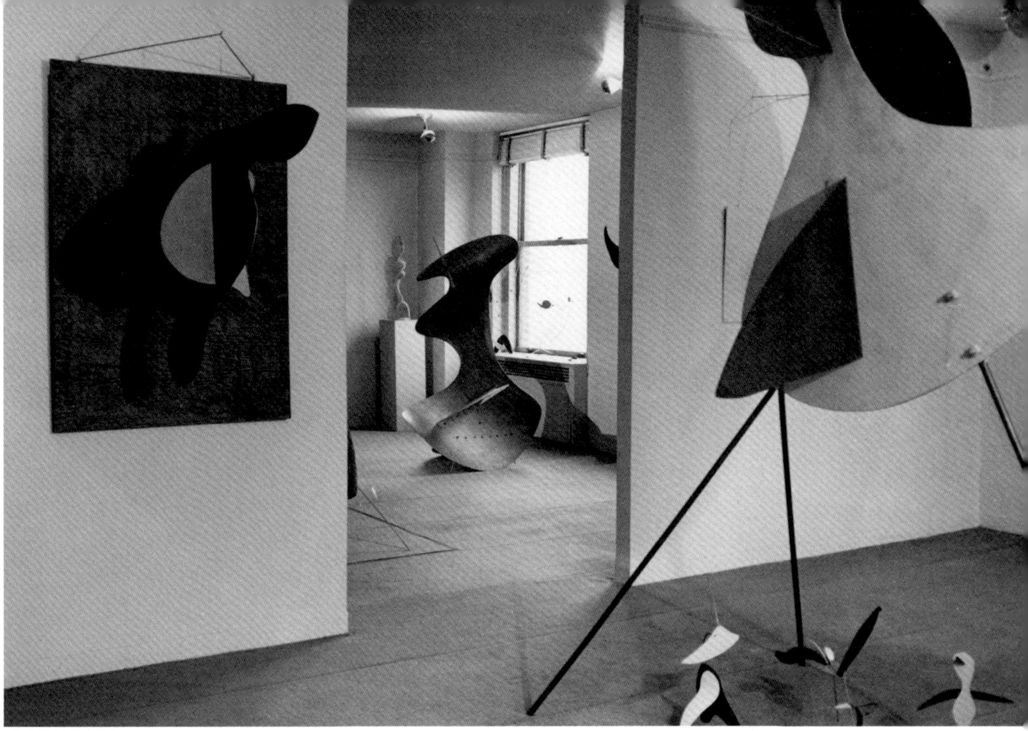

42 Ausstellungsansicht / Installation view, *Calder: Stabiles & Mobiles*, Pierre Matisse Gallery, New York, 1937, Foto / photo Herbert Matter

above the surrounding buildings, against the sky, aiming toward its mark in the great beyond.

Apart from alluding to the sense of elation that accompanies "arriving at a new possibility of beauty,"[22] Calder's process did not specify a destination for that hint of infinity in the movements of his objects—real or implied—or a return route back to the embodied work for that matter. As Jean-Paul Sartre once explained, Calder was working with unseen forces "too numerous and complicated for any human mind, even that of their creator, to be able to foresee all their combinations."[23] It was meant for viewers to chart their own experience. In 1963 Hans Richter, for example, went, he said, from "the circus to the moon," in his eponymous film about Calder's work. As Calder explained: "That others grasp what I have in mind seems unessential, at least as long as they have something else in theirs."[24]

1 When asked why he considered himself a realist, Calder responded, "Because I make what I see. It's only the problem of seeing it. If you can imagine a thing, conjure it up in space—then you can make it, and *tout de suite* you're a realist. The universe is real but you can't see it. You have to imagine it. Once you imagine it, you can be realistic about reproducing it." Alexander Calder, "Alexander Calder," interview by Katharine Kuh, in *The Artist's Voice: Talks with Seventeen Modern Artists* (New York and Evanston, IL, 1962), pp. 38–51, here p. 42.

2 Ibid.

3 Jennifer Roberts, "Introduction: Seeing Scale," in *Scale* (Chicago and Paris, 2016), pp. 10–24, here p. 12.

4 Jed Perl, "Alexander Calder: Multum in Parvo," in *Alexander Calder: Multum in Parvo*, exh. cat. Dominique Lévy Gallery (New York, 2015), pp. 10–19, here p. 19.

5 Alexander Calder, "Comment réaliser l'art?" *abstraction-création: art non figuratif*, no. 1 (1932), p. 6. Translation courtesy Calder Foundation, New York.

6 Calder 1962 (see note 1), p. 39.

7 Alexander Calder, "Que ça bouge—à propos des sculptures mobiles," manuscript, March 8, 1932, Calder Foundation archives. Translation courtesy Calder Foundation, New York.

8 Alexander Calder, *Animal Sketching* (Pelham, NY, 1926), p. 53.

9 André Legrand-Chabrier, "Un petit cirque à domicile," *Candide*, no. 171 (June 23, 1927) p. 7. Also see "Futurist Toys for Advanced Kiddies Created by Calder, Artist-Engineer," *New York Herald* (Paris), August 4, 1927, p. 7.

10 James Johnson Sweeney, "Alexander Calder," in *Calder*, trans. Annick Baudoin and Alain Veinstein, exh. cat. Fondation Maeght (Saint-Paul-de-Vence, 1969), pp. 7–11, here p. 8; James Johnson Sweeney, "Alexander Calder," in *Calder*, trans. Margreth C. Schultz (Boston, 1971), pp. 5–8, here p. 6.

11 Alexander Calder, "What Abstract Art Means to Me," *Museum of Modern Art Bulletin* 18, no. 3 (Spring 1951), pp. 8–9, here p. 8.

12 Calder 1962 (see note 1), p. 42.

13 Alexander Calder, *Calder: An Autobiography with Pictures*, ed. Jean Davidson (New York, 1977), pp. 188–89.

14 Arnauld Pierre, "Staging Movement," in *Alexander Calder: 1898–1976*, ed. Marla Prather, exh. cat. National Gallery of Art, Washington, DC; San Francisco Museum of Modern Art (Washington, DC, 1998), pp. 329–47, here p. 344. See also Calder's description of his stage design for *Socrate* in Alexander Calder, "Mobiles," in *The Painter's Object*, ed. Myfanwy Evans (London, 1937), pp. 62–67, https://calder.org/bibliography/the-painters-object-1937/ (accessed February 26, 2021).

15 Paul Klee: "Sometimes I dream a work of really great breadth, ranging through the whole region of element, object, meaning and style." Paul Klee, *On Modern Art*, with an introduction by Herbert Read, trans. Paul Findlay (1966; repr. Trowbridge, UK, 1987), p. 54.

16 Calder 1937 (see note 14).

17 Alexander S. C. Rower, "Calder in Nature," in *Calder*, exh. cat. Storm King Art Center (Mountainville, NY, 2003), pp. 13–17, here pp. 13–14.

18 Sigfried Giedion, Fernand Léger, and Josep Lluís Sert, "Nine Points on Monumentality (1943)," in *Architecture, You and Me: Diary of a Development*, ed. Sigfried Giedion (Cambridge, MA, 1958), p. 50, cited in Emily Reed, "Sculpture and Architecture: Building Calder's Global Network," in *Alexander Calder: Radical Inventor*, ed. Elizabeth Hutton Turner and Anne Grace, trans. Alexis Diamond, exh. cat. Montreal Museum of Fine Arts; National Gallery of Victoria, Melbourne (Montreal, 2018), pp. 169–78, here p. 176.

19 Calder 1977 (see note 13), p. 258.

20 See Calder's account of his large stabiles in Robert Osborn, "Calder's International Monuments," *Art in America* 51, no. 2 (March–April 1969), pp. 90–100.

21 Alexander Calder, "Memorandum on *Teodelapio*," August 6, 1962, published in *Calder*, ed. Giovanni Carandente, exh. cat. Palazzo Vela, Turin (Milan, 1983), p. 226: "I first caught sight of *Teodelapio* from the train and was delighted at his size and expanse. Dimensions can be deceiving—and I was surprised to learn that the object was taller than it was wide—as I had thought I remembered the contrary."

22 Calder 1932 (see note 7).

23 Jean-Paul Sartre, "Les Mobiles de Calder," in *Alexander Calder: Mobiles, Stabiles, Constellations*, exh. cat. Galerie Louis Carré (Paris, 1946), pp. 9–19. Published in English as "Calder's Mobiles," in *The Aftermath of War: Jean-Paul Sartre*, trans. Chris Turner (Calcutta, 2008), https://calder.org/bibliography/alexander-calder-mobiles-stabiles-constellations-1946/jean-paul-sartre-les-mobiles-de-calder/ (accessed February 8, 2021).

24 Calder 1951 (see note 11), p. 8. I would like to thank Susan Braeuer Dam for this insight: Susan Braeuer Dam, "The Mobile Object," in *Calder: Small Sphere and Heavy Sphere*, exh. cat. Pace Gallery (New York, 2019) pp. 22–37, here p. 34.

43 Calder mit *Teodelapio* (1962) und Modell (1956), Spoleto / Calder with *Teodelapio* (1962) and maquette (1956), Spoleto, Italy, 1962, Foto / photo Ugo Mulas

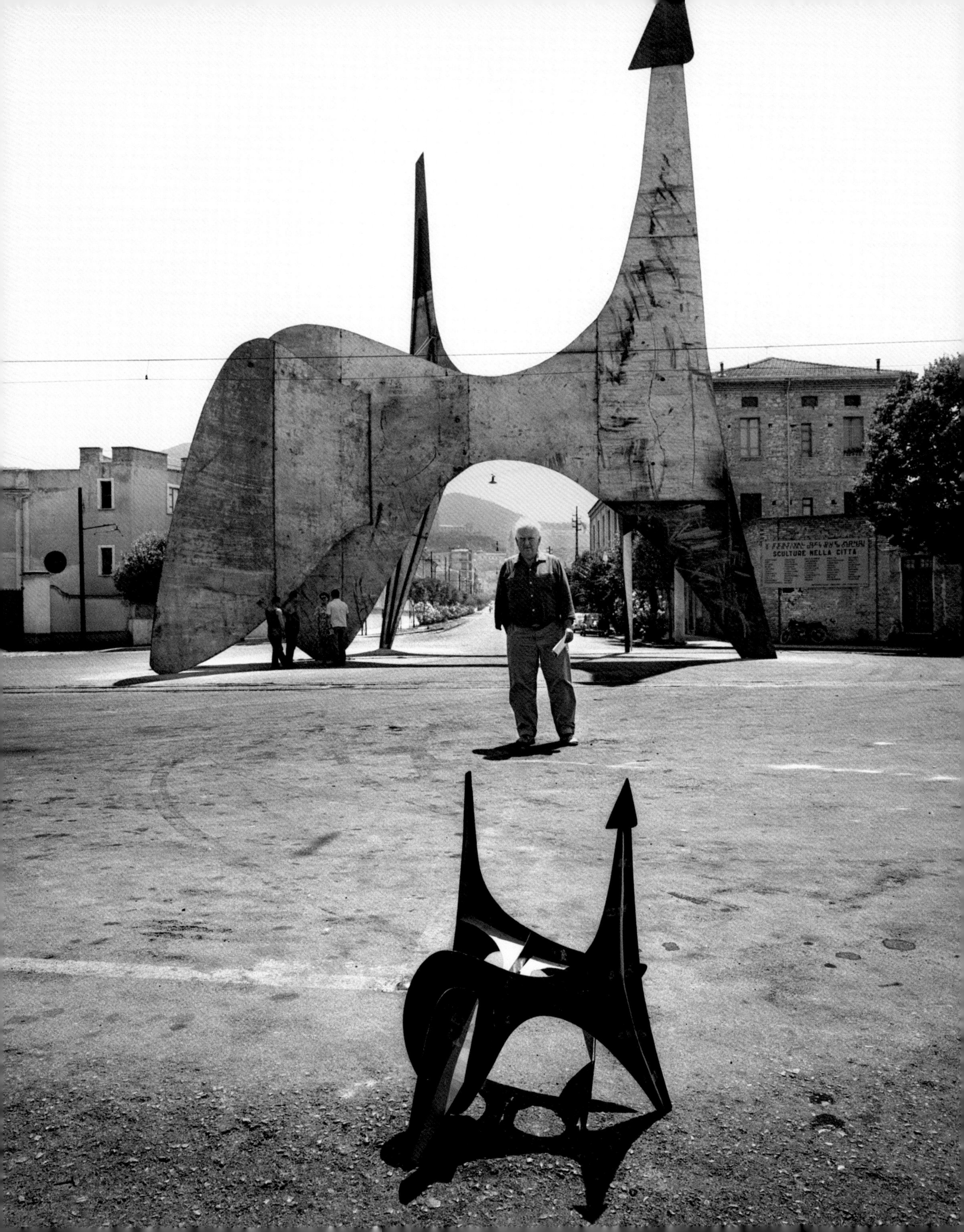
SCULTURE NELLA CITTA

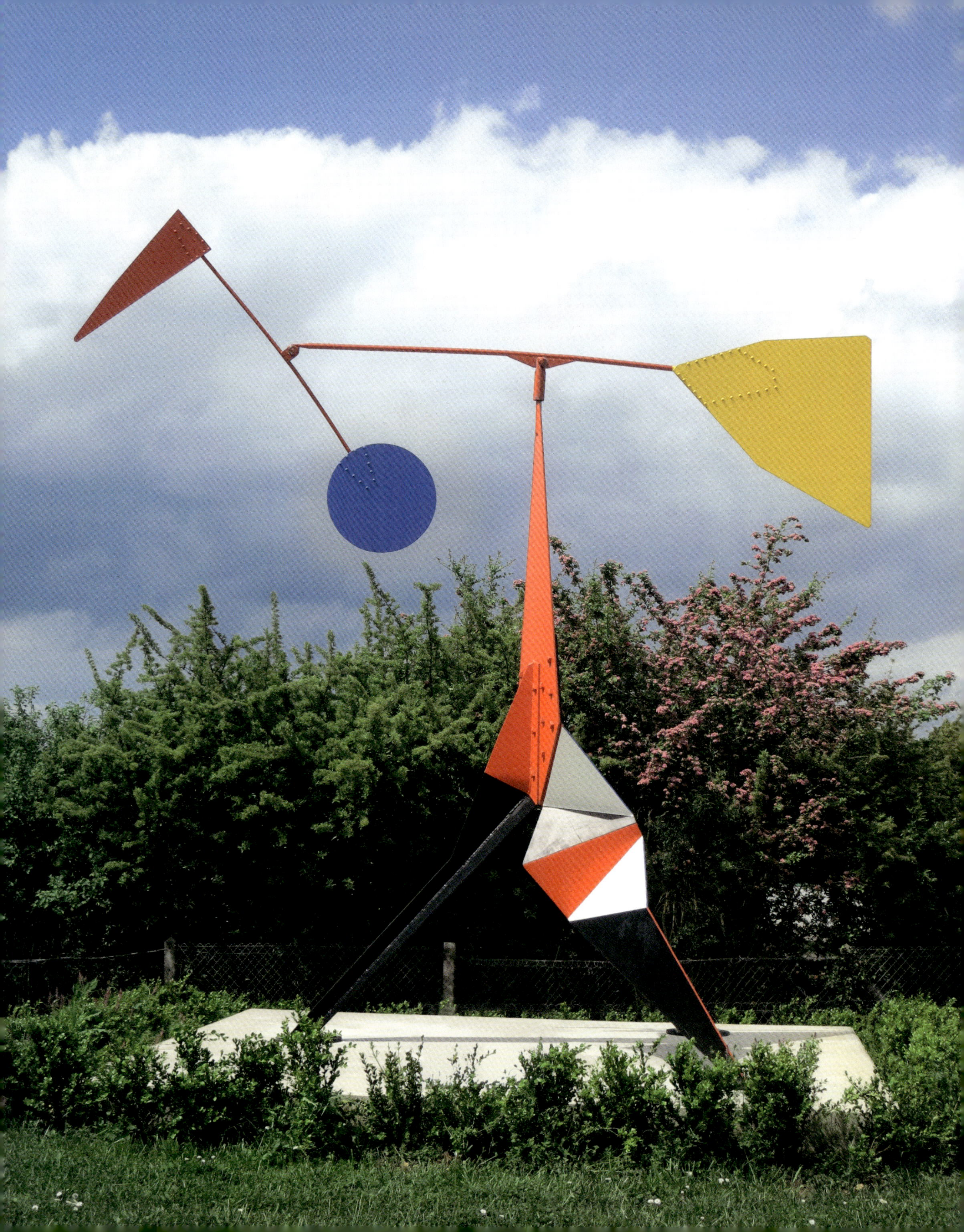

44 *Crinkly*, 1969, Stahl, Stab, Bolzen, Farbe, 350 × 200 cm / sheet metal, rod, bolts, paint, 137 ¾ × 78 ¾ in., Centre National des arts plastiques, France

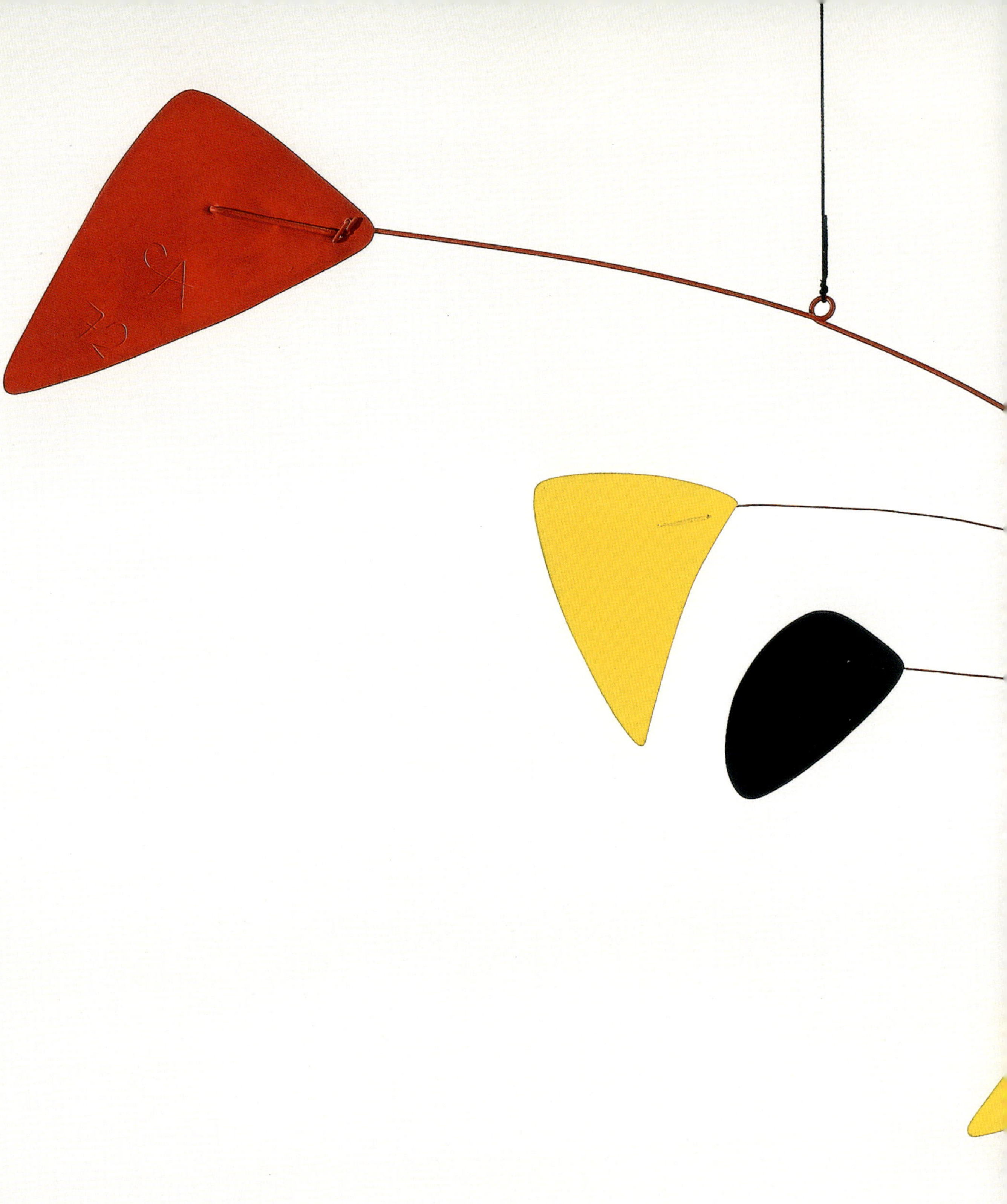

45 *Un de ceux-là*, 1972, Metall, Draht, Farbe, 180 × 100 cm / sheet metal, wire, paint, 70 ⅞ × 39 ⅜ in., Staatliche Museen zu Berlin, Nationalgalerie, Schenkung Sammlung Ulla und Heiner Pietzsch an das Land Berlin 2010

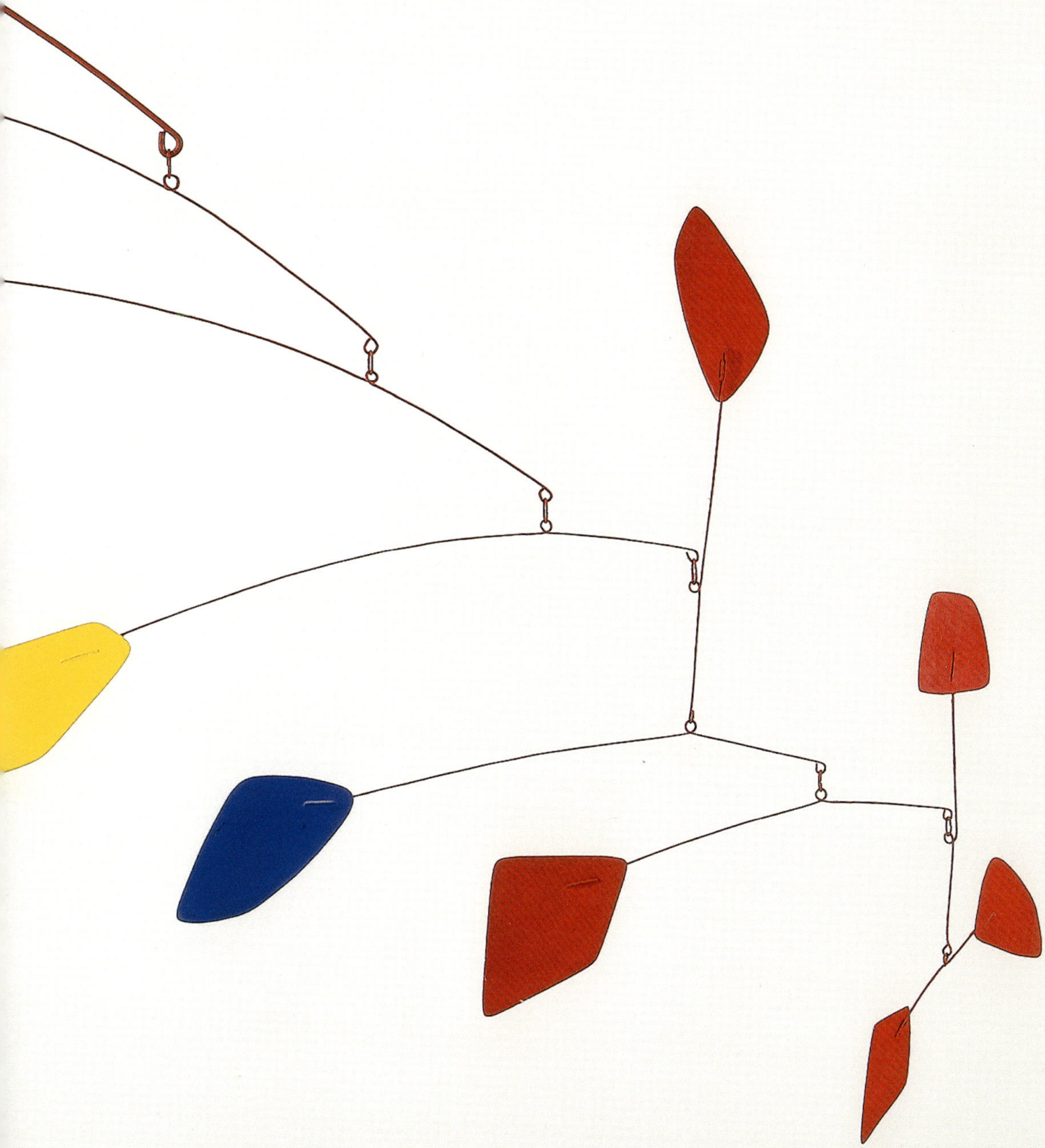

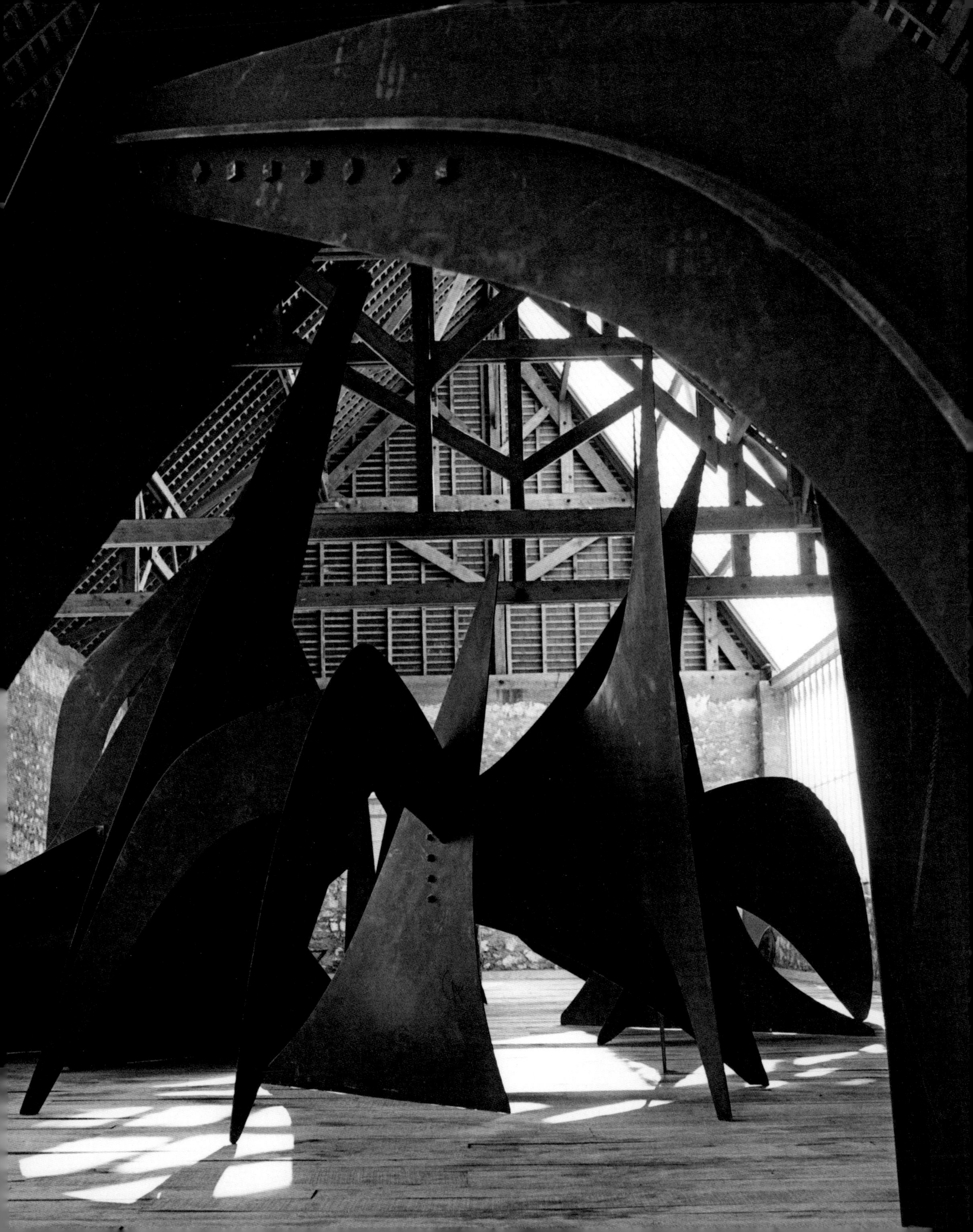

Calders Kathedralen

Beryl Gilothwest

Sieben Beine wölben sich zu steil ansteigenden Bögen, die Alexander Calders großes schwarzes Stabile *Têtes et queue* im Boden verankern. Über ihnen recken sich sieben gegenläufige Streben himmelwärts, außer einer davon mit unterschiedlich großen Scheiben bekrönt: fünf vertikal, eine schräg. Gerade weil sie keinem Schema folgt, ist die Skulptur die perfekte Wahl als Torwächterin vor Ludwig Mies van der Rohes streng geometrisch angelegter Neuer Nationalgalerie in Berlin, wo sie seit über fünfzig Jahren die Museumsbesucherinnen und -besucher empfängt (Abb. 50).[1] Der Architekt Josep Lluís Sert meinte, dass Calders Monumentalskulpturen von ihrem Standort „Besitz ergreifen", ähnlich wie gotische Kathedralen.[2] In diesem Sinne könnte man sagen, dass Calders Stabile für das Berliner Museum dieselbe Rolle spielt wie Notre-Dame für Paris.

Kaum ein Jahr nach der Aufstellung von *Têtes et queue* in Berlin schuf Calder das riesige Stabile *Morning Cobweb*, das die Besucher seiner Retrospektive in Serts Museumsbau für die Fondation Maeght hoch über der Côte d'Azur begrüßte (Abb. 47, 49).[3] Gegenüber dem strengen Raster der Neuen Nationalgalerie erscheinen die Linien von Serts Gebäude einladend biomorph. Und doch ist die Art, wie die spitzen Winkel von *Morning Cobweb* Serts trogförmiges Dach komplementär ergänzen, vergleichbar mit der dramatischen Spannung zwischen den sinnlichen Rundungen und kreisförmigen Abschlüssen von *Têtes et queue* und der nüchternen Geometrie von Mies' Fassade. Beide Skulpturen gehen eine Symbiose mit dem Museum ein, sie sind Totems, energetische Tore zu den von Mies und Sert geschaffenen architektonischen Räumen und der darin gezeigten Kunst.

Von klein auf begeisterte sich Calder für Architektur. In seiner 1966 erschienenen Autobiografie finden sich viele lebendige Äußerungen zu Gebäuden. Im Abschnitt über eine Reise, die ihn 16 Jahre zuvor bis nach Finnland geführt hatte, erwähnt Calder, er habe unterwegs angehalten, „um mir eine schöne alte Kirche aus ganz schlichten Materialien und mit großen Holzskulpturen vor dem Portal anzusehen".[4] Solche bemalten *vaivaisukko*-Figuren, die verarmte Menschen darstellen, stehen vor vielen finnischen Kirchen. In Brusthöhe befindet sich ein Schlitz für Almosen (Abb. 48). Calder hatte zwar keinen Bezug zur institutionalisierten Religion, fühlte sich jedoch zu den groben, eigentümlichen Figuren hingezogen. Sie begrüßten nicht nur die Gläubigen auf ihrem Weg in die Kirche, sondern verkörperten auch die spirituelle Dimension der Gotteshäuser, ähnlich wie *Têtes et queue* diejenige der Neuen Nationalgalerie.

Calders Interesse für architektonische Formen spiegelt sich auch in seinen eigenen Werken wider. 1939 schuf er aus Metallresten eine Skulpturengruppe, die er „Gothic Constructions from Scraps" nannte. Ihre schlanken, hoch aufragenden Bögen erinnern an Strebewerke, die den Gewölbeschub gotischer Kathedralen ableiten (Abb. 51, 52). Ohne unmittelbar auf diese Bauelemente zu verweisen, empfand Calder die Energie der durch sie ermöglichten monumentalen Räume nach. „Architektur nutzt natürliche Formen, Bögen, Pfeiler, Zylinder,

46 *Nervures Minces* (1963) und weitere Stabiles in Calders von ihm selbst entworfenen Atelier Le Carroi in Saché / *Nervures Minces* (1963) and other stabiles in Calder's Le Carroi studio, which he designed himself, Saché, 1963, Foto / photo Ugo Mulas

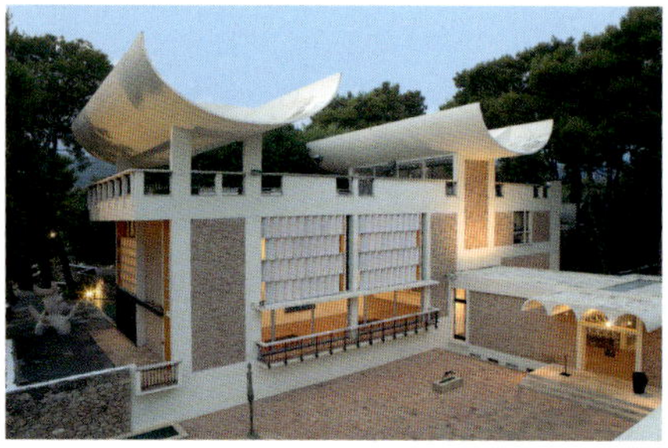

47 Rückwärtige Ansicht der Fondation Maeght, 1964 erbaut von Josep Lluís Sert / View of the rear façade of the Fondation Maeght, built by Josep Lluís Sert in 1964

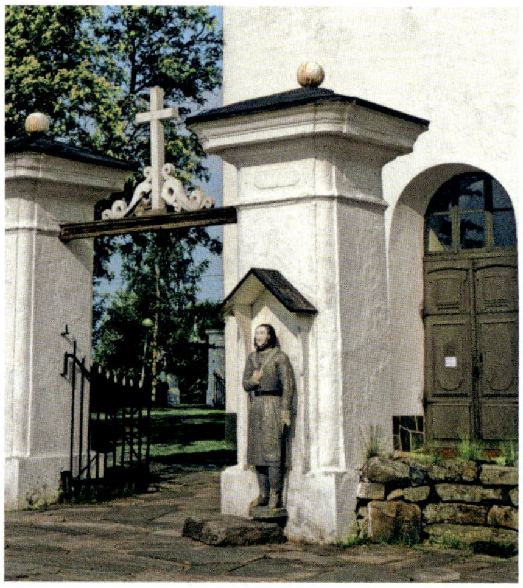

48 *Vaivaisukko* vor dem Eingang zur Kirche der Gemeinde Kaarlela, Kokkola, Finnland / *Vaivaisukko* by the entrance to the church of the Kaarlela parish, Kokkola, Finland

Rechtecke, Kugelsegmente nicht einfach nur", schrieb John Dewey in *Art as Experience*, „sondern sie verleiht deren charakteristischer Wirkung auf den Betrachter Ausdruck."[5] Calder wollte eine sinnliche Erfahrung schaffen, wie sie uns beim Besuch gotischer Kathedralen erwartet, wenn wir uns zwischen den gewaltigen Stützen und Bögen bewegen.

Fast 20 Jahre später beaufsichtigte Calder in Spoleto den Aufbau seiner Bühnenbilder für eine Inszenierung des Balletts *The Glory Folk* von John Butler, in dem es um die evangelikalen Kirchen in den USA geht.[6] Das Kernelement seiner Bühne bildete ein großes Stabile, das seinen „Gothic Constructions" verblüffend ähnlich sah. Darüber kreiste ein reflektierendes Mobile (Abb. 53). In diesem Fall ist die Skulptur die Architektur.[7] Während die in ehrerbietiges Weiß gehüllten Tänzerinnen und Tänzer sehnsüchtig die Arme nach dem ätherischen Mobile ausstreckten, werden sie durch die hohen roten Bögen des Stabiles geerdet. In und unter diesem Heiligtum, in seinem Kraftfeld konnte das Ballettensemble Butlers Choreografie lebendig werden lassen.[8]

Rosalind Krauss stellt fest: „Indem es Aspekte des Körpers beschreibt [...], indem man den Drang verspürt, es in Bewegung zu versetzen, damit es seine Rolle ‚spielt', nämlich die eigene Räumlichkeit auszufüllen und zu bewohnen, setzt das Mobile seine Bedeutung als Skulptur gewissermaßen gleich mit der eines Schauspielers."[9] So gesehen, können Calders Werke den architektonischen Raum auch aus eigener Kraft transformieren. Als das Skulpturverständnis gegen Ende der 1920er-Jahre durch Calders Drahtskulpturen, ein paar Jahre später dann durch die Mobiles und Stabiles neu definiert wurde, gab es kein Vorbild dafür, wie man solche Objekte in einem musealen Umfeld installierte. Um seine Arbeiten dieser Art von Räumlichkeiten einzufügen, musste der Künstler zunächst neue Vorgaben erfinden.[10] Im weitläufigen Ausstellungsraum des Massachusetts Institute of Technology wurden seine Werke 1950 überwiegend von der Decke hängend oder auf dem Boden stehend präsentiert (Abb. 54). Da es nur wenige Sockel und keinerlei Stahlstützen gab, befanden sich die Besucher auf Augenhöhe mit den Werken. Die Fülle an Objekten hatte einen immersiven Effekt und verwandelte die Galerie in einen lebendigen, atmenden Organismus – eine Kathedrale für seine Kunst.

„Ein wirklich funktionales Gebäude", überlegte Sert in einem Harvard-Bulletin, „muss über die materiellen Anforderungen hinaus auch die spirituellen Bedürfnisse der Menschen erfüllen."[11] Seine Fondation Maeght ebenso wie Mies' Neue Nationalgalerie sind Meisterwerke, die sich nahtlos in völlig verschiedene Kontexte einfügen und dabei Umgebungen schaffen, die die moderne Kunst hervorheben, ohne von ihr abzulenken. Aber *Morning Cobweb* und *Têtes et queue* funktionieren materiell und spirituell als Portale zu den jeweiligen Gebäuden. Der Schriftsteller James Jones fürchtete, wenn er eines von Calders Stabiles durchquere, werde er sich in Luft auflösen, doch das Gegenteil geschah: Erleuchtet trat er darunter hervor.[12]

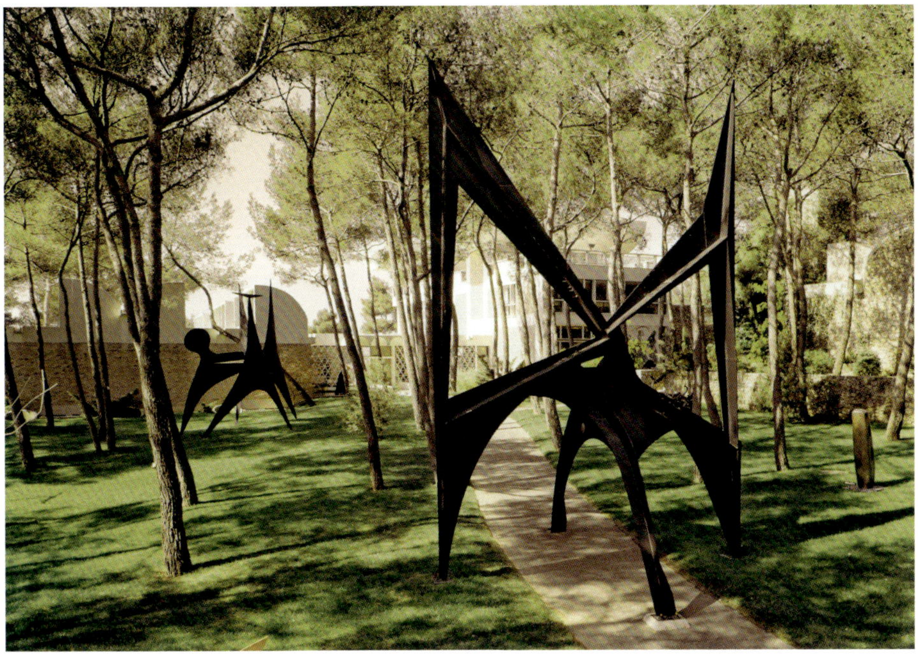

49 *Morning Cobweb* (1969) überspannt den Weg zum Eingang der Fondation Maeght während der Ausstellung *Calder* 1969, Saint-Paul-de-Vence / *Morning Cobweb* (1969) installed over the pathway leading to the entrance of the Fondation Maeght during the exhibition *Calder*, 1969, Saint-Paul-de-Vence, France

1 Seit Juni 1968 steht *Têtes et queue* auf der Terrasse vor der Neuen Nationalgalerie. Calder schuf viele seiner Werke speziell für bestimmte modernistische Architekturprojekte, darunter etwa *Flamingo* (1973) für Mies van der Rohes Kluczynski Federal Building in Chicago, doch war *Têtes et queue* nicht explizit für das Berliner Museum geplant. Für weiterführende Angaben zur Geschichte der Skulptur vgl. den Beitrag von Maike Steinkamp in diesem Katalog.

2 Josep Lluís Sert: „Alexander Calder: 1898–1976", in: *Proceedings of the American Academy of Arts and Letters*, 2. Folge, Nr. 28, 1978, S. 61–64, hier S. 63. Calders *Mercury Fountain* – eines der ersten und wichtigsten Werke für ein Architekturvorhaben – beauftragten Sert und Luis Lacasa für den spanischen Pavillon bei der Weltausstellung 1937 in Paris (Abb. 102). Calder und Sert blieben lebenslang befreundet.

3 Die Ausstellung *Calder* fand vom 2.4. bis 31.5.1969 im Gebäude der Fondation Maeght in Saint-Paul-de-Vence statt. Die Vorlage für die Skulptur bildete das verkleinerte Modell, das Calder 1945 geschaffen hatte, also über zwanzig Jahre zuvor. *Morning Cobweb* (1969) befindet sich heute nicht mehr am damals dafür vorgesehenen Standort.

4 Alexander Calder: *Calder: An Autobiography with Pictures*, hg. von Jean Davidson, New York 1966, S. 207. Die Calders waren auf dem Weg zu einem Besuch bei Maire Gullichsen, der Mitgründerin der Möbelfabrik Artek, in deren privater Villa Mairea in Noormarkku, einem von Alvar Aaltos bedeutendsten Gebäuden. Aalto zählte ebenso zu Calders Freundeskreis wie weitere der bedeutendsten zeitgenössischen Architekten wie Marcel Breuer, Eero Saarinen und Carlos Raúl Villanueva.

5 John Dewey: *Art as Experience*, New York 1934, S. 221. Der Kurator James Johnson Sweeney zitierte Dewey 1943 mehrfach in seinem einflussreichen Essay im Katalog zur Ausstellung *Alexander Calder* im Museum of Modern Art, New York.

6 Calder wirkte an vielen Theaterproduktionen mit, schon Mitte der 1930er-Jahre an zwei Kooperationen mit Martha Graham. *Work in Progress* von 1968 war seine einzige vollständig selbst konzipierte Inszenierung. Siehe Arnauld Pierre: „Staging Movement" in: *Alexander Calder: 1898–1976*, hg. von Maria Prather, Arnauld Pierre und Alexander S. C. Rower, Ausst.-Kat. National Gallery of Art, Washington, D.C., 1998, S. 329–347.

7 Calder entwarf schließlich auf einem Hügel im französischen Ort Saché zwei Gebäude für sich selbst: 1963 ein Atelier und 1969 direkt daneben ein Wohnhaus. Interessanterweise hatte Sert angeboten, das Wohnhaus für die Calders zu planen. Siehe Robert Melvin Rubin: „An Architecture of Making: Saché and Roxbury", in: „Calder in France", hg. von Alexander S. C. Rower, Sonderheft *Cahiers d'Art*, Nr. 1, 2015, S. 30–39.

8 Weitere Angaben zu diesem Vorhaben und anderen Projekten mit spirituellen Bezügen bei Jed Perl: *Calder. The Conquest of Time. The Later Years, 1940–1976*, New York 2020, S. 544–546.

9 Rosalind E. Krauss: *Passages in Modern Sculpture*, Cambridge, MA/London 1981, S. 216–218.

10 Die Ausstellung *Calder* lief in der New Gallery der Charles Hayden Memorial Library im Massachusetts Institute of Technology in Cambridge vom 5.12.1950 bis 14.1.1951. Eine Auswahl von Calders Installationen ist abgebildet in: *Calder and Abstraction: From Avant-Garde to Iconic*, Ausst.-Kat. Los Angeles County Museum of Art, Los Angeles/New York 2013, S. 168–197.

11 Josep Lluís Sert: „Architecture and the Visual Arts", in: *The Writings of Josep Lluís Sert*, hg. von Eric Mumford, New Haven/London 2015, S. 42–46, hier S. 45.

12 James Jones: „Letter Home", in: *Esquire*, 61, Nr. 3, März 1964, S. 28–34, hier S. 34.

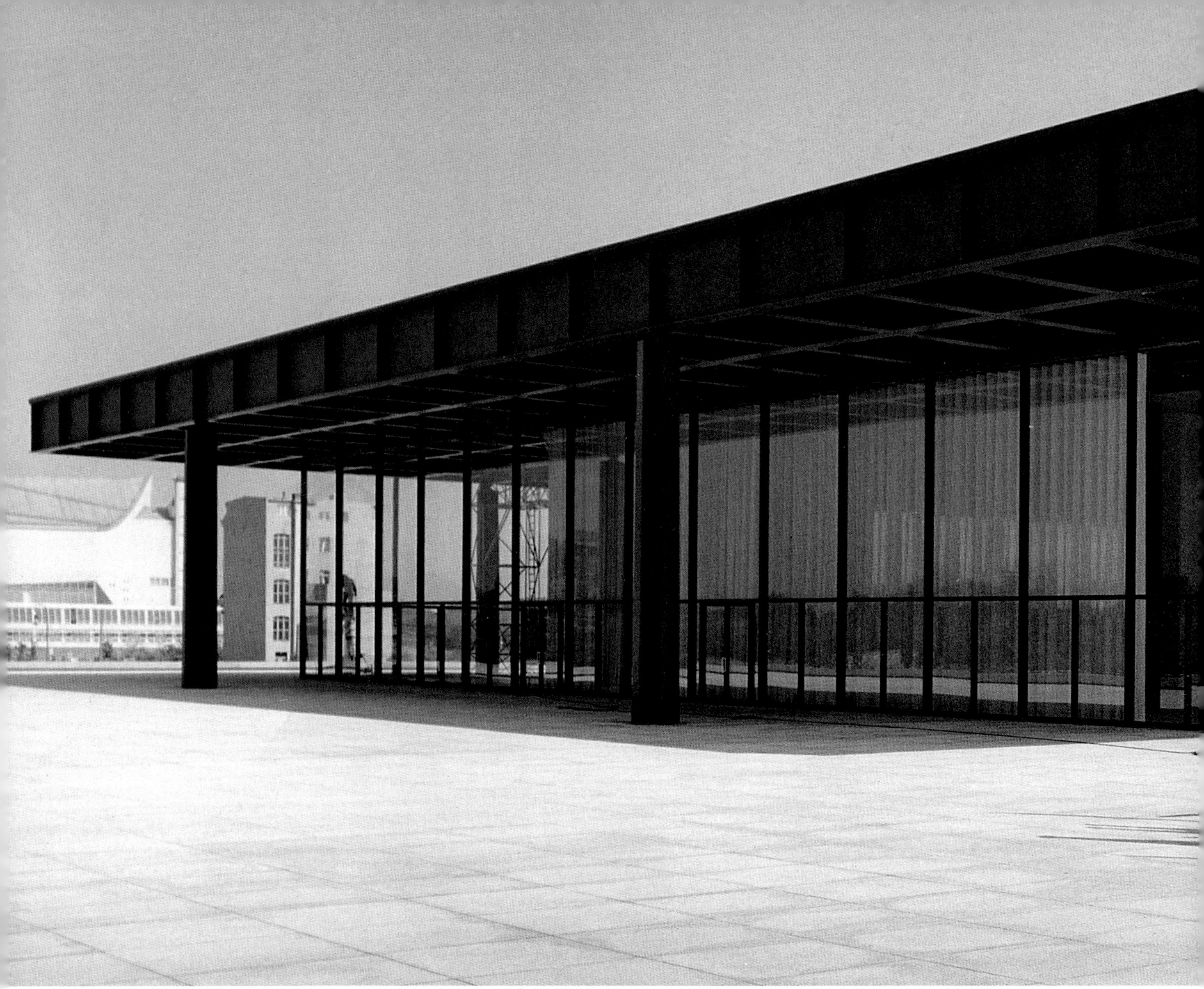

Calder's Cathedrals

Beryl Gilothwest

Seven legs curve into the steeply sloping arches that anchor Alexander Calder's large black stabile *Têtes et queue*. Above them, seven arms extend skyward from inverted arches, all but one capped with variously sized discs; five vertical, one slanted. That the sculpture isn't algorithmic is what makes it such a fitting concierge for Ludwig Mies van der Rohe's gridded Neue Nationalgalerie in Berlin, where it has welcomed visitors for more than fifty years (fig. 50).[1] The architect Josep Lluís Sert has written that Calder's monumental sculptures "take possession" of their sites, and he likens them to Gothic cathedrals.[2] Notre Dame is to Paris what Calder's stabile is to the museum, we could say.

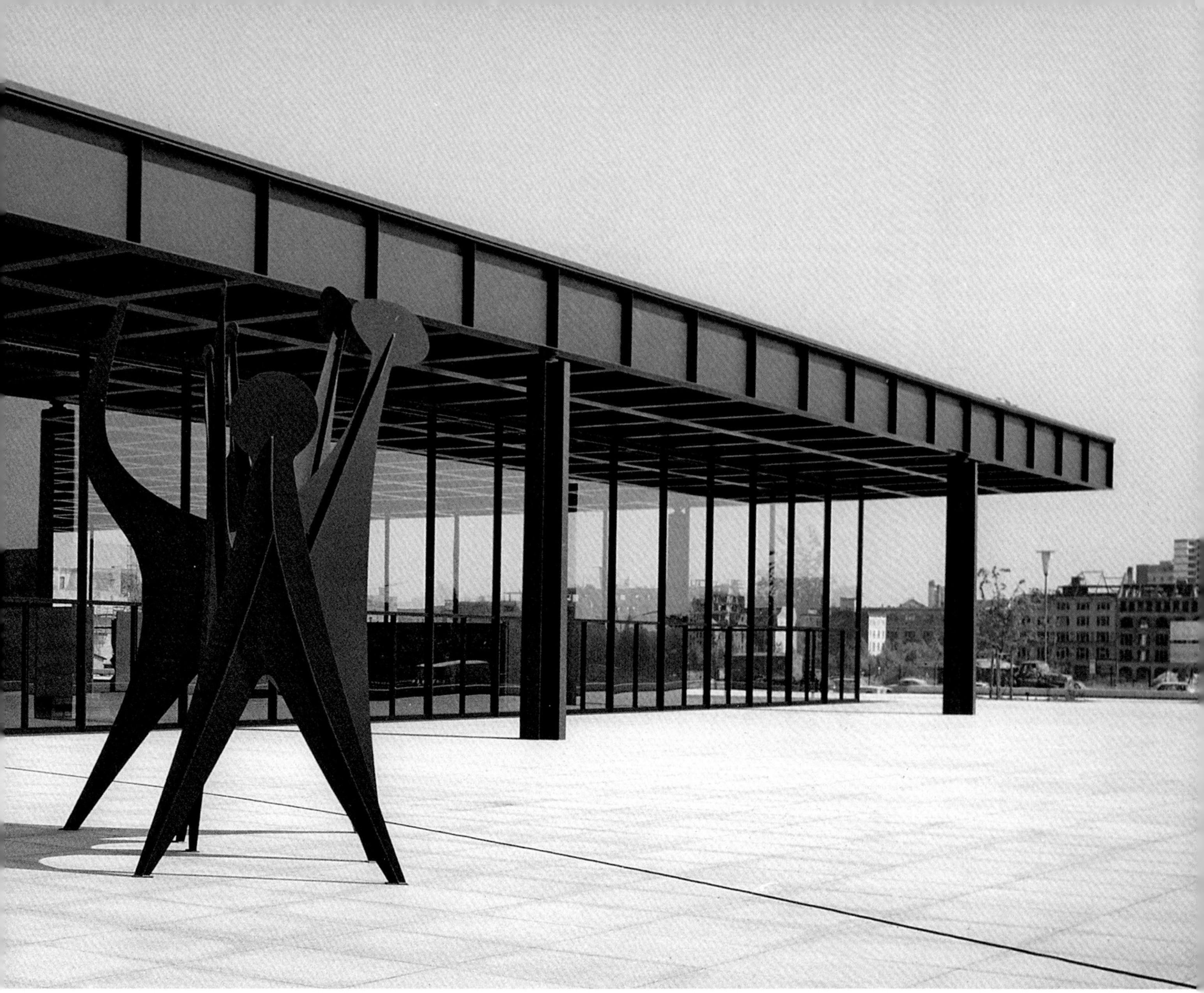

50 Ansicht von *Têtes et queue* (1965) vor der Neuen Nationalgalerie, erbaut von Ludwig Mies van der Rohe 1968 / View of *Têtes et queue* (1965) in front of the Neue Nationalgalerie, built by Ludwig Mies van der Rohe in 1968

Less than a year after *Têtes et queue* was first installed in Berlin, Calder made the enormous *Morning Cobweb* specifically to greet visitors to his retrospective at the Sert-designed Fondation Maeght in the hills above the Côte d'Azur (figs. 47, 49).[3] While that building is as warmly biomorphic as the Neue Nationalgalerie is austerely minimal, the sharp points of *Morning Cobweb* complemented Sert's half-piped roof in the same way that *Têtes et queue*'s sensual curves and bulbed peaks build a dramatic tension with the strict geometries of Mies's façade. Existing in symbiosis with their respective museums, these sculptures are totems, the energetic gateways to Mies's and Sert's architectural spaces and the array of art within.

Calder had a great appreciation for architecture from an early age, and spontaneous observations about buildings abound in the autobiography he published in 1966. In his description of a trip to Finland sixteen years earlier, Calder casually mentions stopping "to see a fine old church, of very modest materials, with large wooden sculptures."[4] A common feature of Finnish churches, painted *vaivaisukko* depict the impoverished and have slots in their chests through which to give alms (fig. 48). With no interest in organized religion, Calder was drawn

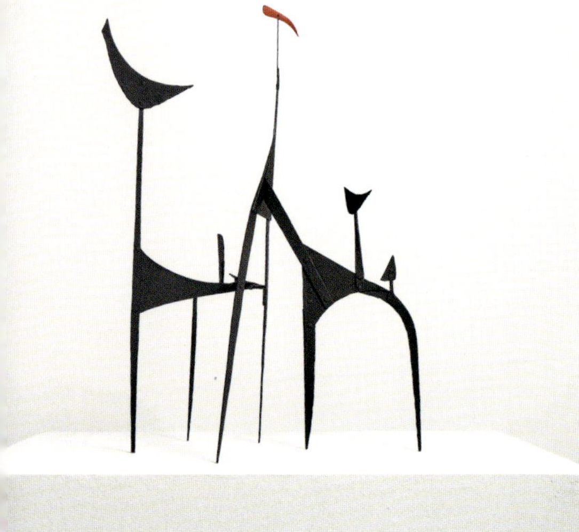

51 *Gothic Construction from Scraps*, 1939, Blech, Draht, Farbe, 86,4 × 61 cm / sheet metal, wire, paint, 34 × 24 in., Calder Foundation, New York

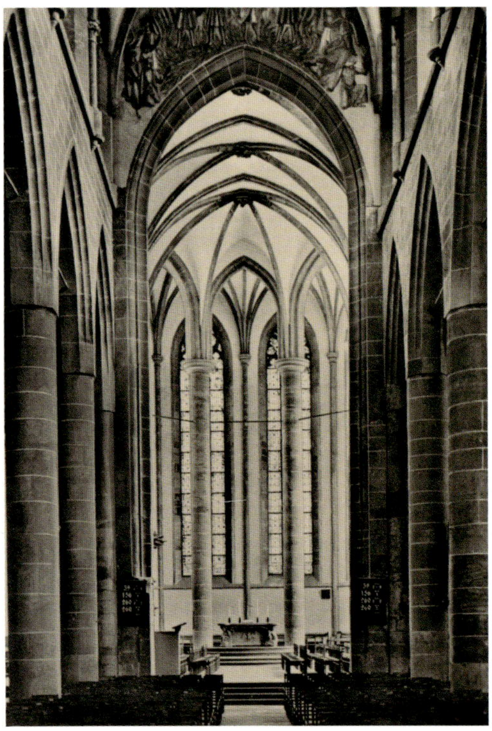

52 Postkarte mit einer Innenansicht der Heiliggeistkirche (1398–1515), Heidelberg, um 1952 erworben von Calder / Interior view of the Church of the Holy Spirit (1398–1515), Heidelberg, postcard acquired by Calder ca. 1952

to these awkward statues for their specificity. They not only welcomed visitors but also functioned as a manifestation of their churches' spiritual intent, much like *Têtes et queue* does for the Neue Nationalgalerie.

An interest in architectural forms also came out in Calder's own work. In 1939, he produced an unusual group of sculptures built from discarded sheet metal found in his studio that he called "Gothic Constructions from Scraps." The thin, soaring arches of these works call to mind the ribs and flying buttresses that support the vaulted ceilings of Gothic cathedrals (figs. 51, 52). Calder wasn't directly referencing those forms, but rather engaging with the energy of the monumental spaces they carved out. "Architecture does more than merely utilize natural forms, arches, pillars, cylinders, rectangles, portions of spheres," John Dewey writes in *Art as Experience*. "It expresses their characteristic effect on the observer."[5] Likewise, Calder's end goal was to achieve the unique sensorial experience derived from walking among the colossal arches of those cathedrals.

Nearly twenty years later, Calder went to Spoleto, Italy, to oversee the construction of sets he had designed for a production of John Butler's ballet *The Glory Folk*, which dealt with evangelical Christianity in the United States.[6] A large stabile, strikingly similar to his "Gothic Constructions," anchored Calder's stage, with a reflective mobile circulating above it (fig. 53). Here, the sculpture *is* the architecture.[7] As the dancers, clad in reverent white, reached up toward the ethereal mobile, the towering red arches of the stabile kept them grounded. It was the sanctuary in, under, and around which the dancers could breathe life into Butler's choreography.[8]

Rosalind Krauss writes: "In that it is a description of aspects of the body . . . in that one feels impelled to set it in motion in order for it to 'perform' the role of filling out and inhabiting its own spatiality, the mobile locates its sculptural meaning as a kind of actor."[9] In this way, Calder's works could also transform architectural space of their own volition. When his wire sculptures in the late 1920s—and the mobiles and stabiles a few years later—redefined the contemporary understanding of sculpture, there was no precedent for how such objects should be installed in a museum setting. Calder had to reimagine installation norms in order to accommodate his work.[10] In the expansive gallery space of an exhibition at MIT in 1950, Calder's sculptures were primarily suspended from the ceiling or placed directly on the ground (fig. 54). With few pedestals and no stanchions, visitors existed on the same plane as Calder's art. The plethora of sculptures was immersive, transforming the gallery into a living, breathing organism—a cathedral for his art.

"If a building is really functional," Sert reflects in a Harvard newsletter, "it should fulfill not only the material requirements but also the spiritual needs of man."[11] Both his Fondation Maeght and Mies's Neue Nationalgalerie are tour de forces, integrating seamlessly into vastly different contexts while providing settings that amplify modern art without distracting from it. But *Morning Cobweb* and *Têtes et queue* are the portals to these buildings, both materially and spiritually. The novelist James Jones worried that if he walked underneath one of Calder's stabiles, he might disappear.[12] Rather, he would emerge enlightened.

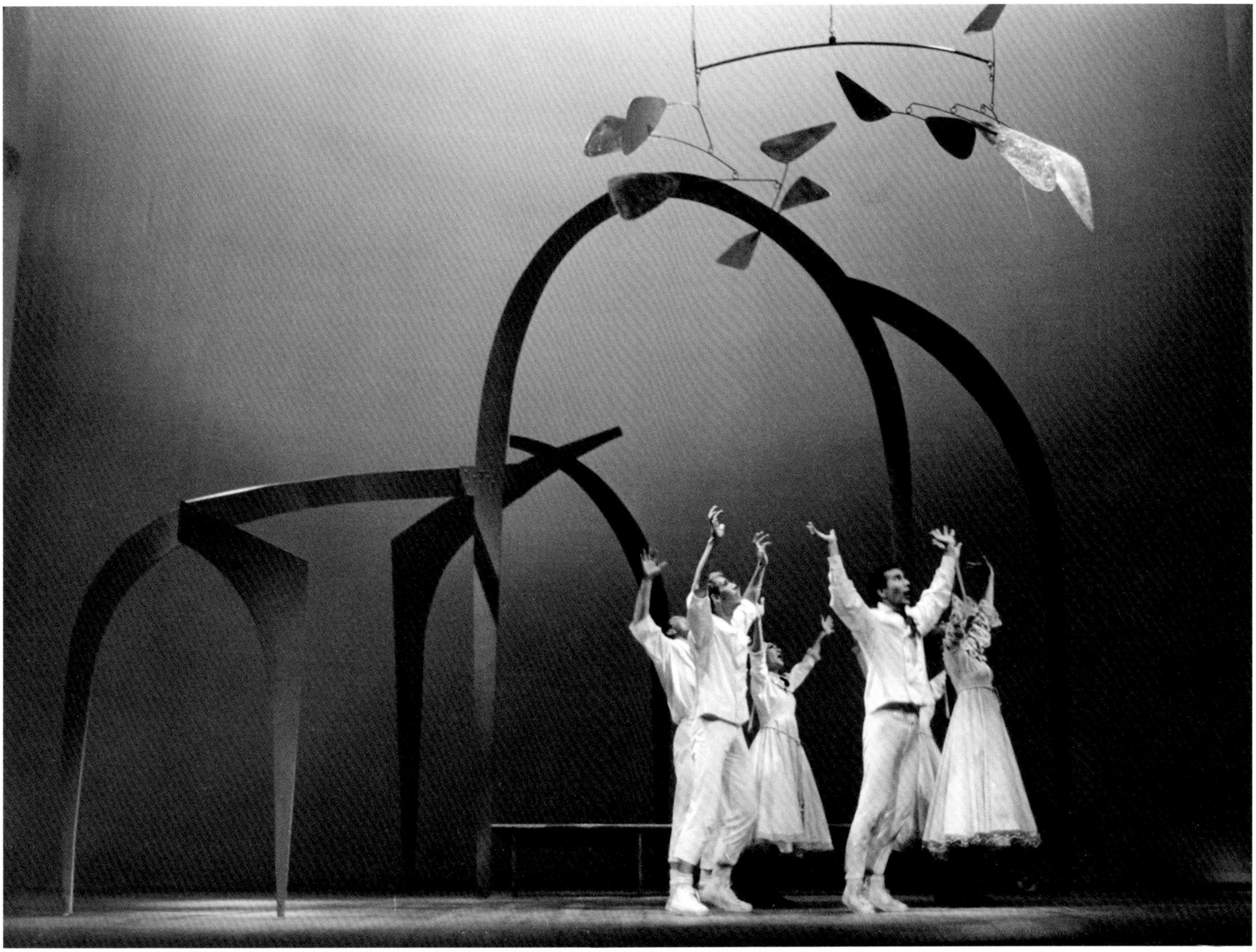

53 Aufführung von *The Glory Folk*, Bühnenbild von Calder, Spoleto / Performance of *The Glory Folk*, stage design by Calder, Spoleto, Italy, 1958

1 *Têtes et queue* (1965) was installed on the terrace in front of the Neue Nationalgalerie in June 1968. While Calder made many site-specific works for modernist architectural projects—including *Flamingo* (1973) for Mies's Kluczynski Federal Building in Chicago—*Têtes et queue* wasn't conceived for the German museum specifically. For more information on the history of the sculpture, see Maike Steinkamp's essay "*Têtes et queue*," in this volume.

2 Josep Lluís Sert, "Alexander Calder: 1898–1976," *Proceedings of the American Academy of Arts and Letters*, 2nd series, no. 28 (1978), pp. 61–64, here p. 63. Calder's *Mercury Fountain*—one of his first and most important works for an architectural project—was commissioned by Sert and Luis Lacasa for their Spanish Pavilion at the 1937 International Exposition in Paris (fig. 102). Calder and Sert went on to become lifelong friends.

3 *Calder* ran from April 2–May 31, 1969, at the Fondation Maeght in Saint-Paul-de-Vence, France. Enlarged from a maquette that Calder made more than two decades earlier, in 1945, *Morning Cobweb* (1969) is no longer installed on the spot for which it was intended.

4 Alexander Calder, *Calder: An Autobiography with Pictures*, ed. Jean Davidson (New York, 1966), p. 207. The Calders were on their way to Noormarkku to stay with the Artek furniture company co-founder Maire Gullichsen at her home, Villa Mairea, one of Alvar Aalto's most important buildings. Calder was friends with Aalto as well as with many of the leading architects of his day, including Marcel Breuer, Eero Saarinen, and Carlos Raúl Villanueva.

5 John Dewey, *Art as Experience* (New York, 1934), p. 221. Curator James Johnson Sweeney liberally quoted Dewey in his important text for *Alexander Calder*, exh. cat. The Museum of Modern Art (New York, 1943).

6 Calder worked on many theatrical productions, beginning with a pair of collaborations with Martha Graham in the mid 1930s and culminating in 1968 with *Work in Progress*, the only performance imagined entirely by the artist. See Arnauld Pierre's "Staging Movement," in *Alexander Calder: 1898–1976*, exh. cat. National Gallery of Art (Washington, DC, 1998), pp. 329–47.

7 Calder ultimately designed two buildings of his own in Saché, France: a hilltop studio in 1963 and an adjacent home in 1969. Interestingly, Sert had offered to design the latter for the Calders. See Robert Melvin Rubin, "An Architecture of Making: Saché and Roxbury," in "Calder in France," ed. Alexander S. C. Rower, special issue, *Cahiers d'Art*, no. 1 (2015), pp. 30–39.

8 For a discussion of this project and others that relate to spirituality, see Jed Perl, *Calder: The Conquest of Space: The Later Years: 1940–1976* (New York, 2020), pp. 544–46.

9 Rosalind E. Krauss, *Passages in Modern Sculpture* (Cambridge, MA, and London, 1981), pp. 216–18.

10 Installed in the New Gallery at the Charles Hayden Memorial Library at the Massachusetts Institute of Technology in Cambridge, *Calder* ran from December 5, 1950–January 14, 1951. For a selection of Calder exhibition installations, see *Calder and Abstraction: From Avant-Garde to Iconic*, exh. cat. Los Angeles County Museum of Art (Los Angeles and New York, 2013), pp. 168–97.

11 Josep Lluís Sert, "Architecture and the Visual Arts," in *The Writings of Josep Lluís Sert*, ed. Eric Mumford (New Haven, CT, and London, 2015), pp. 42–46, here p. 45.

12 James Jones, "Letter Home," *Esquire* 61, no. 3 (March 1964), pp. 28–34, here p. 34.

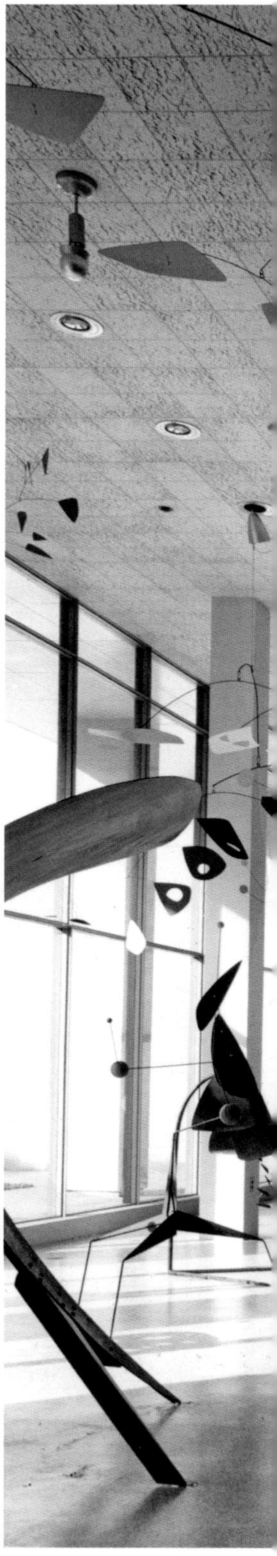

54 Ausstellungsansicht / Installation view, *Calder*, New Gallery, Charles Hayden Memorial Library, Massachusetts Institute of Technology, Cambridge, 1950

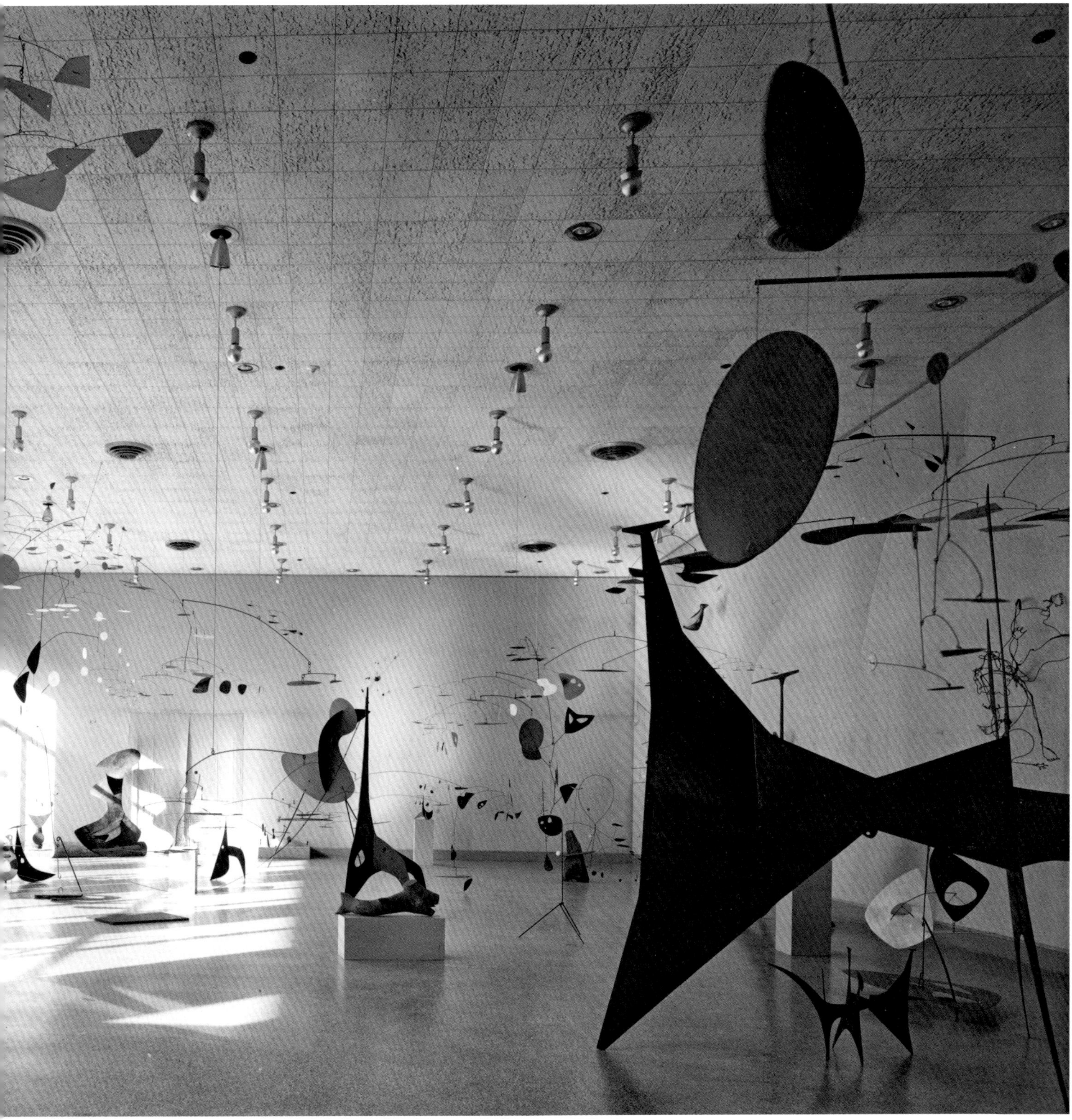

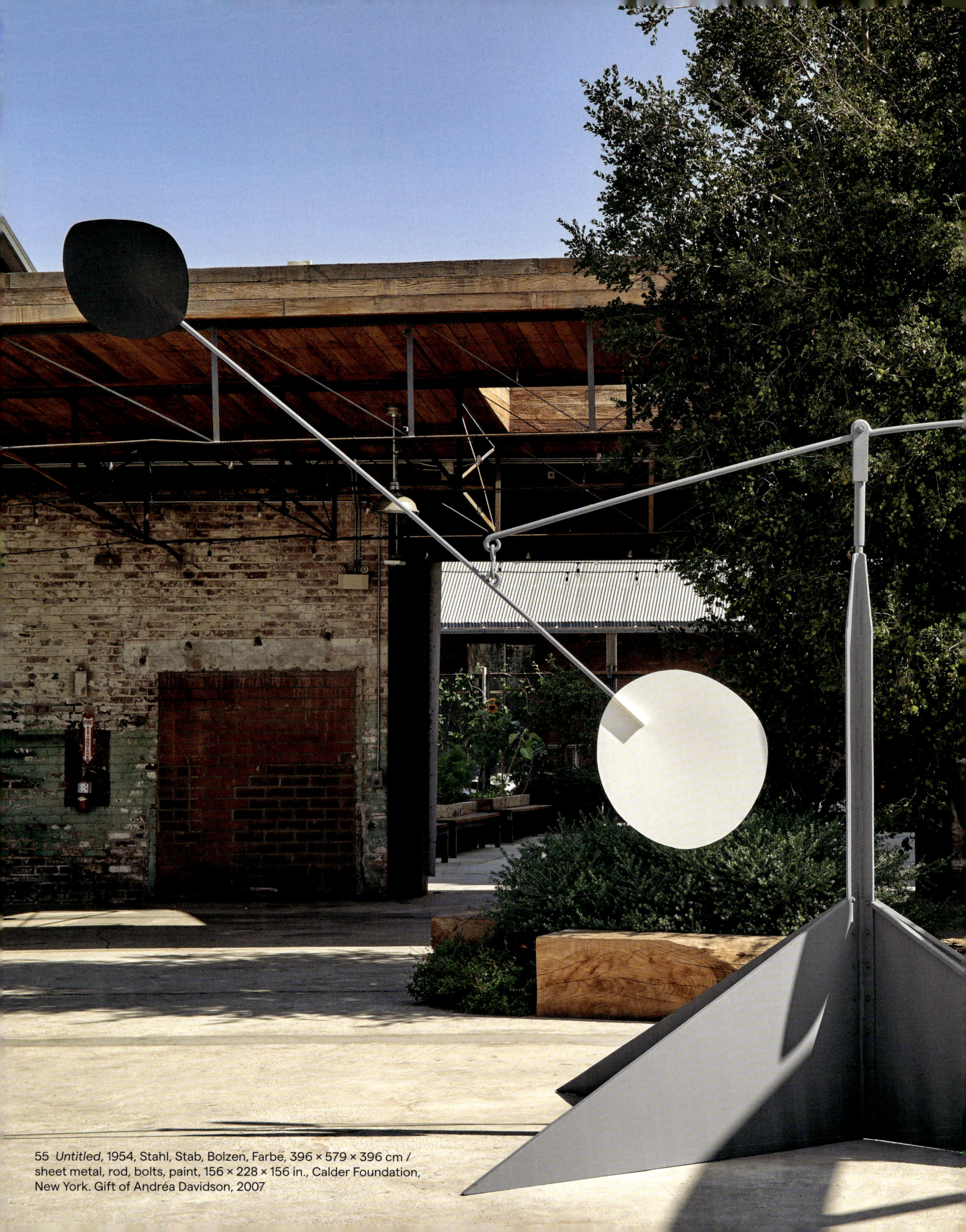

55 *Untitled*, 1954, Stahl, Stab, Bolzen, Farbe, 396 × 579 × 396 cm / sheet metal, rod, bolts, paint, 156 × 228 × 156 in., Calder Foundation, New York. Gift of Andréa Davidson, 2007

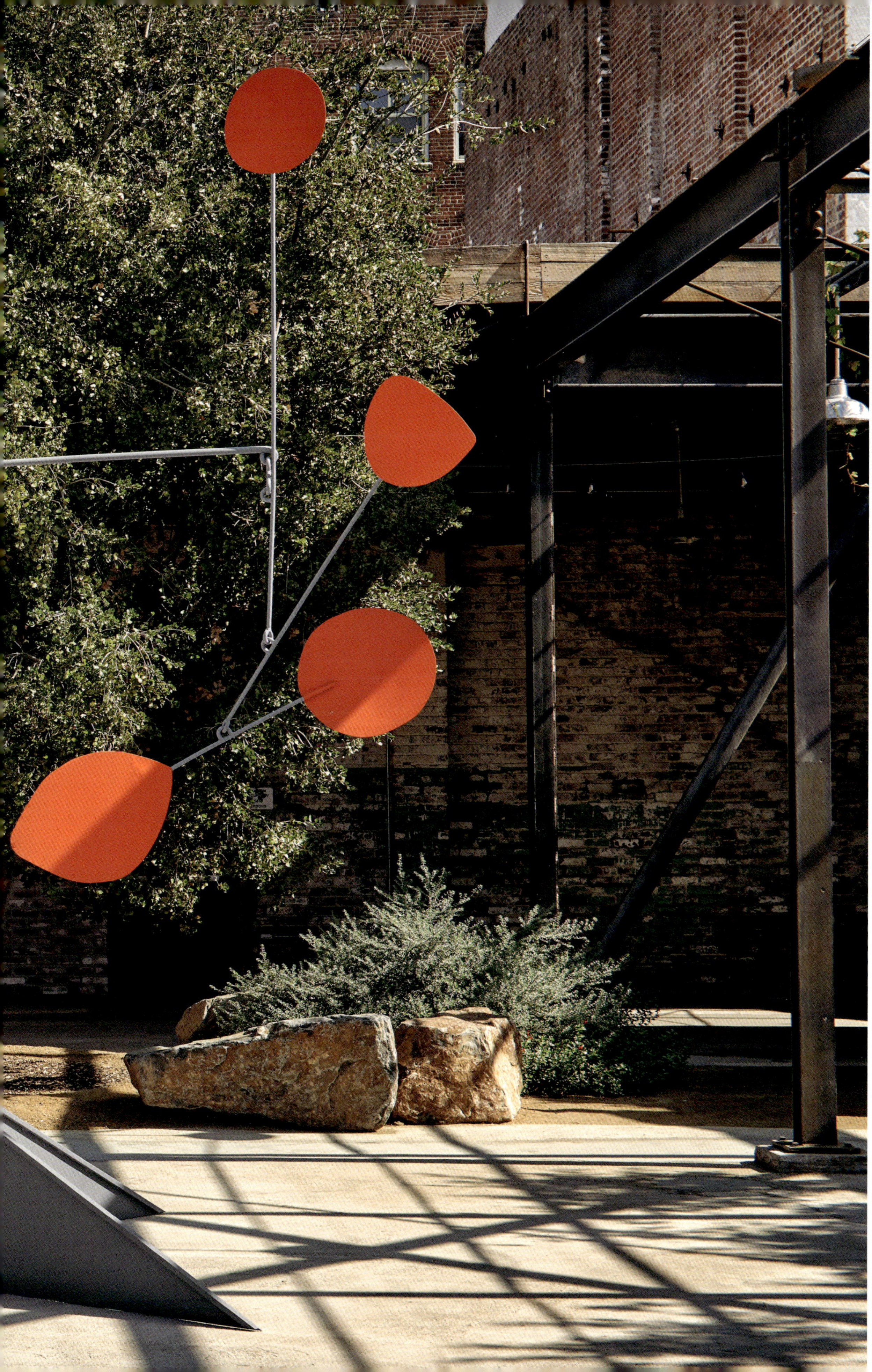

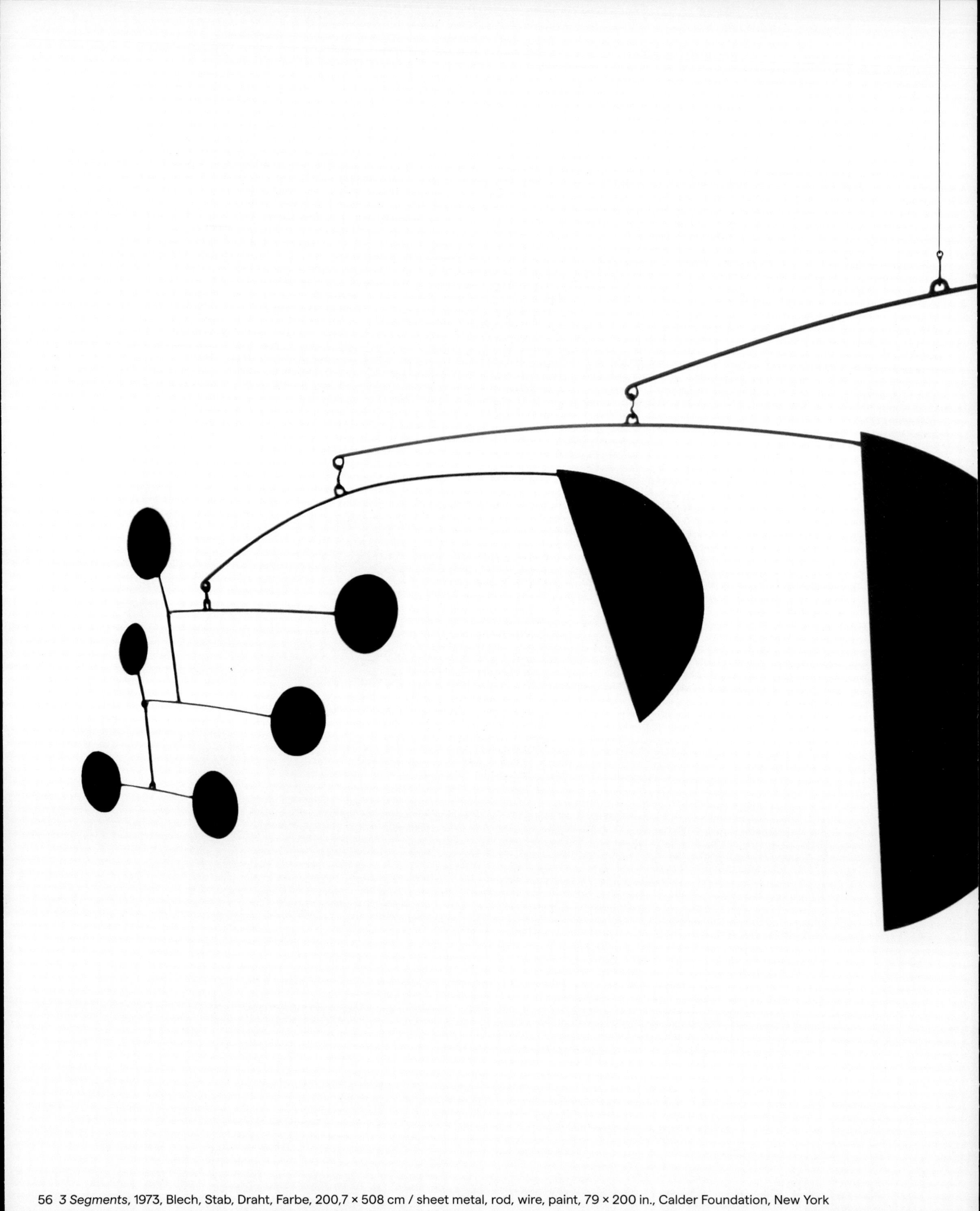

56 *3 Segments*, 1973, Blech, Stab, Draht, Farbe, 200,7 × 508 cm / sheet metal, rod, wire, paint, 79 × 200 in., Calder Foundation, New York

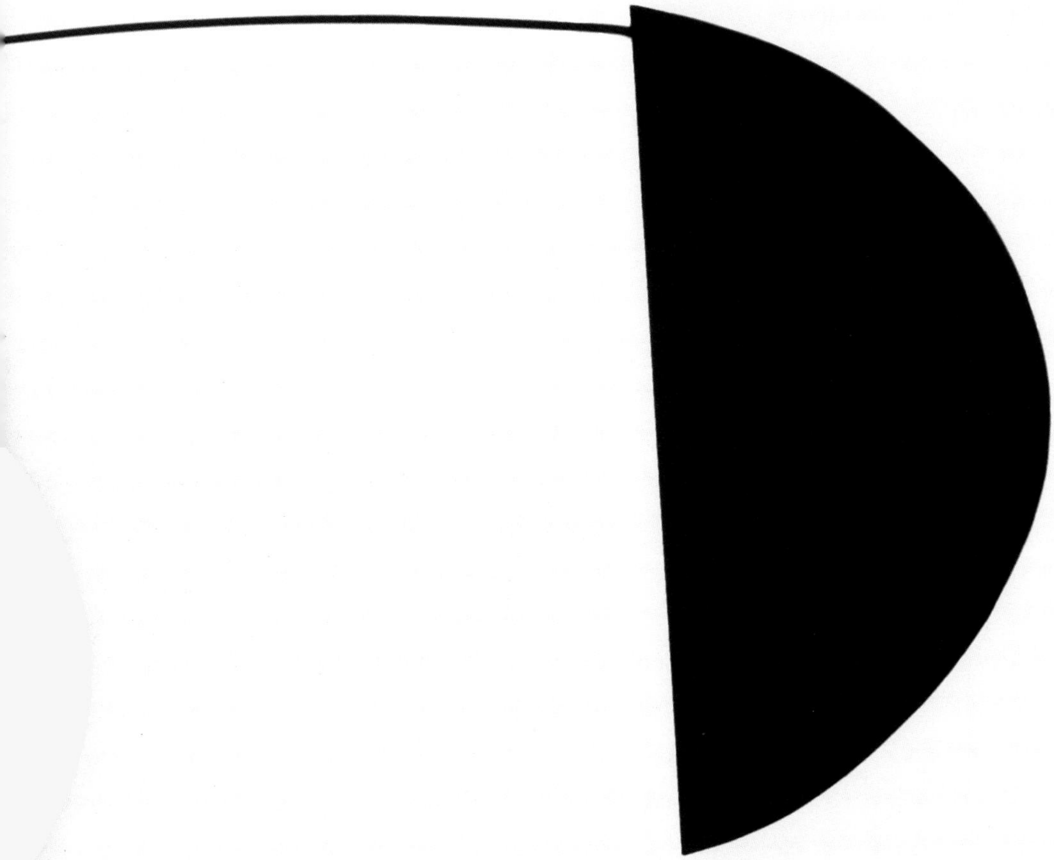

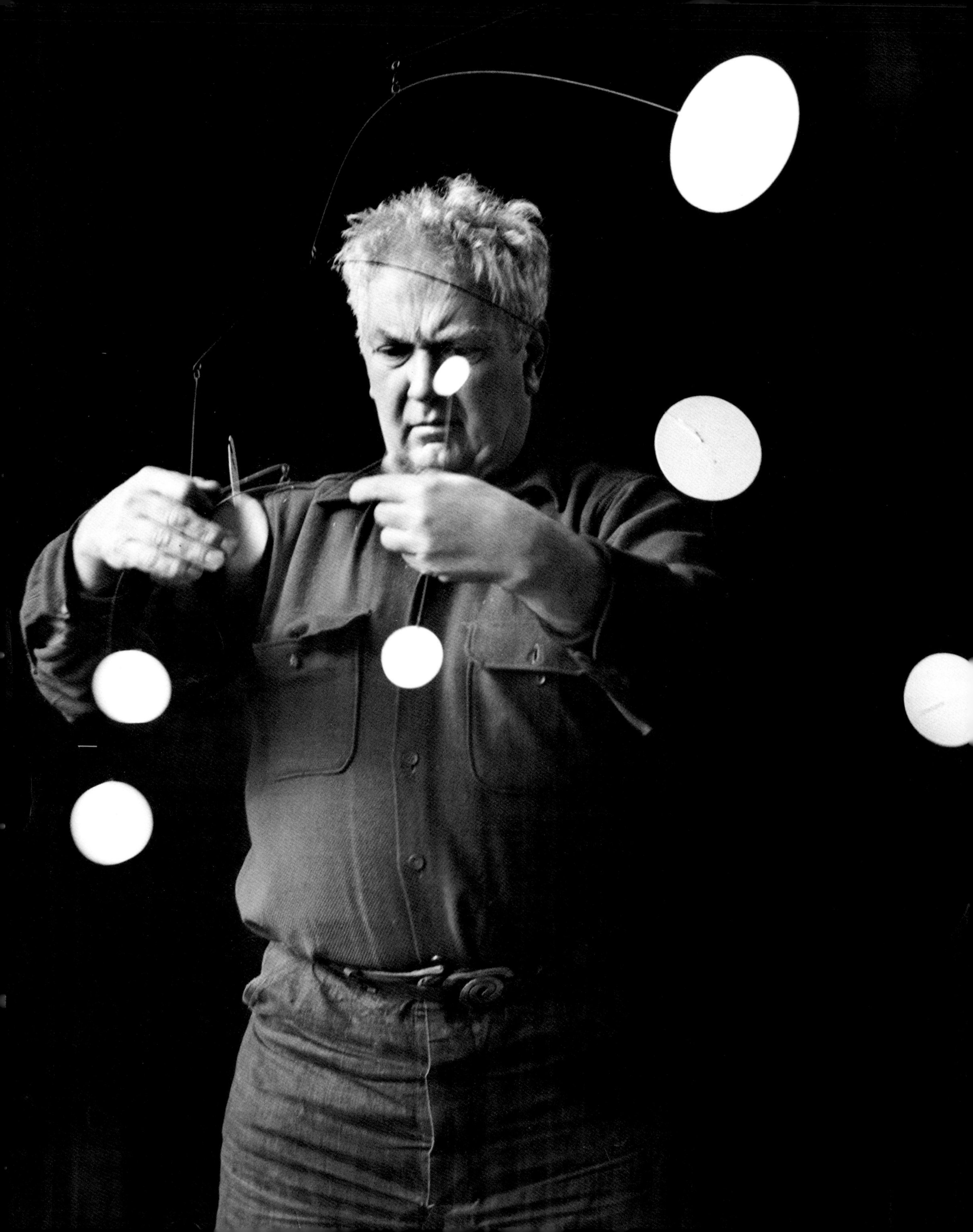

Die Mobiles
Für sich im Raum

Nina
Schallenberg

Mit einer Spanne von mehr als fünf Metern schwebt das zwischen 1959 und 1963 entstandene Mobile *Rouge triomphant* von Alexander Calder im Raum (Abb. 71). Es setzt sich aus drei Ensembles flacher, überwiegend schwarzer Metallelemente zusammen, die durch Walzdrähte miteinander verbunden sind. Wie der Titel besagt, strebt ein rotes Teil triumphierend nach oben. Innerhalb der Gruppen hängen die Elemente jeweils in anderer Weise aneinander, sodass unterschiedliche Figuren und Bewegungen entstehen. Bei zwei der Konstellationen folgen die Metallstäbe in linearer Reihung aufeinander, während sie sich bei der dritten eher verzweigen. Die durch die Anordnungen ermöglichten Bewegungen reichen von sanft kreisenden Runden bis zu einem vibrierenden Auf und Ab. Insbesondere in den Jahren nach dem Zweiten Weltkrieg schuf Calder zahlreiche solcher mehrteiligen, großformatigen Mobiles, deren unterschiedliche Rhythmen und Radien die raumzeitliche Komplexität und Poesie einer jeden Bewegung vor Augen führen (Abb. 59).

Als *Rouge triomphant* entstand, verfügte Calder bereits über eine rund dreißigjährige Praxis in der Herstellung von Mobiles. Bald nachdem er sich 1926 in Paris niedergelassen hatte, erlangte er mit seinen Drahtskulpturen Bekanntheit, die Kritiker damals als „Zeichnungen im Raum“ beschrieben und deren filigrane Strukturen sich bereits jeder traditionellen Vorstellung von Skulptur widersetzten. Während er bei diesen Werken noch figurativ arbeitete, wandte er sich im Jahr 1930 ungegenständlichen Kompositionen zu (Abb. 58). Ein wichtiger Auslöser hierfür war der Besuch des Pariser Ateliers von Piet Mondrian (Abb. 60). Der Niederländer hatte die Wände seines Wohnateliers mit farbigen Paneelen gegliedert, die im Zusammenspiel mit dem

57 Calder mit / with *Snow Flurry I* (1948), Roxbury, 1952, Foto / photo Gordon Parks

ausgesuchten und gezielt platzierten Mobiliar einen Eindruck von harmonischer räumlicher Spannung bewirkten. Diese Anordnung zu erleben, ließ bei Calder die Vorstellung einer realen Bewegung geometrischer Körper im Raum entstehen, die ihn zu einer neuartigen Arbeitsweise inspirierte.

Im Jahr 1931 entstand mit *Object with Red Discs* (Abb. 61) eines der ersten Werke, bei denen Calder mehrere Gleichgewichtsmomente so kombinierte, dass sich die Metall- und Holzelemente stets in latenter Bewegung befinden. Auch die Kombination linear aneinander anschließender Drahtstücke, die in seinen späteren Mobiles häufig zu sehen ist, entwickelte er bereits in dieser frühen Phase. Im selben Jahr schuf er zudem Kompositionen, deren Bewegung durch den Antrieb kleiner versteckter Motoren geleistet wurde – *Two Spheres* war vermutlich die erste davon (Abb. 68). Vor einer rechteckigen, schwarz lackierten Holzplatte befinden sich zwei weiße Kugeln, die mit schwarzen Drähten derart an der Platte befestigt sind, dass ein dahinter liegender Motor Bewegungen von unterschiedlicher Geschwindigkeit in Gang setzt. Vermittelt über die Künstlerin Mary Reynolds, hatte Calder in jener Zeit Marcel Duchamp kennengelernt, der bei einem Atelierbesuch – nicht zuletzt aufgrund seines eigenen Interesses für physikalisch-temporale Phänomene – sehr von den Skulpturen angetan war und sie, Calder zufolge, „Mobile“ taufte.[1]

Der US-Amerikaner zeigte seine neuesten Werke im Rahmen zweier Einzelausstellungen in Paris: 1931 stellte er seine nicht figurativen Arbeiten erstmals in der Galerie Percier aus (Abb. 67), 1932 folgte unter dem Titel *Calder: ses mobiles* die von Duchamp organisierte erste Präsentation seiner Mobiles in der Galerie Vignon. Das positive Echo der Ausstellung bei Percier führte dazu, dass ihn die Gruppe Abstraction Création, der zwischen 1931 und 1936 zahlreiche Künstlerinnen und Künstler angehörten, zum Beitritt einlud. In der ersten Ausgabe der gleichnamigen Zeitschrift skizzierte Calder seine Auffassung von Skulptur, die ebenso materielle wie immaterielle Größen umfasste: „[...] verschiedene

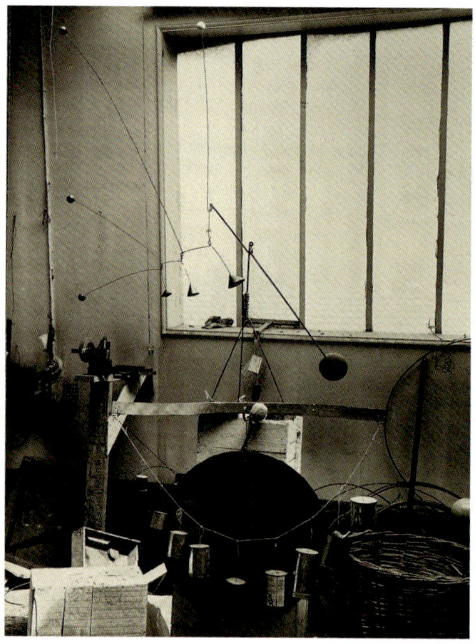

58 Calders Atelier in Paris / Calder's studio in Paris, 1933, Foto / photo Marc Vaux

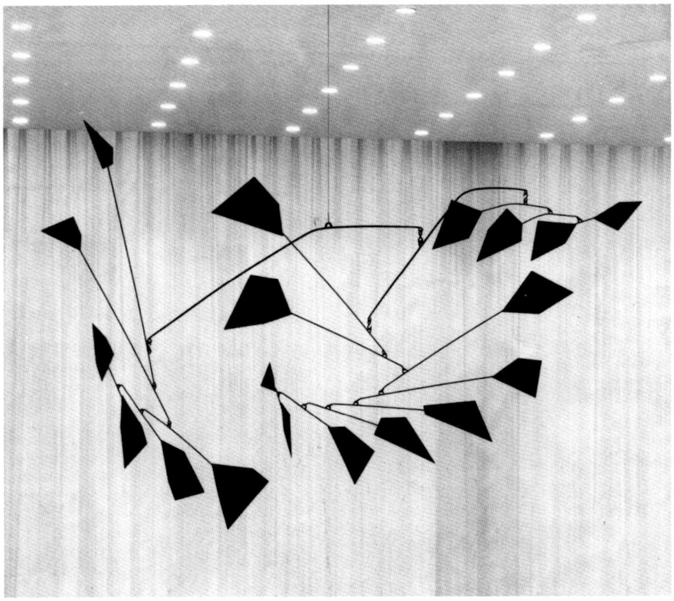

59 *Untitled*, 1959, Blech, Stab, Draht, Farbe, 610 × 610 cm / sheet metal, rod, wire, paint, 240 × 240 in., Chase Manhattan Bank, New York

Massen, leichte, schwere, mittlere – festgelegt durch Variationen der Größe oder Farbe – Richtungen – Vektoren, die Schnelligkeiten, Geschwindigkeiten, Beschleunigungen, Kräfte usw. darstellen […] jedes Element kann sich im Verhältnis zu den anderen Elementen seines Universums bewegen, rühren, schwingen, gehen und kommen. / es soll nicht nur ein ‚momenthafter' Augenblick sein, sondern ein physikalisches Gesetz der Variation zwischen den Ereignissen des Lebens. / kein Auszug, / Abstraktionen / Abstraktionen, die nichts aus dem Leben ähneln, außer in ihrer Art zu reagieren."[2] Mit der Auffassung, dass die Werke keine Abbilder der Realität schaffen, sondern deren Gesetzmäßigkeiten entsprechen sollen, entsprach Calder aktuellen Tendenzen der ungegenständlichen Kunst. Zu erwähnen sind hier die bereits in den späten 1910er-Jahren einsetzenden bildhauerischen Experimente der russischen Konstruktivisten oder auch die 1930 von Theo van Doesburg initiierte Bewegung art concret. Zudem offenbaren Calders Worte die Treffsicherheit Duchamps hinsichtlich der Bezeichnung „Mobile", die im Französischen, wie der Bildhauer in seiner Autobiografie festhielt, eine doppelte Bedeutung hat: „In addition to something that moves, in French it also means motive."[3] Als Mobile wird demnach nicht nur ein in Bewegung begriffener Körper bezeichnet, sondern auch ein Beweggrund, also das innere Motiv für ein Handeln.

Bei den ersten Mobiles lenkten markante Rahmungen und elektrische Motoren von der Konzentration auf die Bewegungen der Objekte ab. In der Folge ließ Calder Rahmen und Hilfsmittel weg und widmete sich der Entwicklung ausgeklügelter Gleichgewichts- und Verbindungslösungen, die den plastischen Elementen ein vielfältiges Spiel zwischen Ruhe und Bewegung ermöglichten. Mit seiner Rückkehr in die Vereinigten Staaten 1933 und der Einrichtung eines Ateliers in Roxbury, Connecticut, eroberten seine Mobiles nun den Raum in neuen Dimensionen (Abb. 66). In der Öffentlichkeit entfalteten sie ihre Wirkung an unterschiedlichen Orten. Im Rahmen von Theaterprojekten dynamisierten sie den Bühnenraum, wie etwa bei der Inszenierung des Stücks

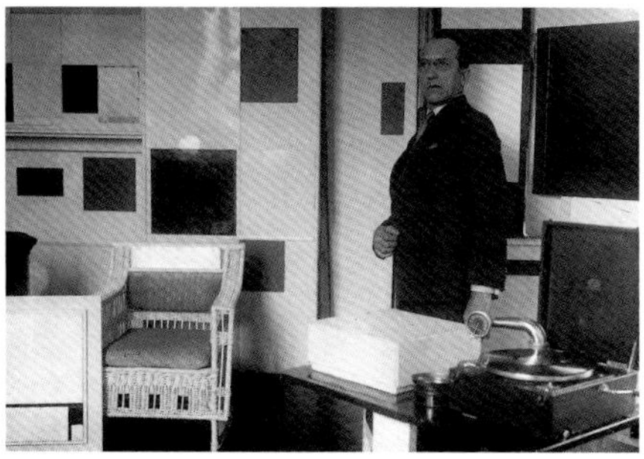

60 Piet Mondrians Atelier in Paris / Piet Mondrian's Paris studio, 1929

Balloon von Padraic Colum, die im August 1946 am Ogunquit Playhouse in Maine Premiere hatte. Für das Bühnenbild schuf Calder *Ogunquit*, das sich heute in der Sammlung des Tehran Museum of Contemporary Art befindet. Einen weiteren Kontext für seine raumgreifenden Mobiles bildeten architektonische Situationen wie etwa das Labyrinth, das die Architekten der Gruppe BBPR 1954 im Mailänder Parco Sempione für die Umgebung des Palazzo dell'Arte entwarfen. Calder präsentierte hier über einem Wasserbassin schwebend das kurz zuvor entstandene Mobile *Le Cagoulard* (Abb. 69, 73). Wenngleich Calders Werke ungegenständlich sind, so eröffnen formale Details und vor allem erzählerische Titel häufig Bezüge zu konkreten Situationen. Sowohl die schwarzen, mit Löchern versehenen Elemente als auch der Titel des Mobiles lassen die rechtsextreme Gruppierung der Cagoulards assoziieren, die in den 1930er-Jahren und während der deutschen Besatzung Frankreichs aktiv war und deren Erkennungszeichen schwarze Kapuzen (*cagoule*) mit Augenlöchern waren.

Während und nach dem Ende des Zweiten Weltkrieges wurde Calders Haus in Connecticut zu einer zentralen Anlaufstelle für Mitglieder der Pariser Avantgarde im Exil. Ein häufiger Gast war André Masson, der wenige Monate nach Kriegsende den französischen Philosophen Jean-Paul Sartre nach Roxbury mitbrachte. Tief beeindruckt von den Mobiles, die im Raum des Ateliers ein eigenes Dasein zu führen schienen, schrieb er einen kurzen Text, der im folgenden Jahr im Katalog einer Ausstellung von Calder in der Pariser Galerie Louis Carré veröffentlicht wurde (Abb. 70). Die beschriebenen Szenen und verwendeten Begriffe erinnern an Sartres Theorie eines Für-sich-Seins, die er 1943 in seinem Hauptwerk *L'Être et le néant* (*Das Sein und das Nichts*) veröffentlicht hatte. Sartre zufolge gründete ein Für-sich nicht allein in sich selbst, sondern es ist in seinem Sein immer abhängig von etwas, das außerhalb von ihm liegt. In diesem Sinne hielt er fest, dass Calder die Bewegungen seiner Mobiles im Kern definierte, sie dann aber den äußeren Einflüssen und damit ihrem Schicksal überließ: „[...] Tageszeit, Sonne, Wärme und Wind bestimmen dann, in welcher Weise sie sich jeweils bewegen; so bleibt das Gebilde immer halbwegs zwischen der Gebundenheit einer Statue und der Unabhängigkeit eines Naturereignisses;"[4] Sartres Beschreibung ergänzt Calders gut zehn Jahre zuvor in *abstraction-création* veröffentlichten Worte. Während der Bildhauer den Akzent auf die in seinen Kompositionen angelegten Bewegungsrichtungen legt, betont der Philosoph den Anteil der äußeren Einflüsse an den Bewegungen der Werke. Unabhängig davon, aus welcher Perspektive das Verharren und Zittern, das Ruhen und Gleiten der Mobiles betrachtet wird, stets macht das Ineinanderwirken von plastischer Form und umgebender Atmosphäre nicht nur das Für-sich-Sein der Mobiles anschaulich, sondern auch die Spannungen im Raum.

1 Alexander Calder: *Calder: An Autobiography with Pictures*, hg. von Jean Davidson, New York 1966, S. 127.

2 „[...] des masses différents, légères, lourdes, moyennes, – indiquées par des variations de grandeur ou de couleur – des directions – vecteurs représentant vitesses, vélocités, accélérations, forces, etc. [...] chaque élément pouvant bouger, remuer, osciller, aller et venir dans ses relations avec les autres éléments de son univers. / que soit, non seulement un instant ‚momentané', mais une loi physique de variation entre les événements de la vie. / pas d'extrations, / des abstractions / des abstractions qui ne ressemblent à rien de la vie, sauf par leur manière de réagir." Alexander Calder, „Comment réaliser l'art?", in: *abstraction-création. art non figuratif*, 1932, Nr. 1, S. 6 (Übers. d. Verf.).

3 Calder 1966 (wie Anm. 1), S. 127.

4 Jean-Paul Sartre, „Les Mobiles de Calder", in: *Calder*, Ausst.-Kat. Galerie Louis Carré, Paris 1946, o. S.; dt. Übersetzung: „Die Mobiles von Calder", in: *Alexander Calder*, Ausst.-Kat. Akademie der Künste Berlin (West), Berlin 1967, S. 21–26, hier S. 22.

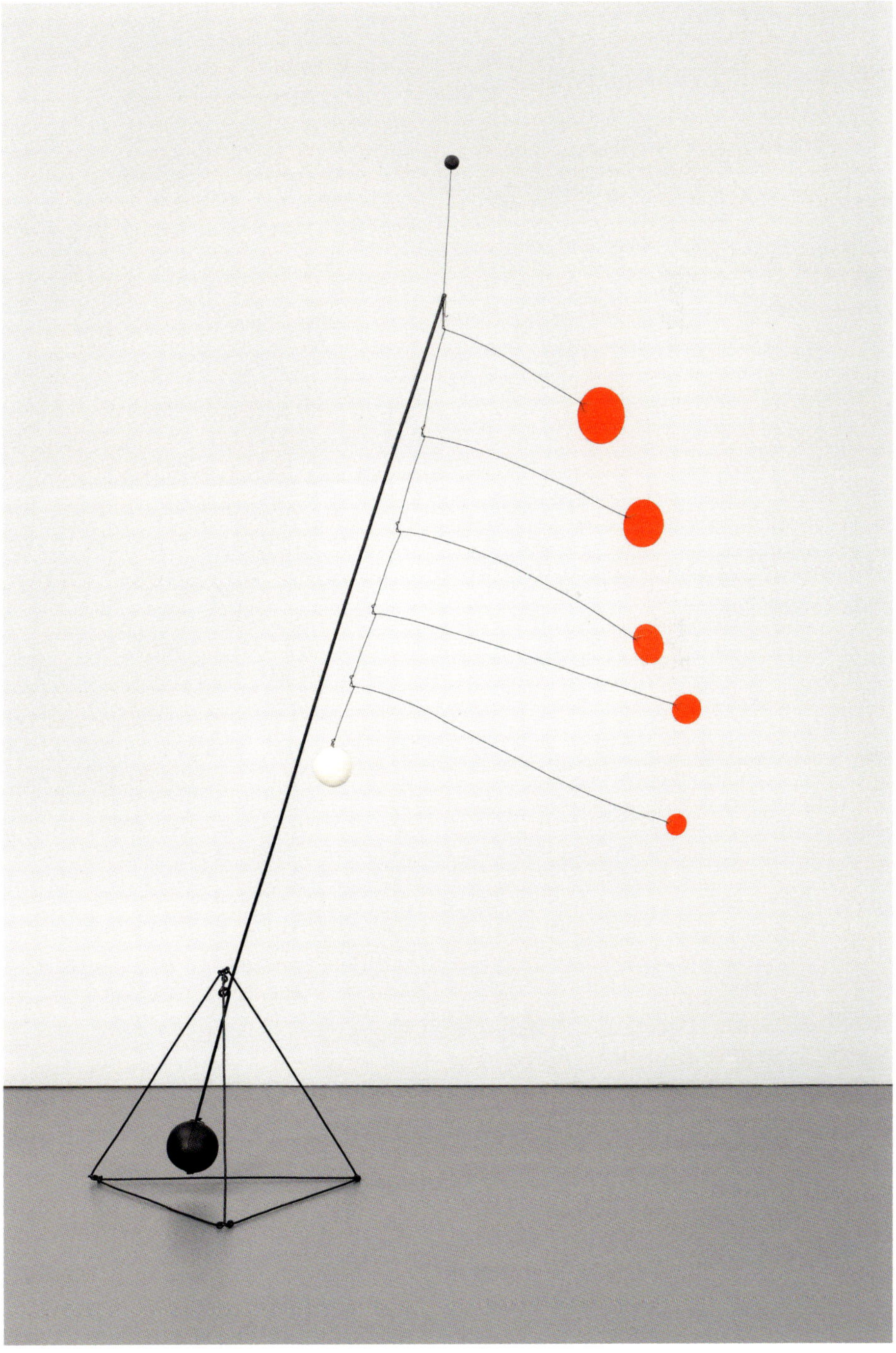

61 *Object with Red Discs*, 1931, Blech, Holz, Draht, Stab, Farbe, 222 × 133 × 62 cm / sheet metal, wood, wire, rod, paint, 87 ½ × 52 ¼ × 24 ½ in., Whitney Museum of American Art, New York

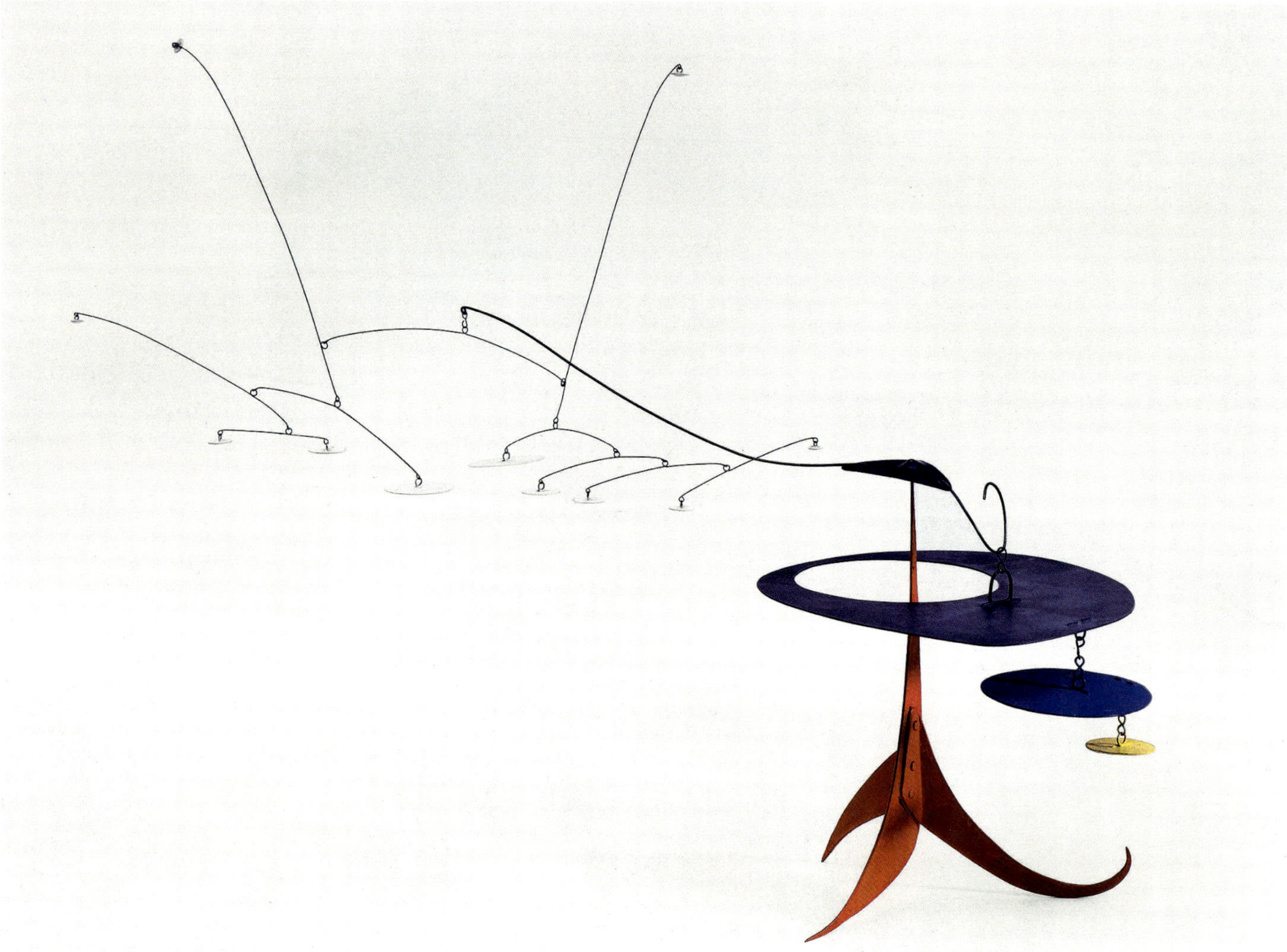

62 *Untitled*, um 1948, Blech, Draht, Farbe, 60 × 100 × 100 cm / ca. 1948, sheet metal, wire, paint, 24 × $39\frac{3}{8}$ × $39\frac{3}{8}$ in., Staatliche Museen zu Berlin, Nationalgalerie

63 *Untitled*, um 1958, Blech, Messing, Draht, Farbe, Höhe 38 cm / ca. 1958, sheet metal, brass, wire, paint, height 15 in., Staatliche Museen zu Berlin, Museum Berggruen

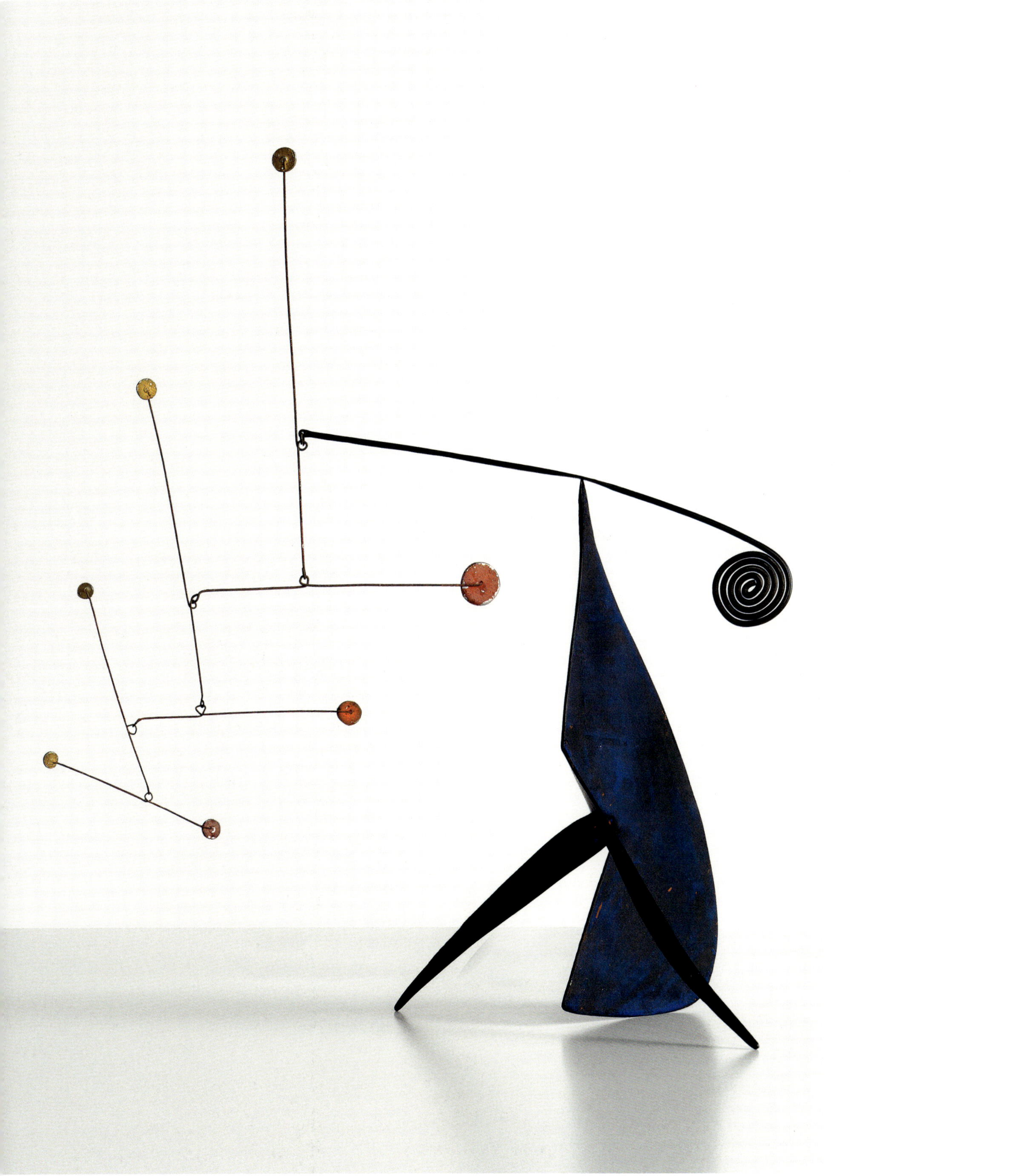

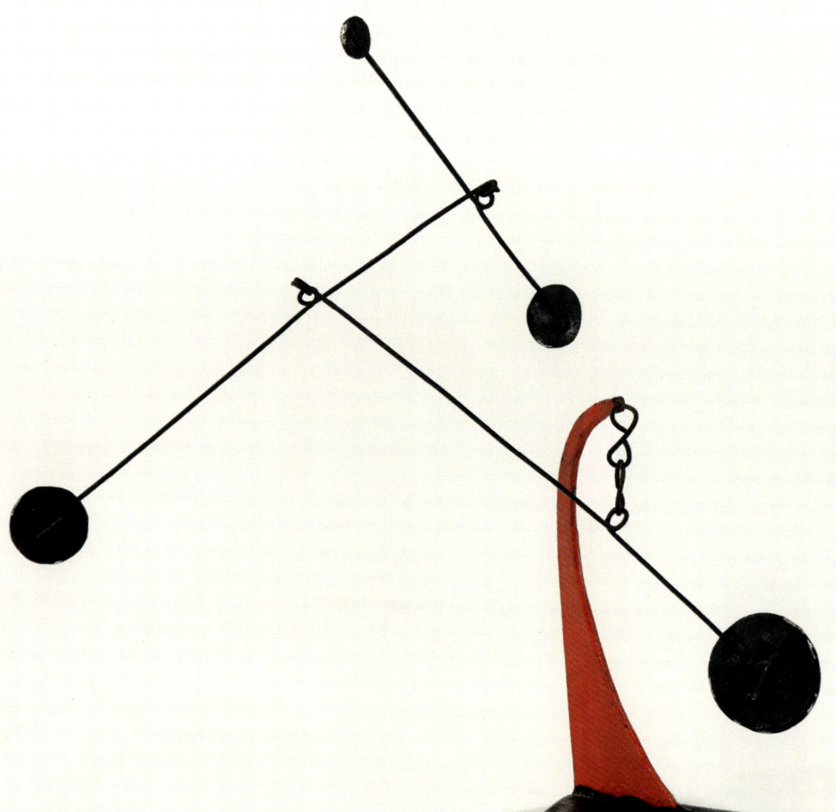

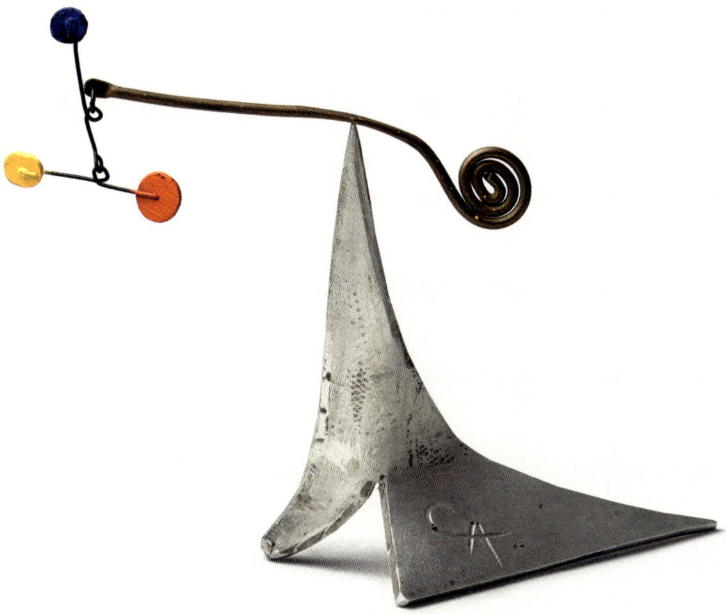

65 *Untitled*, um 1965, Blech, Messing, Draht, Farbe, 15,2 × 14 × 5,7 cm / ca. 1965, sheet metal, brass, wire, paint, 6 × 5½ × 2¼ in., Calder Foundation, New York

64 *Untitled*, um 1940, Blech, Draht, Farbe, 14,5 × 12,1 × 12,1 cm / ca. 1940, sheet metal, wire, paint, 5 11/16 × 4¾ × 4¾ in., Calder Foundation, New York

The Mobiles For Themselves in Space

Nina Schallenberg

With a span of more than five meters, Alexander Calder's mobile *Rouge triomphant* from 1959–63 hovers in space (fig. 71). It consists of three ensembles of flat, predominantly black metal elements that are connected to one another by metal rods. As the title suggests, a red piece strives triumphantly upward. Within the groups, the elements are attached to each other in different ways, thus creating various figures and movements. In two of the constellations, the metal rods are organized in a linear sequence, whereas in the third they tend to branch out. The movements made possible by these arrangements span from a gentle circling to a back-and-forth vibration. Particularly in the years following World War II, Calder created numerous multipart, large-scale mobiles, whose varying rhythms and radii reveal the spatiotemporal complexity and poetry of every movement (fig. 59).

By the time Calder made *Rouge triomphant*, he had already been creating mobiles for some thirty years. Soon after settling in Paris in 1926, he gained recognition for his wire sculptures—described by critics at the time as "drawings in space"—whose delicate structures defied any traditional notion of sculpture. While these works remained figurative, Calder turned to nonobjective compositions in 1930 (fig. 58). A major catalyst for this change was his visit to the Paris studio of Piet Mondrian (fig. 60). The Dutch artist had used colored panels to subdivide the walls of his live-in studio, creating a sense of harmonious spatial tension with the purposeful selection and placement of the furniture. The experience of this arrangement led Calder to conceive of the actual movement of geometric bodies in space, which inspired an innovative shift in his practice.

Created in 1931, *Object with Red Discs* (fig. 61) was one of the first works in which Calder combined multiple moments of equilibrium to set the metal and wood

66 Calder in seinem Atelier in Roxbury mit *Red Disc and Gong* (1940) und *Untitled* (um 1940) / Calder in his Roxbury studio with *Red Disc and Gong* (1940) and *Untitled* (ca. 1940), 1944, Foto / photo Eric Schaal

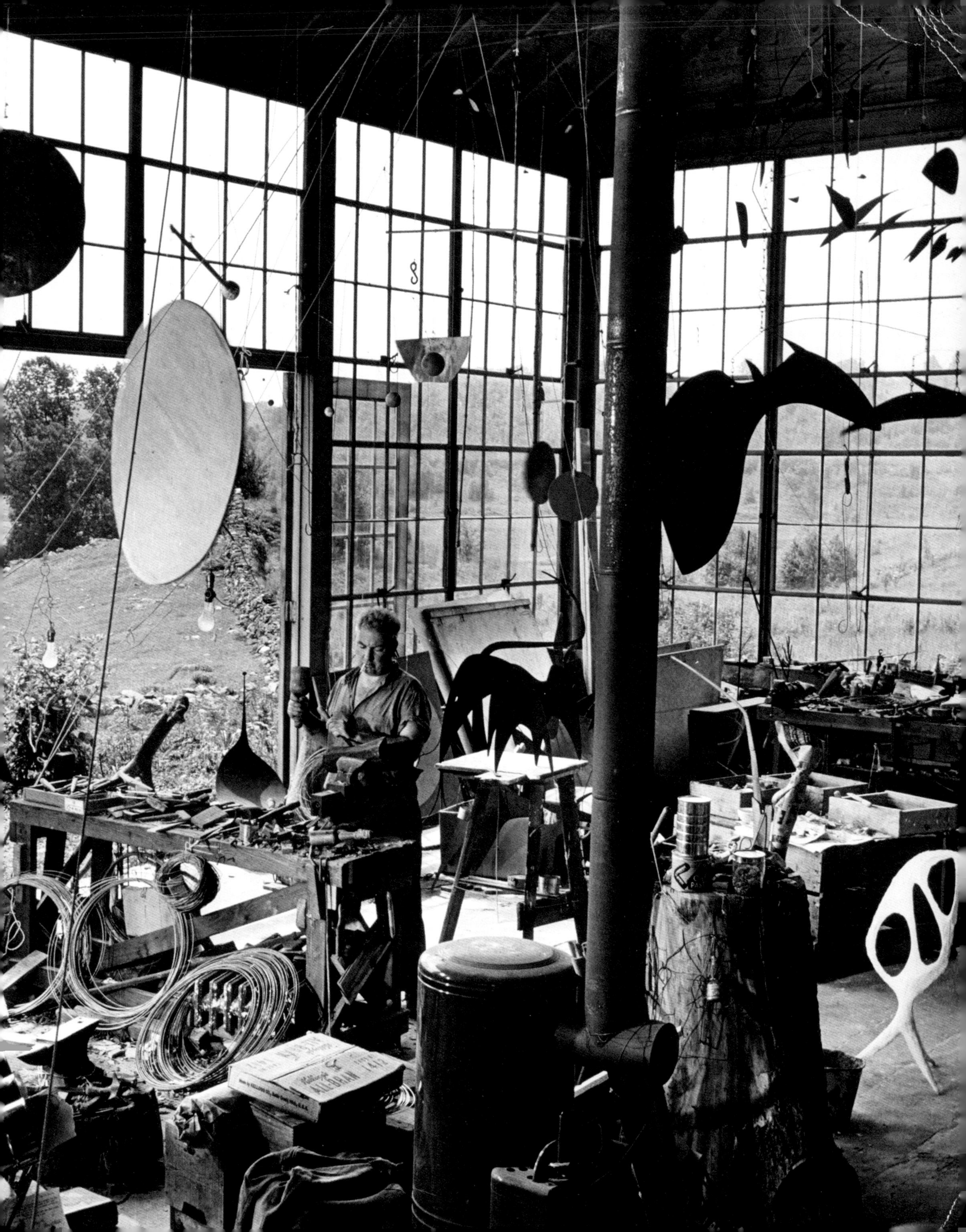

elements into perpetual, latent motion. He also developed the combination of pieces of wire connected in a linear manner, often seen in his later mobiles, during this early phase. That same year, he created other compositions in which movement was generated by small, hidden motors—*Two Spheres* was likely the first of these (fig. 68). Here, in front of a rectangular, black lacquered wooden panel are two white spheres, which are attached to the back with black wire in such a way that the motor behind them sets off movements of varying speed. At the time, the artist Mary Reynolds introduced Calder to Marcel Duchamp, who was taken by the sculptures during a studio visit—not least because of his own interest in physio-temporal phenomena—and, according to Calder, christened them "Mobile[s]."[1]

The American artist presented his latest works in two solo exhibitions in Paris: in 1931, he debuted his nonobjective sculptures at the Galerie Percier in *Alexandre Calder: Volumes-Vecteurs-Densités / Dessins-Portraits* (fig. 67), followed in 1932 by the Duchamp-organized premiere of his mobiles at the Galerie Vignon, *Calder: ses mobiles*. The positive reception at Percier led to an invitation to join the group Abstraction-Création, to which numerous leading abstract artists belonged between 1931 and 1936. In the first edition of the association's eponymous journal, Calder sketched out his conception of sculpture, which encompassed both the material and the immaterial:

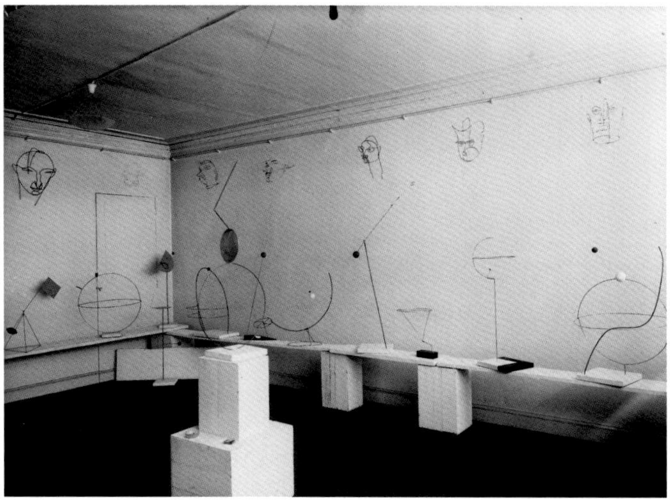

67 Ausstellungsansicht / Installation view, *Alexandre Calder: Volumes-Vecteurs-Densités / Dessins-Portraits,* Galerie Percier, Paris, 1931, Foto / photo Marc Vaux

> Out of different masses, light, heavy, middling—indicated by variations of size or color—directional lines—vectors which represent speeds, velocities, accelerations, forces, etc... / Each element able to move, to stir, to oscillate, to come and go in its relationships with the other elements in its universe. / It must not be just a "fleeting" moment, but a physical bond between the varying events in life. / Not extractions, / But abstractions / Abstractions that are like nothing in life except in their manner of reacting.[2]

With the notion that the works did not reproduce reality but instead should correspond to its laws, Calder addressed then current trends in nonrepresentational art. Here it is worth mentioning the sculptural experiments of the Russian Constructivists, which had already begun by the late 1910s, or the Art Concret movement initiated by Theo van Doesburg in 1930. Moreover, Calder's words reveal the accuracy of Duchamp's term *mobile*, which, as the former noted in his autobiography, has a dual meaning in French: "In addition to something that moves, in French it also means motive."[3] Thus, a mobile is not only a body in motion but also a motivation, or the inner motive for an action.

In the first mobiles, distinctive framing and electric motors diverted attention from the movement of the objects. Calder subsequently abandoned frames and mechanical aids, instead devoting himself to finding

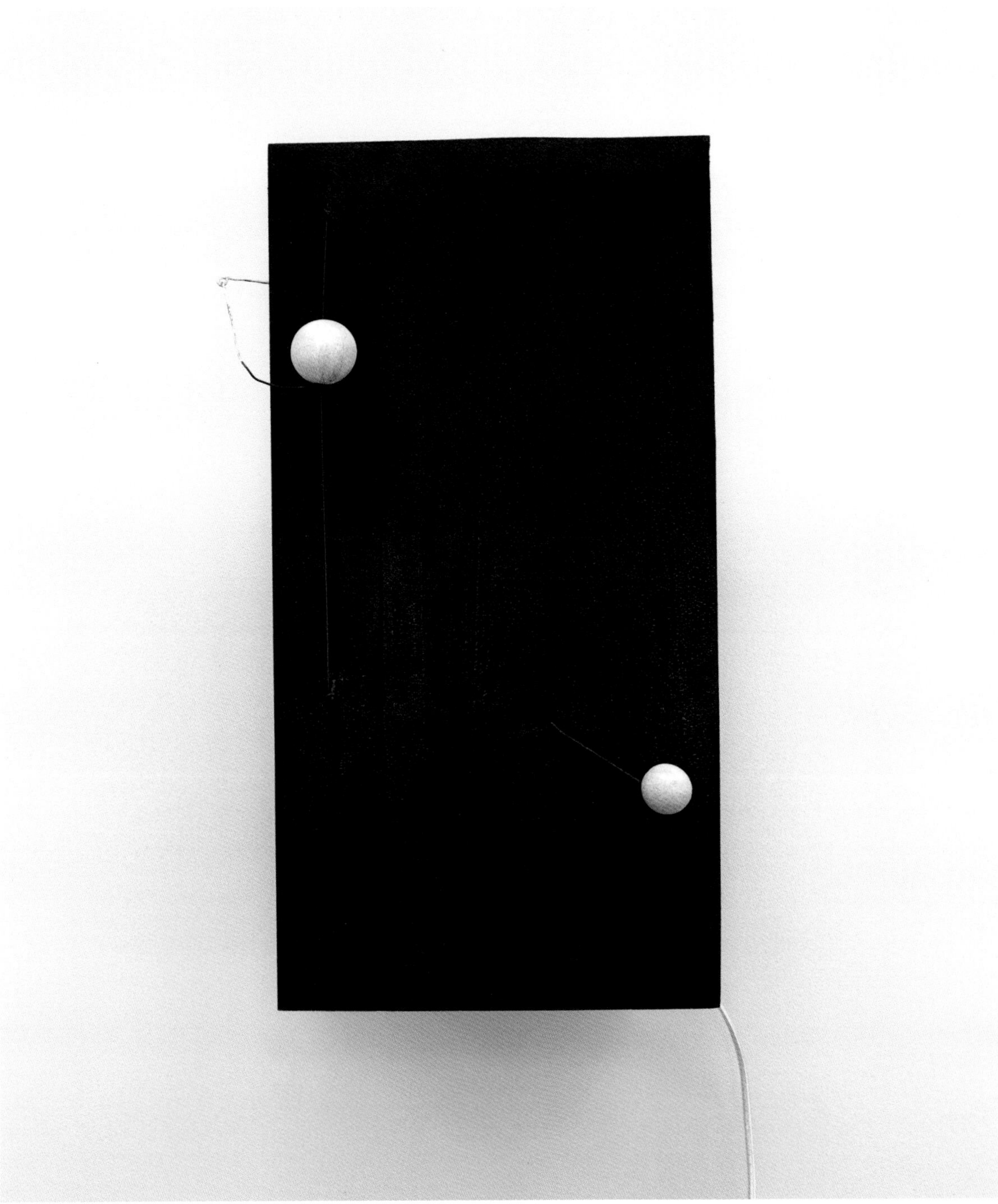

68 *Two Spheres*, 1931, Holz, Draht, Farbe, mit Motor, 54,6 × 27,9 cm / wood, wire, paint, with motor, 21 ½ × 11 in., Calder Foundation, New York

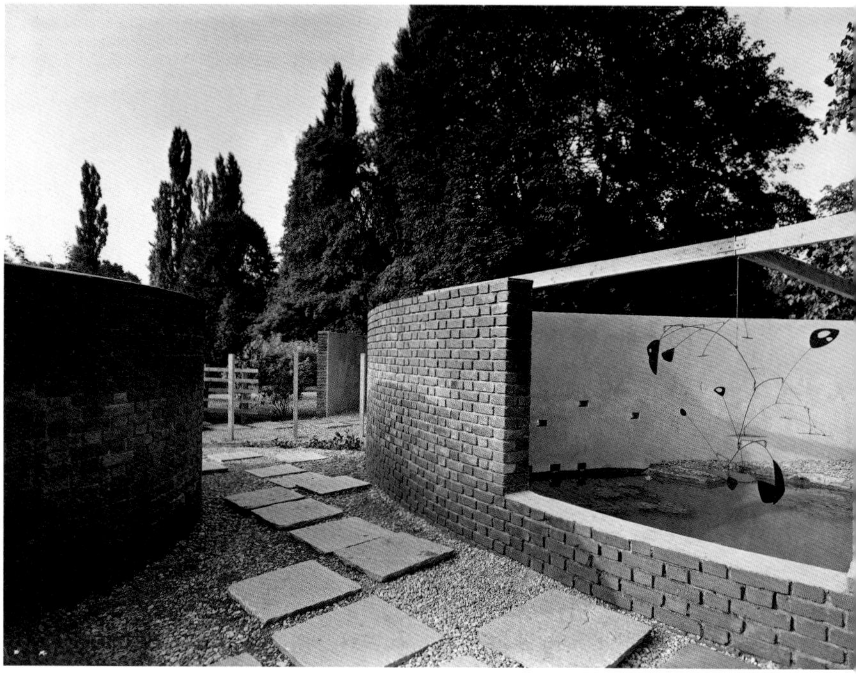

69 *Le Cagoulard*, Parco Sempione, Mailand / Milan, 1954

ingenious ways to use equilibrium and the linkage between the sculptural elements to bring about a multifaceted play between stillness and movement. After the artist returned to the United States in 1933 and established a studio in Roxbury, Connecticut, his mobiles conquered new dimensions (fig. 66). Within the public sphere, these works displayed their effects in various spaces. They dynamized the stage in the context of theater projects, including the production of Padraic Colum's play *Balloon* that premiered at the Ogunquit Playhouse in Maine in August 1946. For the stage set, Calder created *Ogunquit*, which is now in the collection of the Tehran Museum of Contemporary Art. Architectural settings, such as the labyrinth that the architects of the BBPR partnership designed in 1954 for Milan's Parco Sempione near the Palazzo dell'Arte, provided additional environments for his expansive mobiles. There Calder presented his then recent mobile *Le Cagoulard* (figs. 69, 73), suspended above a pool of water. Although his works are nonobjective, some were given narrative titles after the fact of creation that relate to concrete situations; both the perforated black elements as well as the title of the mobile bring to mind the Cagoulards, a secret far-right French terrorist organization that was active during the 1930s as well as the German occupation of France and was known for its signature black hood with eyeholes.

During and after World War II, Calder's house in Connecticut became a central meeting point for exiled members of the Parisian avant-garde. A frequent guest was André Masson, who brought the French philosopher Jean-Paul Sartre to Roxbury a few months after the war's end. Deeply impressed by the mobiles, which seemed to take on an existence of their own in the space of the studio, Sartre wrote a short text that was published the following year in the catalogue accompanying a Calder exhibition at the Galerie Louis Carré in Paris (fig. 70). The scenes described and the terms used are reminiscent of Sartre's theory of being-for-itself, which he published in his 1943 magnum opus *L'Être et le néant* (*Being and Nothingness*). According to Sartre, the "being-for-itself" is not an independent entity. Instead, its existence is always dependent upon something that lies outside of it. Accordingly, he noted that Calder essentially defined the movement of his mobiles but then turned them over to external influences, therefore

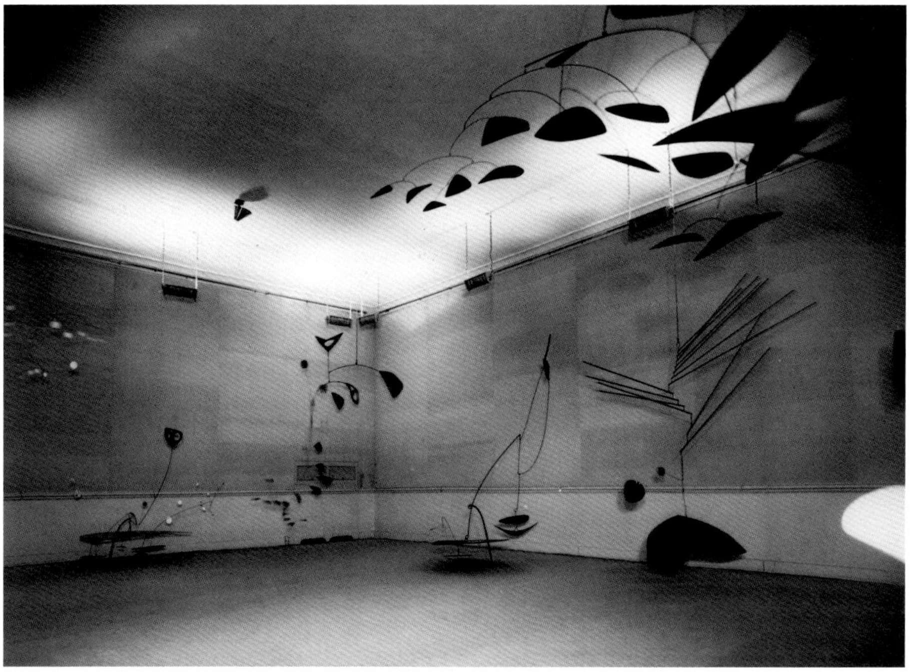

70 Installationsansicht / Installation view, *Alexander Calder: Mobiles, Stabiles, Constellations*, Galerie Louis Carré, Paris, 1946

leaving them to their fate: "Time, sun, heat and wind will determine each particular dance. Thus the object is always midway between the servility of the statue and the independence of natural events."[4]

Sartre's description complements the words Calder had published a good ten years prior in the journal *abstraction-création: art non figuratif*. While the sculptor emphasized the way his compositions were designed for directional movement, the philosopher stressed the role of outside influences on the works' motion. Regardless of the perspective from which the pausing and trembling, stillness and floating of the mobiles are viewed, the interaction between the sculptural form and the surrounding atmosphere reveals not only each mobile's "being-for-itself" but also the tensions within the space.

1 Alexander Calder, *Calder: An Autobiography with Pictures*, ed. Jean Davidson (New York, 1966), p. 127.

2 Alexander Calder, "Comment réaliser l'art?," *abstraction-création: art non figuratif*, no. 1 (1932), p. 6. "Des masses différents, légères, lourdes, moyennes,—indiquées par des variations de grandeur ou de couleur—des directions—vecteurs représentant vitesses, vélocités, accélérations, forces, etc. . . . chaque élément pouvant bouger, remuer, osciller, aller et venir dans ses relations avec les autres éléments de son univers. / que soit, non seulement un instant 'momentané,' mais une loi physique de variation entre les événements de la vie. / pas d'extrations, / des abstractions / des abstractions qui ne ressemblent à rien de la vie, sauf par leur manière de réagir." Translated into English as "How can art be realized?," https://calder.org/bibliography/abstraction-creation-art-non-figuratif-1932/ (accessed March 17, 2021).

3 Calder 1966 (see note 1), p. 127.

4 Jean-Paul Sartre, "Les Mobiles de Calder," in *Calder*, exh. cat. Galerie Louis Carré (Paris, 1946), n.p. Published in English as "Calder's Mobiles," in *The Aftermath of War: Jean-Paul Sartre*, trans. Chris Turner (Calcutta, 2008), https://calder.org/bibliography/alexander-calder-mobiles-stabiles-constellations-1946/jean-paul-sartre-les-mobiles-de-calder/ (accessed March 13, 2021).

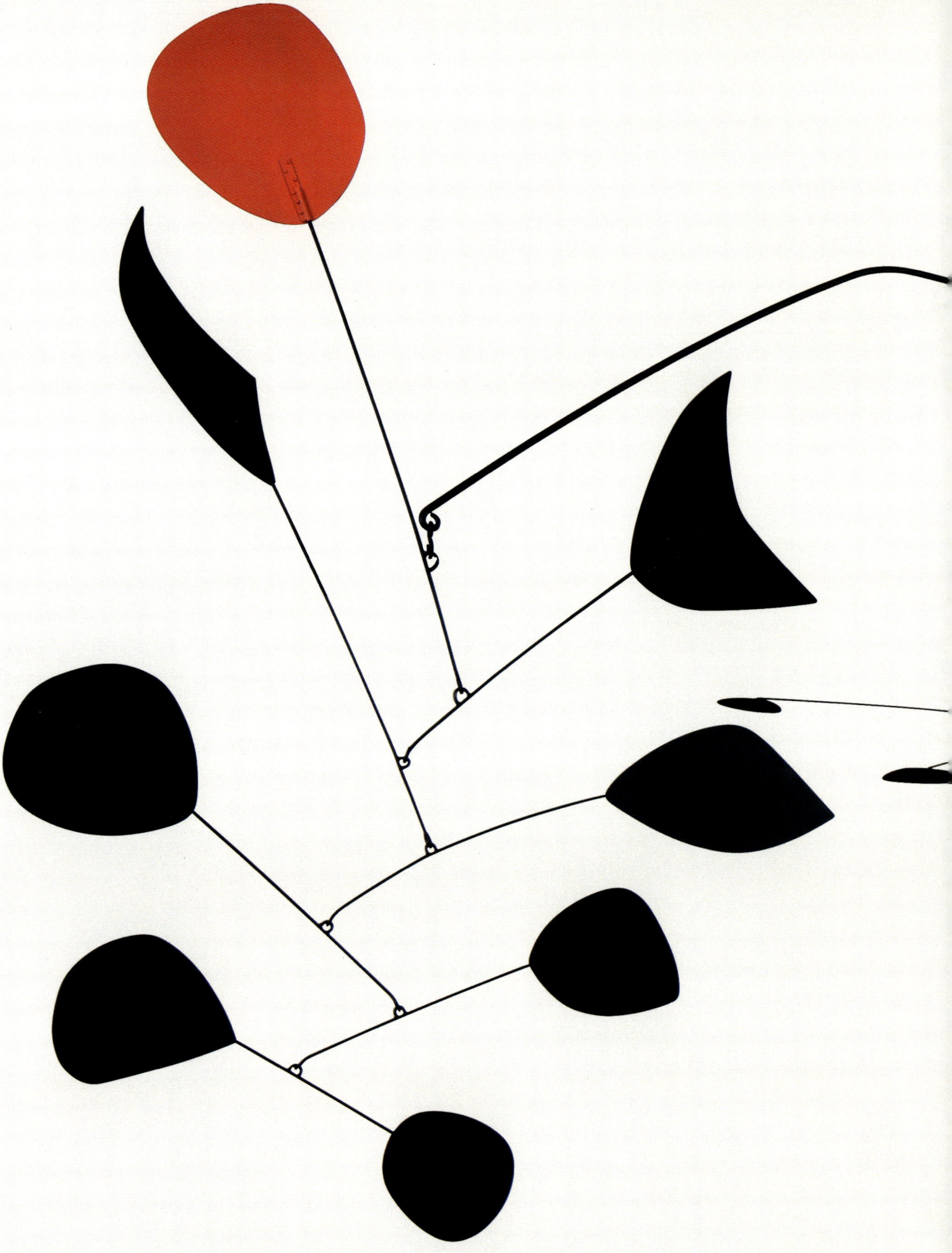

71 *Rouge triomphant*, 1959–1963, Blech, Stab, Draht, Farbe, 279 × 584 × 457 cm / sheet metal, rod, wire, paint, 110 × 230 × 180 in., Collection David and Ezra Nahmad

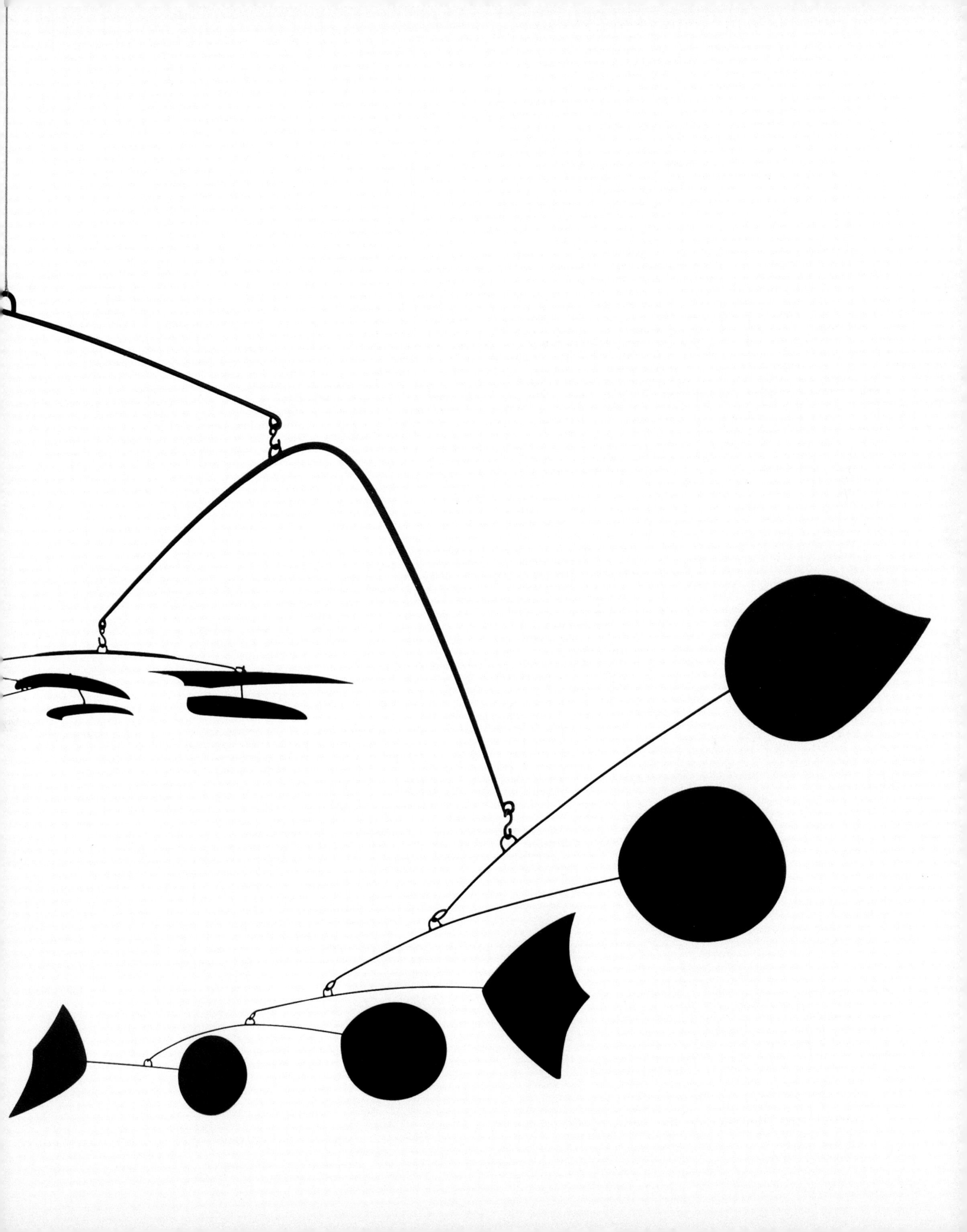

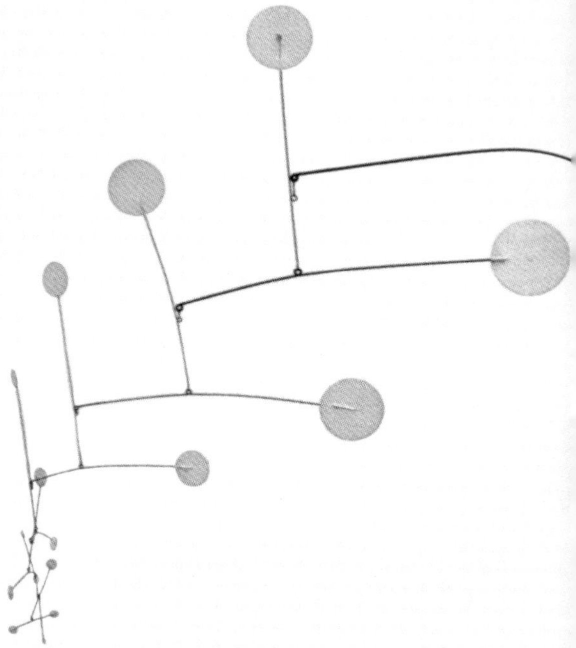

72 *Blizzard*, 1950, Stahl, Draht, Farbe, 320 × 360 × 360 cm / sheet metal, wire, paint, 126 × 141¾ × 141¾ in., Sprengel Museum Hannover, Leihgabe Land Niedersachsen

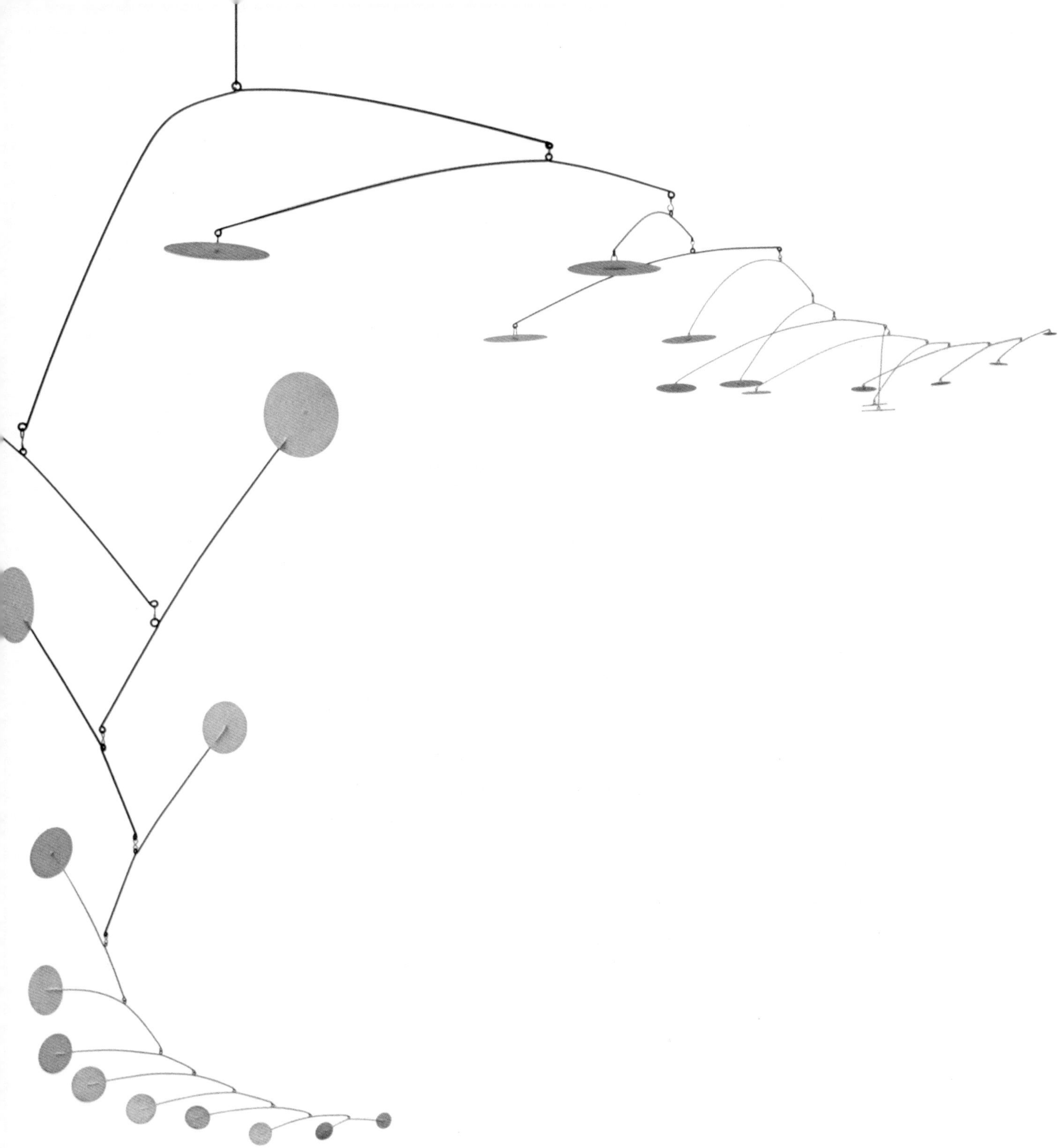

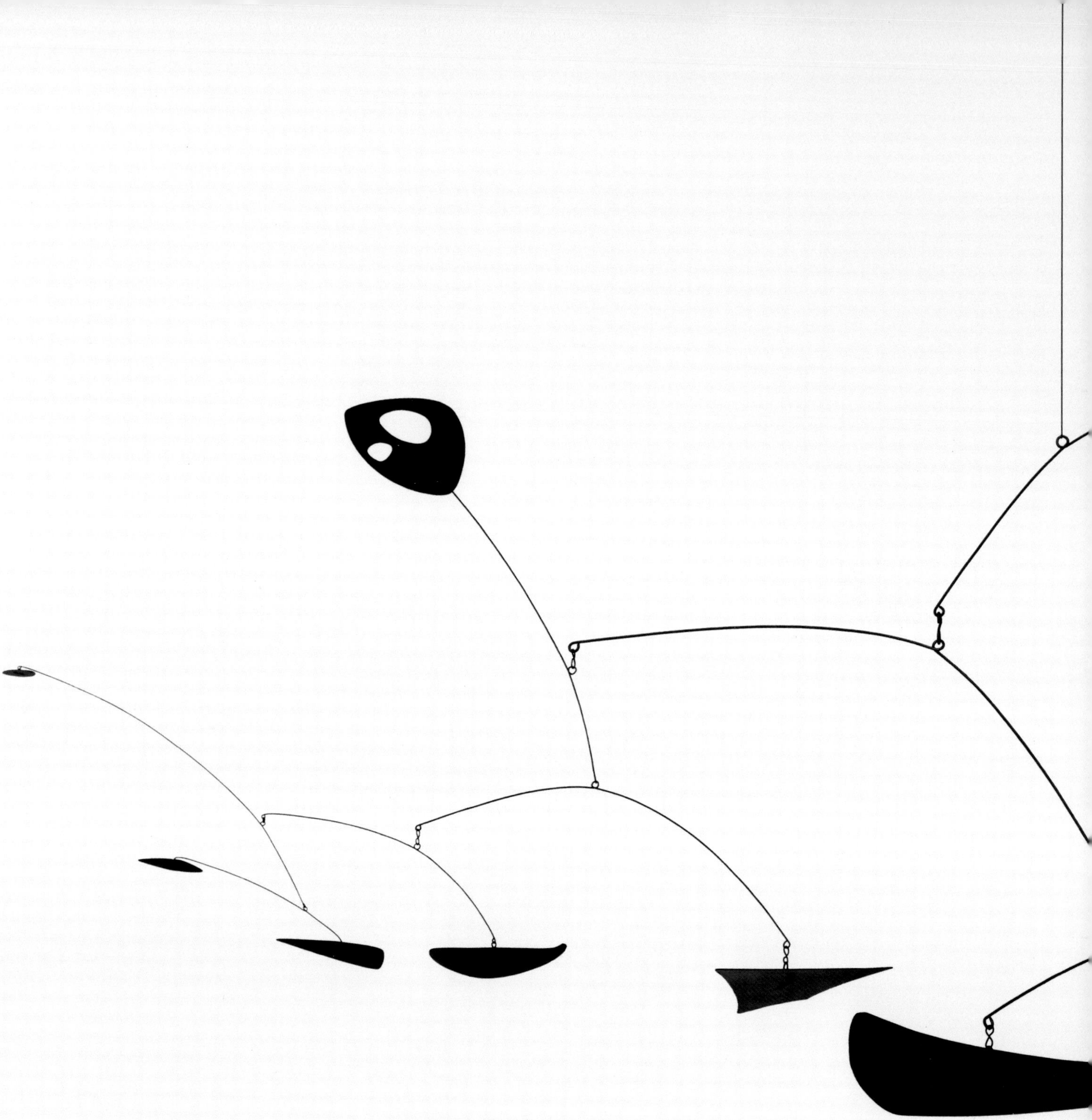

73 *Le Cagoulard*, 1954, Metall, Draht, Farbe, 104 × 345 × 295 cm / sheet metal, wire, paint, 41 × 136 × 116 in., Staatliche Museen zu Berlin, Nationalgalerie, Schenkung Sammlung Ulla und Heiner Pietzsch an das Land Berlin 2010

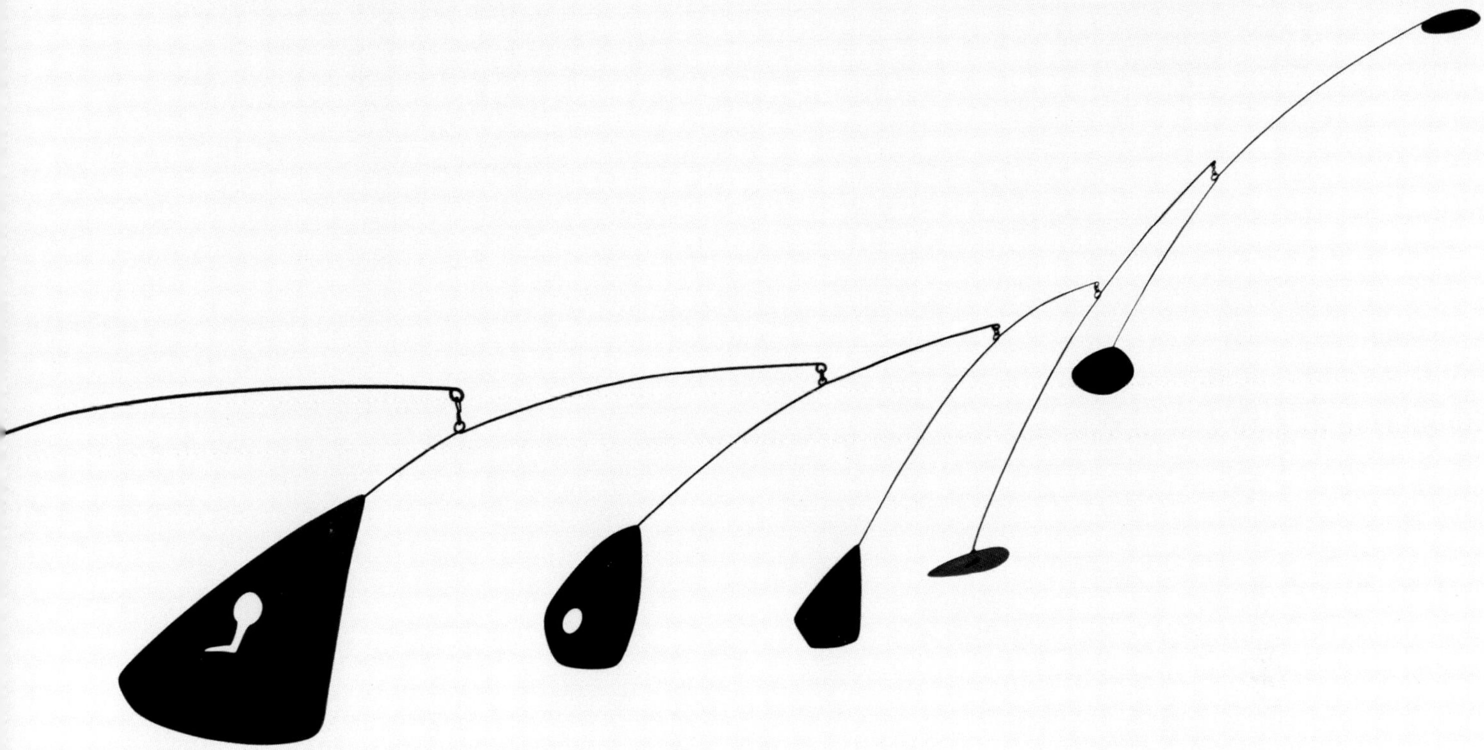

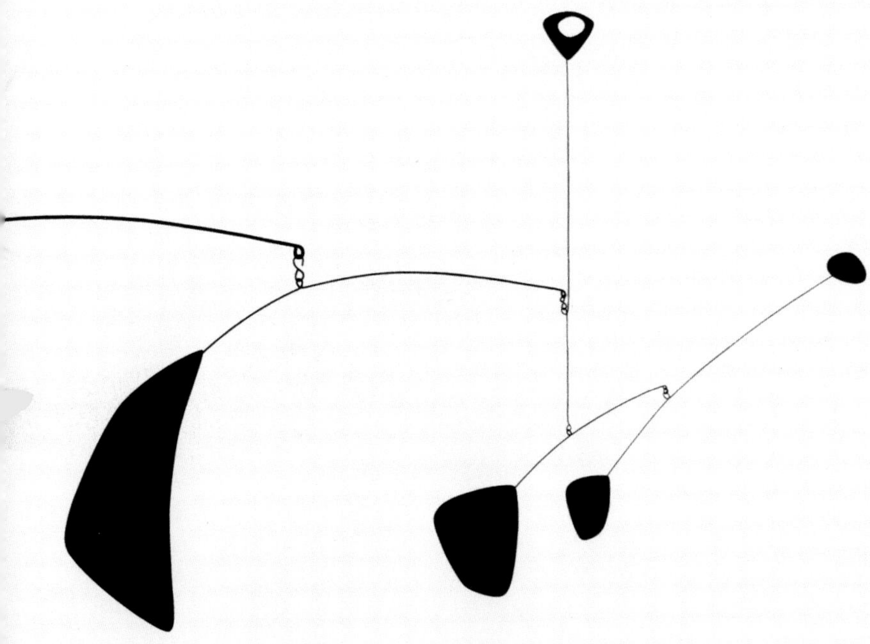

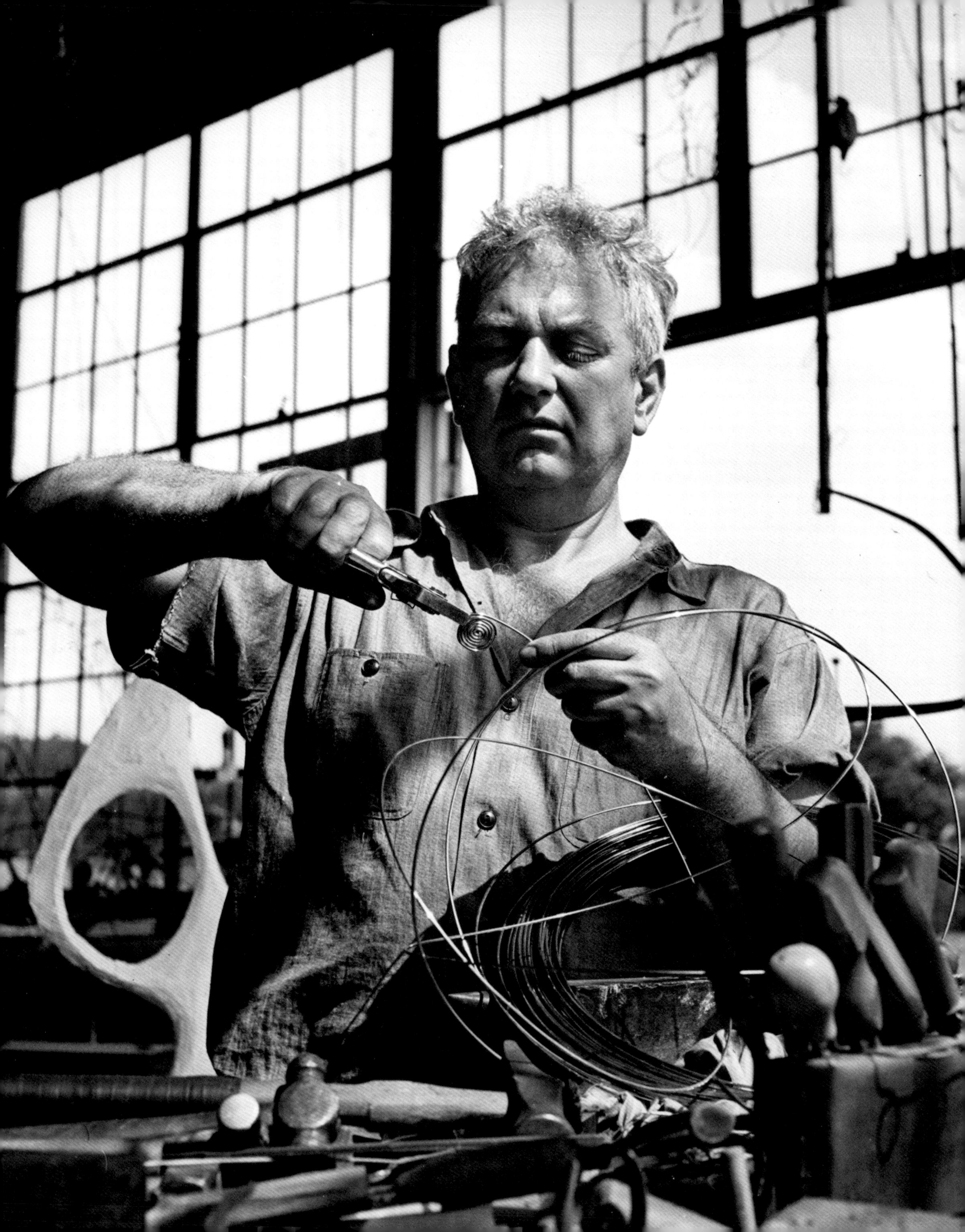

Ästhetische Spiele

Kaitlyn A. Kramer

Strategisch, klar geregelt, belebend, mit Suchtpotenzial: Kein Wunder, dass die Welt des Schachspiels Künstler seit jeher in ihren Bann zieht. Vor allem Marcel Duchamp, sein Leben lang ein passionierter Schachspieler, war von diesem Spiel zutiefst fasziniert und fand in dessen vielen Metaphern Inspirationen für seine Kunstwerke. Anders als er ließ sich Alexander Calder nie vollständig von nur einer Sache einnehmen. Die rastlose Auslotung von Medien und Formen, die sein Kunstschaffen antrieb, prägte auch sein Privatleben. Er durchstreifte die gesellschaftlichen Kreise von New York bis Frankreich und zurück nach Connecticut und sog die Geschehnisse der Zeit auf, nur um sein Leben in seiner eigenen, unverwechselbaren Weise zu gestalten.

Calders Werke sind enorm einfallsreich und schwer einzuordnen, was häufig dazu führte, dass man ihn kurzerhand in eine der großen zeitgenössischen Kunstströmungen einsortierte. In den 1940er-Jahren fiel sein Name oft in einem Atemzug mit jenen der Surrealisten, vor allem, seit er sich 1942 auf Einladung von André Breton an der Ausstellung *First Papers of Surrealism* im Whitelaw Reid Mansion in New York beteiligt hatte. Julien Levy richtete zwei Jahre später in seiner Galerie in Manhattan unter dem Titel *Imagery of Chess* eine Ausstellung zum Thema Schach aus (Abb. 77). Calder, der 1932 bei Levy in seiner ersten New Yorker Einzelausstellung verschiedene Mobiles gezeigt hatte, steuerte dazu einige Schachspiele sowie vier provokante Zeichnungen obszöner Schachfiguren bei. Die überlieferten Aufnahmen der Ausstellung veranschaulichen die wiedererkennbaren künstlerischen Ausdrucksformen der beteiligten Künstler, von André Bretons und Nicolas Calas' verspiegeltem Schachbrett mit einer Ansammlung von teils mit Rotwein, teils mit Weißwein gefüllten Cocktailgläsern über Isamu Noguchis elegantes Schachtischchen mit skurrilen Figuren bis zu Max Ernsts gedrungenen geometrischen Totemwesen.[1]

Calders Schachspiele lösten bei vielen sicher Erstaunen aus. Zwar verarbeitete er zu dieser Zeit bereits geschnitzte Holzstücke und Draht zu den feingliedrigen, komplexen Tisch- und Wandarbeiten, die er Konstellationen nannte, doch haben die vorwiegend aus Holz gefertigten Spielbretter und Figuren wenig mit seinem sonstigen Stil zu tun. Vor allem das Spiel von 1944 (Abb. 82) wirkt befremdlich: Es besteht aus bearbeiteten,

74 Calder in seinem Atelier in Roxbury / Calder in his Roxbury studio, 1944, Foto / photo Eric Schaal

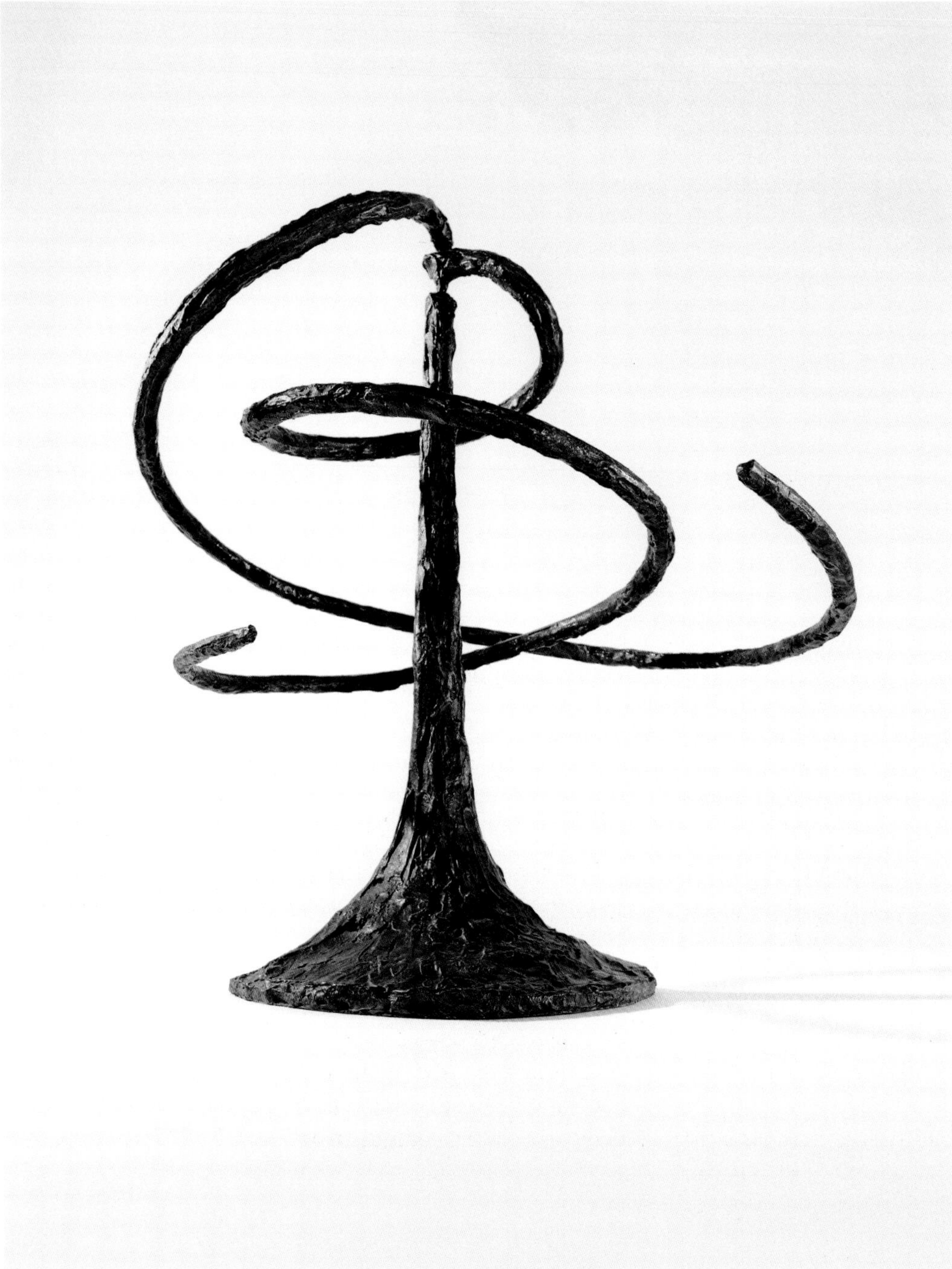

75 *The Helices*, 1944, Bronze (dreiteilig), 80 × 79,4 × 61 cm / bronze (in three sections), 31½ × 31¼ × 24 in., Calder Foundation, New York

unkonventionell rot und blau lackierten, ausgedienten Möbelteilen auf einem Brett mit schwarzen Quadraten, die ungenau auf die grob zugeschnittene Sperrholzplatte aufgemalt sind. Auf deren Oberfläche sieht man hier und da weiße Farbkleckse, doch machte sich Calder nicht die Mühe, die Schlichtheit seines Konstrukts zu kaschieren. Das Spiel ist von seinen Materialien her nicht kostbar, bezeugt jedoch die Kreativität, die bei seiner Erschaffung freigesetzt wurde. Entgegen den klaren Regeln des Schachspiels und dessen bedächtigem Charakter scheinen Calders Spiele einen grenzenlosen Bewegungsradius zu fordern.

Die auffälligsten Figuren bei diesem Exemplar sind die ausladenden Springer, die viel breiter sind als die ihnen zugewiesenen Felder. Beim Spielen stoßen die abstrahierten Pferdeköpfe gegen die minimalistischen Türme und Läufer und überragen die Bauern. Zwar sind auch die Damen ungewöhnlich groß, doch wirken vor allem die klobigen Springer neben den Königen und Damen, die an ihren Kronen erkennbar sind, ein wenig deplatziert.

Eine Parallele zu diesem Spiel mit Größe und Maßstab findet sich in Calders Experimenten mit Bronze aus demselben Jahr. Wiederum ein Freund, diesmal der Architekt Wallace K. Harrison, bestellte bei ihm „einige große Objekte für den Außenbereich, vielleicht aus Zement".[2] Calder nutzte die Gelegenheit, um einer seiner vielen Ideen plastische Form zu verleihen. Aus Gips schuf er Strukturen, die gleichermaßen bodenständig und verschmitzt erscheinen. In Bronze gegossen, veranschaulichen diese kinetischen Objekte den überraschenden Widerspruch zwischen Masse und Schwerelosigkeit, wie etwa *The Helices* (1944, Abb. 75), dessen schwungvollen spiralförmigen Arme sich wie bei einem Mobile rings um den konischen Standfuß im Kreis drehen. Die Modelle wurden nie als monumentale Skulpturen ausgeführt, trotzdem imaginierte Calder sie in Zeichnungen als turmhohe ausbalancierte Körper im öffentlichen Raum, zwischen denen sich die Menschen tummeln oder die riesigen Metallarme der Skulpturen als Rutsche benutzen (Abb. 76). Es ist diese Art von Fantasie, die auch die Figuren auf dem Spielfeld charakterisiert, wenn sie sich auf die trügerischen Strategien des Spiels einlassen.

Ein weiteres seiner Schachspiele ist in Hans Richters Episodenfilm *8×8: A Chess Sonata in 8 Movements* von 1957 zu sehen.[3] Während in den übrigen Segmenten des Films skurrile Metaphern und explizite Verweise auf Schach überwiegen, beginnt der Teil über Calder mit einer ebenso seltsamen wie fesselnden Szene. Im charakteristischen roten Oberhemd rollt er einen riesigen Baumstumpf über eine Wiese bei Roxbury in Connecticut. Darunter kommt ein Löffel zum Vorschein, dessen Stiel er umbiegt. Schritt für Schritt führt er vor, wie er das Utensil mit müheloser Präzision in eines seiner typischen Stand-Mobiles verwandelt (siehe zum Vergleich Abb. 80). Diese Miniaturplastik stellt er zu einer umfangreichen Sammlung ähnlicher Tischskulpturen, deren mobile Aufsätze er durch Anpusten tanzen lässt. Die orchestrierten Bewegungen werden sodann abgelöst von Klängen, wenn Calder zu Richters experimenteller Filmmusik eine selbstgefertigte gläserne Glocke läutet und aus Bierdosen Rumbarasseln konstruiert, die er zum Tönen bringt. Die Idee leitet über zu einem regelrechten Blechdosenballett, für das Calder ausgediente Olivenölkanister in Streifen schneidet und daraus Vögel formt, die sich wie bei einem Hochseilakt drehen und wiegen. Zu diesem Ensemble gesellen sich Mobiles, die durch Calders Hände und den Wind von Roxbury in Bewegung versetzt werden.

Das Thema Schach kommt erst in den allerletzten Sekunden des Filmsegments vor, als die Hand eines Spielers auf Calders Schachbrett eine Dame aufnimmt und damit den gegnerischen König schlägt. Der Angriff ist so kurz, dass man den entscheidenden Akt leicht verpasst.[4] Genau in diesem Augenblick jedoch bildet das Sammelsurium der vorangehenden Szenen ein kohärentes Ganzes. Die Schachfiguren sind genial umfunktionierte Holzelemente, die sich durch die sorgfältig gewählten Aufsätze aus gewöhnlichen Eisenwaren unterscheiden (Abb. 78). Calder schuf das transportable Spiel in den Kriegsjahren um 1942 für Duchamp, damit dieser es auf Reisen mitnehmen konnte. Im Film stülpt die Dame die Öse ihres Schraubhakens über die aufragende Holzschraube des Königs und wirft ihn seitlings auf das Spielbrett. Als Schachzug ausgewiesen ist die kurze Szene durch spezifische Indikatoren wie das Schachbrett oder den Filmtitel, aber ebenso wie der zur Plastik gewordene Löffel oder mit wenigen Handgriffen belebtes Blech – auch ohne konkreten Kontext sind die Utensilien von Calders Kunstfertigkeit beseelt; sie verleiht ihnen weit über ihre ursprüngliche Funktion hinaus Macht.

Der Galerist Levy erinnerte sich an eine von Duchamps zahlreichen Aussagen zum Thema Schach: „Es war kein Kriegsspiel, sondern ein ästhetisches Spiel. Man spürt die Form des Schachbretts, wenn das Muster sich zu verändern beginnt, und kann es noch schöner machen, auch wenn man [dabei] verliert."[5] Dieser Gedanke schwingt mit in Richters Wiedergabe von Calders Schaffensprozess, bei dem mehr entsteht als Objekte. Mit seinen einzigartigen Werken, von minimalen, jedoch innovativen Modifikationen von Haushaltsartikeln bis hin zu fesselnden Skulpturen, die jeden Innenraum verwandeln, schenkte Calder uns Erfahrungen und Teilhabe. Seine Skulpturen zu betrachten bedeutet, immer wieder neue, stetigen Veränderungen unterworfene Aspekte ihrer Schönheit zu entdecken. Calder hauchte Metall Leben ein und verlieh ihm Flügel. Seine Strategie eröffnet das Spiel.

1 Für weiterführende Informationen zur Ausstellung *The Imagery of Chess* siehe Larry List (Hg.): *The Imagery of Chess Revisited*, New York 2005.

2 Alexander Calder: *Calder. An Autobiography with Pictures*, hg. von Jean Davidson, New York 1966, S. 195.

3 https://www.youtube.com/watch?v=gMIBbesWJDA (abgerufen am 11.6.2021)

4 Ebd., Min. 25:50.

5 Jed Perl: *Calder. The Conquest of Space. The Later Years, 1940–1976*, New York 2020, S. 62.

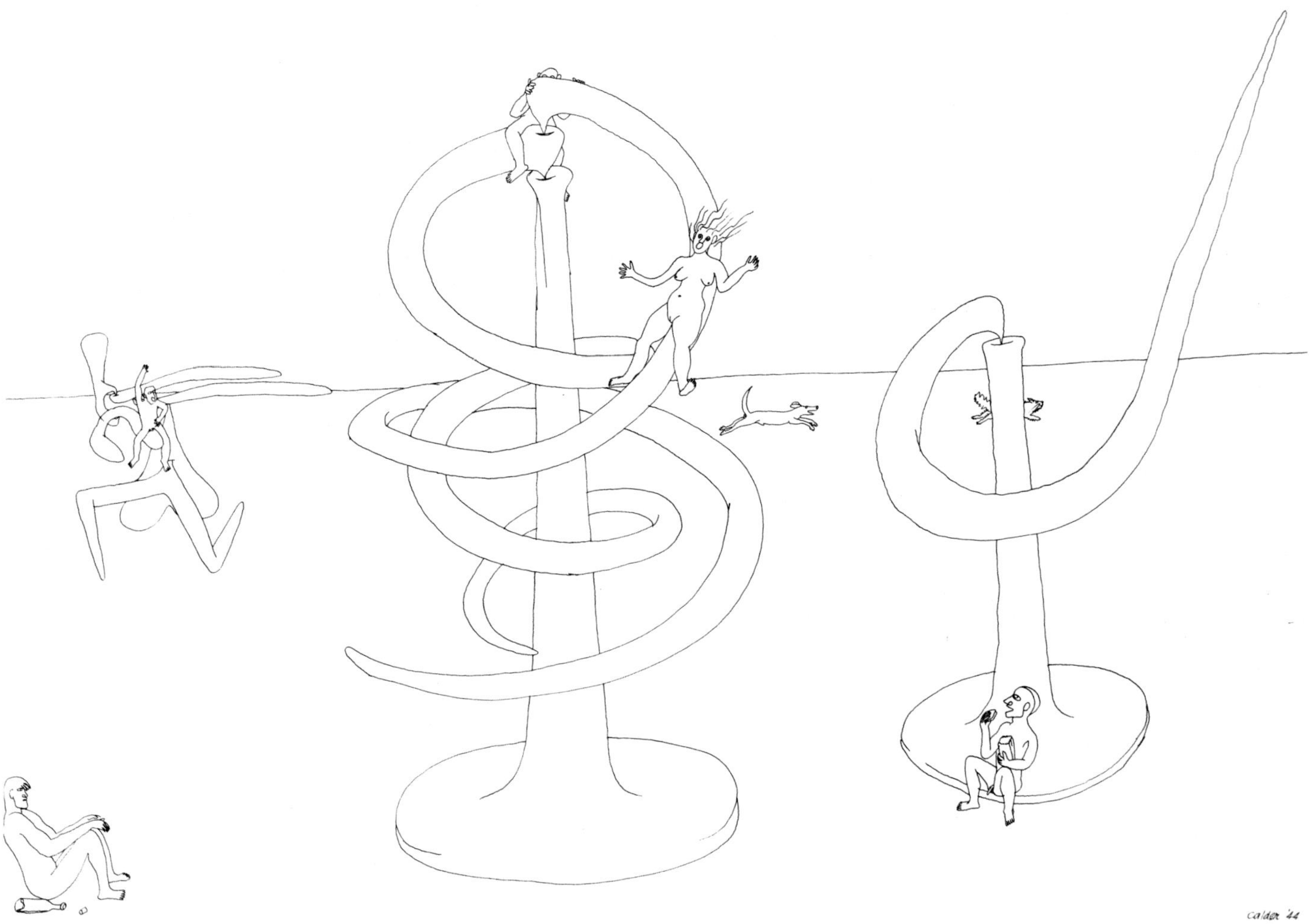

76 *Helix Slide*, 1944, Tinte auf Papier, 57,2 × 78,7 cm / ink on paper, 22 ½ × 31 in.

Aesthetic Games

Strategic, determinate, activating, addictive: there's no mystery why artists have long been seduced by the world of chess. Marcel Duchamp was especially intoxicated by its charms, finding inspiration for his artwork in the game's many metaphors, and was a devoted player throughout his life. Unlike Duchamp, Alexander Calder was not consumed by any one thing. The roving exploration of media and form evident in his art making complemented his personal life, during which he traversed social scenes from New York to France to Connecticut, absorbing the times only to forge his own distinct way of living through and beyond them.

The hard-to-place ingenuity evident in Calder's work often caused him to be shoehorned in the definitive art movements of his time. In the 1940s his work was often considered alongside the Surrealists, notably with his inclusion in the 1942 *First Papers of Surrealism* exhibition at the Whitelaw Reid mansion in New York at the invitation of André Breton. Two years later, when Julien Levy organized an exhibition devoted to chess at his Manhattan gallery (fig. 77), Calder—whose first New York solo show of mobiles was hosted at Levy's gallery in 1932—contributed a few chess sets in addition to four provocative drawings of naughty chess pieces. Documentation of the works included in the *Imagery of Chess* show illustrates the recognizable styles and sentiments of various artists involved, from a mirrored board supporting a collection of cocktail glasses filled with both red and white wine by Breton and Nicolas Calas to Isamu Noguchi's sleek chess table supporting whimsical pieces and Max Ernst's set of squat, geometric totems.[1]

To many, Calder's chess sets would have seemed unexpected. While he had been working with carved

Kaitlyn A. Kramer

wood and wire at the time for his delicate and complexly arranged tabletop and wall works known as Constellations, the predominantly wooden sets don't readily recall the artist's distinctive style. One set in particular (fig. 82), from 1944, stands out as uncanny: comprising discarded bits of hewn furniture parts, the unconventionally painted red and blue pieces are arranged on a board where black squares are imprecisely painted onto a coarsely cut sheet of plywood. A few white paint smears are visible on the surface, where Calder took no pains to hide its rough-cut construction. While the set is not made of precious materials, it's clear that an imaginative force was at play in its realization. For a game so determinate and paced, Calder's sets seem to require infinite motion.

The most noticeable and peculiar pieces in this example are the oversized knights, spilling out over their designated squares. When the game is in play, the abstracted horses' knobbed noses bump into the minimal structures of the castles and bishops and hover over the pawns. Aside from the queen and king pieces, which boast identifiable crowns in spite of the queen's irregularly larger size, the knights stand out as bulky things, like figures out of place.

This play with scale recalls a similar preoccupation from the same year, in the artist's experiments in bronze. Created as the result of another invitation—from another friend, the architect Wallace K. Harrison, who suggested that the artist make "some large outdoor objects which could be done in cement"[2]—this series of bronzes was an excuse for Calder to solidify one of his many roving curiosities. With plaster, Calder worked the material into textural forms at once grounding and mischievous. Cast in bronze, kinetic specimens such as *The Helices* (1944; fig. 75) suggest the unexpected contradiction of being dense yet weightless, the curving tendrils floating like a mobile above the sloping base. The monumentally scaled sculptures were never realized, yet Calder nonetheless envisioned them as towering public works in drawings that depict characters gallivanting around the balancing masses, some sliding down the imagined sculptures' mammoth curves (fig. 76). In the chess set, this imaginative force is evident in his figures' movement across the board as they engage in the deceptive puzzle of the game.

Another of Calder's chess sets makes an appearance in Hans Richter's 1957 anthology film *8×8: A Chess Sonata in 8 Movements*.[3] Unlike the quirky metaphors and explicit chess imagery present in the other contributions, Calder's segment begins with a peculiar yet engrossing scene where the artist, clad in his iconic red

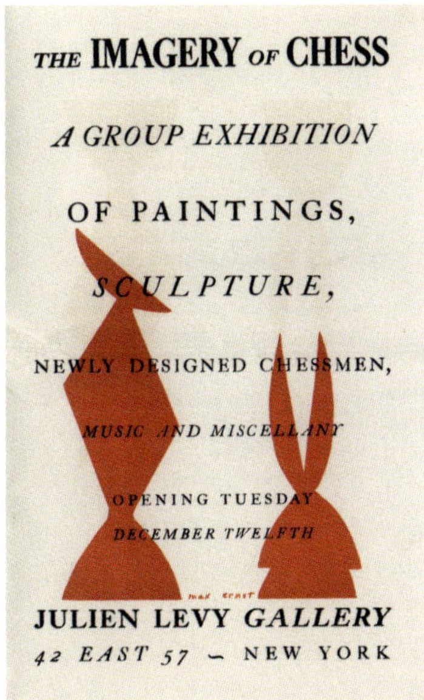

77 Umschlagvorderseite des Ausstellungskataloges / Front cover of the catalogue *The Imagery of Chess: A Group Exhibition of Paintings, Sculpture, Newly Designed Chessmen, Music, and Micellany*, Julien Levy Gallery, New York, 1944

button-up shirt, rolls a massive tree stump across the Roxbury, Connecticut, landscape, uncovering a metal spoon buried underneath. The artist bends the spoon and slowly reveals, with effortless precision, the utensil's transformation into an intimate, animated standing mobile (for comparison, see fig. 80). The petite sculpture is added to a prolific collection of other tabletop works whose mobile tops Calder activates with his breath. This orchestra of movement makes way for one of sound, with Richter's experimental score enlivening images of Calder ringing his custom glass dinner bell as well as constructing and then playing a beer can samba rattle. He builds on the handmade rattle with another tin can dance, cutting repurposed olive oil containers into birds that twist and sway on a tightrope aviary. Calder's mobiles join the ensemble, provoked by both the artist's physical instruction and the Roxbury breeze.

A nod to chess only appears in the last few seconds of the film's segment, in which a chess player's hand advances his queen in a move to take his opponent's king on Calder's set. The capture occurs in a matter of seconds; blink, and you risk missing the concluding action.[4] It is in this moment that the eclectic buildup of the previous scenes coheres. The chess set itself is another one of the artist's ingenuities, fashioned for Duchamp from repurposed wooden bits, each piece distinguishable by its deliberate metal hardware topper (fig. 78). Assembled around 1942, during the war, the set was transportable, made to accompany Duchamp throughout his travels. In the film, we see the queen's screw eye hook loop around the king's protruding wood screw, toppling him over onto the board. The brief scene reads as a game of chess through specific codes—the checkerboard, the film's subject—but even without this context, the utilitarian objects are imbued with Calder's artistry, allowing them to yield power beyond their intended functions. In the artist's dexterous hand, the spoon becomes a sculpture and sheet metal springs to life.

On chess, the gallerist Levy recalled one of Duchamp's many musings, in which the artist proposed: "it wasn't a war game, it's an aesthetic game, and you feel the shape of the board as it begins to shift its pattern and you make it become beautiful, even if you lose."[5] This sentiment sings through Richter's portrait of Calder's process, which resulted in the creation of more than mere objects. He occasioned the gift of experience and participation through his unprecedented works—from slight yet innovative modifications to household objects to arresting sculptures that can transform the space of any interior they meet—and to behold them is to discover continuous instances of their beauty, everchanging. Calder breathed air into metal, encouraging it to take flight; his strategy begets the game.

1 For an in-depth history of *The Imagery of Chess*, see Larry List, ed., *The Imagery of Chess Revisited* (New York, 2005).

2 Alexander Calder, *Calder: An Autobiography with Pictures*, ed. Jean Davidson (New York, 1966), p. 195.

3 https://www.youtube.com/watch?v=gMIB-besWJDA (accessed June 11, 2021).

4 Ibid., min. 25:50.

5 Jed Perl, *Calder: The Conquest of Space: The Later Years*: 1940–1976 (New York, 2020), p. 62.

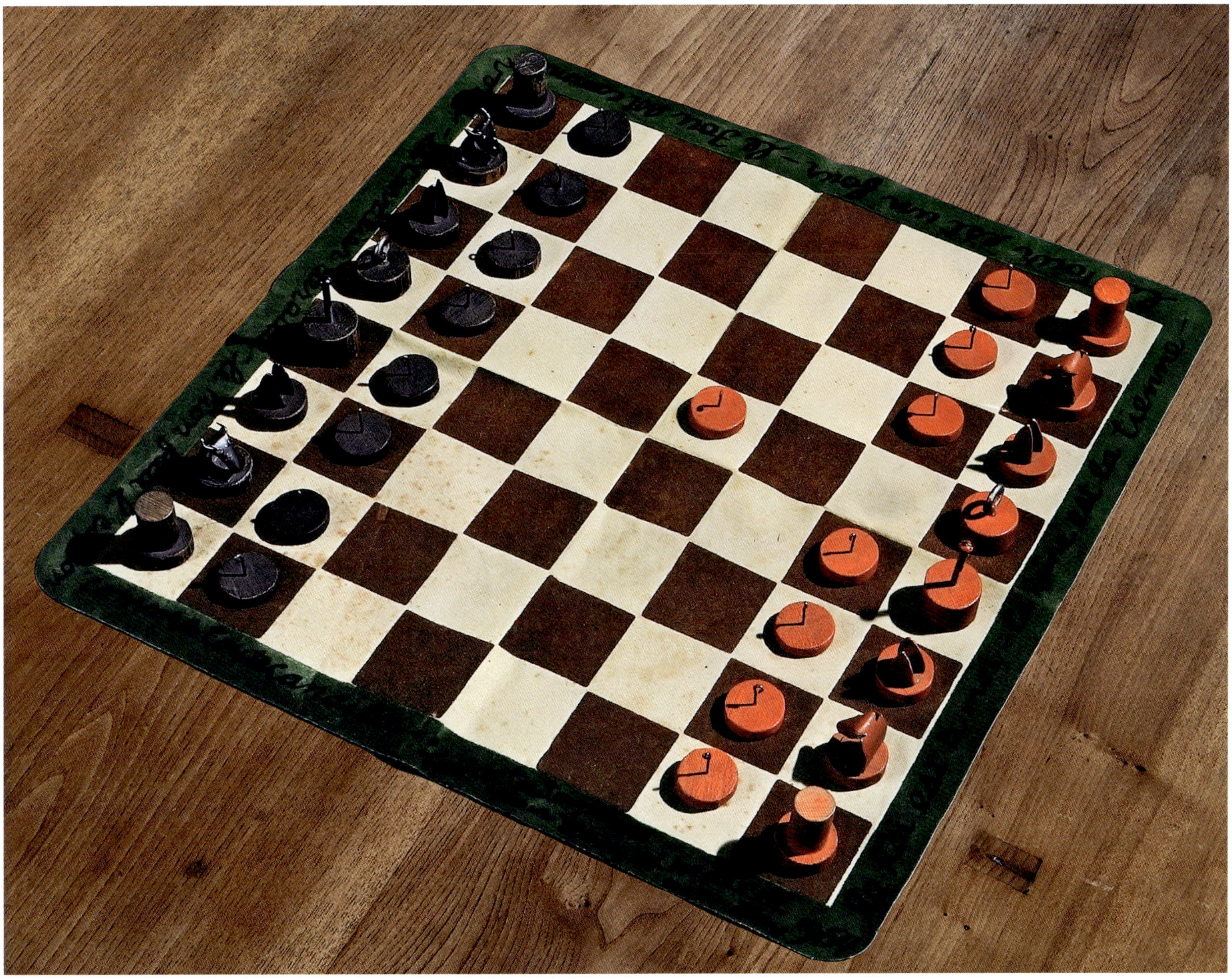

78 Schachspiel, um 1942, Holz, Blech, Draht, Schrauben, Ösen, Farbe. Geschenk Calders an Marcel Duchamp, fotografiert auf einem 1964 von Man Ray gefertigten Spielfeld aus Leinwand / Chess set, ca. 1942, wood, sheet metal, wire, screws, screw-eyes, paint. Gifted by Calder to Marcel Duchamp, photographed on a canvas board made by Man Ray in 1964

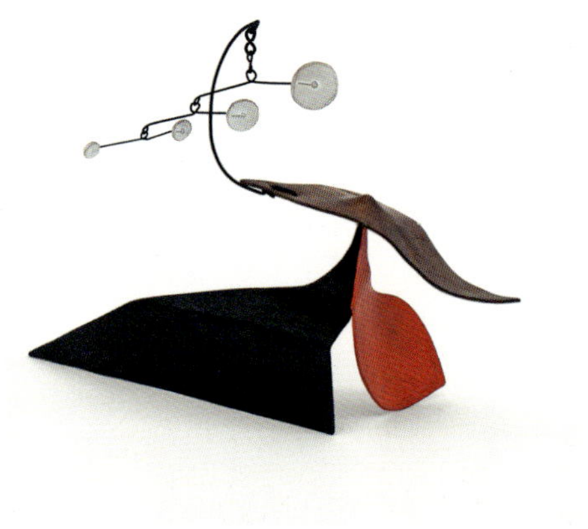

79 *Four Dots and Brass Tail*, um 1953, Blech, Messing, Draht, Farbe, 15,9 × 24,1 × 7,6 cm / ca. 1953, sheet metal, brass, wire, paint, 6¼ × 9½ × 3 in., Calder Foundation, New York

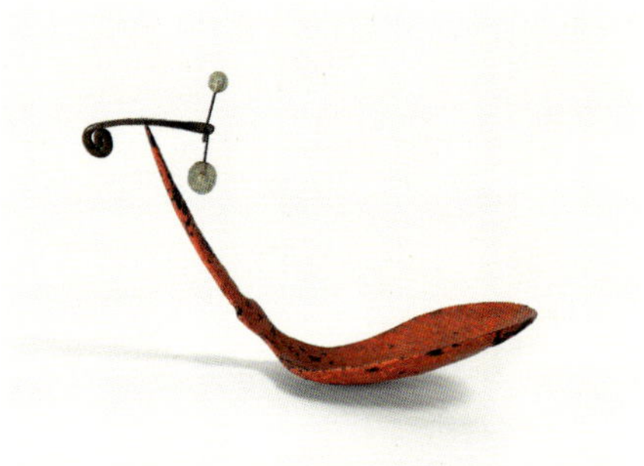

80 *La Cuiller*, 1954, Löffel, Messing, Draht, Blech, Farbe, 8,3 × 13 × 2,9 cm / spoon, brass, wire, sheet metal, paint, 3¼ × 5⅛ × 1⅛ in., Calder Foundation, New York

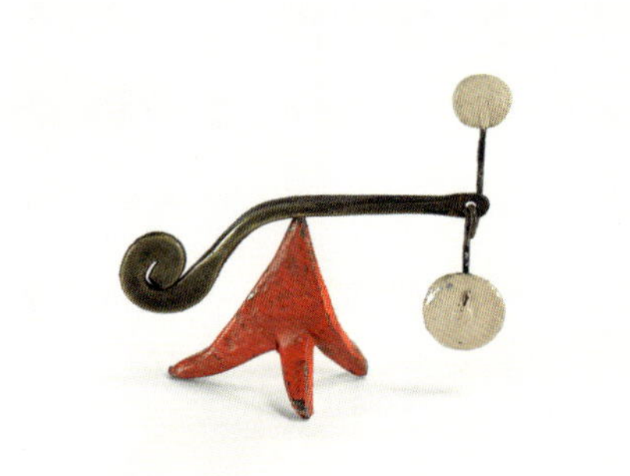

81 *Untitled*, um 1954, Blech, Messing, Draht, Farbe, 3,5 × 6,5 × 1,6 cm / ca. 1954, sheet metal, brass, wire, paint, 1⅜ × 2 9⁄16 × ⅝ in., Calder Foundation, New York

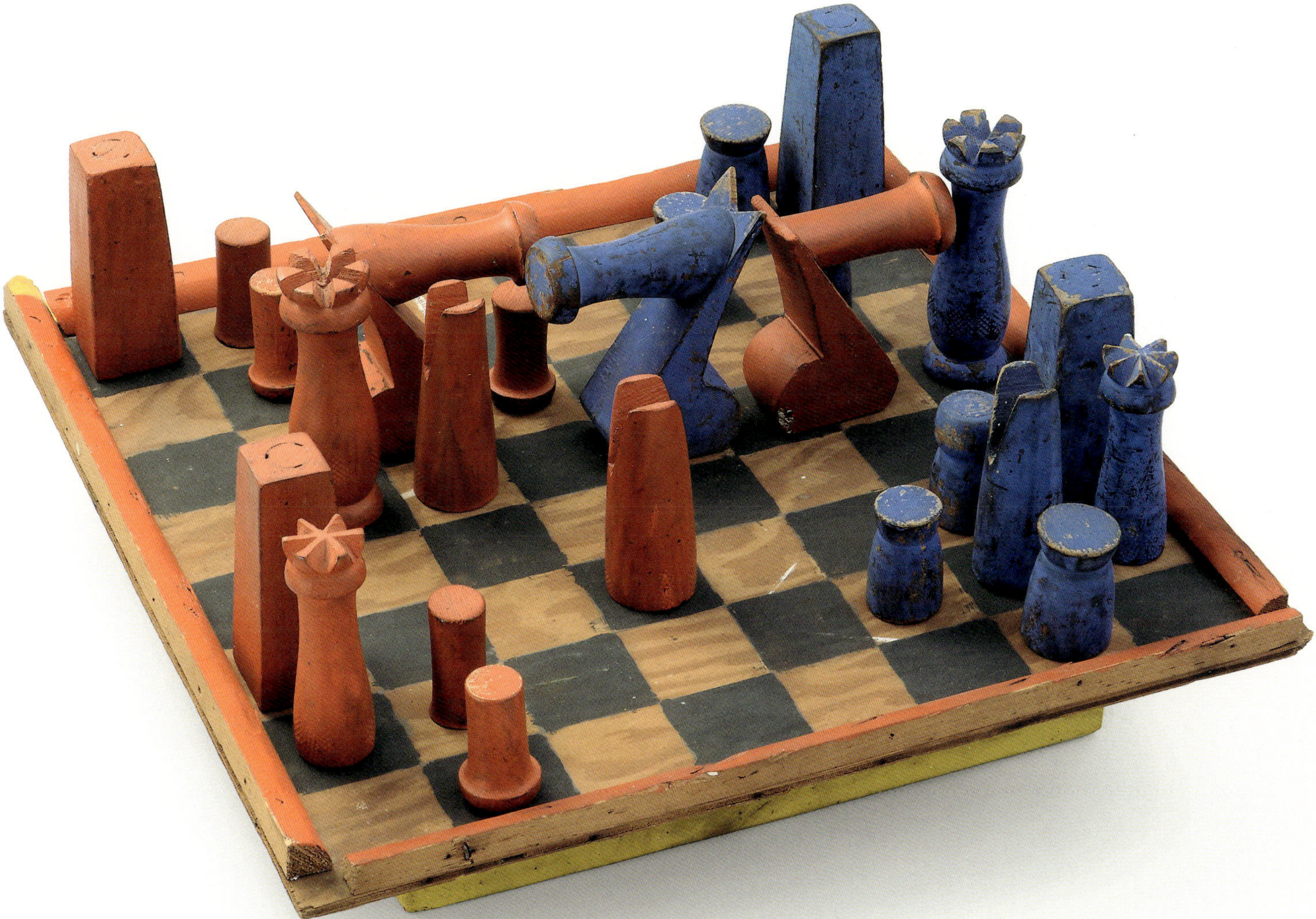

82 Schachspiel, 1944, Holz, Farbe; Spielbrett: 45,7 × 45,7 cm / Chess set, 1944, wood, paint; board: 18 × 18 in., Calder Foundation, New York. Mary Calder Rower Bequest, 2011

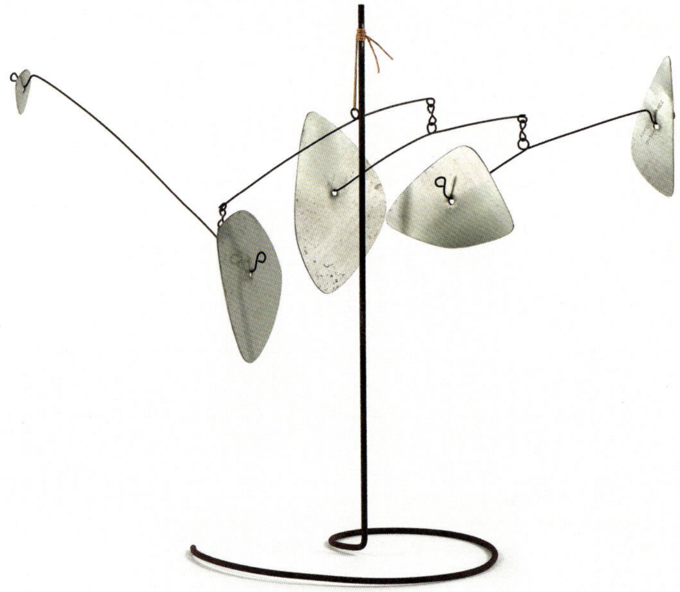

83 *Untitled*, um 1942, Blech, Draht, Schnur, 29,2 × 33 × 17,8 cm / ca. 1942, sheet metal, wire, string, 11½ × 13 × 7 in., Calder Foundation, New York

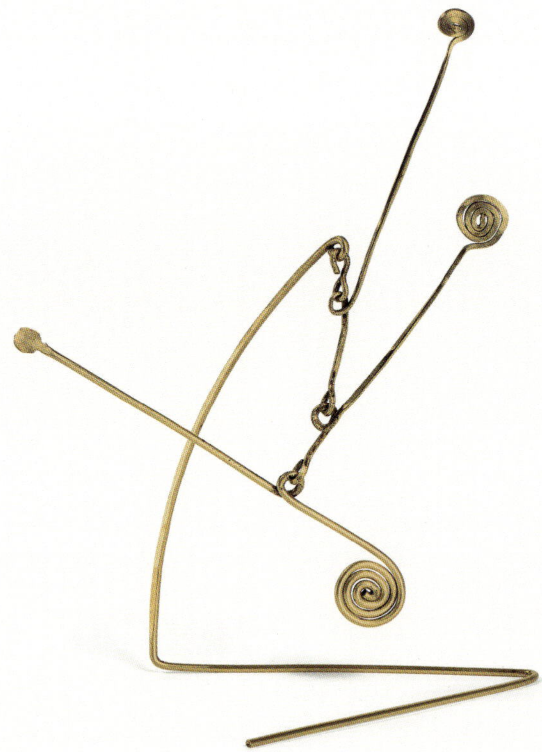

84 *Untitled*, um 1942, Messingdraht, 17,5 × 13,3 × 7,6 cm / ca. 1942, brass wire, 6⅞ × 5¼ × 3 in., Calder Foundation, New York

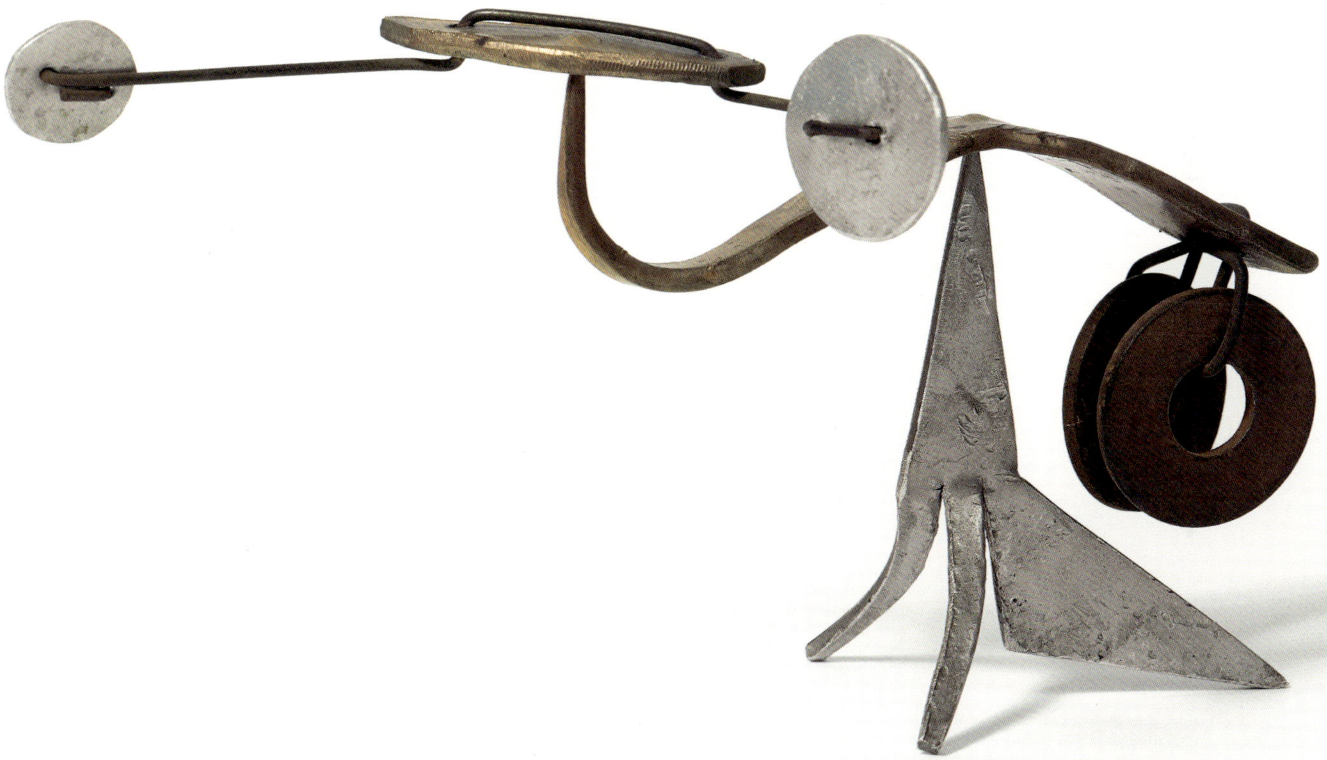

85 *Untitled*, um 1970, Blech, Messing, Unterlegscheiben, Draht, 10,2 × 19 × 6,4 cm / ca. 1970, sheet metal, brass, washers, wire, 4 × 7 ½ × 2 ½ in., Calder Foundation, New York

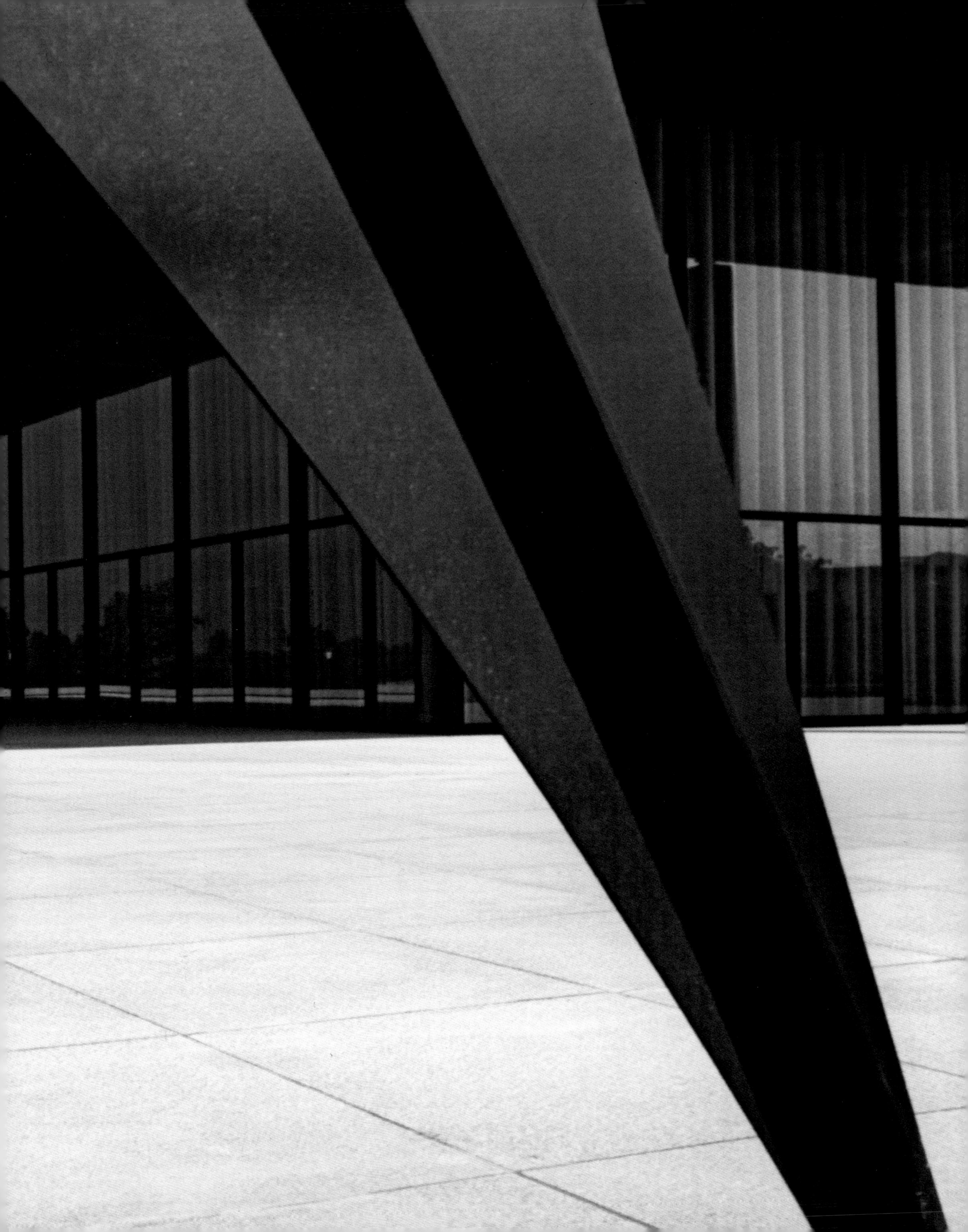

Têtes et queue

Maike Steinkamp

Seit Juni 1968 steht *Têtes et queue* (1965) auf der Terrasse der Neuen Nationalgalerie (Abb. 1). Rund zwei Monate später, am 15. September, wurde das Haus feierlich eröffnet. Die Plastik besteht aus sechs vertikal aufgestellten, sich auffächernden, schwarz lackierten Stahlplatten. Ihre aufstrebenden, geschwungenen und gleichsam architektonisch wirkenden Glieder werden an den oberen Enden von runden Flächen abgeschlossen. Nur eine Platte ragt schweifförmig mit einer schmalen, abgerundeten Spitze nach oben, was auch den Titel erklärt, den Alexander Calder dem Werk in Anlehnung an die an Köpfe und einen Schwanz erinnernden Formen nach Fertigstellung gab. Die abstrakte Konstruktion weckt bei manchen Betrachterinnen und Betrachtern – nicht zuletzt durch eben diesen Schwanz und die runden Abschlüsse – Assoziationen an ein mehrköpfiges Fabeltier.

Stephan Waetzoldt, der damalige Generaldirektor der Staatlichen Museen zu Berlin, beschrieb die Skulptur als das „große, freundliche Tier aus dem Stahl, der unser technisches Zeitalter prägt“, und rechnete das Werk mit dem „vielfältigen Spiel seiner scharf gespannten Konturen und der gelösten Eleganz des Standes“ uneingeschränkt zu den großen und bleibenden Gestaltungen der Gegenwart.[1] Für ihn war Calder einer der wenigen (wenn nicht der einzige) Bildhauer, dem eine „überzeugende künstlerische Interpretation des technisch bestimmten Lebensgefühls unserer Zeit“ gelungen war.[2]

Diese Betrachtung Waetzoldts kann unter anderem auf den Produktionsprozess bezogen werden, den Calder vor allem für seine großformatigen Stabiles wählte. Seit Anfang der 1960er-Jahre ließ er seine monumentalen Arbeiten nicht nur in den USA, sondern

86 *Têtes et queue* (1965), Detail, 1968

gleichermaßen in dem Stahlwerk Biémont im französischen Tours herstellen. Als Grundlage dienten vom Künstler gefertigte Modelle, welche die Metallbauer dann in die gewünschte Größe übertrugen. Calder begleitete diese Arbeitsschritte stets eng, um die Kontur der Formen zu verfeinern und gegebenenfalls Konstruktionselemente wie Rippen und Platten anzupassen oder hinzuzufügen (Abb. 95).

Seit Anfang der 1950er-Jahre war Calder mit seinen Stabiles zunehmend in den öffentlichen Raum vorgedrungen. Seine organisch-abstrakten oder tektonischen Formen nahmen urbane Plätze ein und ermöglichten nicht zuletzt durch ihre Mehransichtigkeit immer neue Seh- und Raumerfahrungen. Internationale Aufträge, Preise und Ausstellungsbeteiligungen trugen weiter zur Popularität des Bildhauers bei. Auch in Westdeutschland war er in zahlreichen Ausstellungen präsent, teilweise unterstützt von staatlichen Institutionen, die in der Förderung US-amerikanischer Kunst und der ihr zugesprochenen künstlerischen Autonomie einen Akt der Internationalisierung und Demokratisierung sahen.[3] So war Calder im September 1952 unter anderem vom Auswärtigen Amt eingeladen worden, eine Reise durch die Bundesrepublik zu unternehmen. Zur gleichen Zeit fand eine von der Galerie Parnass in Wuppertal organisierte Schau seiner Mobiles statt, die zwei Jahre durchs Land tourte und 1953 auch in der West-Berliner Galerie Springer zu sehen war.[4] In den Folgejahren reüssierte der Künstler gleich mehrfach auf der documenta in Kassel: 1955, 1959 und vor allem 1964, als er mit seinen großformatigen Stabiles *Les Triangles* (1963), *Les Trois Ailes* (1963), *Le Faucon* (1963) und *Tamanoir* (1963) hervorstach (Abb. 87). Bereits vor dem Zweiten Weltkrieg hatte Calder jedoch schon seinen ersten Auftritt in Deutschland absolviert. 1929 präsentierte er in der Berliner Galerie Neumann-Nierendorf in einer Einzelausstellung seine neu entwickelten Drahtplastiken. Der Kunstkritiker Adolf Behne zeigte sich damals begeistert von der Schau und bewunderte, wie Calder mit einem „Minimum“ an Material erstaunliche Effekte „hext“. Aus seiner Sicht bewies der Künstler damit großes Talent zur Gestaltung und „Ausbeutung der Luft“,[5] Fähigkeiten, die auch für seine späteren Arbeiten zentral werden sollten.

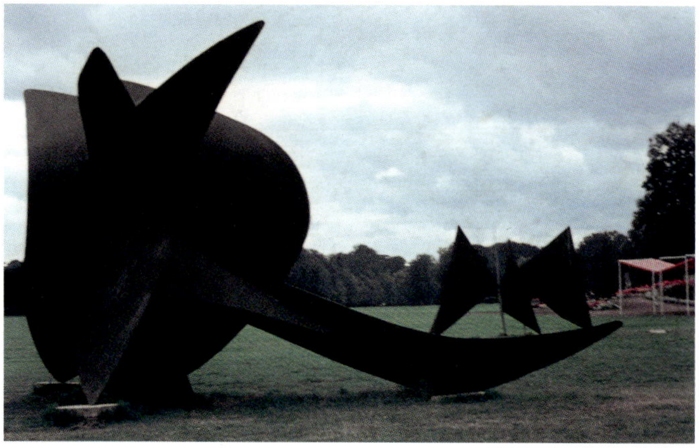

87 Calders Stabiles *Le Faucon* (1963) und *Les Triangles* (1963) auf der documenta 3 / Calder's stabiles *Le Faucon* (1963) and *Les Triangles* (1963) at documenta 3, Kassel, 1964

Sowohl 1929 als auch 1952 reiste Calder nach Berlin. Ein letztes Mal kehrte er im Mai 1967 anlässlich einer Retrospektive seiner Arbeiten in der West-Berliner Akademie der Künste in die geteilte Stadt zurück (Abb. 89, 91). Stephan Waetzoldt hielt die Eröffnungsrede.

Bereits zu diesem Zeitpunkt hatte Waetzoldt sich mit Werner Haftmann, dem frisch gekürten Direktor der im

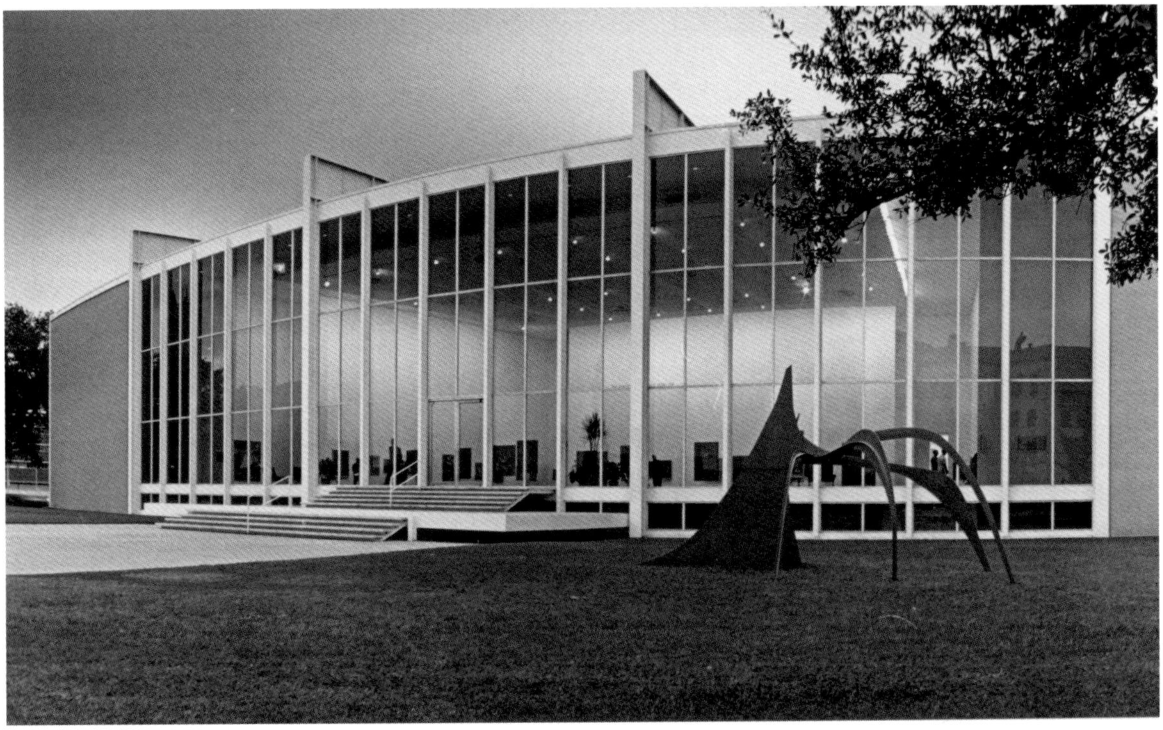

88 *The Crab* (1962) vor dem Anbau des Museum of Fine Arts, Houston / *The Crab* (1962) in front of the expansion of The Museum of Fine Arts, Houston

Bau befindlichen Neuen Nationalgalerie, über den Ankauf von *Têtes et queue* verständigt.[6] Haftmann hatte das schwarze Stabile 1965 auf einer großen Retrospektive Calders im Musée National d'Art Moderne in Paris gesehen und war augenblicklich davon eingenommen. Aufgestellt in den gewaltigen Innenräumen des Palais de Tokyo entfaltete die Skulptur zusammen mit weiteren Stabiles eine eindrückliche Präsenz (Abb. 94).

Auch Waetzoldt war begeistert. Die kraftvolle Monumentalskulptur sollte ihren Platz auf der granitbedeckten Terrasse des Neubaus erhalten, wo sie von allen Seiten weithin sichtbar sein würde und in ihrer vertikalen Dynamik in einen spannungsreichen Dialog mit der minimalistischen Architektur treten konnte. An den Springer Verlag, den man als Sponsor für den Ankauf zu gewinnen hoffte, schrieb Waetzoldt im Oktober 1966: „Sie [die Skulptur] wird dort im Kontrast zu den gelagerten stereometrischen Formen der Stahl-Glas-Konstruktion von Mies van der Rohe zu besonderer Wirkung gelangen. Dies ist auch die Meinung von Mies selbst, mit dem zusammen wir die Aufstellung des Bildwerkes von Calder am maßstabsgetreuen Modell untersucht haben."[7]

In der Tat scheint Mies das Zusammenspiel von Calders großformatigen Stabiles mit seiner Architektur gefallen zu haben. Seinem Entwurf für die Neue Nationalgalerie hatte er ein Foto von seinem 1958 vollendeten Anbau für das Museum of Fine Arts in Houston beigefügt, vor dem sich bereits ein Stabile von Calder befand, *The Crab* (1962, Abb. 88).[8]

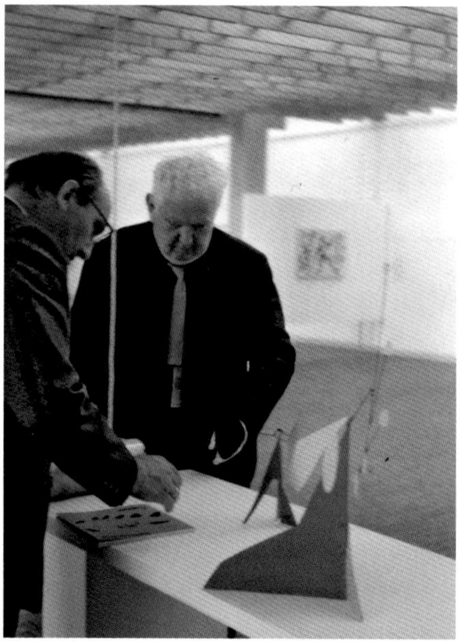

89 Calder während des Aufbaus seiner Retrospektive in der Akademie der Künste / Calder during the installation of his retrospective at the Akademie der Künste, Berlin (West), 1967

Waetzoldt konnte die Axel Springer Stiftung mit seiner Argumentation überzeugen. Sie erwarb *Têtes et queue* und übergab die Skulptur dem Generaldirektor der Staatlichen Museen offiziell am 17. Mai 1967. Es sollte jedoch noch einige Zeit dauern, bis sie ihren endgültigen Platz auf der Terrasse der Neuen Nationalgalerie einnehmen konnte. Erst am 27. Juni 1968 wurde sie mit großer medialer Begleitung dort installiert, nachdem sie knapp anderthalb Jahre vor dem Verlagshaus des Springer-Konzerns gestanden hatte (Abb. 92).[9] Mit ihrer Aufstellung auf der Terrasse wurde *Têtes et queue* zum Wahrzeichen der Neuen Nationalgalerie. Schon zur Eröffnung des Hauses wurde mit dem Werk geworben (Abb. 90, 93). Mit ihrer monumentalen Struktur, die „frei ist von Rhetorik sowie von aufgeblasenem oder falschem Pathos", wie der Kritiker John Russell 1965 über die Arbeiten Calders geschrieben hatte,[10] repräsentierte *Têtes et queue* ebenso wie der Bau der Neuen Nationalgalerie selbst mit seinem Standort nahe dem Potsdamer Platz und der Grenze zu Ost-Berlin eine damals als freiheitlich und demokratisch empfundene westliche Moderne. Zusammen mit der Bronze *Bogenschütze* (1964) des Briten Henry Moore wurde *Têtes et queue* zu einem Aushängeschild der von Werner Haftmann entwickelten Idee einer im Kontext des Kalten Krieges vor allem auf Westeuropa und die USA ausgerichteten „Weltgalerie"[11], die in dem neuen Museumsgebäude ihren adäquaten Platz erhalten sollte.

1 Rede von Stephan Waetzoldt anlässlich der Eröffnung einer Ausstellung von Werken des 19. Jahrhunderts der Nationalgalerie im Axel Springer Haus, zit. nach: *Morgenpost*, 18.11.1966.

2 Brief von Stephan Waetzoldt an Hans Wallenberg, Axel Springer Verlag, 14.10.1966, Neue Nationalgalerie, Archiv, Bildakte Calder.

3 Alex J. Taylor: „Unstable Motives. Propaganda, Politics, and the Late Work of Alexander Calder", in: *American Art*, 26, Nr. 1, Frühjahr 2012, S. 24–47, hier 29f.

4 Vgl. Alexander Calder: *Calder: An Autobiography with Pictures*, hg. von Jean Davidson, New York 1966, S. 211.

5 Adolf Behne: „Plastik als Luftakt: Alexander Calder in der Galerie Neumann-Nierendorf", in: *Welt am Abend*, 11.4.1929.

6 Vgl. Robert Osborn: „Calder's International Monuments", in: *Art in America*, 57, Nr. 2, März/April 1969, S. 32–49, Abb. S. 42.

7 Brief Waetzoldt an Wallenberg (wie Anm. 2).

8 Ich danke Uta Caspary für den Hinweis auf das Foto (HdZ 12386, 26) in Mies van der Rohes Präsentationsmappe, Staatliche Museen zu Berlin, Kunstbibliothek, R 119/Kasten 3603c.

9 Mein Dank geht an Dipl. Rest. Anke Klusmeier, die mir Einblick gab in ihre gründlichen Recherchen zur Entstehung, Erwerbung und Aufstellung von *Têtes et queue* anlässlich ihrer Restaurierung des Werkes 2015–2020.

10 John Russell: „Russia to the Louvre", in: *Sunday Times*, 26.9.1965, zit. in Jed Perl: *Calder. The Conquest of Space. The Later Years, 1940–1976*, New York 2020, S. 403.

11 Vgl. Christina Thomson: „Neubau und Fusion. Der Weg zur Neuen Nationalgalerie und den Vereinigten Kunstsammlungen 1961 bis 1968", in: Christina Thomson und Petra Winters (Hg.): *Die Galerie des 20. Jahrhunderts in Berlin 1945–1968. Der Weg zur Neuen Nationalgalerie*, Berlin 2015, S. 114–148, hier S. 135.

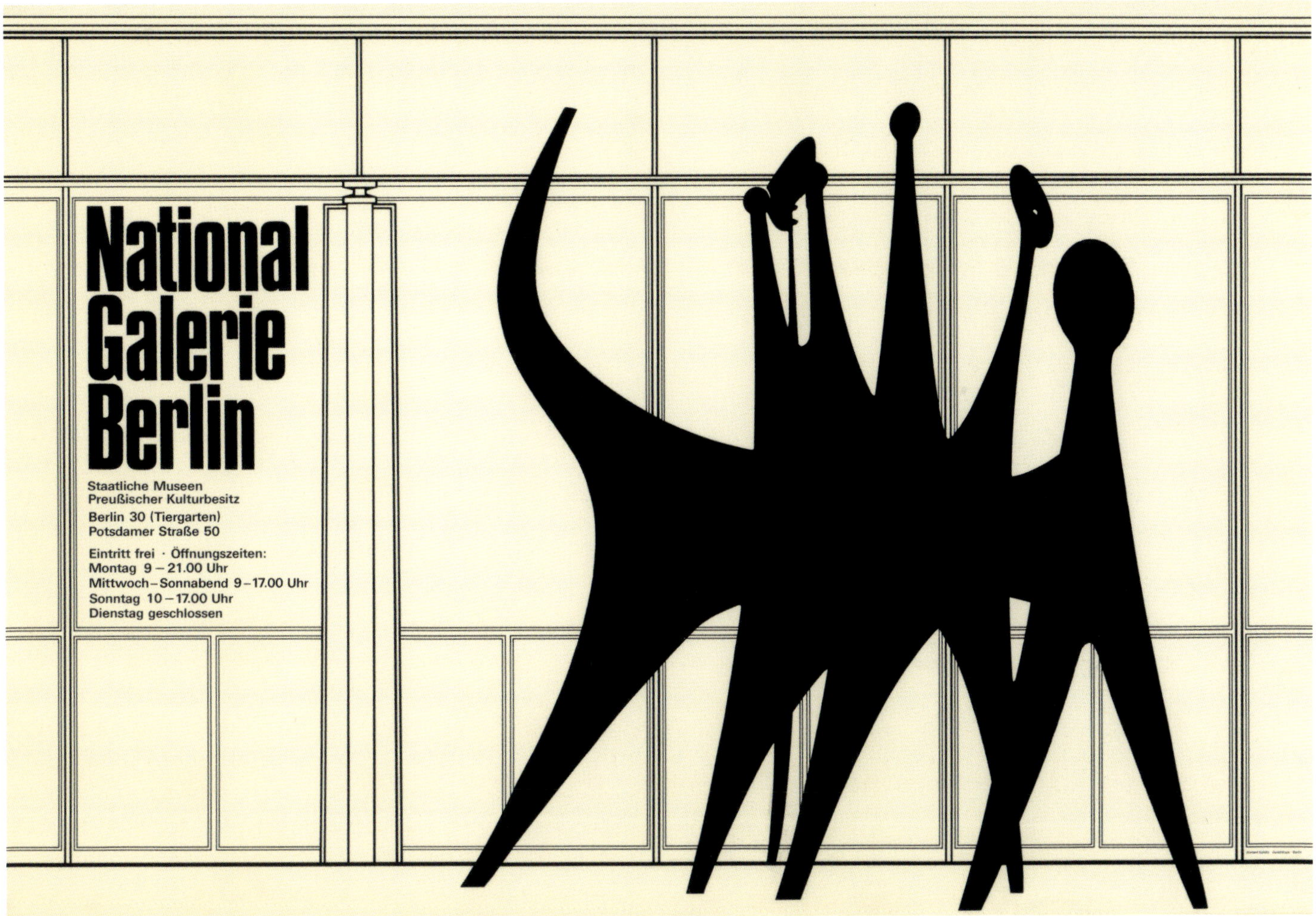

90 Wieland Schütz, Plakat der Neuen Nationalgalerie mit *Têtes et queue*, 1970, 59,4 × 84 cm / poster for the Neue Nationalgalerie with *Têtes et queue*, 1970, 23 2/8 × 33 1/8 in., Staatliche Museen zu Berlin, Kunstbibliothek

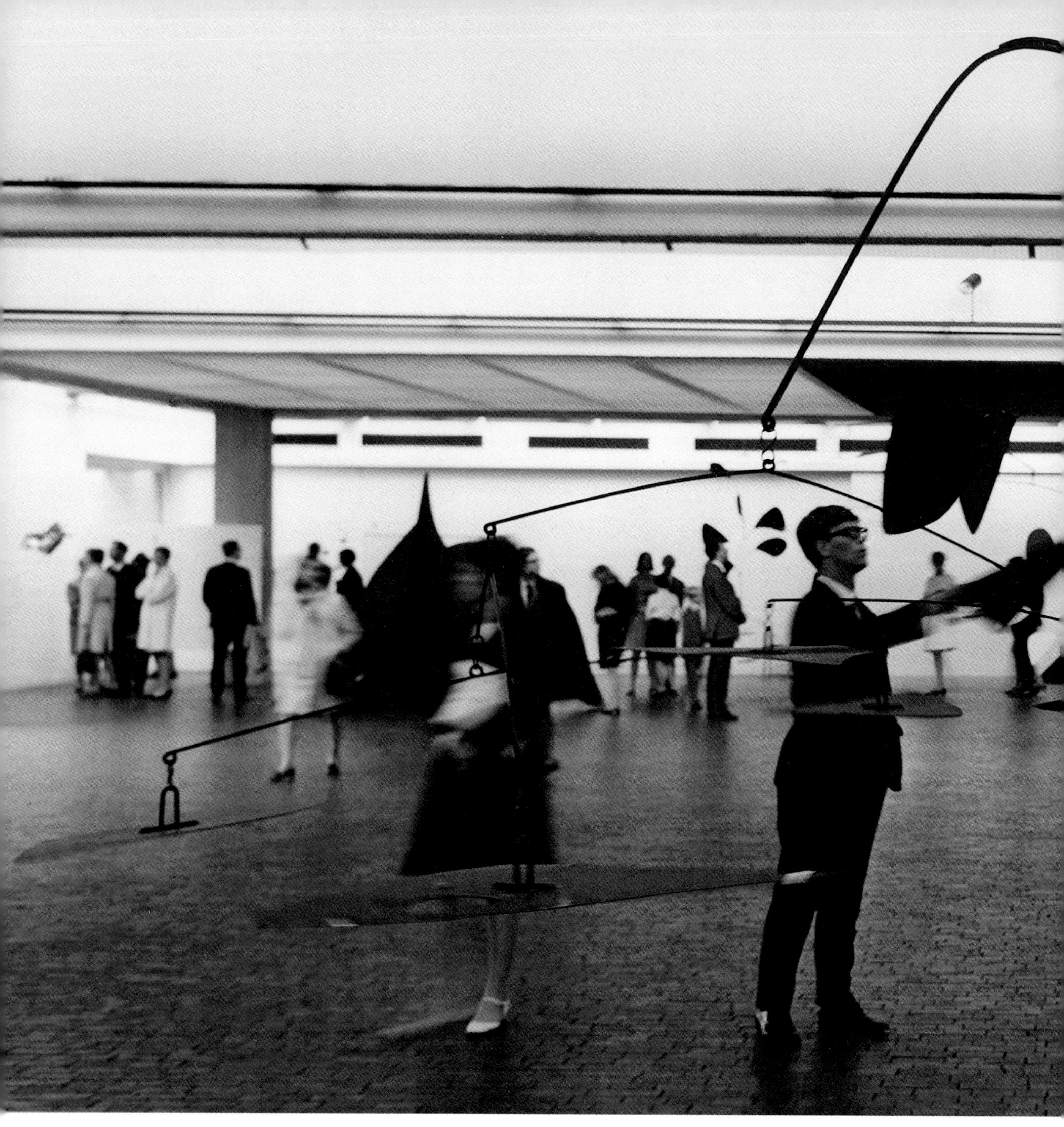

91 Ausstellungsansicht / Installation view, *Alexander Calder*, Akademie der Künste, Berlin (West), 1967

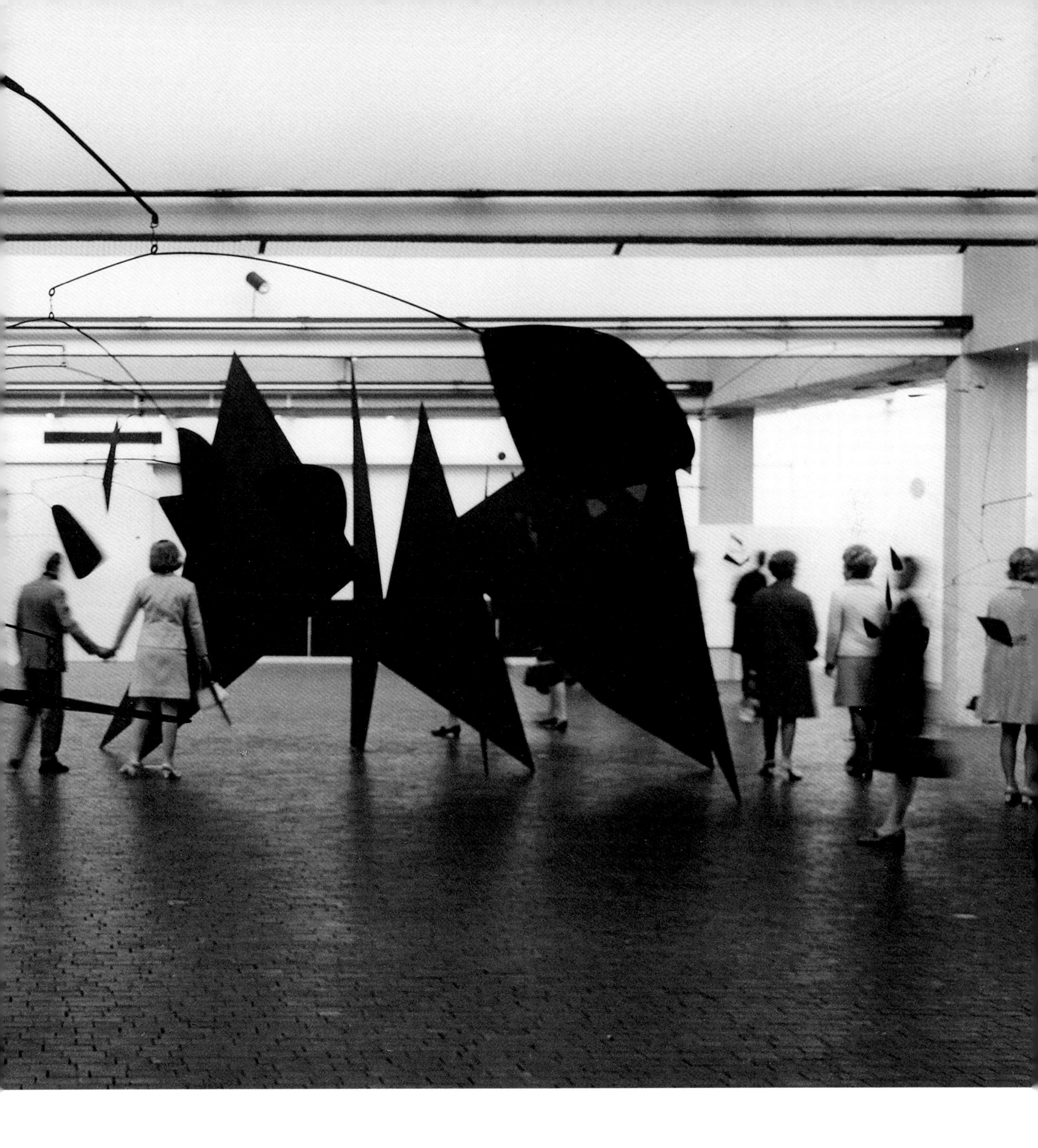

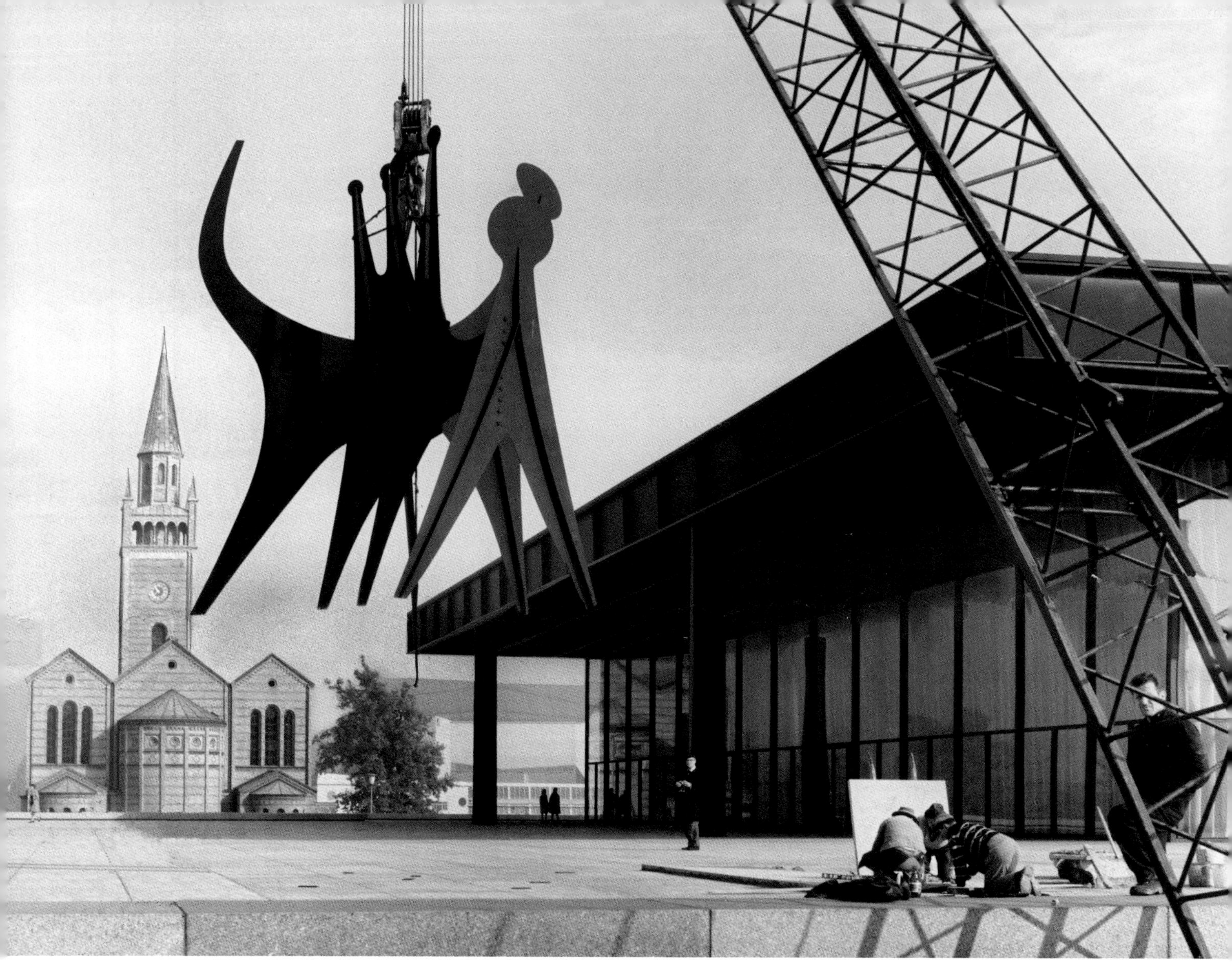

92 Aufbau von *Têtes et queue* auf der Terrasse der Neuen Nationalgalerie / Installation of *Têtes et queue* on the terrace of the Neue Nationalgalerie, 1968

Maike Steinkamp

Têtes et queue

Têtes et queue (1965) has stood on the Neue Nationalgalerie's terrace since June 1968 (fig. 1). The museum's opening ceremonies took place some two months later, on September 15. The sculpture consists of six black, vertically oriented steel plates that fan out. Its soaring, curved elements simultaneously appear architectonic and culminate in round surfaces. A single plate with a small, rounded tip projects upward, which also helps explain the sculpture's title, given after the fact of creation based on a vague description of forms, such as heads and a tail. The abstract construction evokes to some a multiheaded mythical creature, especially with this tail and the circular forms at the end of each limb.

Stephan Waetzoldt, then the general director of the Staatliche Museen zu Berlin, described the sculpture as the "large, friendly steel animal that characterizes our technological age," and unreservedly counted the work, with "its multifaceted play of sharply taut contours and the relaxed elegance of its stance," among the great and everlasting designs of the present age.[1] For him, Alexander Calder was one of the few sculptors—if not the only one—who successfully created a "convincing artistic interpretation of the technologically driven attitude toward life in our time."[2]

Waetzoldt's observation relates, among other things, to the mode of production that Calder chose for his large-scale sculptures. Since the early 1960s, he had several of his monumental works fabricated not only in the US but also at the Biémont iron foundry in Tours, France, where metalworkers transposed models by the artist into the desired size. Calder always followed each step of the process closely, in order to refine the shape profiles and to incorporate or add structural elements, such as ribs or plates, when necessary (fig. 95).

Since the early 1950s, Calder's stabiles had become increasingly prominent in public spaces. His organic abstract or tectonic forms occupied urban squares and, particularly because they could be viewed from multiple angles, offered ever-new visual and spatial experiences. The artist's international commissions, prizes, and participation in exhibitions further contributed to his popularity. He also showed his work in numerous exhibitions in West Germany, sometimes with the backing of state institutions that considered supporting American art and the artistic autonomy granted to it as an act of internationalization and democratization.[3] Against this backdrop, the German Federal Foreign Office invited Calder to tour the nation. At that time, an exhibition of his mobiles organized by the Galerie Parnass in Wuppertal was on view, which traveled throughout the country for two years; in 1953 it was shown at the Galerie Springer in West Berlin.[4] In the following years, the artist had several successes at documenta in Kassel: in 1955, 1959, and especially in 1964, when his large-scale stabiles *Les Triangles* (1963), *Les Trois Ailes* (1963), *Le Faucon* (1963), and *Tamanoir* (1963) received prominent attention (fig. 87). Yet Calder had already made his first appearance in Germany before World War II. In 1929 he had a solo exhibition of his then-new wire sculptures at the Galerie Neumann-Nierendorf in Berlin. At the time, the art critic Adolf Behne was enthusiastic about the show and praised how Calder "conjured" striking effects with a "minimum" of material. As he saw it, the artist thus demonstrated his talent for giving form to and "exploiting air,"[5] abilities that would also be central to his later works.

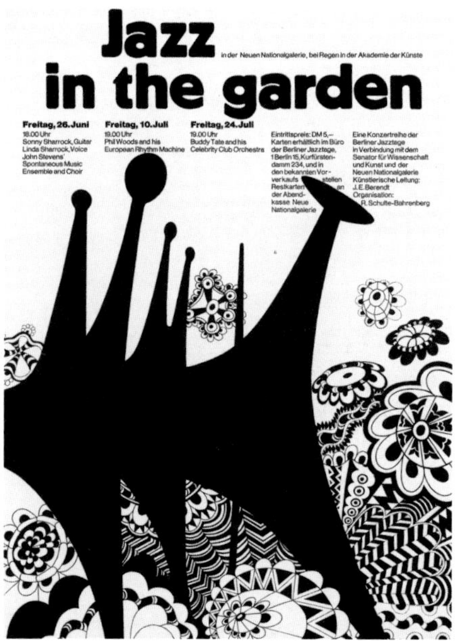

93 *Jazz in the Garden*, 1969, Plakat, 84 × 59,4 cm / poster, 33⅛ × 23⅜ in., Staatliche Museen zu Berlin, Kunstbibliothek

Calder traveled to Berlin in 1929 and 1952. In May 1967 he returned to the divided city one last time for a retrospective of his work at the Akademie der Künste in West Berlin (figs. 89, 91), for which Stephan Waetzoldt delivered the opening address.

By this time, Waetzoldt had already reached an agreement with Werner Haftmann, the newly appointed director of the Neue Nationalgalerie, about the acquisition of *Têtes et queue*.[6] Haftmann had seen the black stabile at a large Calder retrospective at the Musée National d'Art Moderne in Paris in 1965 and was immediately taken by it. Installed in the vast interiors of the Palais de Tokyo, the sculpture, together with other stabiles, had a striking presence (fig. 94).

Waetzoldt was also enthusiastic. The powerful monumental sculpture was to be placed on the granite-paved terrace of the new building, where it would be visible from all sides and its dynamic verticality could enter into an exciting dialogue with the minimalist architecture. In October 1966, Waetzoldt wrote to the Springer Verlag, a publishing house he hoped to gain as a sponsor for the acquisition: "It [the sculpture] will have a special effect there in contrast to the stereometric forms of [Ludwig] Mies van der Rohe's steel and glass construction. This is also the opinion of Mies himself, with whom we studied the placement of Calder's sculpture using a scale model."[7]

Indeed, Mies seems to have liked the interplay between Calder's large-format stabiles and his own architecture. Along with his design for the Neue Nationalgalerie, the architect had included a photograph of his addition to the Museum of Fine Arts, Houston, which was completed in 1958 and already had a stabile by Calder, *The Crab* (1962; fig. 88), on display outside.[8]

Waetzoldt's argument won over the Axel Springer Stiftung, and the foundation acquired *Têtes et queue*, officially transferring the sculpture to the general director of the Staatliche Museen on May 17, 1967. It would be some time, however, before the sculpture would move to its final location, on the Neue Nationalgalerie's terrace. On June 27, 1968, to great media fanfare, it was installed there, after having stood in front of the Springer publishing house for almost a year and a half (fig. 92).[9]

After it was placed on the terrace, *Têtes et queue* became an icon of the Neue Nationalgalerie. As early as the building's opening, the sculpture was

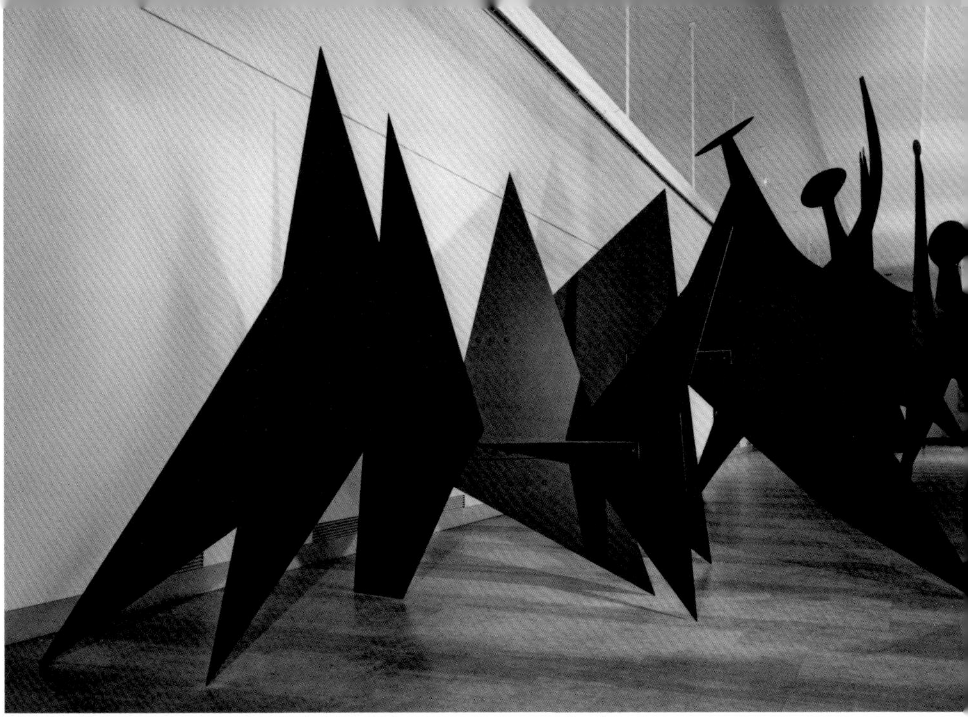

94 *Les Triangles* und *Têtes et queue* in der Ausstellung / *Les Triangles* and *Têtes et queue* at the exhibition *Calder*, Musée National d'Art Moderne, Paris, 1965

used in advertisements for the museum (figs. 90, 93). With a monumental structure that "is free from rhetoric, inflation or false pathos," as the critic John Russell wrote of Calder's work in 1965,[10] *Têtes et queue*, like the building of the Neue Nationalgalerie, itself located near Potsdamer Platz on the border to East Berlin, represented a form of western modernism perceived at the time as liberal and democratic. *Têtes et queue*—together with the bronze *Archer* (1964) by British artist Henry Moore—became a figurehead for Werner Haftmann's Cold War concept of a "world gallery"[11] largely oriented on Western Europe and the United States, which was to be given its rightful place in the new museum building.

1 Speech by Stephan Waetzoldt at the opening of an exhibition of nineteenth-century works from the Nationalgalerie at the Axel Springer Haus, quoted from *Morgenpost*, November 11, 1966.

2 Stephan Waetzoldt to Hans Wallenberg, Axel Springer Verlag, October 14, 1966, Calder image file, archive, Neue Nationalgalerie.

3 Alex J. Taylor, "Unstable Motives: Propaganda, Politics, and the Late Work of Alexander Calder," *American Art* 26, no. 1 (Spring 2012), pp. 24–47, here pp. 29–30.

4 See Alexander Calder, *Calder: An Autobiography with Pictures*, ed. Jean Davidson (New York, 1966), p. 211.

5 Adolf Behne, "Plastik als Luftakt: Alexander Calder in der Galerie Neumann-Nierendorf," *Welt am Abend*, April 11, 1929. Translated into English as "Sculpture as Aerial Act: Alexander Calder at the Galerie Neumann-Nierendorf," https://calder.org/bibliography/welt-am-abend-1929/ (accessed May 19, 2021).

6 See Robert Osborn, "Calder's International Monuments," *Art in America* 57, no. 2 (March/April 1969), pp. 32–49, here fig. p. 42.

7 Waetzoldt 1966 (see note 2).

8 I thank Uta Caspary for the reference to the photo (HdZ 12386, 26) in Mies van der Rohe's portfolio, Staatliche Museen zu Berlin, Kunstbibliothek, R 119/Kasten 3603c.

9 My thanks to the conservator Anke Klusmeier, who offered insight into her thorough research on the origin, acquisition, and installation of *Têtes et queue* conducted while restoring the work from 2015 to 2020.

10 John Russell, "Russia to the Louvre," *The Sunday Times*, September 26, 1965, quoted from Jed Perl, *Calder: The Conquest of Space: The Later Years: 1940–1976* (New York, 2020), p. 403.

11 See Christina Thomson, "Neubau und Fusion: Der Weg zur Neuen Nationalgalerie und den Vereinigten Kunstsammlungen 1961 bis 1968," in *Die Galerie des 20. Jahrhunderts in Berlin 1945–1968: Der Weg zur Neuen Nationalgalerie*, ed. Christina Thomson and Petra Winters (Berlin, 2015), pp. 114–48, here p. 135.

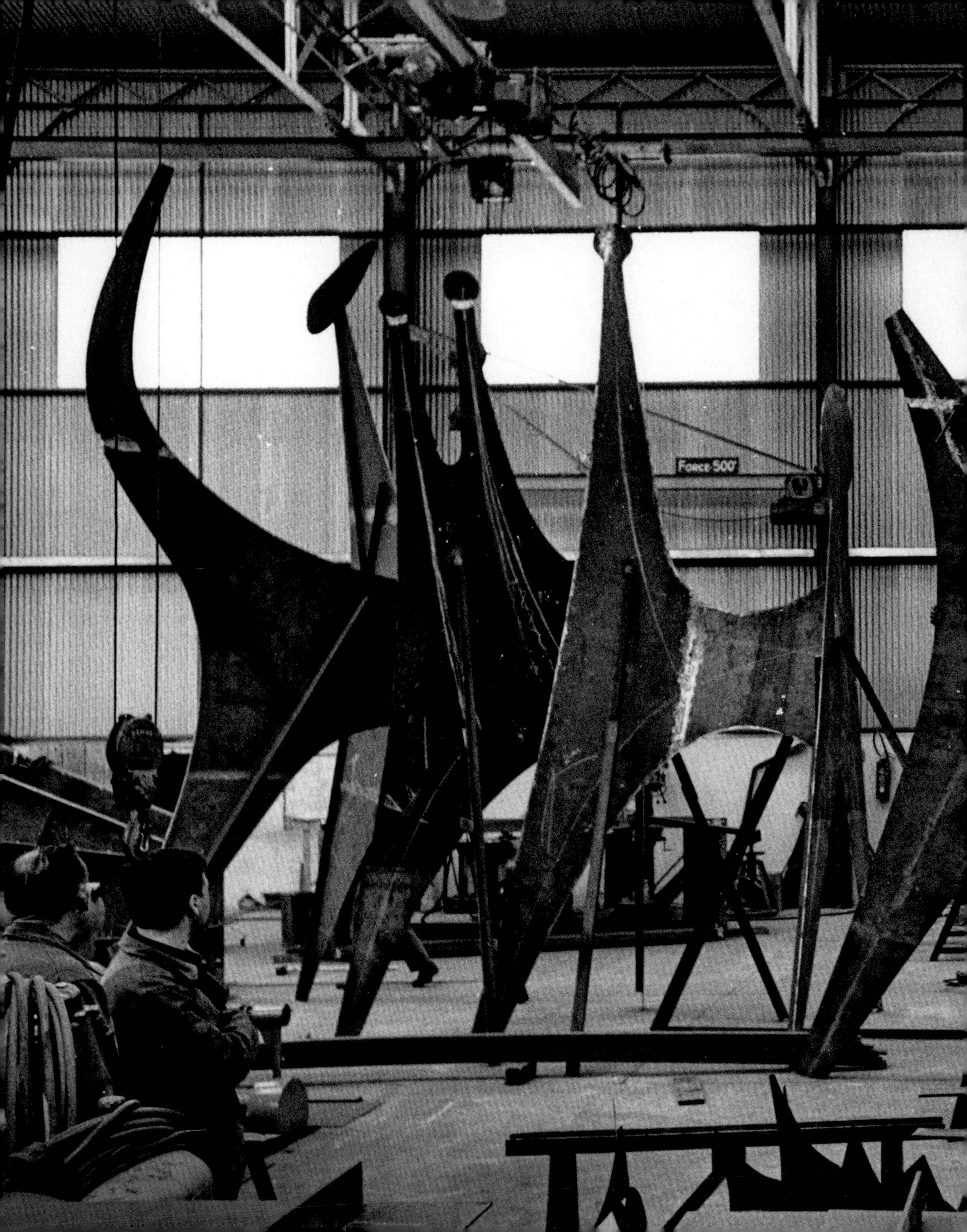

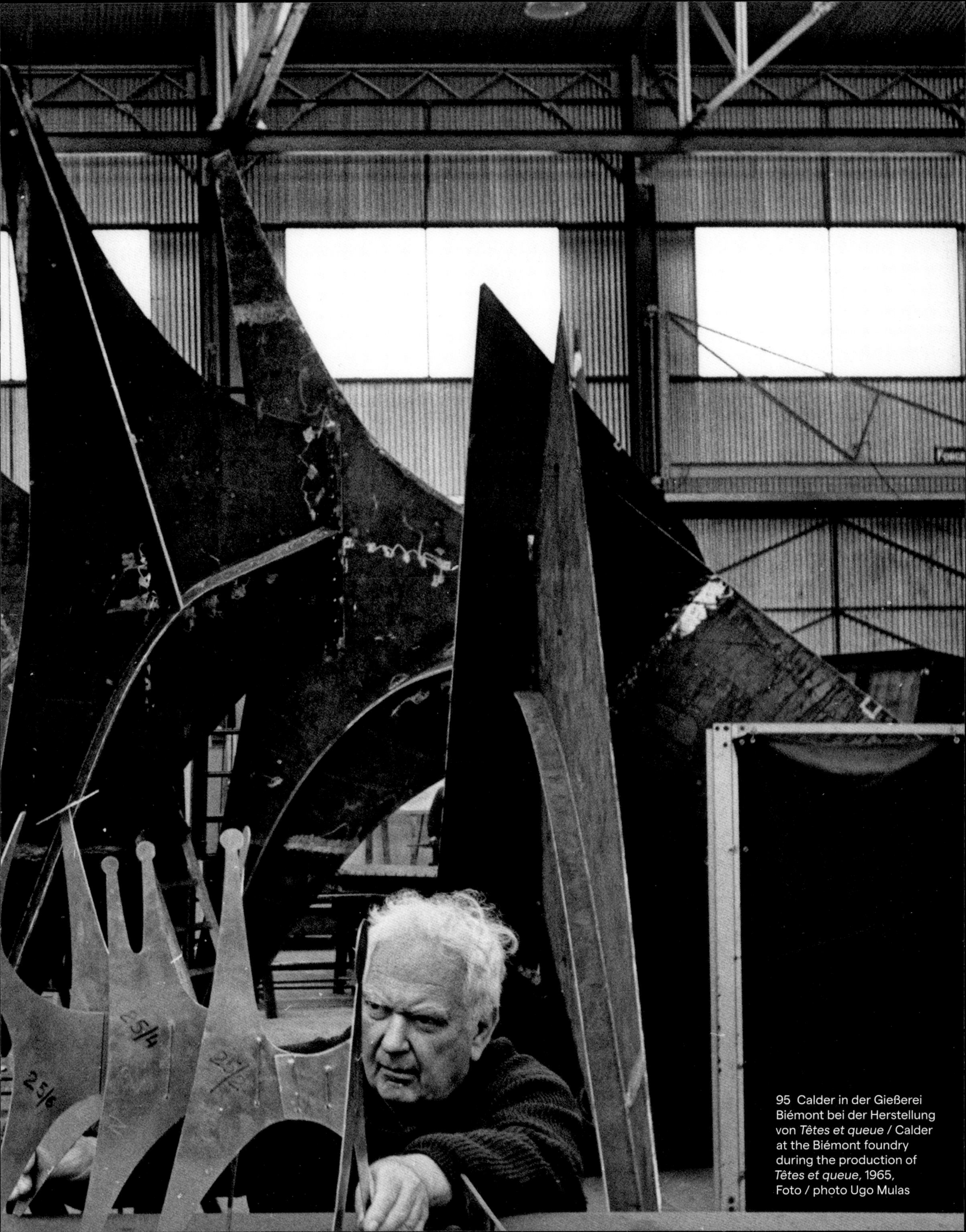

95 Calder in der Gießerei Biémont bei der Herstellung von *Têtes et queue* / Calder at the Biémont foundry during the production of *Têtes et queue*, 1965, Foto / photo Ugo Mulas

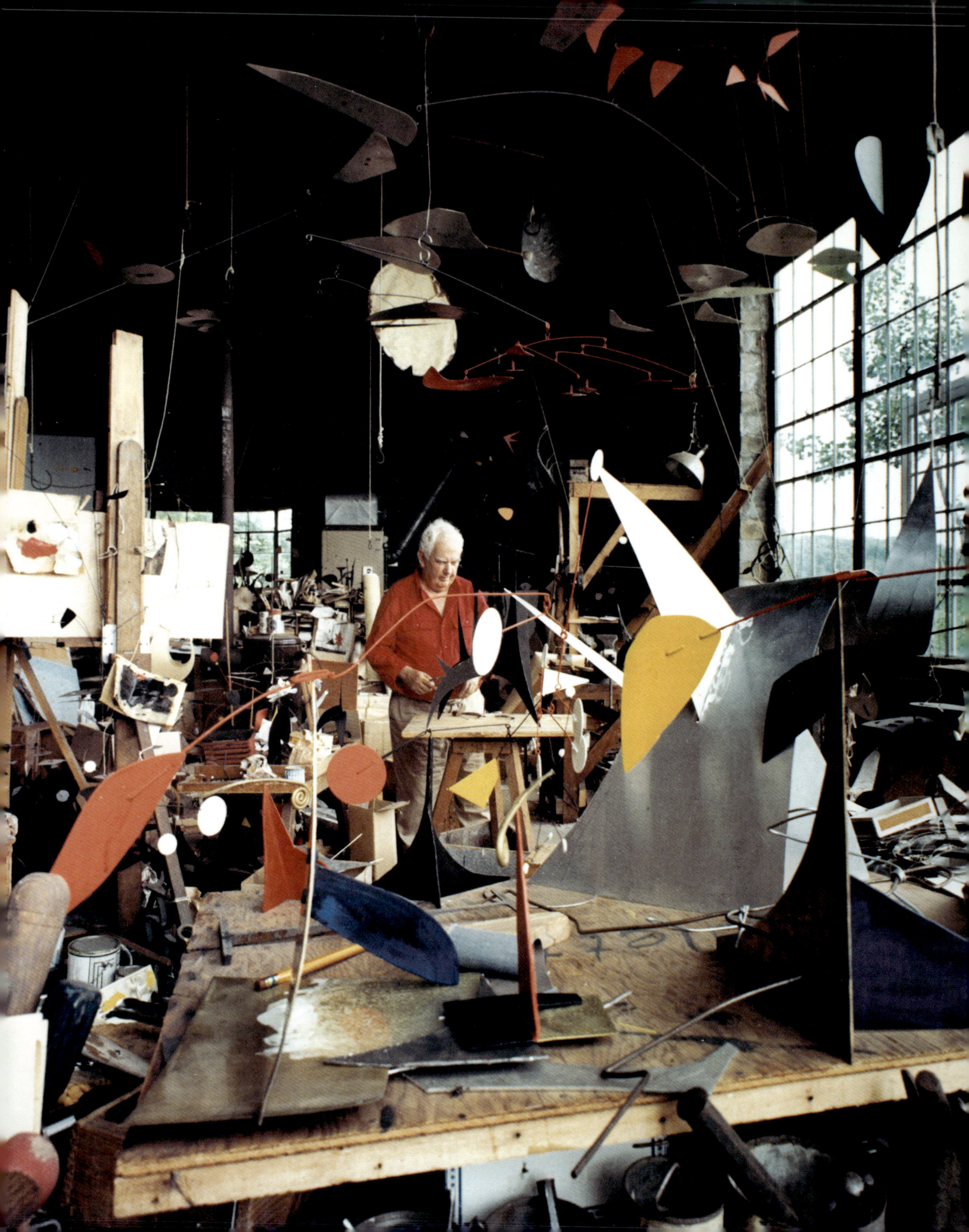

Biografie Alexander Calder

1898, Lawnton, PA – 1976, New York, NY

Alexander Calder kam 1898 als Sohn eines Künstlerehepaares zur Welt. Sein Vater war Bildhauer, seine Mutter Malerin. 1906, als die Familie im kalifornischen Pasadena mitten in der florierenden Arts-and-Crafts-Bewegung lebte, begann Alexander, in einer eigenen kleinen Werkstatt Spielzeug und Schmuck für die Puppen seiner Schwester zu gestalten. Weihnachten 1909 schenkte Calder seinen Eltern zwei seiner frühesten Skulpturen, einen Hund und eine Ente aus gebogenem Messingblech (Abb. 98). Nach dem Abschluss der Highschool studierte er am Stevens Institute of Technology in Hoboken, New Jersey, Maschinenbau und machte dort 1919 sein Diplom. Es folgte eine mehrjährige Tätigkeit bei verschiedenen Firmen, unter anderem als Hydraulik- und als Automobilingenieur. 1923 zog Calder nach New York und besuchte dort Kunstkurse der Art Students League. Die Gemälde, die während dieser Zeit entstanden, lehnten sich eng an die Ästhetik der Ashcan School an, die im frühen 20. Jahrhundert für realistische New Yorker Straßenszenen bekannt war. Zeitgleich illustrierte er für die *National Police Gazette* Sportereignisse und Vorstellungen des Ringling Bros. and Barnum & Bailey Circus. Schon in dieser Phase fertigte er Skulpturen und andere Objekte an, oftmals aus Blech und Draht.

1926 übersiedelte Calder nach Paris. Kurz darauf entstand aus Draht und einer Vielzahl von vorgefundenen Materialien der *Cirque Calder* (1926–1931, Abb. 12). Die erste „Vorstellung" fand in Paris vor einem Publikum aus Freunden und Kollegen statt, und schon bald präsentierte Calder seinen Zirkus mit großem Erfolg sowohl dort als auch in New York. Die Veranstaltungen dauerten nicht selten rund zwei Stunden und waren sehr aufwendig gestaltet. Der *Cirque Calder* nahm die Performancekunst um 40 Jahre vorweg und spiegelt vielleicht Calders lebenslange Vorliebe für das Theater, für das er eine Reihe von Bühnenbildern schuf.

Seine innovative Idee der Arbeit mit Draht entwickelte er weiter. Er „zeichnete" dreidimensionale Porträts von Freunden ebenso wie Tiere, Zirkusmotive und Prominente seiner Zeit aus Draht. Um den radikalen Bruch mit der stabilen Festigkeit von Ton, Bronze und Marmor zu unterstreichen, nannte er diese figurativen Drahtgebilde „Objekte" statt „Skulpturen".

1928 lud die New Yorker Weyhe Gallery Calder zu seiner ersten Einzelausstellung ein. Ihr folgten in schneller Folge weitere in New York, Paris und 1929 auch in Berlin (Abb. 101), sodass Calder häufig auf Ozeandampfern zwischen Amerika und Europa pendelte. Bei einer dieser Atlantiküberquerungen lernte er Louisa James kennen, die Großnichte des Schriftstellers Henry James, und die beiden heirateten im Januar 1931. Er unterhielt freundschaftliche Beziehungen zu vielen prominenten Künstlern und Intellektuellen aus der ersten Hälfte des 20. Jahrhunderts wie Hans Arp, Fernand Léger, James Johnson Sweeney und Marcel Duchamp.

96 Calder in seinem Atelier in Roxbury / Calder in his Roxbury studio, 1964, Foto / photo Andreas Feininger, Saint Louis Art Museum. Gift of the Feininger Family

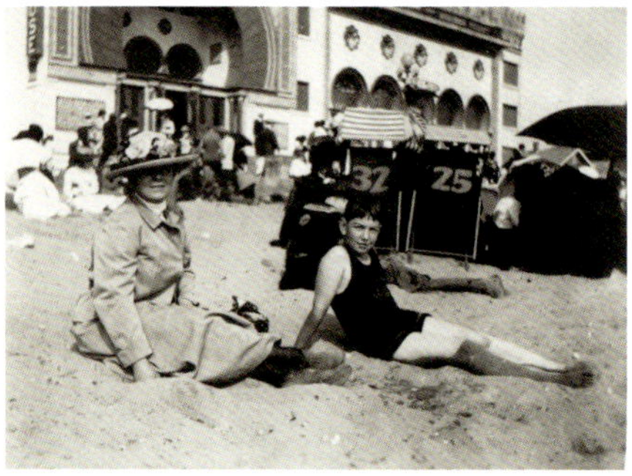

97 Calder mit seiner Mutter am Strand in Kalifornien / Calder and his mother on the beach in California, 1909

Im Herbst 1931 vollzog sich in Calders künstlerischem Schaffen eine radikale Wende. Die ersten abstrakten kinetischen Skulpturen begründeten eine völlig neue Kunstform. Diese Objekte, die Marcel Duchamp „Mobiles“ taufte, bewegten sich anfangs noch mithilfe von Motoren, doch ließ Calder diese Idee wieder fallen und legte die folgenden Werke so an, dass sie nur noch auf Luftströme, Licht, Feuchtigkeit und menschliche Interaktion reagierten. Für Calders stationäre Objekte prägte Hans Arp als Antwort auf Duchamps Etikett „Mobile“ den Ausdruck „Stabile“.

1933 kehrten Alexander und Louisa Calder in die USA zurück und kauften in Roxbury, Connecticut, ein altes Bauernhaus. Ihre älteste Tochter, Sandra, kam 1935 zur Welt, ihre Schwester Mary 1939.

1937 entstand das Stabile *Devil Fish*, bei dem Calder erstmals ein Modell zu einer Großplastik ausarbeitete (Abb. 41). Im selben Jahr folgten zwei wichtige Auftragsarbeiten: *Mercury Fountain* für den spanischen Pavillon der Pariser Weltausstellung von 1937 (Abb. 102) und 1939 *Lobster Trap and Fish Tail* für das Treppenhaus im neuen Gebäude des Museum of Modern Art in New York. Seine erste Retrospektive fand 1938 in der George Walter Vincent Smith Gallery in Springfield, Massachusetts, statt, eine weitere folgte 1943 im Museum of Modern Art in New York, kuratiert von James Johnson Sweeney mit Unterstützung von Marcel Duchamp. Calder war zu dieser Zeit der jüngste Künstler, dem das MoMA eine komplette Werkschau widmete. Diese entpuppte sich als solcher Publikumsmagnet, dass sie bis ins folgende Jahr verlängert wurde.

Während des Zweiten Weltkrieges arbeitete Calder weiter, doch da Metall Mangelware war, griff er immer

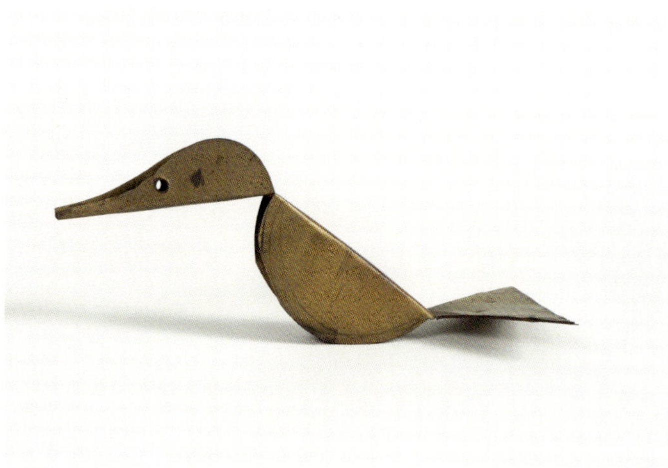

98 *Duck*, 1909, Messingblech, 4,5 × 10,8 × 5,1 cm / brass sheet, 1 ¾ × 4 ¼ × 2 in., Calder Foundation, New York. Mary Calder Rower Bequest, 2011

häufiger auf Holz als Werkstoff zurück. So entstanden neuartige, originelle Skulpturen, die Sweeney und Duchamp „Konstellationen" tauften. 1945 schuf Calder eine Reihe kleinformatiger Plastiken, für viele davon nutzte er aus Sparsamkeit den Verschnitt von Blechplatten, die er zu größeren Skulpturen verarbeitet hatte. Duchamp kam auf die Idee, wie sich Calders Arbeiten problemlos nach Europa verschicken ließen und machte Pläne für eine Schau in der Galerie Louis Carré in Paris. Calder begann, dafür zerlegbare größere Objekte zu konzipieren, die man nach der Ankunft in Paris wieder zusammensetzen konnte. Die wegweisende Ausstellung fand im Jahr darauf statt; zum Katalog steuerte Jean-Paul Sartre seinen berühmten Essay über Calders Mobiles bei (Abb. 103).

1948 unternahm Calder die erste von drei ausgedehnten Reisen durch Brasilien und zeigte seine Werke in überaus erfolgreichen Ausstellungen in Rio de Janeiro und São Paulo. 1952 übernahm er den Auftrag für die

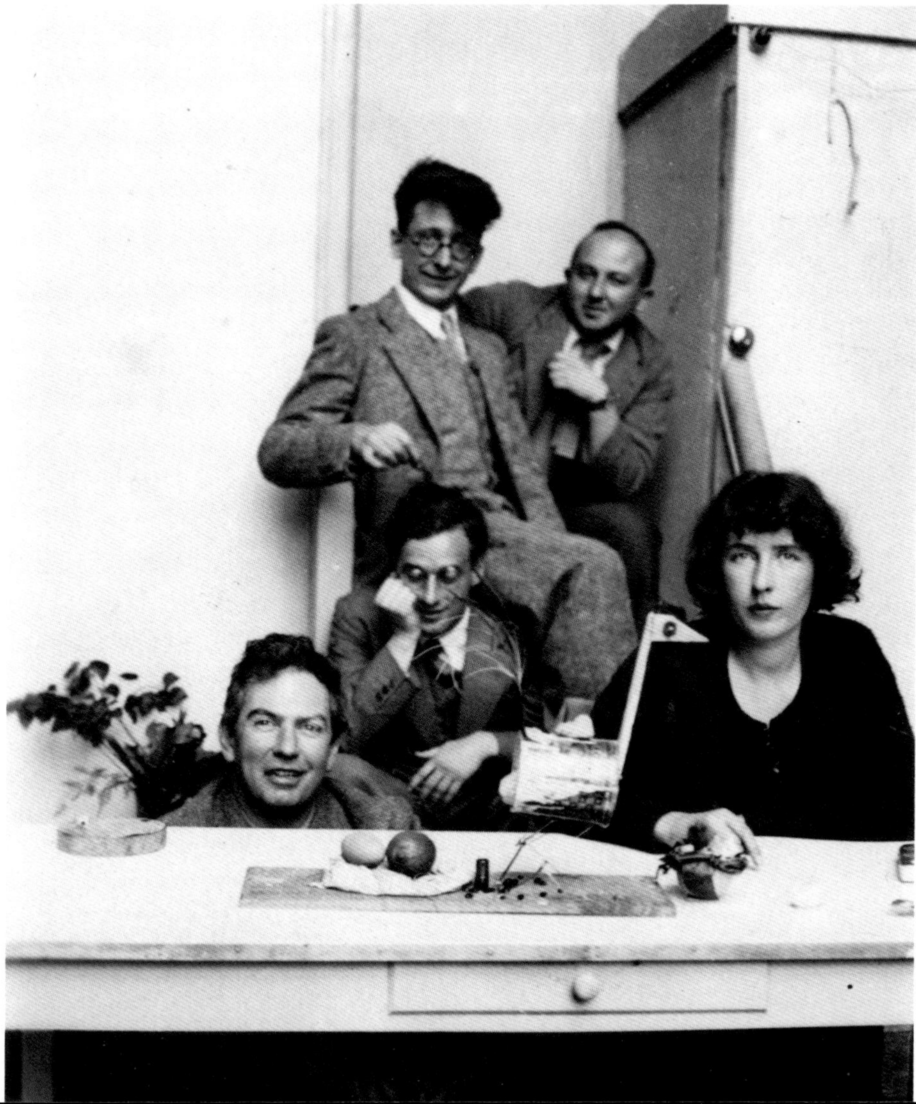

99 Im Atelier von Jean Hélion / In Jean Hélion's studio, Paris, 1933, vorn, von links / front row, from left: Alexander Calder, William Einstein, Louisa Calder, hinten / back row: Jean Hélion, Anatole Jakovsky, Foto / photo Jean Blair-Hélion

Acoustic Ceiling (1954) in der „Aula Magna", dem Auditorium maximum der Universidad Central de Venezuela. Im selben Jahr vertrat er die Vereinigten Staaten bei der Biennale von Venedig und wurde dort mit dem Hauptpreis für Bildhauerei ausgezeichnet.

Während eines einjährigen Aufenthalts in Aix-en-Provence schuf Calder 1953 die erste Gruppe monumentaler Freiluft-Skulpturen, diesmal ohne kleinere Modelle direkt im Maßstab 1:1. Zudem interessierte er sich in dieser Phase für die Gouache-Malerei. 1954 und 1955 unternahm er Reisen nach Vorderasien, Indien und Südamerika, zwischendurch immer wieder nach Paris. Während dieser Zeit fertigte er Arbeiten in einer erstaunlichen Fülle und Vielfalt. Für US-amerikanische wie auch internationale Auftraggeber entstanden kurz darauf mehrere typische „Calders" wie das Mobile *.125* (1957, Abb. 11) für den John F. Kennedy Airport in New York und die riesige bewegliche *Spirale* (1958, Abb. 39) für das UNESCO-Gebäude in Paris. In Italien schuf Calder für das Festival dei Due Mondi 1962 in Spoleto das rund 18 Meter hohe Stabile *Teodelapio* (Abb. 43).

1963 stellte Calder in Saché ein neues großes Atelier mit Blick über das Indre-Tal fertig und bekräftigte damit seine noch immer enge Bindung an Frankreich. Die ältere Tochter der Calders, Sandra, wohnte ganz in der Nähe mit dem Journalisten Jean Davidson, den sie 1955 geheiratet hatte. Gemeinsam mit seinem Schwiegersohn publizierte Calder 1966 seine vielgelesene Autobiografie. Die jüngere Tochter Mary blieb in den USA und heiratete dort 1961 Howard Rower.

Mit Unterstützung durch eine industrielle Eisengießerei hatte Calder bereits in den 1950er-Jahren die Gestaltung monumentaler Skulpturen in Angriff genommen. Während seiner letzten Schaffensjahre arbeitete er großenteils an Werken für institutionelle Auftraggeber. Zu seinen wichtigsten Objekten gehören *Trois disques* für die Weltausstellung 1967 in Montreal, *El Sol Rojo* für die Olympischen Spiele 1968 in Mexico City und *La Grande Vitesse* für Grand Rapids, Michigan, im Jahr 1969. Umfangreiche Retrospektiven von Calders Œuvre veranstalteten das Guggenheim Museum in New York (1964/65), das Museum of Fine Arts in Houston (1964), das Musée National d'Art Moderne in Paris (1965, Abb. 94) und die Fondation Maeght im südfranzösischen Saint-Paul-de-Vence (1969). 1967 zeigte auch die Akademie der Künste im damaligen West-Berlin eine große Calder-Ausstellung (Abb. 89, 91).

Bei der Eröffnung der Retrospektive *Calder's Universe* im Whitney Museum of American Art in New York 1976 war der 78-Jährige noch persönlich zugegen. Mit seinem Tod nur wenige Wochen darauf endete eine der produktivsten und innovativsten Künstlerlaufbahnen des 20. Jahrhunderts.

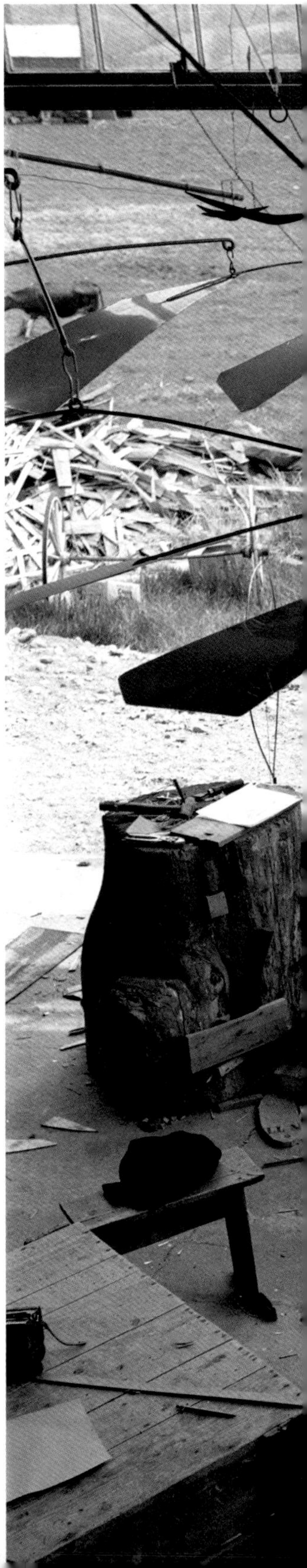

100 Calder in seinem Atelier in Roxbury / Calder in his Roxbury studio, 1941, Foto / photo Herbert Matter

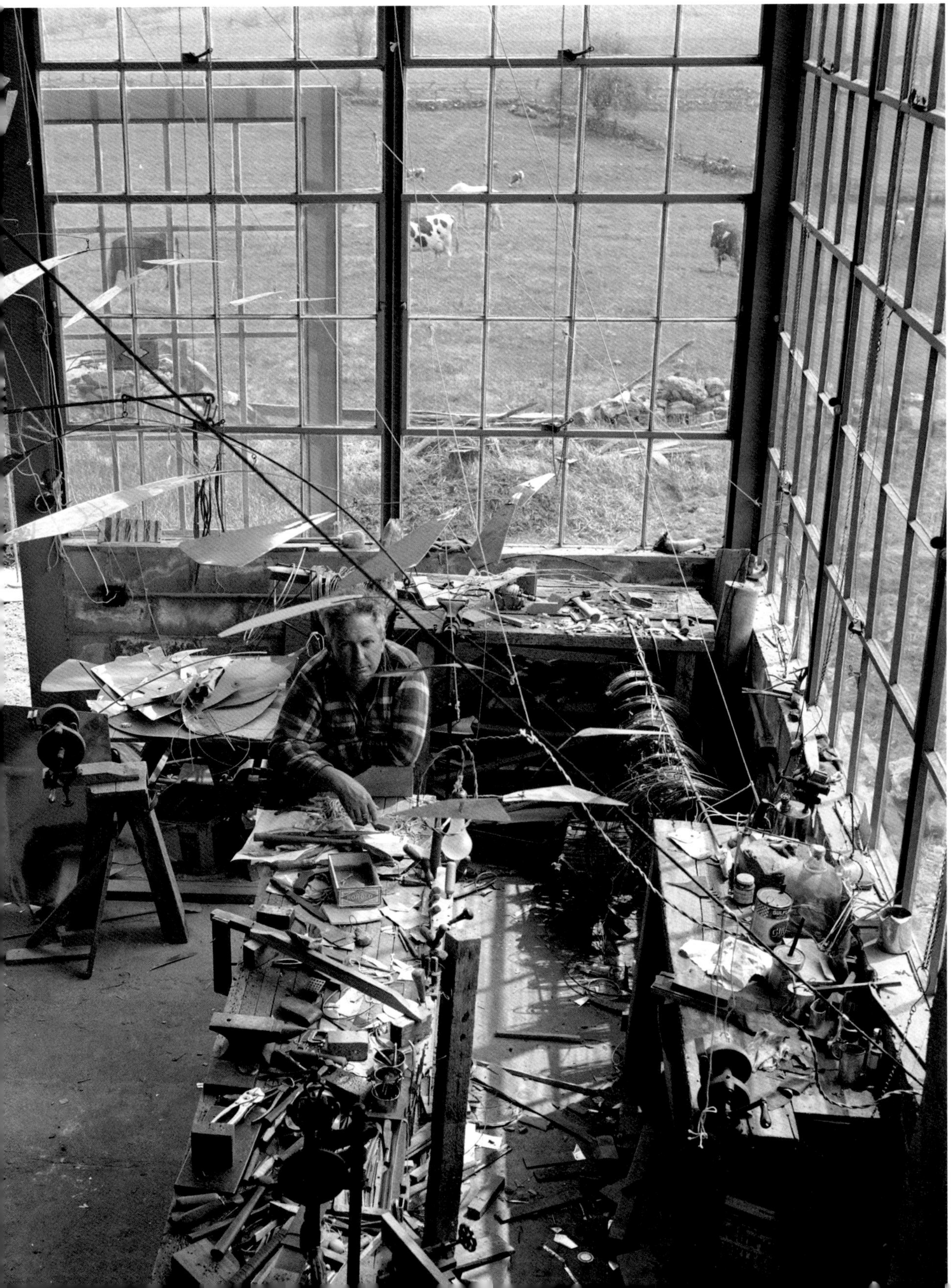

Biography Alexander Calder

1898, Lawnton, PA—1976, New York, NY

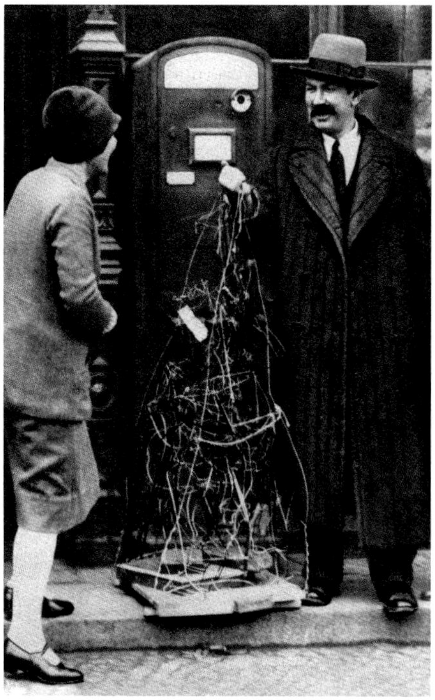

101 Calder kommt mit einem Bündel seiner Drahtskulpturen zur Präsentation in der Galerie Neumann-Nierendorf / Calder arriving with a bundle of his wire sculptures to exhibit at the Galerie Neumann-Nierendorf, Berlin, 1929

Alexander Calder was born in 1898 to artist parents—his father was a sculptor, and his mother a painter. In 1906, while living in Pasadena amid the flourishing Arts and Crafts movement, Calder was given his first tools and a workshop, where he made toys and jewelry for his sister's dolls. For Christmas in 1909, Calder presented his parents with two of his earliest sculptures, a dog and a duck made out of bent brass sheet (fig. 98). After high school, he enrolled at the Stevens Institute of Technology, in Hoboken, New Jersey, graduating in 1919 with a degree in mechanical engineering. He subsequently worked for several years at various jobs, including as a hydraulics and automotive engineer. In 1923 Calder

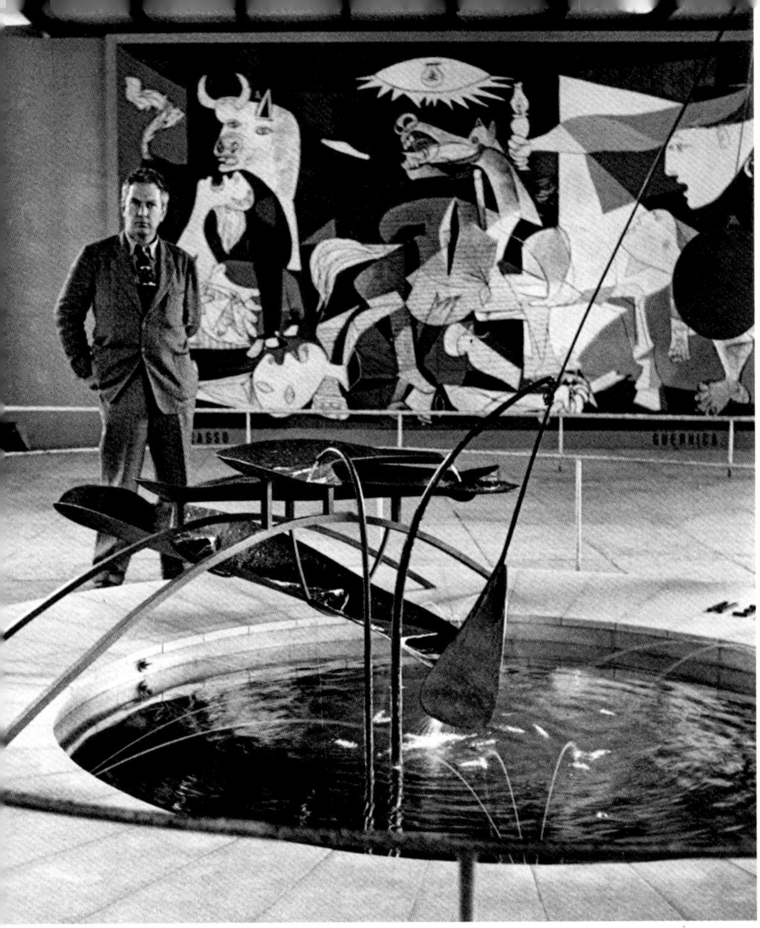

102 Calder mit *Mercury Fountain* (1937) im spanischen Pavillon auf der Weltausstellung in Paris, Juli 1937 / Calder with *Mercury Fountain* (1937) in the Spanish Pavilion at the Paris World's Fair, July 1937, Foto / photo Hugo Herdeg

moved to New York and studied at the Art Students League, where he produced paintings congruous with the realist aesthetic of the Ashcan School of the early twentieth century, known for its scenes of urban life in New York. He worked concurrently at the *National Police Gazette*, illustrating sporting events and the Ringling Bros. and Barnum & Bailey Circus. During this period, he frequently used sheet metal and wire for sculptures and other projects.

Soon after moving to Paris in 1926, Calder created *Cirque Calder* (1926–31; fig. 12), made of wire and a spectrum of found materials. Its first performance was held in the French capital for an audience of friends and peers, and soon Calder was presenting the circus in both Paris and New York to much success. Calder's renderings of his circus often lasted about two hours and were quite elaborate. In fact, the *Cirque Calder* predated performance art by forty years and possibly explains in part his lifelong interest in theater, for which he created numerous stage designs.

Calder continued to explore his invention of wire sculpture, using wire to "draw" in space three-dimensional portraits of friends, animals, circus themes, and personalities of the day. He called these figurative wire works "objects" as opposed to "sculpture," to signify his decisive break from the solidity of clay, bronze, and marble.

In 1928 Calder was given his first solo gallery show at the Weyhe Gallery in New York. This exhibition was soon followed by others in New York, Paris, and Berlin (fig. 101); as a result, Calder spent much time crossing the ocean by ship. On one of these steamer journeys, he met Louisa James (a grandniece of the writer Henry James), and the two were married in January 1931. He became friendly with many prominent artists and intellectuals of the early twentieth century at this time, including Jean Arp, Fernand Léger, James Johnson Sweeney, and Marcel Duchamp.

In the fall of 1931, a radical shift in Calder's artistic career occurred when he created kinetic abstract sculpture and gave form to an entirely new type of art. Some of the earliest of these objects moved by systems of motors and were dubbed "mobiles" by Marcel Duchamp. Calder soon turned away from the motorized compositions of his earliest mobiles, developing works that respond to air currents, light, humidity, and human interaction. Arp, in a sarcastic response to Duchamp's term "mobile," named Calder's stationary objects "stabiles."

In 1933 Calder and Louisa left France and returned to the United States, where they purchased an old farmhouse in Roxbury, Connecticut. Their first daughter, Sandra, was born in 1935, and a second daughter, Mary, followed in 1939.

In 1937 Calder completed *Devil Fish* (fig. 41), his first stabile enlarged from a model. He received two important commissions: *Mercury Fountain* for the Spanish pavilion at the 1937 Paris World's Fair (fig. 102), and *Lobster Trap and Fish Tail* for the main stairwell of the new Museum of Modern Art building in New York in 1939. His earliest retrospective was held at the George Walter

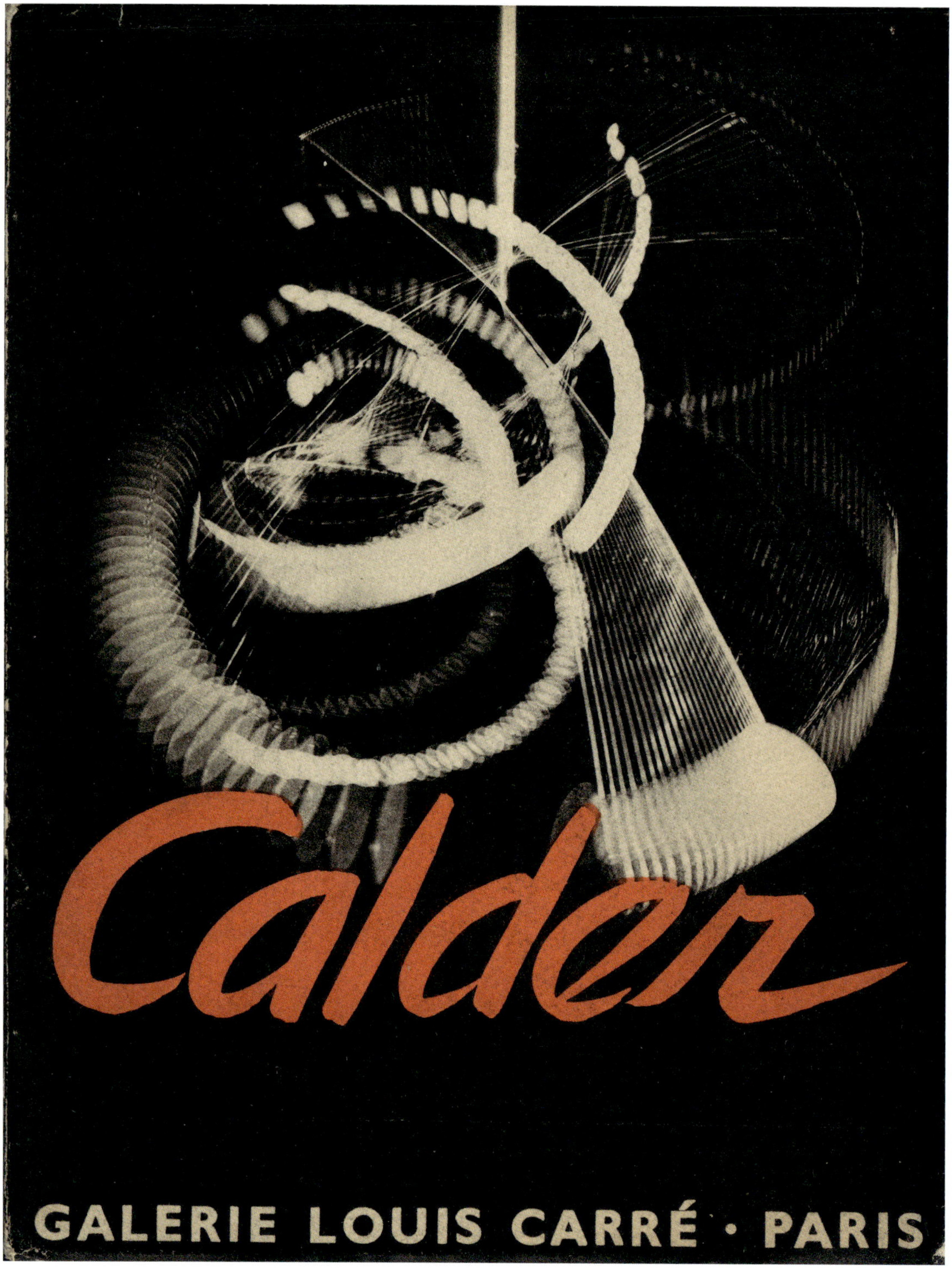

103 Ausstellungskatalog / Exhibition catalogue, *Alexander Calder: Mobiles, Stabiles, Constellations*, Galerie Louis Carré, Paris, 1946

Vincent Smith Gallery in Springfield, Massachusetts, in 1938. Another retrospective followed in 1943 at the Museum of Modern Art in New York, curated by Sweeney, with the assistance of Duchamp. At that time, Calder was the youngest artist ever to whom the museum had dedicated a full-career survey, which was so popular that it was extended into 1944.

During World War II, Calder continued to create. Because metal was in short supply, he turned increasingly to wood as a sculptural medium. Working in wood resulted in yet another original form of sculpture, works referred to as "constellations" by Sweeney and Duchamp. In 1945 Calder made a series of small-scale works; in keeping with his economy, many were made from scraps of metal that he had trimmed while making larger pieces. Inspired by the idea that the works could be easily mailed to Europe, Duchamp planned a Calder show at Galerie Louis Carré in Paris; Calder soon began to make larger works for the show that were collapsible and intended to be reassembled upon arrival in Paris. This important show was held the following year, and Jean-Paul Sartre wrote his famous essay on Calder's mobiles for the exhibition catalogue (fig. 103).

Calder made the first of three extended trips to Brazil in 1948, where he held highly successful exhibitions in Rio de Janeiro and São Paulo. In 1952 he accepted the commission for *Acoustic Ceiling* (1954) for the Aula Magna auditorium at the Universidad Central de Venezuela. That same year, Calder represented the United States at the Venice Biennale, winning the Grand Prize for sculpture.

During a yearlong stay in Aix-en-Provence in 1953, Calder executed his first group of large-scale outdoor works, which were realized in direct scale, as opposed to being enlarged from maquettes. The artist also concentrated on painting gouaches. In 1954 and 1955 he visited the Middle East, India, and South America, with trips to Paris in between, resulting in an astonishing output and range of work. Calder soon turned his attention to commissions both at home and abroad, producing such recognizable works as *.125* (1957; fig. 11), a mobile hung in the John F. Kennedy Airport in New York, and *Spirale* (1958; fig. 39), a major commission for UNESCO in Paris. In Italy, Calder created *Teodelapio* (fig. 43), a stabile over fifty-eight-feet tall, for the 1962 Festival dei Due Mondi (Festival of the Two Worlds), in Spoleto.

In 1963 Calder completed the construction of a large studio overlooking the Indre Valley in Saché, manifesting his strong relationship to France. Calder and Louisa's daughter Sandra, who married the journalist Jean Davidson in 1955, was living close by; together with his son-in-law, Calder published a well-received autobiography in 1966. The Calders' younger daughter, Mary, lived in the US and married Howard Rower in 1961.

With the assistance of a full-scale, industrial iron foundry, Calder began to fabricate monumental works and devoted much of his later career to public commissions. Some of his most important projects include *Trois disques* for the 1967 exposition in Montreal; *El Sol Rojo* for the 1968 Mexico City Olympic Games; and *La Grande Vitesse* for Grand Rapids, Michigan, in 1969. Major retrospectives of Calder's work were held at the Guggenheim Museum in New York (1964–65); The Museum of Fine Arts, Houston (1964); the Musée National d'Art Moderne, Paris (1965, fig. 94); and the Fondation Maeght in Saint-Paul-de-Vence, France (1969). In 1967 he also had a major show at the Akademie der Künste in (West) Berlin (figs. 89, 91).

In 1976 the artist attended the opening of yet another retrospective of his work, *Calder's Universe*, at the Whitney Museum of American Art in New York. Just a few weeks later, Calder died at the age of seventy-eight, ending the most prolific and innovative artistic career of the twentieth century.

104 Calder mit / with *Snow Flurry* (1948), Saché, 1963, Foto / photo Ugo Mulas

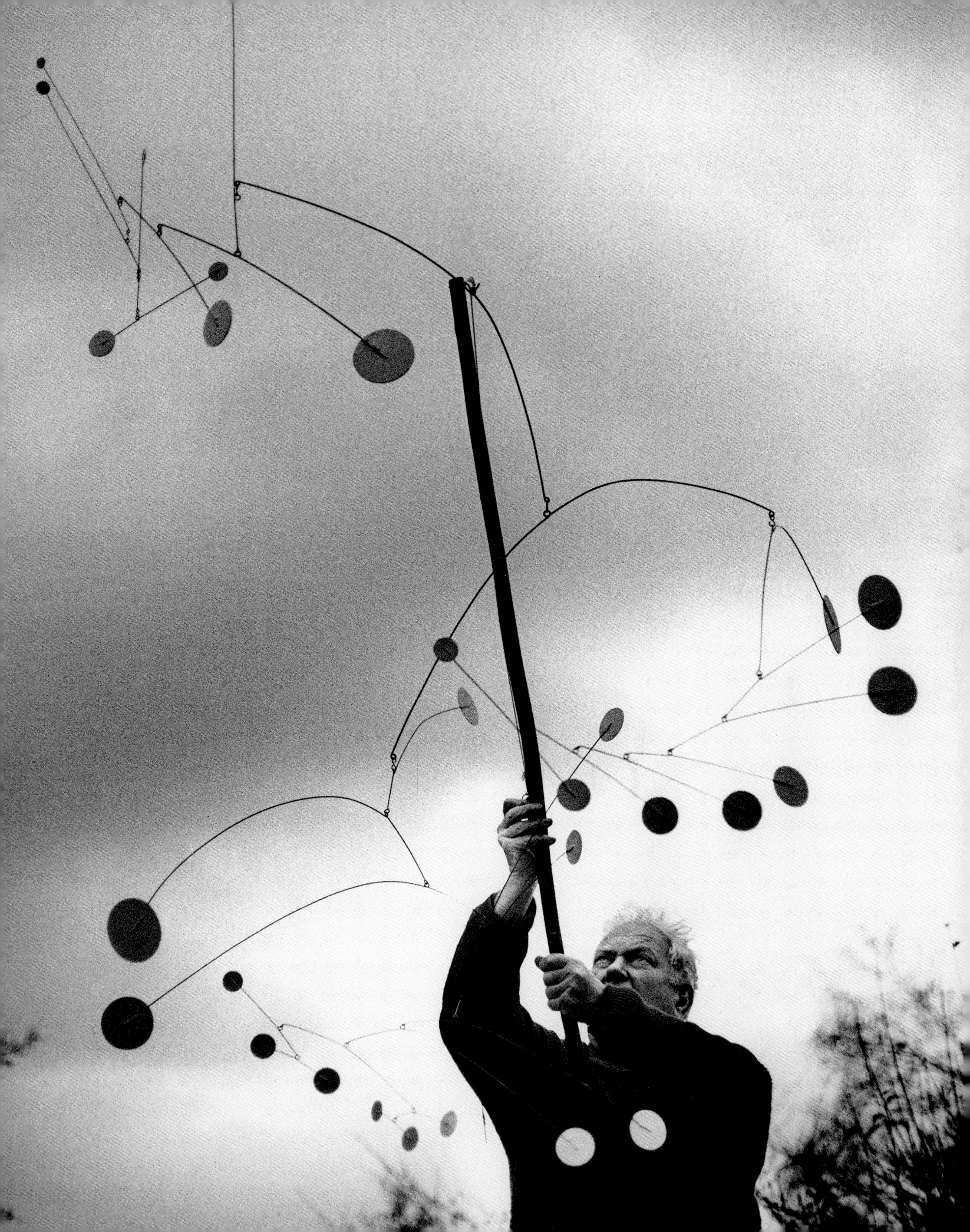

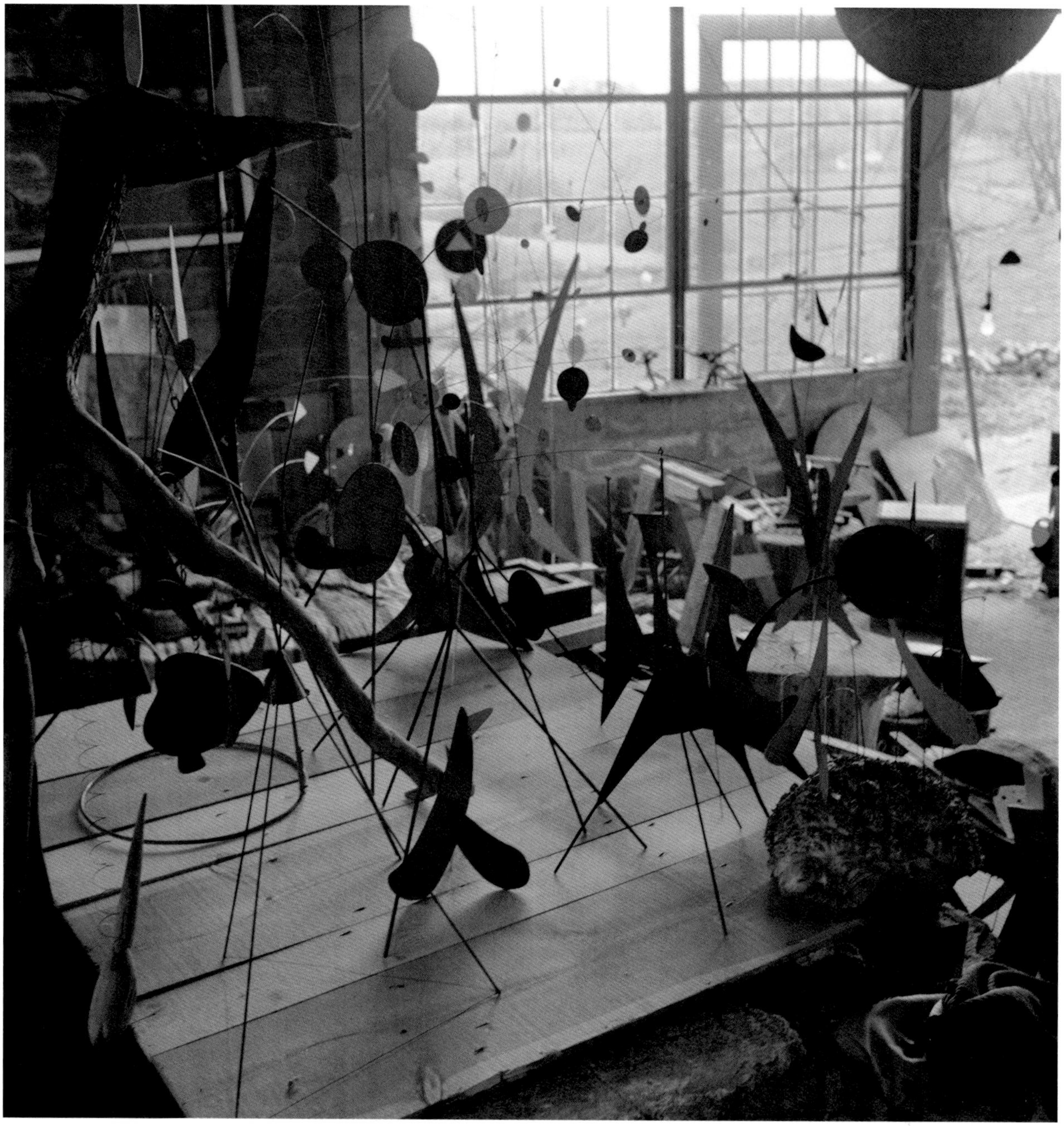

Verzeichnis der ausgestellten Werke

List of Exhibited Works

105 Calders Atelier in Roxbury / Calder's Roxbury studio, 1941, *Apple Monster* (1938), *Tadpole* (Modell, um 1936 / maquette, ca. 1936), *Yucca* (1941), *Black Beast* (Modell, 1939 / maquette, 1939), *Myrtle Burl* (1941), Foto / photo Herbert Matter

Maximal

Untitled, 1954, Stahl, Stab, Bolzen, Farbe, 396 × 579 × 396 cm /
Untitled, 1954, sheet metal, rod, bolts, paint, 156 × 228 × 156 in.

Calder Foundation, New York. Gift of Andréa Davidson, 2007
Abb. / fig. 55

Les Triangles, 1963, Stahlplatten, schwarz lackiert, 330 × 470 × 210 cm /
Les Triangles, 1963, sheet metal, black paint, 130 × 185 × 106 ⅓ in.

Museum Ostwall im Dortmunder U, Dortmund
Abb. / fig. 31 (historische Aufnahme / historical photo)

Les Trois Ailes, 1963, Stahl, Bolzen, Farbe, 380 × 450 × 266 cm /
Les Trois Ailes, 1963, sheet metal, bolts, paint, 149 ⅝ × 177 ⅛ × 104 ¾ in.

Musée National d'Art Moderne – Centre de création industrielle,
Centre Pompidou, Paris. Transfer 1983
Abb. / fig. 25

Têtes et queue, 1965, Stahl, Bolzen, Farbe, 550 × 470 × 330 cm /
Têtes et queue, 1965, sheet metal, bolts, paint, 216 ½ × 185 × 130 in.

Staatliche Museen zu Berlin, Nationalgalerie
Abb. / fig. 1

Crinkly, 1969, Stahl, Stab, Bolzen, Farbe, 350 × 200 cm /
Crinkly, 1969, sheet metal, rod, bolts, paint, 137 ¾ × 78 ¾ in.

Centre National des arts plastiques, France
FNAC 9719
Abb. / fig. 44

Five Swords, 1976, Stahl, Bolzen, Farbe, 541 × 671 × 884 cm /
Five Swords, 1976, sheet metal, bolts, paint, 213 × 264 × 348 in.

Calder Foundation, New York
Abb. / fig. 8

Small Sphere and Heavy Sphere, 1932/33, Gusseisen, Stab, Draht, Holz, Schnur, Faden, Farbe, Hindernisse, Höhe 317 cm /
Small Sphere and Heavy Sphere, 1932/33, cast iron, rod, wire, wood, cord, thread, paint, impedimenta, height 125 in.

Calder Foundation, New York. Mary Calder Rower Bequest, 2011
Abb. / fig. 23

Blizzard, 1950, Stahl, Draht, Farbe, 320 × 360 × 360 cm /
Blizzard, 1950, sheet metal, wire, paint, 126 × 141 ¾ × 141 ¾ in.

Sprengel Museum Hannover, Leihgabe Land Niedersachsen
Abb. / fig. 72

Otto's Mobile, 1952, Metall, Aluminium, bemalt, 533,4 × 243,8 cm /
Otto's Mobile, 1952, sheet metal, aluminum, painted, 210 × 96 in.

Fondation Beyeler, Riehen/Basel, Sammlung Beyeler
Abb. / fig. 2

Le Cagoulard, 1954, Metall, Draht, Farbe, 104 × 345 × 295 cm /
Le Cagoulard, 1954, sheet metal, wire, paint, 41 × 136 × 116 in.

Staatliche Museen zu Berlin, Nationalgalerie, Schenkung Sammlung
Ulla und Heiner Pietzsch an das Land Berlin 2010
Abb. / fig. 73

Rouge triomphant, 1959–1963, Blech, Stab, Draht, Farbe, 279 × 584 × 457 cm /
Rouge triomphant, 1959–1963, sheet metal, rod, wire, paint, 110 × 230 × 180 in.

Collection David and Ezra Nahmad
Abb. / fig. 71

Un de ceux-là, 1972, Metall, Draht, Farbe, 180 × 100 cm /
Un de ceux-là, 1972, sheet metal, wire, paint, 70 ⅞ × 39 ⅜ in.

Staatliche Museen zu Berlin, Nationalgalerie, Schenkung Sammlung
Ulla und Heiner Pietzsch an das Land Berlin 2010
Abb. / fig. 45

3 Segments, 1973, Blech, Stab, Draht, Farbe, 200,7 × 508 cm /
3 Segments, 1973, sheet metal, rod, wire, paint, 79 × 200 in.

Calder Foundation, New York
Abb. / fig. 56

Minimal

Untitled, um 1940, Blech, Draht, Farbe, 14,5 × 12,1 × 12,1 cm /
Untitled, ca. 1940, sheet metal, wire, paint, $5\frac{11}{16} \times 4\frac{3}{4} \times 4\frac{3}{4}$ in.

Calder Foundation, New York
Abb. / fig. 64

Untitled, um 1942, Blech, Draht, Schnur, 29,2 × 33 × 17,8 cm /
Untitled, ca. 1942, sheet metal, wire, string, $11\frac{1}{2} \times 13 \times 7$ in.

Calder Foundation, New York
Abb. / fig. 83

Untitled, um 1942, Messingdraht, 17,5 × 13,3 × 7,6 cm /
Untitled, ca. 1942, brass wire, $6\frac{7}{8} \times 5\frac{1}{4} \times 3$ in.

Calder Foundation, New York
Abb. / fig. 84

Untitled, um 1945, Draht, Farbe, 14 × 10,2 × 10,2 cm /
Untitled, ca. 1945, wire, paint, $5\frac{1}{2} \times 4 \times 4$ in.

Calder Foundation, New York
Abb. / fig. 16

Grand Piano, Red, 1946, Blech, Draht, Farbe, 24,5 × 25,4 × 7,6 cm /
Grand Piano, Red, 1946, sheet metal, wire, paint, $9\frac{5}{8} \times 10 \times 3$ in.

Calder Foundation, New York
Abb. / fig. 40

Untitled, um 1946, Blech, Messing, Draht, Farbe, 21,6 × 21,6 × 10,2 cm /
Untitled, ca. 1946, sheet metal, brass, wire, paint, $8\frac{1}{2} \times 8\frac{1}{2} \times 4$ in.

Calder Foundation, New York
Abb. / fig. 17

Untitled, um 1946, Blech, Farbe, 12,7 × 17,8 × 8,9 cm /
Untitled, ca. 1946, sheet metal, paint, $5 \times 7 \times 3\frac{1}{2}$ in.

Collection David and Ezra Nahmad
Abb. / fig. 30

Louisa's 43rd Birthday Present, 1948, Blech, Holz, Draht, Filz, Zigarrenkiste, Farbe; Kiste: 6,4 × 22,1 × 12,9 cm; Mobile rechtes Fach: 13,8 × 3,7 × 14 cm; Mobile Fach hinten Mitte: 6,5 × 4 × 3,5 cm; Mobile Fach hinten links: 6,4 × 3 × 3,5 cm; Mobile Fach vorne links: 5,6 × 5,2 × 7,1 cm; Mobile vorne Mitte: 4 × 4,5 × 2,9 cm /
Louisa's 43rd Birthday Present, 1948, sheet metal, wood, wire, felt, cigar box, paint; box: $2\frac{1}{2} \times 8\frac{11}{16} \times 5\frac{1}{16}$ in.; mobile from right compartment: $5\frac{7}{16} \times 1\frac{7}{16} \times 5\frac{1}{2}$ in.; mobile from back center compartment: $2\frac{9}{16} \times 1\frac{9}{16} \times 1\frac{3}{8}$ in.; mobile from back left compartment: $2\frac{1}{2} \times 1\frac{3}{16} \times 1\frac{3}{8}$ in.; mobile from front left compartment: $2\frac{3}{16} \times 2\frac{1}{16} \times 2\frac{13}{16}$ in.; mobile from front center compartment: $1\frac{9}{16} \times 1\frac{3}{4} \times 1\frac{1}{8}$ in.

Calder Foundation, New York
Abb. / fig. 15

Toadstool with Feather, 1948, Blech, Draht, Farbe, 18,4 × 12,1 × 10,8 cm /
Toadstool with Feather, 1948, sheet metal, wire, paint, $7\frac{1}{4} \times 4\frac{3}{4} \times 4\frac{1}{4}$ in.

Calder Foundation, New York
Abb. / fig. 28

White Counterbalance, 1948, Blech, Draht, Farbe, 26,7 × 25,4 × 7,6 cm /
White Counterbalance, 1948, sheet metal, wire, paint, $10\frac{1}{2} \times 10 \times 3$ in.

Calder Foundation, New York
Abb. / fig. 26

Untitled, um 1948, Blech, Draht, Farbe, 60 × 100 × 100 cm /
Untitled, ca. 1948, sheet metal, wire, paint, $24 \times 39\frac{3}{8} \times 39\frac{3}{8}$ in.

Staatliche Museen zu Berlin, Nationalgalerie
Abb. / fig. 62

Untitled, um 1950, Blech, Farbe, 5,1 × 10,2 × 4,8 cm /
Untitled, ca. 1950, sheet metal, paint, $2 \times 4 \times 1\frac{7}{8}$ in.

Calder Foundation, New York
Abb. / fig. 29

Four Dots and Brass Tail, um 1953, Blech, Messing, Draht, Farbe, 15,9 × 24,1 × 7,6 cm /
Four Dots and Brass Tail, ca. 1953, sheet metal, brass, wire, paint, $6\frac{1}{4} \times 9\frac{1}{2} \times 3$ in.

Calder Foundation, New York
Abb. / fig. 79

La Cuiller, 1954, Löffel, Messing, Draht, Blech, Farbe, 8,3 × 13 × 2,9 cm /
La Cuiller, 1954, spoon, brass, wire, sheet metal, paint, $3\frac{1}{4} \times 5\frac{1}{8} \times 1\frac{1}{8}$ in.

Calder Foundation, New York
Abb. / fig. 80

Untitled, um 1954, Blech, Messing, Draht, Farbe, 3,5 × 6,5 × 1,6 cm /
Untitled, ca. 1954, sheet metal, brass, wire, paint, $1\frac{3}{8} \times 2\frac{9}{16} \times \frac{5}{8}$ in.

Calder Foundation, New York
Abb. / fig. 81

Untitled, um 1955, Blech, Messing, Draht, Farbe, 16,5 × 17,8 × 10,2 cm /
Untitled, ca. 1955, sheet metal, brass, wire, paint, $6\frac{1}{2} \times 7 \times 4$ in.

Calder Foundation, New York
Abb. / fig. 18

Untitled, um 1958, Blech, Messing, Draht, Farbe, Höhe 38 cm /
Untitled, ca. 1958, sheet metal, brass, wire, paint, height 15 in.

Staatliche Museen zu Berlin, Museum Berggruen
Abb. / fig. 63

Untitled, um 1965, Blech, Messing, Draht, Farbe, 15,2 × 14 × 5,7 cm /
Untitled, ca. 1965, sheet metal, brass, wire, paint, $6 \times 5\frac{1}{2} \times 2\frac{1}{4}$ in.

Calder Foundation, New York
Abb. / fig. 65

Untitled, um 1970, Blech, Messing, Unterlegscheiben, Draht, 10,2 × 19 × 6,4 cm /
Untitled, ca. 1970, sheet metal, brass, washers, wire, $4 \times 7\frac{1}{2} \times 2\frac{1}{2}$ in.

Calder Foundation, New York
Abb. / fig. 85

Schachspiel, 1944, Holz, Farbe; Spielbrett: 45,7 × 45,7 cm /
Chess set, 1944, wood, paint; board: 18 × 18 in.

Calder Foundation, New York. Mary Calder Rower Bequest, 2011
Abb. / fig. 82

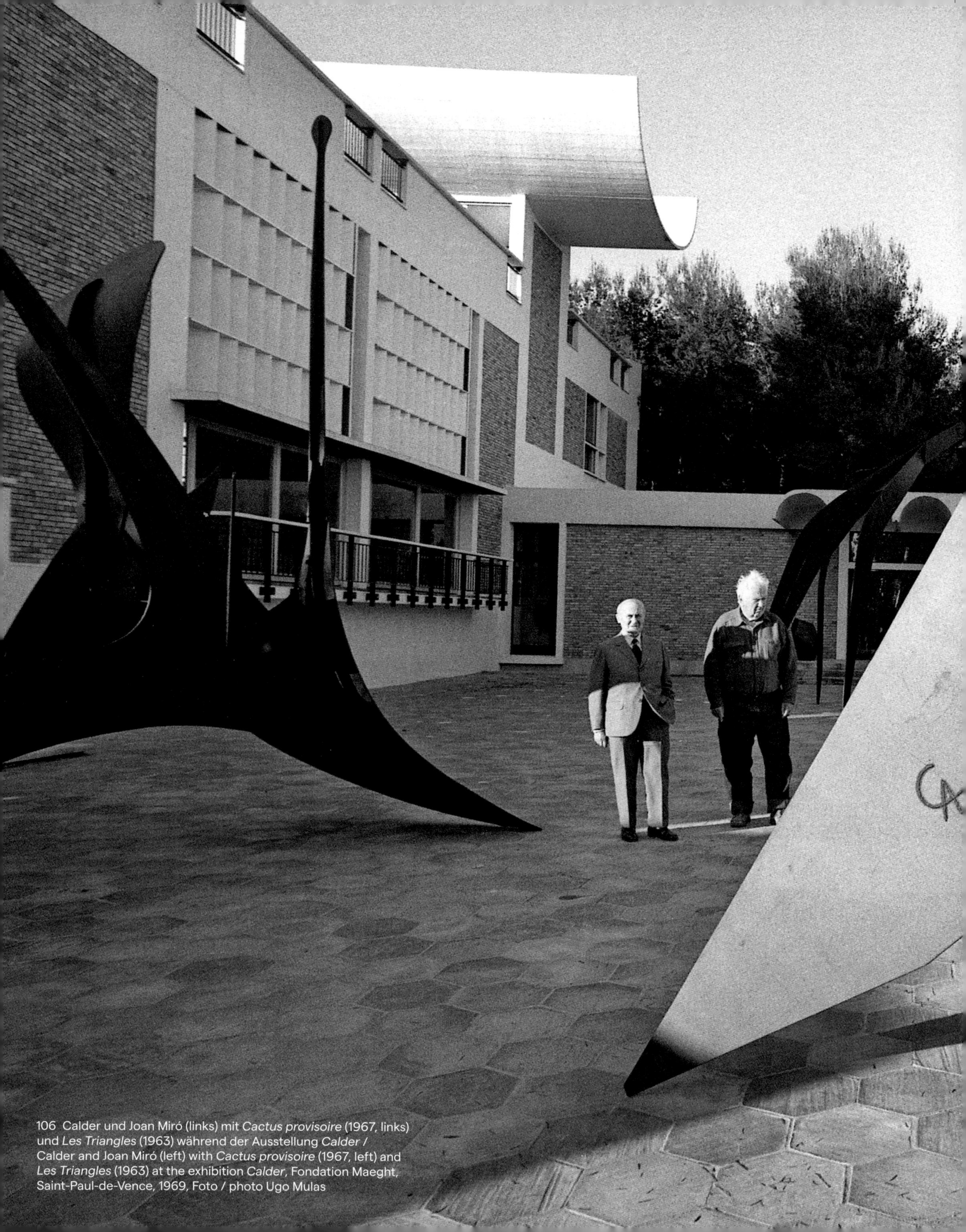

106 Calder und Joan Miró (links) mit *Cactus provisoire* (1967, links) und *Les Triangles* (1963) während der Ausstellung *Calder* / Calder and Joan Miró (left) with *Cactus provisoire* (1967, left) and *Les Triangles* (1963) at the exhibition *Calder*, Fondation Maeght, Saint-Paul-de-Vence, 1969, Foto / photo Ugo Mulas

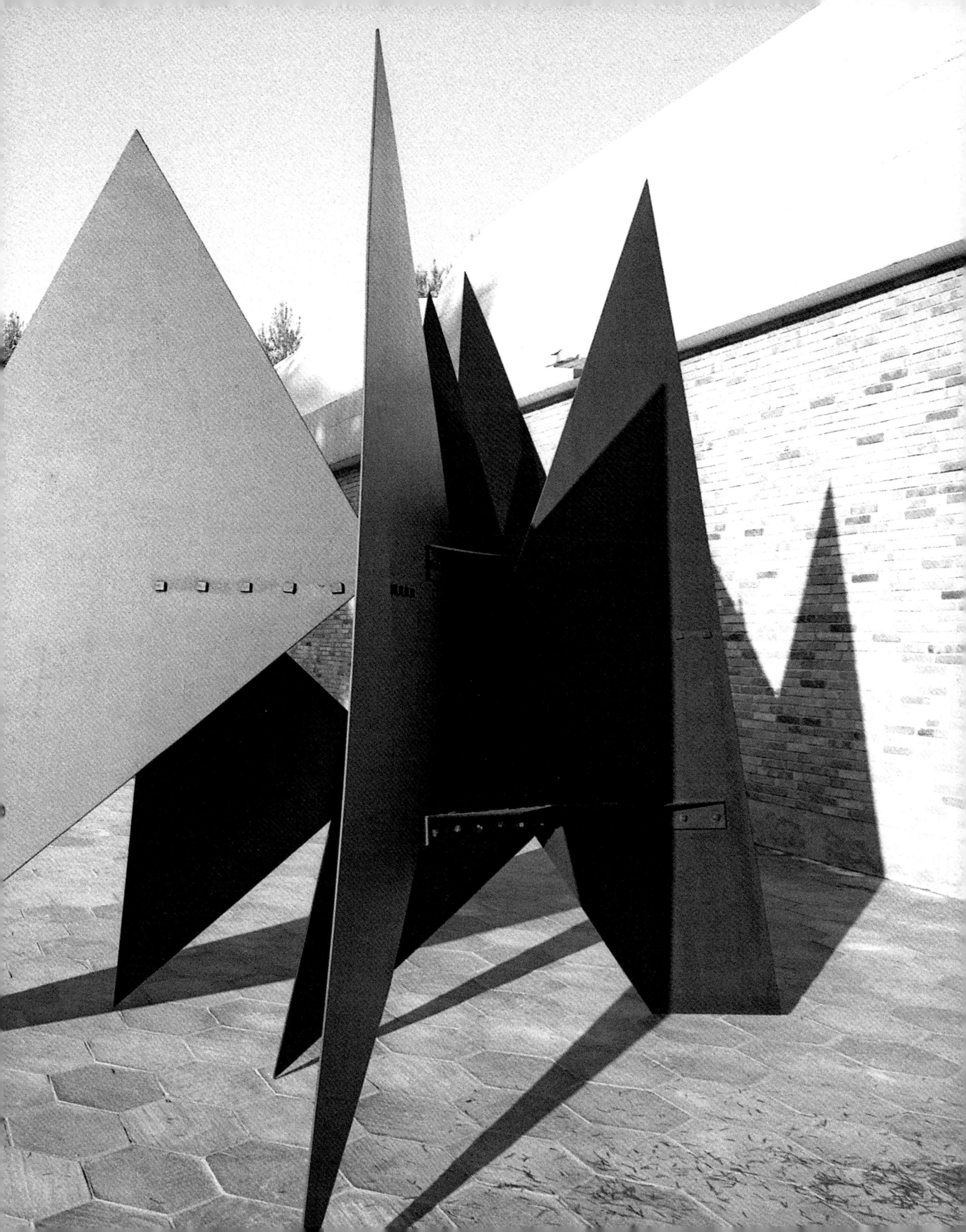

Copyrights

Fotonachweis

Photo Credits

Akademie der Künste, Berlin/Reinhard Friedrich, S./p. 147

© AKG Images/Walter Limot, S./p. 25

Alamy Stock Foto, S./pp. 58–59; PvE, S./p. 94 u./b.

Foto Ancillotti/ Triennale Milano – Archivio Fotografico, S./p. 120

Archives du Ministère de l'Europe et des Affaires étrangères – La Courneuve/ Hélène Hoppenot, S./p. 32

Archives Fondation Maeght (France), S./pp. 95; Stéphane Briolant, S./p. 94 o./t.

Archives of American Art, Smithsonian Institution, Alexander Calder papers, 1926–1967, S./p. 41; Marc Vaux, S./p. 108; Dwan Gallery Records, 1959 – ca. 1982 © The Estate of Robert Morris, S./p. 57

Fondation Beyeler, Riehen/Basel, Sammlung Beyeler/Robert Bayer, S./pp. 16–17

bpk/Nationalgalerie, SMB/Jens Ziehe, S./p. 112; Neue Nationalgalerie, SMB/ Liselotte und Armin Orgel-Köhne, S./p. 142; Museum Berggruen, Privatbesitz/ Roman März, S./p. 113

The Eli and Edythe L. Broad Collection, Los Angeles, S./p. 75

Earle Brown Collection, Paul Sacher Foundation, Basel/ Bruce Kiefer, S./p. 35

Stuart Byrom, S./p. 88

Courtesy Calder Foundation, New York/ Art Resource, New York, S./pp. 24, 36, 49, 53, 66 (beide/both), 72, 74, 76, 77, 79, 84, 98 (beide/both), 99, 102–103, 104–105, 109, 115, 119, 121, 124–125, 126–127, 133, 135, 137, 138 o./t., 139, 153, 158 o./t., 162, 164; Claude Gaspari, S./p. 65; Jean Blair-Hélion, S./p. 159; Herbert Matter, S./pp. 18, 27, 46, 85, 160–161, 168; Hugo P. Herdeg © Christian Herdeg, S./p. 163; Gordon Parks © The Gordon Parks Foundation, Pleasantville, S./p. 106; Tom Powel Imaging, S./pp. 42–43, 44 (beide/ both), 45, 64, 73, 83, 114, 130, 138 u.l., u.r./ b.l., b.r., 140 (beide/both), 141, 158 u./b.; John G. Ross, S./p. 40; Alexander S. C. Rower, Umschlag/cover, S./pp. 30–31; Eric Schaal © Life Magazine, S./pp. 117, 128; Ezra Stoller © ESTO, S./pp. 100–101; Sacha Stone, S./p. 38

© Centre Pompidou, MNAM-CCI Bibliothèque Kandinsky, Dist. RMN-Grand Palais, Marc Vaux, S./p. 118

© documenta archiv/Herbert Blochel, S./p. 144

Photo Ugo Mulas © Ugo Mulas Heirs. All rights reserved, S./pp. 68–69, 70, 87, 92, 154–155, 167, 172–173, 176

© 2021. Digital image The Museum of Modern Art, New York/Scala, Florence, S./p. 50 u./b.

Collection David and Ezra Nahmad, S./pp. 67, 122–123

National Gallery of Art, Washington 1979.51.1, S./p. 50 o./t.

Photo Collection RKD – Netherlands Institute for Art History, The Hague, S./p. 110

Saint Louis Art Museum © Courtesy of The Andreas Feininger Estate and Bonni Benrubi Gallery, New York City, S./p. 156

Staatliche Museen zu Berlin (SMB): Roman März, S./pp. 5, 7; Kunstbibliothek, S./p. 147; Dietmar Katz, S./p. 152; Neue Nationalgalerie/ Simon Menges, S./pp. 22–23; Neue Nationalgalerie, S./p. 145; Nationalgalerie/Jochen Littkemann, S./pp. 90–91

Ullstein Bild, Harry Croner S./pp. 96–97; Wieczorek S./p. 150

Georg Wegner, S./p. 146

© 2021. Digital image Whitney Museum of American Art/Licensed by Scala, S./p. 111

Impressum

Die Publikation erscheint anlässlich der Ausstellung /
This catalogue is published in conjunction with the exhibition

Alexander Calder

Minimal Maximal

22. August 2021–13. Februar 2022
August 22, 2021–February 13, 2022

Staatliche Museen zu Berlin,
Neue Nationalgalerie

Die Ausstellung wird ermöglicht durch die /
The exhibition has been made possible by the

Freunde der Nationalgalerie
www.freunde-der-nationalgalerie.de

Colophon

Ausstellung / Exhibition

Kurator*innen / Curators: Joachim Jäger, Udo Kittelmann, Maike Steinkamp

Ausstellungskoordination / Exhibition coordinator: Katharina Wippermann

Projektmanagement / Project management: André Odier, Katharina von Chlebowski

Assistenz / Assistance: Marie Probst, Stefanie Meisgeier

Finanzen / Finances: Lutz Driever

Kommunikation / Communication: Fiona Geuß

Konservatorische Betreuung / Conservation: Hana Streicher, Thomas Lucker

Kunstvermittlung / Education: Veronika Deinzel

Ausstellungsdesign / Exhibition design: mvprojekte, Meyer Voggenreiter, Nicole Miller

Ausstellungsbau / Exhibition construction: LICHTblick Bühnentechnik

Katalog / Catalogue

Für die / For the Nationalgalerie, Staatliche Museen zu Berlin herausgegeben von / edited by Joachim Jäger, Udo Kittelmann, Maike Steinkamp

Katalogkoordination / Catalogue coordination: Barbara Delius

Bildredaktion / Image editing: Barbara Delius, Jacek Slaski

Redaktion und Lektorat / Editing and copy-editing: Barbara Delius (Deutsch / German), Joann Skrypzak-Davidsmeyer (Englisch / English)

Übersetzung / Translation: Birgit Lamerz-Beckschäfer (Biografie, Gilothwest, Kramer, Rower, Slifkin, Turner), Sarah McGavran (Jäger/Kittelmann/Steinkamp, Schallenberg, Steinkamp, Quandt), Russell Stockman (Jäger/Steinkamp)

Grafische Gestaltung und Satz /
Graphic design and layout: Ta-Trung, Berlin (www.ta-trung.com)

Projektmanagment / Project management: André Odier

Projektleitung Prestel / Prestel project direction: Andrea Bartelt-Gering

Herstellung Prestel / Prestel production management: Cilly Klotz

Repro / Separations: Reproline mediateam GmbH & Co. KG, Unterföhring

Druck und Bindung / Printing and binding: Eberl & Kösel GmbH & Co. KG, Krugzell

Schrift / Typeface: Matter SQ / Stanley

Papier / Paper: Profibulk 1,1 f., 150 g/qm

Penguin Random House Verlagsgruppe FSC® N001967

A member of Penguin Random House Verlagsgruppe GmbH
Neumarkter Strasse 28 · 81673 Munich

Umschlagabbildung / Cover illustration
Five Swords, 1976 (Detail)
Abb. / fig. 8

Bibliografische Informationen der Deutschen Nationalbibliothek

Die Deutsche Nationalbibliothek verzeichnet diese Publikation in der Deutschen Nationalbibliografie, detaillierte bibliografische Daten sind über http://dnb.de abrufbar

Library of Congress Control Number: 2021940459
A CIP catalogue record for this book is available from the British Library.

Printed in Germany

ISBN 978-3-7913-7929-6
(Buchhandelsausgabe / trade edition)

ISBN 978-3-88609-859-0
(Museumsausgabe / museum edition)

www.smb.museum

www.prestel.de

www.prestel.com

FSC www.fsc.org
MIX
Paper from responsible sources
FSC® C013736

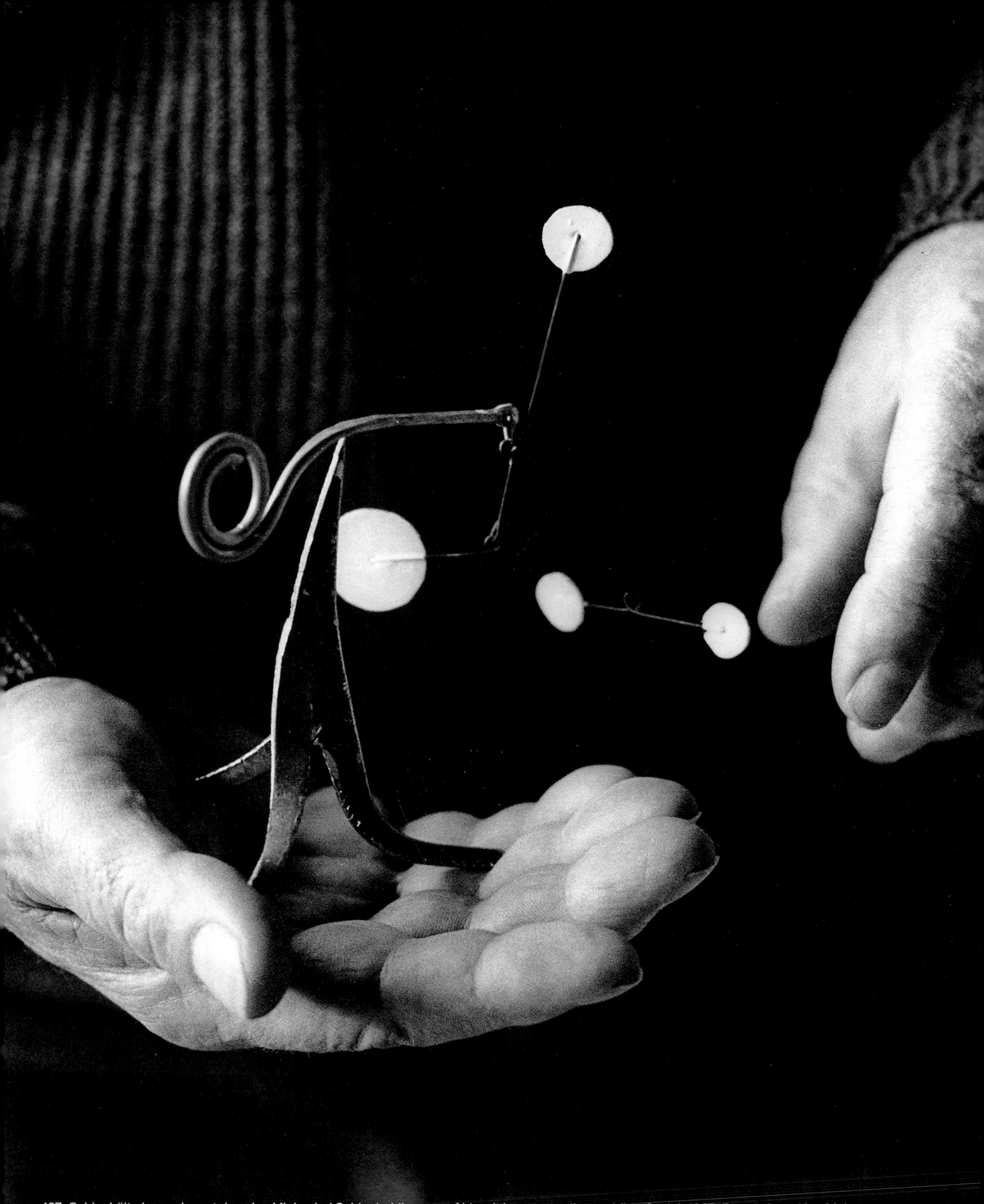

107 Calder hält eines seiner stehenden Minimals / Calder holding one of his miniature standing mobiles, Saché, 1963, Foto / photo Ugo Mulas